Lines of Most Resistance

Lines of Most Resistance

EDWARD PEARCE

LITTLE, BROWN AND COMPANY

A *Little, Brown* Book

First published in Great Britain in 1999
by Little, Brown and Company

Copyright © 1999 by Edward Pearce

The moral right of the author has been asserted

A CIP catalogue record for this book
is available from the British Library.

ISBN 0 316 64850 7

Typeset in Sabon by
Palimpsest Book Production Limited,
Polmont, Stirlingshire
Printed and bound in Great Britain by
Clays Ltd, St Ives plc

Little, Brown and Company (UK)
Brettenham House
Lancaster Place
London WC2E 7EN

Contents

For Peter Hennessy,
an example to all of us.

'The moment the very name of Ireland is mentioned, the English seem to bid adieu to common feeling, common prudence and common sense, and to act with the barbarity of tyrants and the fatuity of idiots!'

Sydney Smith

Introduction

After this book was written but while I was still caught up in (and complaining about) thickets of footnoting and corrections, I found myself talking to a distinguished historian at a party. 'Ah well,' he said, 'another hundred or so, and you'll get your Ph.D.'

Lines of Most Resistance has far too broad a scope – three Home Rule Bills and the Parliament Act across twenty-eight years – to hope for the high-focus heaven of academic election. However, if I felt the temptation to murmur something about quality and width, another historian met at another party put paid to that by asking about the length. 'About 150,000 words,' I said.

'Ah, a *medium*-sized book!'

But this book does represent primary research – chiefly into the press of the day – and does invite a reconsideration of history. It is, first and last, a book about Conservative opposition. I am arguing, and, I hope, demonstrating, from the depths of *Hansard* and the pages of furiously right-wing Victorian and Edwardian journals, that the stand against Irish Home Rule was something more than tactics.

I argue that the resistance was so bitter, with ultimate overtones of counter-revolution voiced in the circumstances of cautious reform, that it is best seen as the paroxysmal end to a political order. It was an order with which the late nineteenth-century Conservative Party, imperial but also desperately anxious, identified itself.

'The purpose of an opposition is to oppose' is a glib phrase one gets from the sort of politician who lives by ready-cooked thinking. It implies resisting the best of an opponent's plans equally with the worst precisely because they come from an opponent. No one reading the speeches and comments of Lord Salisbury will charge him with that. For all that he could see great domestic advantages and came to enjoy them through thirteen years of office, both his tactics and reflexes were overwhelmed by opinion and prejudice, those of party and of leader.

Salisbury detested the Irish, and saw coercion as the proper expression of sacred union. Equally, no one reading the debates and press articles surrounding the Lloyd George budget of 1909 and their lordships' suicidal rejection of it will think that opposition to that was some kind of routine twitch.

Opposition to Lords Reform and all three attempts at Home Rule was visceral. Certainly elements of cyncism occurred: Randolph Churchill impresses as a man working up extremism in order to show it off. But although there was furious distress among Tories at ever and again losing elections after 1906, Conservative politicians and journalists did believe that union and Empire were threatened. They did have anti-Catholic, anti-Irish prejudices; the House of Lords did, for most of them, assume the qualities of a tribal totem.

We are discussing a period of Empire and its attendant racial arrogance, but also an acknowledged, subtly diminishing British world strength. The right wing in Britain had passed out of effortless superiority into a sort of bullying self-pity. The notion of acting generously from strength was intolerable precisely because they lacked assurance about that strength.

Introduction

I have attempted to trawl the record of opposition to both major reforms and to catch the climate of unreason, highlighting *inter alia* the extraordinary paranoia of A.V. Dicey, the distinguished academic constitutional lawyer who, despite the colour of dispassion and high scholarship, would spend thirty years on and off in frantic protest, starting with calls for meeting Gladstone's temperate devolution with armed resistance.

Salisbury told a political meeting that civil representative institutions were not granted to Hottentots. In the *Saturday Review*, John Morley, Gladstone's chief secretary for Ireland, was seriously compared with Jean-Paul Marat. During the proceedings of the 1893 Home Rule Bill, an Irish member who had called Joseph Chamberlain 'Judas' was punched by a Tory, starting a fight among sixty MPs before the Speaker's chair.

Over Lords reform, the Liberal Winston Churchill was variously called 'adventurer', 'traitor' and 'potboy' and the prime minister, Asquith, accused of seeking to set up a despotism. The prospective 500 new peers who, had it been rejected, should have been created to pass the Parliament Bill were described as making the nobility of Louis Napoleon look like Plantagenets. Charles Whibley, a literary critic and Tory, said after the bill passed that in the good old days Mr Asquith would have stood in the dock indicted for treason.

This was no ordinary period of party politics, its feelings expressed by no routine badinage. Over Ireland and Lords reform, Conservative opposition went slightly mad. I have read the debates and the journals of the time, chiefly the *Saturday Review, Blackwood's* and the *National Review*, to quote *in extenso* what normally appears by way of evidential nibbles. The full blast of fear and malevolence is here almost anthologised, and with it the formal arguments against reform in words most of which have not seen print for anything between eighty and 110 years.

I think that such evidence, known but not focused upon,

should alter our view of how reform happens. We tend rather complacently to treat political liberalisation from 1832 onwards as inevitable. Worried about and foot-dragged over, no doubt, it must essentially have been the natural, moderate, incremental British thing we were always going to do.

It was more like death. Opposition to Irish Home Rule had a quality of violent unreason, with overtones of illegality and possible violence, something which is not our image of our country. This would, of course, show itself at its most blatant in the resistance after 1912 led by Bonar Law, leader of the Conservative Party, to what proved the final bid for a peaceful compromise with Ireland. One MP stored weapons on his premises (while being suspended briefly from the Commons for calling Asquith a traitor). The possibility that a bluff, if called, might have convulsed into shooting and killing resistance to the mildest of devolutionary bills escaped testing only by the outbreak of the First World War.

But the Tory Party of this era was in every sense prewar. National pride was bubbling along with resentment, paranoia and belief that opponents *were* traitors and enemies. The record of resistance to reform here is a miserable one, surely not in need of hindsight to be seen as self-defeating and very stupid nonsense. The contrast with the Churchill, Butler, Macmillan response to the Labour Party's actions after 1945 is eloquent.

As far as Ireland is concerned, men who had denounced the constitutionalist John Redmond succeeded to the point of stopping Home Rule and getting instead an independent Irish state governed by extreme physical-force nationalists. Opposition had run against all rational Conservative instincts, all shrewd compromise and half-loaf wisdom – the true genius of that party. Arguably *that* Conservative Party died in 1918, or perhaps in 1922.

What emerged afterwards, the party of Stanley Baldwin, ready to devolve powers in India (ironically infuriating a metamorphosed Winston Churchill), was something generally vaguer, nicer and without the same certainties; above all, saner. And it represents a key historical shift.

Lines of Most Resistance tries to catch in some day-to-day detail the voice and style of that deceased Tory party, triumphalist about the old order at the approach of its dissolution. It also seeks to show that the notion of change broadening down from generation to generation is, here anyway, a complacency inspired by distance. It is not doctoral or written at heavenly length, but it tries to show this period of our history as involving more protracted and endemic pain and folly than we generally suppose.

Thanks are owed to the eternally helpful staff of the London Library, from which I have fetched and carried back several hundredweight of eighty-year-old bound volumes, also to the Newspaper Library at Colindale; to Caroline North, an editor of immaculate and patient organisation, to Alan Samson and Bill Hamilton, my editor and agent respectively, who helped develop the idea and made it possible; and to my wife, who sweetly endures authorship. Thanks also to Linda Silverman for her brilliant picture research and to Perviz Seabrook for an excellent index.

I have no research assistant to thank, though after that weight of bound volumes and having read hundred-year-old, eight-point print on microfilm from an imperfectly focused viewer, I have sometimes wished that I did.

PART I

Irish Home Rule 1886 and 1893

I

'A Separate Nation! Surely Gladstone Could Not Mean It'

'*Signal*! Special edition! Mester Gladstone's Home Rule Bill. Full report. Gladstone's speech. Special!' The dark running figures approached, stopping at frequent gates, and their hoarse voices split the night. The next moment they had gone by in a flying column, and Edwin and the other man found themselves with fluttering paper in their hands . . .

. . . In his room he settled himself once more under the gas, and opened the flimsy newspaper with joy. Yes, there it was – columns, columns, in small type! . . . As he read the speech, slowly disengaging its significance from the thicket of words, it seemed incredible. A parliament in Dublin! The Irish taxing themselves according to their own caprices! The Irish controlling the Royal Irish Constabulary! The Irish members withdrawn from Westminster! A separate nation! Surely Gladstone could not mean it! . . . the wondrous legend of the orator's divine power – the long-stretching, majestic, misty sentences gave him faith. Henceforward he was a Home Ruler . . .

. . . 'I'm going this road' said Darius when they were

safely out of the bank pointing towards the Sytch.

'What for?'

'I'm going this road' he repeated, gloomily, obstinate
. . . the idea occurred to him that his father was bound
for the Liberal Club. It was so . . .

. . . 'Well Mr Clayhanger' said the steward in his
absurd boniface way, 'you're quite a stranger.'

'I want my name taken off this club' said Darius
shortly 'Ye understand me. And I reckon I'm not the
only one these days.'

The steward did indeed understand. He protested in
a low, amiable voice, while the billiard players affected
not to hear; but he perfectly understood. The epidemic
of resignations had already set in, and there had been
talk of a Liberal-unionist Club. The steward saw that
the grand folly of a senile statesman was threatening
his own prospects. But at Edwin as they were leaving,
he smiled in a quite peculiar way, and that smile clearly
meant 'Your father goes dotty, and the first thing he
does is to change his politics.' This was the steward's
justifiable revenge . . . At the top of Duck Bank, Darius
silently and without warning, mounted the steps of the
Conservative Club. Doubtless he knew how to lay his
hand instantly on a proposer and seconder. Edwin did
not follow him.

Clayhanger, Arnold Bennett

The brilliant eye of the novelist has caught a great political
crisis in a few sentences. The reaction of Darius Clayhanger
in taking his name off the books of the Bursley Liberal Club
spoke for a great body of English opinion, conservative by
instinct if not formally Conservative in politics. But his son
Edwin's response, that here was something visionary, creating
in the best minds faith for a vast undertaking, would be
validated when Home Rule had been three times furiously
rejected by such conservative opinion and an independent

Irish state consequently and dismally achieved by violence and exhaustion.

Gladstone came to Irish Home Rule in 1886 after he had long brooded on Ireland and after Ireland herself had been shaken by disaster and in desultory conflict with the mainland for decades. The options of violence and reform were not new (and they could splash across each other). There existed a pattern of misery, reform, violence (of an ineffective but unpleasant kind), repression, more misery and the start of a new cycle of the same.

A hundred years before, a still independent Irish Parliament, Protestant and oligarchic but responding to the handsome, hopeful leadership of Henry Grattan, had seemed poised to call up the Enlightenment and disregard religious barriers and bans. Grattan had been an advanced Whig as Gladstone was now an advanced Liberal. His frustration in the shadow of a species of cold-war hysteria about the French revolutionaries spreading their tentacles into Ireland had been followed by the events of 1798.

In that year, a rising (at its strongest in County Wexford) had been suppressed, speeches had been made, rank and file fired on, people hanged, songs written and bitter memories set up for cherishing in the most exemplary way imaginable. The forenames 'Robert Emmett' are still given – mostly to Irish American children – in honour of a rebel leader executed as rebel leaders would be executed in 1916, thirty years after Gladstone's first Home Rule bill. 'The Wearing of the Green' said, with less distinction but as much effect, what Yeats' 'Easter 1916' – 'I have met them at close of day' – would say about another rising, other executions. The profound and endearing observation of Winston Churchill that 'grass grows over the battlefield, but over the scaffold, never' was its own sufficient terse truth. The great fantail of Irish mourning rhetoric had again been ornamented.

As for development, the executions of 1798 were followed by 'union', the absorption of the old Dublin Parliament, intolerable now that it had indeed functioned as a parliament, into the Westminster 'imperial' one. This had been achieved at a price – one varying according to the member bribed. But the bringing about of union in 1801 had had a rhetoric of its own, not insincere for being unfulfilled. John Fitzgibbon, Earl of Clare, wished to bring his country 'to her proper station in the rank of civilised nations . . . from the degraded post of a mercenary province to the proud station of an integral and governing member of the greatest Empire in the world'.

Thus exalted, Ireland would wait twenty-eight years for the promised emancipation of Catholics, the great majority of her people, to citizenship of that great Empire. And this would be achieved only after an extensive and menacing campaign under a national leader aroused the latent power of the peasantry. It was, moreover, something done during another short phase of Liberal sentiment and power. To be exact, it was the pre-achievement of Reform, conceded by the Conservative but realistic Duke of Wellington just before the Radical Parliament of 1830.

O'Connell, the 'liberator' whose agitation had achieved this, had toyed with Home Rule but he had also been willing, thirty years on, to take Clare's words at their face value and to employ citizenship of that great Empire for the advancement of Irishmen within a genuine union. Reasonably enough, the portrait of Daniel O'Connell hangs today in the hall of the Reform Club. But Reform had benefited Ireland, so it seemed, largely on paper. Before the liberator died in 1847, failure of the potato, staple of a near monoculture, starved perhaps a million, perhaps a million and a half, and drove a larger number into exile, preponderantly to America, from which country most impetus (and money and weapons) for violent revolt would come.

The famine (or as Irishmen reasonably say, 'Famine'), which started up late in 1845 was *not* genocide. The British government did not seek or desire the potato blight *phytophthora infestans* which, rotting the crop, left multitudes of Irish starving. They didn't have to; belief sufficed. As John Bright observed, 'Let us think of the half-million who within two years past have perished miserably in the workhouses, on the highways and in their hovels – more, far more than ever, fell by the sword in any war this country ever waged; let us think of the crop of nameless horrors which is even now growing up in Ireland, and whose disastrous fruit may be gathered in years and generations to come.'[1] (Ironically, by the time of Gladstone's Home Rule Bill, Bright would join with Tories and Liberal Unionists in opposing it.)

In fact, according to the leading modern historian of Ireland, the lowest grand bill of mortality is 750,000, and the ceiling is 1.5 million.[2] The potato crop failed in 1845 and again in 1846, preventing the sowing of a new crop. The disease fell back in 1847 and returned in 1848 and 1849.

The response of government to the crisis was not so much cruel as doctrinaire. Peel and Russell, who had the handling of it, were Manchester School men, arithmetical Ricardians with a sustaining stratum of Malthus. In the face of a crop disease which induced starvation, they feared that relief would create dependency. The Poor Law, designed in England to suppress such weakness, operated in Ireland with its full rigours to discourage slackness and pauperism in the destitute. William Gregory, an esteemed civil servant, later an MP, introduced a rule by which no one possessed of a quarter-acre plot might be admitted to a workhouse. There was a strong, correct belief that small landholdings were entirely wrong for the long-term efficiency of the Irish economy. Clearances by act of God made sense.

Not that the poor were wilfully neglected. Food depots were established, Indian meal was distributed. M. Alexis Soyer, chef of the Reform, mindful of expense, famously introduced his costed soup. But relief itself, as against public works requiring proof of physical labour by the claimant, did not appear until 1847. In the name of what is now termed 'workfare', piers were built at which no ship would dock, walls built to contain nothing. Yet money *was* spent – half a million in the hard currency of mid-century in the first year alone. But plans to build railways as both public works and infrastructure investment were abandoned. And as Roy Foster, scrupulously fairminded towards the British government, observes, 'There was also an attitude, often unconcealed, that Irish fecklessness and lack of economy were bringing a retribution that would work out best in the end' – Malthusianism with extreme prejudice. The term 'holocaust' has taken on the meaning of planned, intended slaughter, so there was no holocaust, but hundreds of thousands of people did starve to death.

The historic effect upon Ireland is best measured in numbers, numbers which acquire a rhetorical force of their own. A population of 8,200,000 in the early 1840s stood at 4,400,000 in 1911. And in the period during and immediately after the famine, the population decline has been put at 2.25 million. For to the people dead were added the numbers of those who emigrated, and in conditions of supplementary atrocity – ships perfectly suited to completing what the famine had begun. Coffin ships packed beyond the call of political economy produced mortality, on the Cork to Quebec run, of 20 per cent. The Ireland of the second half of the nineteenth century was preoccupied with vivid memories of endemic death. Also of dispossession: Irishmen abroad, chiefly in the United States, had known also the concluding experience of slums and slum fever on water, regarding themselves with no great self-indulgence as men expelled from their own country.

Ireland would slowly make a recovery of sorts and money would come to her from abroad by way of remittance – £34 million all told between 1848 and 1867.[3] The diaspora would also finance, encourage, and where possible direct, extreme nationalist politics, up to and very much including violence.

The dynamite which preceded the Semtex of our times was an Irish American amenity, commonly supplied or paid for by

Irish America. The Irish American mood was well caught by a visitor: 'Animated by a spirit of nationality beyond all belief: the dynamite-loving ex-Fenian soldier, the respectable lawyer and the affluent merchant – all contribute their money to the common idea; namely that of obtaining at the very least for their country the same privileges which each state in the union possesses in relation to the central American government.'[4]

The union which Gladstone sought to modify and would be accused of repealing had seen in the fifty years before he proposed Home Rule annihilatory famine, the loss of nearly half the population and a steady recurring campaign of violence. Conservative politicians and journalists would speak indignantly of Ireland being 'disloyal'. Given dependency, given Britain's pre-eminent power in the world and the deference which power and habituation bring, she was more loyal than anyone had any reason to expect. But where O'Connell had been a constitutionalist, however threatening his mass movement, his tradition of reform within the system, achieved by amending the system itself, now made up only one wing of nationalism. Destruction wasn't new, but the violence which had existed across the eighteenth century in the form of rural groups – White Boys, Ribbon Men – had been spasmal, localised (and rurally localised at that). The new movement 'Fenianism' – though 'organised' was the last word for its squabbling and erratic activities – was international, had access to money and to a press, notably the *Irish People*, and had leaders with education and concentrated purpose. John O'Leary, John O'Mahony, Michael Davitt (who had lost an arm in a Lancashire cotton mill), the business mind of Patrick Egan, the violent oratory of O'Donovan Rossa and the quiet competence of John Devoy were all directed at the creation of an Irish nation.

And the language of terrorist violence was present waiting to become the reality. 'Dynamite, Greek fire or Hell fire, if it could be had' were acceptable to O'Donovan Rossa if they would remove England from Ireland. Rossa, the least of these men, was a disoriented noisy speechmaker, so it was apt enough that his funeral in 1915 should provide the occasion for an oration during the First World War hiatus by another speechmaker, Patrick Pearse, heralding the Easter Rising the following year.

The 1860s were marked by what the British press called 'outrages', though compared with our last three decades' promiscuous killings of citizens and soldiers in blood a hundred years cold, these were human and more readily understandable. An attempt to release prisoners from Clerkenwell Prison killed innocent people entirely unintentionally, occasioning Britain's last public hanging. Another attempt at a prison rescue led to the death of a policeman, Sergeant Brett. For this, almost certainly accidental, killing, three men, Allen, Larkin and O'Brien, were, with the consolation of privacy, also hanged. New songs were written, the grass grew no better.

Underlying all politics in Ireland lay the land. It was not merely that so much land was in English or Protestant ascendancy hands – which actually varied a great deal in their conduct towards tenants – but there had emerged what was called the 'strong farmer'. He was Irish, Catholic and replete with memories, but also the residual beneficiary of emigration and consolidation and as such the occupant of 10 to 30 acres. He was better off, better able to make difficulties and not at all grateful. He was also the object of Mr Gladstone's concern for Ireland. Gladstone's Land Act of 1870 compelled evicting landlords to pay compensation for any dispossessions other than for non-payment of rent. This was done to protect the tenant farmer from what Gladstone characterised as 'the terrible weapon of undue and unjust eviction'. The act failed for a number of reasons – loopholes in the text and a fall in product prices which made previously moderate rents unpayable.

For in the mid-seventies, Ireland, along with the rest of the union, entered the agricultural depression. A combination of open-ended cheap foreign supply from newly flowering North American prairies slashing prices out of sight and five years of execrable weather – seasons of vertical, inveterate rain which left grain green in late August – did terrible things. The fears of the English protectionists in Peel's time thirty years before were realised: this whirligig of time brought in revenge to Disraeli, defender of the Corn Laws, now ironically (and indifferent) in office. The price of wheat, which had for nearly thirty years knocked about on a range of 47 to 53 shillings per quarter measure, fell in that calamitous half-decade to a low point of 17s 4d. Land values collapsed in England and arable farming with them. Essex, from being a grain bowl, saw the arrival of highland scrub cattle, the only livestock which could live on stubble. As for land and its lordships, Oscar Wilde's remark of the mid-nineties was to the point. 'It gives one position and prevents one from keeping it up.'

The Irish small farmer scarcely saw the joke. Loss of what had been so hardly won fell on a small farmer desperate but not submissive. Gladstone's attempt in 1870 to create equitable rights for him in his land was totally bypassed when crashing prices meant that rents could not be paid and that lawful dispossession followed. Finally, by way of a sadism in nature, in 1878 and 1879 the miserable weather created in the south-west substantial areas of potato blight. The condition of the land and its ownership had an immediate impact upon politics. The sort of moderation which the English always admire too late had offered itself in the early seventies before weather and economy turned. Isaac Butt, Protestant, professor of political economy, courtroom lawyer, enlightened (and embarrassed) Donegal landlord and a man much loved, had picked on the idea of Home Rule, a phrase coined by the Trinity College academic J.A. Galbraith.

Butt represented Ireland with intelligence and persuasive sense. An English government should have been able to respond to a man who, in Roy Foster's words, 'shared in and helped create a sense of Irishness that accepted historic English influence while claiming realistic autonomy'.[5] He would launch at Bilton's Hotel in Dublin the Home Government Association of Ireland. Becoming the Home Rule Association, it would have instant political impact. MPs began to be elected the very next year, 1871. And the Ballot Act of 1872 realised, in Ireland at least, the worst fears of those who had argued that removal of the requirement to stand up in a manly way under the eyes of a land agent taking notes would allow cowardly tenants and labourers to vote the wrong way. But ironically, in the General Election of 1874, the Liberal Party was annihilated in Ireland while the Tories hung on to a core of support in Ulster. The chief secretary, Chichester Fortescue, who had had the grace to represent an Irish seat, lost it, and with precious little national organisation, fifty-nine Home Rulers were elected.

Isaac Butt offered the Parliament of 1874 the motion 'that it is expedient and just to restore to the Irish nation the right and power of managing all exclusively Irish affairs in an Irish Parliament; and that provision should also be made at the same time for maintaining the integrity of the empire and the connection between the countries by reserving to this imperial Parliament full and exclusive control over all imperial affairs.'

Butt has had poor treatment from history. A moderate man, he has been treated as a weak one. Lacking the charisma of revolt and imprisonment, he makes a poor legend, but he talked profound good sense and first brought forward an option which, if taken up, would have taken Irish history and English history in Ireland into a benign spiral. Engaged 120 years on, in our latest armistice in three decades of killing, we are not placed to patronise Isaac Butt. He was being civil and rational and was met by the new prime minister, Disraeli, with an early example of that combination of patronage and apprehension which over forty years would mark Conservative reaction to Home Rule. It was all, said Disraeli, 'perilous stuff'. And if we did not 'cleanse the parliamentary bosom' of it, we should 'bring about the disintegration of the Kingdom and the destruction of the Empire'.[6] The words are a sort of perfunctory hysteria, a reaction of instant, absolute fear expressed with a slight shrug. The motion would be defeated by 458 votes to 61, the atrocity of federalism averted. 'A united people', in Disraeli's vapid words, was still 'welded in one great nationality'. But the question would continue to be raised again and the hysteria of the response would mount.

So in 1874, before the wheel of the economy had run across Irish (and English) rural feet, a straightforward political request without menaces had been scorned. It would be scorned again and again in the way of a blocking batsman as in successive years Butt presented and re-presented his bill. And that wheel was turning in Ireland, turning economically with rents unpayable, dispossession and avid acceptance of tenancies by men anxious for land. By the end of Disraeli's government in 1880, orthodox parliamentary tactics had failed and the mood of tenant farmers, though distressed, was drily apt for lighting.

Rational civility describes Isaac Butt's approach. In better worlds rational and civil approaches are met. But as one of his parliamentary colleagues observed, Butt was too gentlemanly – 'We're all too gentlemanly.' Joseph Biggar, a self-made Belfast grocer without genteel inclinations, put it plainly. 'The English stop our bills. Why don't we stop their bills? . . . No Irish bills, but stop English bills. No legislation. That's the policy, sir.'[7]

What Biggar began on his own, other Irish members joined him in doing. On 22 April 1875 he took on coercion – the recurring suspension of constitutional liberties, otherwise called a Crimes Bill – by means of which British governments, with greater and less satisfaction, restored Ireland to order at the expense of law. Four hours reading from blue books and the daily press followed a day or two later by 'spying strangers', something which involved the Prince of Wales being apologetically removed from the Distinguished Strangers' Gallery, did not stop that coercion bill, but it was a nasty warning. The time would come twenty years on when a Speaker would be reduced by an intransigence which had turned into football violence to contemplate summoning the Metropolitan Police. But that was an excess; regular practice perfected what Biggar had begun, turning it into a formation dance in which each successive intervener in a debate spoke – for hours at a time – to be succeeded by yet other Irishmen equipped with interminable texts who also spoke. There was no closure procedure at this time. Biggar's injunctions were four: to work only in government time; to aid anybody to spend government time; 'whenever you see a government bill, block it' and 'whenever you see a raw, rub it'.[8]

The effect upon government and English members, thus blocked and rubbed, was what might have been expected. A minority recognised a great issue provoking infuriating tactics, most others an intolerable pest inducing a greater general contempt for all the Irish. Yet oddly, unionists (Conservatives and those Liberals who would join them), those who had least tolerance for the Irish members' conduct, were most loath to lose them. Per contra, advanced Gladstonian Liberals who had essential understanding and whose party usually benefited from Irish votes in the Commons wanted their departure to a Dublin Parliament.

Events were too bitter for Isaac Butt's mild ways. He totally opposed parliamentary obstruction, but had no means of stopping it. The object of great affection, but getting no results for his impeccably constitutional overtures, he had lost control of the party he had created before he was, more or less gently, superseded. The bitter events were not merely parliamentary. Parliament for Irishmen functioned in parallel with the conflict on the land.

Potato blight was back in 1878. Dispossession for non-payment of rents unpayable, given glut prices during dearth, had been back longer. The potato crop of 1879 fetched just above a quarter of what had been earned in 1876. More than 1,200 familes (6,000 people) had been made homeless by eviction during 1879. In the years 1879 to 1883 14,600 tenants would be evicted, the highest number for thirty years. And thirty years before had been the Famine time.

The Land League was the consequence, parliamentary tactics a kind of commentary on the new nightmare. The Land League, subject of Anthony Trollope's last, unfinished and irascible novel, *The Land Leaguers* (1883), had been created in 1877 and directed first to preventing dispossession. Landlords, themselves reeling from the depression, would respond to an inevitable rent default by serving notice to quit, usually through an agent, and lease the land to a new tenant. The league targeted sometimes the agent, always the new tenant taking up the lease.

The first, most important effect of the league over a period of years was to show the British government impotent to uphold its own laws when challenged at key points. In the famous episode of Captain Charles Boycott, an honest if stiff and tactless agent serving Lord Erne's estates in County Mayo, the neologising troublemakers who 'boycotted' the estate with a withdrawal of goods and, more important, labour would demonstrate the economic vulnerability of an interdicted farm. Only ludicrous overkill of volunteers entrained from Ulster with police standing behind them could get the harvest in. The costs of production to a boycotted farm instantly rendered it uneconomic to reap grain, a sort of revenge for the sad returns which had caused dispossession.

The Land League worked because it had a natural constituency. Agricultural misfortunes had different roots in different parts of Ireland, potato blight hitting the south-west, tillage prices the concern in Ulster, a huge fall in butter prices affecting Tipperary and Cork. But the central idea of intimidation making the life of a boycotted tenant not worth living, reinforced by latent intimidation – what was done in that farm that could be done in this – had a natural body of support. A conspiratorial Fenian minority based in America was given credit and took it. But it was an open conspiracy, with many joining. Comfort taken by British politicians from 'tiny minorities' and among Fenians at their exclusive triumph was delusive. This was a peasants' revolt, and a peasants' revolt needs peasants.

Vicious and brutal things would be perpetrated over the next few years: a savage maiming of cattle, cases of arson and serious assault. Intimidation involving delivery of coffins and shots fired into houses was aimed at landlords a little, at the takers-up of eviction tenancies very much. Murder would occur. Things were done which might not be excused, and majority English opinion, itself violently mercurial, would not, in a snapshot of that time, have rejected Lord Salisbury's remarks about Hottentots or George Saintsbury's description of the Irish parliamentarians as 'these Yahoos'.

What English public opinion did not comprehend was that a man who might have been ten at the height of the famine in 1848, might have struggled through, acquired land, made a go of it, been protected from unreasonable eviction by the 1870 act and then, at the age of forty, see the return of the potato blight, sell his crop for a fraction of a normal year's price, have no money for rent and finally face destitution. English public opinion was insufficiently lit by English public imagination. Roy Jenkins has caught the public mood in relation to Ireland in the late seventies and early eighties by comparing it with France during the war in Algeria in the late 1950s.[9] People there who recognised that that war should not be pursued either kept the thought to themselves or were quickly told what traitors, communists, enemies of France and probably Jews they were. We did better than that, though a reading of the right-wing press during all the periods of Home Rule debate discourages complacency. Revulsion at things revolting was converted into unreasoning and essentially racial contempt, all vicious spirals would be given a twist. The idea of distinguishing between Irishmen and between Irish organisations, like the notion of understanding that desperate acts might be rooted in desperation, was a very sophisticated one. Any politician talking coercion or Hottentots or, as soon happened, extending a hand (or incitement) to those sound, unIrish Irishmen of Ulster was on political velvet. And high motives and sincerity lay easily to hand for the politician doing it.

But revulsion would find its essence, its concentrated form, a year or two later at a time when the Land League was still active, the Irish members still obstructive. Gladstone, who had succeeded Disraeli, to the childish resentment of Queen Victoria, was not yet proposing Home Rule. He had coped with the Land League as best he could through the offices of W.E. Forster. The extent of Anglo-Irish understanding was measured in the chief secretary's nickname. It was a humane act, apologists argued, that police dispersing danger-ous crowds should fire only buckshot, which injures, rather than bullets, which kill. It was typical of Forster's repressive rule, said Irishmen, that he proposed firing at all. 'Buckshot Forster' he became, responsible for a policy of dedicated coercion and repression, the equivalent perhaps of Robert Lacoste, the hard man (from the Socialist Party, naturally) who governed Algeria to the entire satisfaction of its French colonists.

But Forster, though stern, was no brute. Indeed there was something rather magnificent about him. He was, after all, the creator, ten years before, of Forster's Education Act. And his response in Ireland was one of deeply felt emotion. He had seen for himself in the remote depths of County Clare a farmer dying in the local workhouse after being wounded in the legs, ironically with gunshot, for the crime of having paid his rent. 'God save Ireland,' said the chief secretary from a hotel balcony in Tullamore in Queen's County. 'God save Ireland from cruel men of whatever class they may be . . . grasping landlords or midnight marauders. God save Ireland from the pestilence that walketh at noon and the terror that stealeth at night.'[10]

The implications of the unrest for the political leadership were at once frightening and enthralling. But the new political leadership since the fall of Butt was Charles Stewart Parnell, and Parnell, like Dryden's Achitophel, was 'a daring pilot in extremity'. Parnell was a Protestant and a landlord. A great acreage of speculation has essayed and revised his personality, motives and inner nature. What matters here is that Parnell was a sort of genius, someone in whom that blown-rose expression 'charisma' was in bright bloom. Gladstone would, in the end, think him the greatest man he had ever met; the cool young Asquith considered him one of the three or four great men of the century. (He was also broke, and his brother expressed wry fellow feeling for Captain Boycott when he collected rents with a couple of policemen in tow.) He induced obsession after his death: characters of James Joyce in *Portrait of the Artist as a Young Man* debate Parnell and the MPs and priests who betrayed him after the notorious divorce case. He was cold and attracting warmth, aloof and loved, single-purposed, unIrishly given to dark silences, significantly armed with the scorn and nonchalance of the inheriting class and turning it upon that class. Parnell's motivation may be worth any number of seminars; his impact was ferocious. He was a gentleman but, as it were, no gentleman. As the still obscure member for Meath in the mid-seventies, he had spoken crushingly against moderation. 'Why was some measure of protection given to the Irish tenant? It was because there was an explosion at Clerkenwell and because a lock was shot off a prison van at Manchester.'[11]

These were the outrages which politicians either deplored or looked the other way from. Parnell never had any trouble with the unsayable. Like a true Machiavellian, he asked succinctly what caused what. Tim Healy, a key lieutenant (and one of the 'betrayers' of 1890) spoke long afterwards as a critic of Parnell, but the bigness and difference of the man still comes out. 'We created Parnell and he created us. We seized very early in the movement the idea of this man with his superb silences, his historic name, his determination, his self-control, his aloofness – we seized that as the canvas of a great national hero.'[12]

Parnell and the Land League were different chemicals combining improbably. Peasants in County Kerry wanted to keep their farms and pay low rents. Home Rule was a remote abstraction to them. Equally, Parnell felt 'utter disgust' at the big meetings he was addressing in the west. Disgust arose from his conviction of 'how hollow and wanting in solidarity everything connected with the movement was'.[13] For ironically, Parnell did have vague but sincere hopes for landlord-and-peasant reconciliation through a large element of state intervention. The ideas of the Common Agricultural Policy – directed after all at inception in 1957, Algeria time, chiefly at poor farmers in the south-west of France with a quite Irish ability to be frightening about farm prices – would have been up Parnell's street.

The Land League had produced a running jacquerie and it served conservative peasants indifferent to great ideas of government. But it enraged and frightened the English – and focused Ireland in English eyes. Parnell had earlier spoken contemptuously of conciliation: Ireland 'would never gain a single sixpennyworth from her by conciliation'.[14] Whatever the Land League might be – reactive, emigré-inspired, brutal, unvisioned – it was not conciliatory.

2

Long Surgical Knives

Combined with the ambushing and talking down of legislation at Westminster, unrestful Ireland was becoming a preoccupation, *the* preoccupation, of British governments. They yo-yoed between listening and shouting, between making overtures and locking people up. The chief secretary Forster, horrified at the dying man in County Clare, was responding to the pressure of intolerable things, shifting from reform to coercion. There would develop a fundamental split in Gladstone's 1880 government between Forster and the GOM himself.

Gladstone offered his great Land Act of 1881 with fair rent, fixed tenure and free sale of tenancies, all governed by a Land Commission with the status of a High Court. The historic effect would be enormous. The power of landlords would be finite, motives had been created for those landlords to divest themselves of estates so restricted and, ironically, Conservative rule from 1885 would be rich in land-purchase schemes deriving from Gladstone's initiative. Against this, Forster, shocked and affronted by the violence of the west, offered an Irish Crimes Act – more coercion. Long-term, Gladstone had brought off a transformation, though the effect would be slow. Short-term, events would be given a distinct

Algerian twist by coercion. Forster had been magnificent on that Tullamore balcony, but he had been too grieved to be wise.

Forster and Gladstone were hawk and dove. Gladstone was prime minister, but Forster, with the neglible Viscount Cowper as viceroy, ruled Ireland. Parnell in Ireland was an orator who, starting with his famous Westport speech, was giving comfort to the western rural revolt. Parnell in Westminster was now member for Cork and leader of the Irish Party. By executive fiat, without trial and under the emergency laws, the chief secretary arrested the leader of the parliamentary party and put him into Kilmainham Jail.

Parnell, like all leaders of colonial revolts, was the beneficiary of arrest. He understood well enough the fundamental benefit of the Land Act, but he was balanced between potential understanding with this English government and the Irish American patrons, arm's-length extremists to a man, but the providers of cash. (Irish members were men of few means, for whom, unlike those of the parliamentary Labour Party after 1910, no state salary was available.) Anyway, with Forster using his powers to arrest supporters, Parnell could not afford reasonableness. Martyrdom was a professional duty which Forster, plagued in the Commons by the Irish Party, furious with *United Ireland*, the vivid and offensive press vehicle of Parnell's protégé, William O'Brien, was ready to offer. And at this juncture, he carried Gladstone with him. In a speech in Leeds, the prime minister spoke of a conflict 'between law on the one side and sheer lawlessness on the other', adding words which became famous in mocking Irish mouths: 'I say, gentlemen, without hesitation, that the resources of civilisation against its enemies are not yet exhausted.' 'The resources of civilisation,' '*mission civilisante*': the grim Algerian analogy continues.

It is always a mistake for rulers of recalcitrant peoples to respond to baiting. Parnell now baited the government in a speech at Wexford, calling Gladstone 'the greatest coercionist, the greatest and most unrivalled slanderer of the Irish nation that ever undertook the task'. That was politics and noise. But another sentence in the Wexford speech was historic. Parnell spoke of the 'determination of the Irish people to regain for themselves their lost land and their lost legislative independence'. In five years' time, Gladstone would do everything in his power to restore that legislative independence. For the time being, he authorised Forster to return to Dublin and send police into Morrison's Hotel with warrants for the detention of Parnell in Kilmainham Jail.

Gladstone was in a false position doing that, and Kilmainham itself another false, if advantageous, place for Parnell to be. The Land Act represented a major advance for the people Parnell represented. The sparring and noisemaking done respectively to appease intransigent expatriate bank-rollers and to assert the resources of civilisation obscured convergence between the two men. The deal or 'treaty' of Kilmainham which would be achieved through intermediaries six months later recognised this reality. It also alienated Forster. To him its terms, vague and insubstantial on Parnell's part, represented a triumph for the Irishman, something the natteringly resentful Queen also felt. Again, the inconsiderable Cowper had been replaced as viceroy by Spencer, who would prove a serious reformer. Forster felt himself betrayed, and resigned.

Two things were happening: the pieces were falling into place for the ultimate move to Home Rule, and Gladstone was making an enemy, the first of a great number in his own party. Home Rule would be fought for in 1886 to the sound of votes cast with departing feet, Liberal Unionists, Old Whigs, Joseph Chamberlain. Gladstone was an inspirational statesman and a terrible personnel manager.

But within days, Forster's view of Ireland as a place where pestilence walked at noon and terror stole by night was to be given jarring and horrific credibility. His replacement was to be Frederick Cavendish, a Devonshire, the younger brother of a key minister, Lord Hartington, and himself a protégé of Gladstone and husband of Gladstone's beloved niece, Lucy Lyttleton. Lord Frederick was best known as a pleasant and competent financial secretary deputising to Gladstone, who, in the middle of all this, was also his own chancellor of the exchequer. Lord Frederick was a personal appointment, someone whom Gladstone trusted and could guide. His was thus an appointment directed at liberalisation. For 'the greatest coercionist of the Irish people', in Parnell's Wexford rhetoric, had been seen by John Morley at a Downing Street dinner at the very end – New Year's Eve – of 1880. He 'took me into a corner and revealed his coercion [scheme] much as a man might say in confidence that he found himself under the painful necessity of slaying his mother – it was downright piteous.'[1]

Lord Frederick had not been in Dublin above twelve hours when, walking in Phoenix Park with Thomas Burke, the permanent under-secretary, en route for the viceroy's lodge, he was stabbed to death, and Burke with him. The murder, committed by a group of men – Brady, Kelly, Delaney, Caffrey, Fagan and Hanlon – calling themselves 'the Invincibles' and with transatlantic links, employed long surgical knives, a fact which lingered with resplendent horror in the public imagination. When four years later George Saintsbury wished to abuse the parliamentary Irish Party in a ranting piece for the Tory *Saturday Review*, he called them 'the party of surgical knives'.

The reaction of Gladstone to the news brought to him by Edward Hamilton, his private secretary, was first to fall on his knees and pray, and second to make straight for his niece's home to comfort her. Ten days later, with heroic offensiveness, Arthur Balfour, ablest of the Tories, denounced the Kilmainham treaty and the government: 'I do not think any such transaction can be quoted from the annals of our political history. It stands alone in its infamy . . . They have negotiated in secret with Treason . . .'[2] It was not the first

Tory virulence on Ireland, but there was an infinity of it to come. Gladstone, who had liked him, was bitterly wounded; Balfour, in the classic style, never apologised.

The murders aborted the developments implicit in the Kilmainham understanding. Not only that, but the policy of Forster was necessarily restored with a new Coercion Bill and with Forster himself, apparently validated in his crushing instinct, lauded by the Tories and held up as the scapegoat for Gladstone's scheming. Parnell would later become the victim of the Pigott forgeries – false allegations published triumphantly in *The Times* alleging his approval of the murders – much later, after a parliamentary commission's exhaustive inquiry and the suicide of the forger, humiliatingly refuted.

Parnell was in fact prostrated by Phoenix Park, thought his life's work destroyed and offered to resign from seat and leadership. The Irish Party, though it went through the motions of opposing the 1882 Crimes Bill, had no real heart for doing so. As Conor Cruise O'Brien would later put it in his classic study, 'For two years from the summer of 1880 to the summer of 1882, Ireland had held a foremost position in the politics of the United Kingdom. By the end of 1882, she had ceased to be a major concern.' The Irish Party's policy meanwhile 'became a waiting one'.[3]

Yet the Kilmainham treaty remained operative. Parnell and Gladstone, two of the great men of their century, were moving uneasily towards one another. For that matter, the idea that the Tories might make some kind of Home Rule deal themselves did not seem unthinkable. Lord Carnarvon, who would briefly be Salisbury's viceroy, was certainly drawn to the idea. And Balfour, he of the infamy and treason speech, would also say in 1887, 'After all, when it comes, I shall not be sorry. Only let us have separation as well as Home Rule; England cannot afford to go on with the Irishmen in her Parliament.' (It was not a compliment, and the desire to see the back of the people who had turned Parliament into a siege struggled in Conservative minds with the sanctity of the union.) Then again, Michael Hicks Beach was a moderate man, capable of listening, and there was Lord Randolph Churchill, the rising if eclectic Tory who had derided Forster's early resort to coercion and who had spent his adolescence in the viceregal lodge developing Irish Catholic contacts.

The Conservatives were about to become involved, for in 1885, Gladstone, electoral reform and the death of General Gordon behind him, finally resigned after a defeat on, of all things, beer duty. Salisbury, the Tory leader – 3rd Marquess, descendant of Elizabeth's Cecil and in Roy Jenkins' phrase, 'a cynical pessimist as well as a skilful statesman', formed a government.

Irish votes had been cast against that budget and early in the career of the new government Carnarvon, Salisbury's viceroy, held a meeting with Parnell. Gladstone responded to this with austere approval. He remained unresponsive to Parnell's inquiries to him and urged co-operation with the Conservative government. The virtue of a Conservative move supported by the Liberals was that the Tories were able to get things through the House of Lords. This unreformed bundle of negative antiquity under the restraints of convention only over money bills (which in 1909, it would brush aside), was so completely the creature of the Conservative Party that the Holy Innocents (Slaughter) Bill would have had a clear passage if sent up by a Salisbury majority.

Conservative opinion, which saw only knavishness in anything Gladstone did, assumed that he meant to split them. Salisbury wrote to Lord Bath, fearful of any meddling with the union, at the end of 1885: 'I am quite of your mind and so are the members of the government generally. I never admired the political transformation scenes of 1829, 1846, 1867; and I certainly do not wish to be the chief agent in adding a fourth to the history of the Tory Party.'[4] The dates mentioned had involved respectively Catholic emancipation, abolition of the corn laws and urban manhood suffrage. But all had injured the Conservatives as a political party. The cynical pessimist in Salisbury was very strong, so was the narrowest spirit of party.

Besides, setting his own estimate of Gladstone's motives as his model, Salisbury was attentive to a Liberal split, something which, given the view of so many Old Whigs that Gladstone was a dangerous Red, was waiting to happen. Writing to Lord Randolph Churchill on 9 December 1885, Salisbury concurred with that compulsive young cynic. 'I entirely agree that our leaning must be to the moderate Liberals and that we can have nothing to do with any advance toward the Home Rulers.' Such actions would follow their convictions and pledges, he remarked piously, before adding that anything else would also 'be quite fatal to party cohesion'. Contemplating Hartington, unhappy lieutenant to Gladstone, who had just made an affirmation of loyalty, Salisbury observes equably: 'He evidently said what he did to prevent his friends from suspecting him of any intention under any circumstances to join us. His resolves are not eternal, but he has effectually barred himself from any such new course until some little time has passed, or something new has happened.' Carnarvon was permitted his private initiative to sound out the Irish, but it was unanimously rejected across two Cabinet meetings at the end of the year.

The dimensions of what Gladstone would attempt to do, the grain against which he was cutting, can be glimpsed from the judgements of England's greatest contemporary historian, James Anthony Froude. Froude, a specialist on Tudor England, was in the Macaulay mode, a stylist who wrote a relaxed, arm-swinging, highly readable prose and made history at a high level into popular reading. He held, not discreditably, the old English Protestant assumptions which hardly helped him to a balanced view of Ireland, though he had moments of describing both the landscape and people of Irish localities lyrically. That said, he had a cut-and-dried racist view of history which stops the modern reader dead.

But Froude was comfortably in tune with his age. The 'Preliminary Essay' to his three-volume *The English in Ireland* (1881) will suffice. The work, by the way, is dedicated to an Ulsterman, Sir Garnet Wolseley, the 'Most Distinguished representative of The English in Ireland'. English intellectual Conservatives at this time were frequently hero-worshippers of generals – Gordon, Roberts, Wolseley and later the calamitous Kitchener – something reflecting an oddly Prussian style.

Froude tells us that 'the better sort of men submit willingly to be governed by those who are nobler than themselves, organisation creates superiority of force; and the ignorant and the selfish may be and are justly compelled for their own advantage to obey a rule which rescues them from their natural weakness ... and the rights of man – if such rights there be – are not to liberty, but to wise direction and control.'

That, for Froude, was the general theory, but those who rule, being stronger, would tend to be better men: 'On the whole and as a rule, superior strength is the equivalent of superior merit.' Froude admits that 'a nobler people may, through force of circumstances, or great numerical inferiority, be oppressed for a time by the brute force of baser adversaries.' But that, he thinks, cannot stick. 'An oppressed cause, when it is just, attracts friends and commands moral support which converts itself sooner or later into material strength.'[5] He had told an American audience in 1872 that if the time ever came when Celt and Saxon were to live together in quiet, it would be 'when America tells the Irish that they have no longer a grievance which legislation can redress, and that they must depend for their future prosperity on their own industry'.[6]

Virtue and truth for Froude have a way of being deftly subsumed into strength, for 'nature has allotted superiority of strength to superiority of intellect and character; and in deciding that the weaker shall obey the more powerful, she is in reality saving them from themselves, and then confers true liberty when she seems most to be taking it away.' If a nation is strong enough to keep its liberty, he says, it deserves liberty; if not, not.

These general principles are then examined in relation to the Irish. Starting out from the three captains in Henry V, Fluellen the Welshman, Jamy the Scot and Macmorris the Irishman, comparisons are made. The Welsh are conquered but are not to be thought inferior for that reason. They were simply fewer, geographically vulnerable and remote from allies. So, 'neither slaves nor cowards', they had fought, but realised the odds and 'when resistance became obviously hopeless, they loyally and wisely accepted their fate', and 'though vain with true Celtic vanity of pedigrees which lose themselves in infinity', they learned the score and 'ceased to pine after after political liberty which they were consciously unable to preserve; and finding themselves accepted on equal terms as joint inheritors of a magnificent empire, the iron chain became a magnificent ornament'. Not contributing as much to that magnificent empire as the Scots, 'they have never been its shame or its weakness; and their retention of a few harmless peculiarities has not prevented them from being wholesome or worthy members of the united Common-wealth.'[7]

The Scots were something else. They were 'a race of men who had been hammered to a temper which made them more valuable than mountains of gold'.[8] The 'Lowland Scots', he added 'were Teutons. They offered effective resistance for a long time; accordingly, union with Scotland 'was effected on equal terms. Two separate self-governed peoples entered slowly and deliberately into voluntary partnership on terms of mutual respect.'

There were no mountains of gold in Ireland and no native Teutons. Certainly they were brave. 'The hardihood of the Irish kern was proverbial throughout Europe'[9] and they had been a large and effective contingent in British armies. But at home in Ireland it was different. 'An unappeasable

34

discontent has been attended with the paralysis of manliness.'[10] Accordingly, 'recurring insurrections have only issued in absolute and ever disgraceful defeat'. If, says Froude bluffly, Ireland had fought effectively like Scotland, she would have prospered – alone, choosing then to be united with England or in her own continental alliances. Equally, if, like Wales, she had understood her weak position and had sensibly submitted, she would not have been the loser. Given that submission, it was in England's interests to treat her well and 'there was not originally any one advantage which England possessed which she was not willing and eager to share with her'.[11]

But Ireland fell between stools and 'would neither courageously do battle nor would she honourably submit', and 'when insurrection finally failed, [the Irish] betook themselves to assassination and secret tribunals; and all this while they were holding up themselves and their wrongs as if they were the victims of the most abominable tyranny, and inviting the world to judge between them and their oppressors.'

Such behaviour upset England. 'Everything she most valued for herself – her laws and liberties, her orderly and settled government, the most ample security for person and property – England's first desire was to give to Ireland in fullest measure. The temper in which she was met exasperated her into harshness and at times to cruelty; and so followed in succession alternations of revolt and punishment . . . till it seemed at last as if no solution of the problem was possible *save the expulsion or destruction of a race which appeared incurable* [my italics].'[12]

Having apparently toyed with extermination, Froude turns his attention to the general Irish character.

Lighthearted, humorous, imaginative, sensitive, susceptible through the entire range of feeling, from the profoundest pathos to most playful jest, if they possess some virtues, they possess the counterfeits of a hundred more. Passionate in everything – passionate in their religion, passionately courageous, passionately loyal and and affectionate – they are without the manliness which will give strength and solidity to the sentimental part of their dispositions.

Courageous but unmanly, the Irish had aesthetic sense: 'If they have never produced a tolerable drama, it is because imagination cannot outstrip reality . . .' They had no architecture. 'No lines of beauty soften anywhere the forbidding harshness of their provincial towns; rarely does climbing rose or creeper dress the naked walls of a farmhouse cottage.' And the Irish were to blame for their climate, having 'pared its forests to the stump till it shivers in damp and desolation'.

Froude, just a little inclined to be judgemental, swells magisterial. 'The perceptions of taste which belong to the higher orders of understanding is absent – or cleanliness of person and habit. The Irish are the spendthrift sister of the Aryan race.'

Possibly a compliment at this point might have been taken amiss, but Froude wants to be fair. The Irish are charming. 'They have a power of attraction which no one who has felt it can withstand.' And besides, the Irish were loyal, something which no one appreciated better than the Norman barons who conquered Ireland. Unfortunately, the baron was so comfortable with such followers that he went native. 'He forgot more and more that he was come to Ireland to introduce English law and manners' though there were 'efforts from the nobler part of the English settlers to arrest the downward progress'. By the statute of Kilkenny in 1367, 'intermarriage with the Irish or fostering with the Irish was made treason'. In a footnote, Froude speaks of fostering as 'entrusting the children to Irish foster-nurses, the most fatal of all the means by which the degeneracy was brought about'.

Froude has conceded that the Irish at this time had capable leaders like Hugh O'Neill, men who had served in French or

Spanish armies, 'taken degrees at Oxford and Cambridge' or 'at the Inns of Court'. 'The force of circumstances,' he confides, had 'carried Ireland forward in spite of herself in the general stream of civilisation.'

However, the bad effect of the Irish upon those who come to govern them is invoked a little later to explain the crimes of Elizabethan soldiery in Ireland. Froude has just impressed us by his disgust at this when basic principles catch up with him.

> Placed in the country to repress banditti they were little better than banditti themselves . . . Too few to take prisoners or hold a mutinous district in compelled quiet, their only resource was to strike terror by cruelty. When sent to recover stolen cattle or punish a night foray, they came at last to regard the Irish peasants as unpossessed of the common rights of human beings, and shot and strangled them like foxes or jackals . . . something related with a calmness more frightful than the atrocities themselves; young English gentlemen describing expeditions to the mountains 'to have some killing' as if a forest was being driven for a battue.

Conceding an abandonment of common civilisation by English soldiers, Froude then insouciantly reaches the conclusion that 'the best and only hope for the country was the extension of English influence over it.' After all, 'the worst cruelties of the garrisons were but the occasional copies of the treatment of the Irish by one another'.

In discussing Norman rule and the problems encountered by Elizabeth's representatives in Ireland, Froude, writing in 1880–81, was mindful of his own times, those of the Land League and coercion. He has remarked already on the shifts between what he calls 'severity' and tolerance. The early Stuart kings were to attempt the latter course – 'a wet sponge was passed over all the crimes committed against the late Queen'. But of course it couldn't last. There were to be new risings. 'Experience was to show that the Irish did not understand forbearance, that they interpreted lenity into fear, and respected only an authority that they dare not trifle with.'

3

The Kite and Joe

W hat followed prejudice was debate, much of it prejudiced. Carnarvon's interest in a Conservative response
to Parnell and the Irish was not allowed to come to anything.
It was barred for the good reason that Salisbury, heading a
minority government in 1885, had no intention, as he had told
Lord Bath, of giving anything up to mankind that was meant
for party. A letter from Gladstone to Balfour, Salisbury's
nephew and successor, had expressed the view that 'it will
be a public calamity if this great subject falls into the lines
of party conflict', that accordingly, he desired 'specially on
grounds of public policy that it should be dealt with by the
present Government'[1] and offering a bipartisan approach.

But Salisbury had already resolved against any advance
towards Home Rule. He held office for six months, the latter
half of 1885. By December he was through with Carnarvon
and his Irish soundings for good. Parnell would later allege
in the Commons that he 'had been informed the previous
summer by a Minister of the Crown that the Conservative
Party intended if they won the elections, to offer a statutory
legislature to Ireland'.[2] Carnarvon would deny anything so
concrete or authorised, insisting that he had been making
only his own preliminary explorations. Salisbury, he would

say, warned him, 'most properly, to be cautious, but did not as head of the government, interpose to prevent the meeting.'[3] Salisbury and Carnarvon were writing each other polite, exculpatory and embarrassing letters in June 1886, Salisbury sticking to the line that his viceroy had no certain views when he began exploration, so he, Salisbury, could not have objected, but that when Carnarvon's views did harden in November and on their being expressed to Cabinet, 'You were met by a strong expression of dissent from two or three members, and the subject dropped – and I think, was not resumed.'[4]

Salisbury had never been the man for risking party unity. He would in due course express views on the Irish people cruder than Froude's. How much this sort of ranting came from conviction is uncertain. More importantly, the proprietor of the Hotel Cecil did not think in bipartisan terms for the accomplishment of a major reform. With a certain aristocratic vulgarity, he would remark that Gladstone 'would give the oyster to the Parnellites and leave the shell to his own party'. That Parliament was delicately balanced. The Irish held the exact balance, so anyone working with and for them stood open to charges of owing office *to* them. As that Parliament stood, Salisbury was placed to remain in office, let Carnarvon have his head over Home Rule and enjoy Liberal support and risk a grave split in the Tory Party. He was damned if he would do any such thing.

Gladstone, by a mirror image, faced the same choice. He could, on coming to power, have pulled back from Home Rule and preoccupied his administration with the local government schemes (not least in Ireland) which Joseph Chamberlain, his overarchingly ambitious and outstanding new lieutenant, was proposing. The Liberal Party would have been intact, the disappointed Irish would have abused him moderately – as they had before the election, something which was no great disadvantage in mainland politics – and the Tories, denied a handle and an election, would have been out of office for the rest of the decade.

In a third option, the two leaders, by working together, could have put agreed reform through independently of Irish support and to the frustration of all the negative voices.

Salisbury was an intelligent, shrewd politician who would do very well in his own time by remaining resolutely if comfortably wrapped in conventional thinking. He was, in a limited sense, a Machiavellian, always doing what made sense in terms of party self-interest. But the Florentine directed his mind to grand designs. And Salisbury, who did not, was essentially a provincial Machiavelli. Gladstone would be naïve in Cabinet-making, failing, unlike the Vicar of Wakefield, to choose one for the qualities which would last. He would make a series of mistakes about the importance of both Ulster and opinion in England; about Darius Clayhanger. But when he had declared, long before, that to solve the problem of Ireland was his mission, he had told the plain truth, and surely, it had to be *someone's* mission.

In the Parliament elected in 1885, Gladstone had lost ground, but, with Irish support, had a majority. He had done well in the country and badly in the suburbs, which were turning Tory. After defeat on the beer duty technicality, that majority lay dormant, admitting a minority Tory ministry. When six months later (in December, announced 16 January 1886) Carnarvon resigned, and with him Hart Dyke, chief secretary, Dyke's replacement in Ireland, W.H. Smith, would request the only option to negotiations with Parnell – a Coercion Bill – and everyone in that finely balanced Parliament knew exactly where they were. Salisbury wanted to be out of office because Ireland could harm a Conservative government only if tackled imaginatively; could indeed harm any government only if tackled imaginatively. A call for a Coercion Bill was by way of affronting the Irish bloc, a means to being out. Gladstone was ready and not calculating.

'Not perhaps in mere logic,' he wrote, 'but practicably, it was now plain that Ireland had no hope from the Tories . . . I determined on taking any and every legitimate opportunity to remove the existing Government from office.' His colleague Sir William Harcourt, a very modified Home Ruler himself, asked if Gladstone was willing to go forward without the support of either Hartington or Chamberlain. Gladstone believed that he 'was prepared to go forward without any body. That is to say without any known and positive assurance of support.' This was 'one of the great imperial occasions which call for such resolutions'.[5]

Being without Hartington or Chamberlain would be a serious prospect. The Marquess of Hartington, elder brother of Lord Frederick Cavendish, was not so much motivated by recollection of the murder as by convictions which had been carrying him ever further away from the man whose decent, unglamorous lieutenant he had been for so long. Hartington was a Whig. The Whigs were a diminishing force electorally in parliaments new-crafted by reform acts. They themselves had brought about the Act of 1832, the Great Reform Act, but not for nothing had the nickname of Lord John Russell, one of those responsible for it, been 'Finality Jack'.

The Whigs were just a little like the Institutional Revolutionary Party which ruled Mexico until almost yesterday. There had been one true revolution which prevented the necessity – beyond tempering amendments – for any more. And besides, it was *their* revolution, and they would defend it against dangerous innovations. Whig landlords still influenced elections in county seats, an influence which would, after the 1884 Act, slip away from them. The urbanisation of the nineteenth century was part of a progress of which they theoretically approved, but could not control. It carried the implication of more radical demands and a larger volume of government and expenditure and thus tax. They were against that. Like rural workers leaving for the towns, Whigs would depart from the Liberal Party in successive waves. Ireland would precipitate one of the major splashes. Rather like Darius Clayhanger, working man turned small capitalist, they were showing the conservatism of age.

And Ireland was, of all issues, historically tender to the Whigs, for their true revolution had been 1688, with 1832 as a sort of grand adjustment (perhaps the word 'reform' was psychologically the apt word), and they were a party of establishment. They were not aggressive Protestants on the Ulster or Froude model. Catholic emancipation had given them few problems in 1829, while union itself had been the creation of Pitt the Younger, a Tory. But the British state itself was arguably a creation of 1688. Any weakening of it, for whatever good reasons, worked against their own foundations.

More prosaically, they were landowning noblemen threatened by taxes and by manufacturers with the working classes coming up, and they had more in common with the heroic lethargy of Salisbury than with Gladstone's tribulating visions. They were about to create from all these negatives an entity, Liberal Unionism, of which Oscar Wilde would make Lady Bracknell say nine years later, 'Oh, they count as Tories and dine with us – or come in the evening at any rate.'*

Hartington, who would make a good, balanced Commons speech against the bill, did not even come into the government that Gladstone would now form. The 'Hawarden Kite', an unauthorised, well-meaning and cack-handed briefing about Home Rule proposals by Herbert, Gladstone's youngest son, through a news agency and a newspaper in his Leeds constituency, precipitated that. The gaffe made the occasion but the breach would have happened anyway. Hartington had with difficulty been reconciled to the extension of the national franchise in 1884. His vote and those of an undefined number of other Whigs could not be cast for Home Rule. Yet in melancholy and reluctant fashion, the Liberal Unionists would, long after this, sit on the same side of the chamber, proximate and

---

* Yet Lansdowne, a southern Protestant landowner and former Whig, caught years later in a sudden torrential downpour, preferred to get soaked rather than take refuge in the Tory Carlton Club.

confusing opponents. All this had been apparent to Gladstone in the months of waiting, but it had not weighed. He was, after all, losing in addition the services of another Whig, Lord Richard Grosvenor, his chief whip.

Gladstone, more than most party leaders, thought reclusively. The logical extension of his longstanding concern for Ireland into a belief in Home Rule makes sense looked at in retrospect, but the mental steps by which it was reached were not spelled out as they were ascended. The statement was to come biblically from the summit. Thus, almost inadvertently, the shift to Home Rule would be proclaimed as Revelation, in this case revelation in the *Leeds Mercury* and the *Pall Mall Gazette*. It was not good politics. The quartermastering of information is now over-refined as a legion of smart briefers do their dubious work. For Gladstone, possessed of a high purpose to be milled in his own mind, such precautions were beneath consideration. So, unprompted by him, the *Pall Mall Gazette* reported the Hawarden Kite on 17 December: 'Mr Gladstone has definitely adopted the policy of Home Rule for Ireland . . .' This wonderfully innocent interview, in which the nineteenth-century tape-recorder seems to have been left on and the term 'off the record' entirely overlooked, indicated that there was 'reasonable expectation that both Lord Hartington and Mr Goschen will come round to Mr Gladstone's view . . .' The kite was the result of Herbert's inexperience, but its views and its grand-scheme optimism were those of William Gladstone.

He was to bring just such inept politics to his dealings with the other great defector, Chamberlain. Joseph Chamberlain, screwmaker, revolutionary municipalist, creator of the Birmingham caucus and electrifier of local government while still in his early thirties, represented the very highest abilities resting upon a more modest ethical foundation. Like Gladstone, he was a man of destiny, though much more self-consciously so, and unlike Gladstone, when Chamberlain cut a corner he actively meant to cut a corner. Disraeli would never have applied to Chamberlain his quip about Gladstone insisting that the ace of spades had been put in his sleeve by God. When it suited him, Joe played off the bottom of any deck.

Chamberlain, though the representative of Birmingham Nonconformity – unitarianism, actually – was troubled by neither religious prejudice nor Hibernophobia. (English and Welsh Nonconformity would have a broadly honourable approach to Ireland, despite religious differences.) Again, Chamberlain at that stage of his career, was a motorised reformer and as far from the deep constitutional repose of Hartington as could be. In Ireland he was solidly on the record as an opponent of coercion. During the 1880–85 government, he had been, with his ally Dilke, an advocate of greater devolution for Ireland and a resister of crimes acts. There were differences, and important ones. Chamberlain had favoured a Central Board handling independently education, communications and land, together with extensive local government.

He was a freelance on Ireland, not only pushing himself forward in 1884 as a mooter of schemes, but also acting as a communication channel for Captain O'Shea, supposed if unreliable spokesman for Parnell. Chamberlain, who would produce for Britain his 'Unauthorised Programme' of 1884, was putting his best efforts into unauthorised activity at this time. Spencer, who as viceroy *was* authorised in Ireland, had entertained the Control Board scheme thoughtfully, but had come to the conclusion that it was too dependent on Westminster and that Irish administration, subordinate to English policy direction, would never work. Spencer's own development was to become more radical and to press for the full Home Rule package.

Chamberlain, both frustrated of a personal triumph and personally resentful of Spencer as he tended to become when thwarted, slipped towards conservative immobilism. He had been firmly on the record as an opponent of Irish separation.

At Warrington he had compared Ireland with London as having no better claim upon autonomy. 'It is said by him [Parnell] that justice requires that we should concede to Irishmen the absolute right of self-government . . . I cannot admit that five millions of Irishmen have any greater inherent right to govern themselves without regard to the rest of the United Kingdom than the five million inhabitants of the metropolis.'[6] With all his other motives, Chamberlain lacked the sympathy to make an imaginative leap or even to begin to see how Irishmen might see themselves. Even at his most sympathetic, an English self-preoccupation betrayed him into a condescension as obtuse as it would be popular. The Chamberlain of the South African War was already lurking.

'Separation' now tended for him to merge with any form of autonomy which went beyond his own Central Board. What had effectively happened during the negotiations and the rejection of the Central Board scheme was that Chamberlain had been given motives for not developing his thinking, not coming to terms with Home Rule in the way that most of the Cabinet would actually do. For a man proudly calling himself a radical, he became in 1884–5 strangely reliant upon old speeches which argued his consistency and masked his pique.

Circumstances over ten years would turn Radical Joe into Imperial Joe, but the coming separation – from Gladstone and later from the Liberal Party – would be in part a product of Gladstone's extraordinary ineptitude at man-management – and of the overweening and impatient ambition of Joseph Chamberlain. The Hawarden Kite, to quote the *Pall Mall Gazette* again, complacently proclaimed of the Home Rule scheme that 'Mr Chamberlain and Sir Charles Dilke could not consistently oppose it'.

The way in which policy would be formulated was naturally disruptive of good relations. Gladstone had not responded to Chamberlain's early plans, but had come up with his own which went further, and moreover had made his own contacts with Parnell. The Irish leader had advised Irishmen to vote against Liberals in the 1885 election despite Chamberlain's unofficial efforts, yet here was Gladstone producing what Captain O'Shea in his conversations with Chamberlain called 'a better offer'. There were reasons for Gladstone's closeness, and Parnell had, very reasonably, been listening to all offers – from Chamberlain, Gladstone and Carnarvon. But Chamberlain was a man affronted, outbid and bypassed by his elderly chief, who, at seventy-six, should have been living up to his often-repeated talk about retirement. His words to his friend Dilke were: 'I don't like him. I really hate him.'[7]

But Chamberlain was not out yet and, ironically, the Liberals would regain power at the start of 1886 through the offices of his camp. Jesse Collings, a Birmingham MP and very much the ruffian on Chamberlain's personal stair, introduced a motion on the absence of any provision in Salisbury's Queen's Speech for rural workers. Chamberlain had, eighteen months before in that 'Unauthorised Programme', advocated small-holdings for those coming new voters, the country labourers, the so-called 'three acres and a cow' scheme, an oddly Irish notion recalling the Chartist Feargus O'Connor.

The motion was picked up by Gladstone, made the subject of a major Commons speech of his own and pressed to a division on the address where, on 25 January 1886, the government was defeated and fell. No one thought the Commons was debating smallholdings. They were debating Ireland, and who should govern; debating also who should take risks and who avoid them. Defeated and resigning office, Salisbury had won.

When it came to forming a government, it might still have been open to Gladstone to reclaim Chamberlain. And having already lost Hartington, Grosvenor and his former attorney-general, Henry James, from his right wing, he could not afford to alienate the radical faction leader. He did, though. For a start, Chamberlain might have been offered the treasury, a measure of his real and self-perceived standing, but that was wanted for Harcourt, who, a natural partisan Liberal if no friend of the Irish, would always have remained grumblingly loyal. The Queen was insisting on Rosebery, one of the great vacancies of political history, for the Foreign Office. But the Colonial Office which Chamberlain requested, foreshadowing his imperial future and a vital and preoccupying job to keep him fascinated and out of revolt, produced from Gladstone five calamitous words, 'Oh, a secretary of state!'

'No man,' wrote Johnson to Lord Chesterfield, 'is content to have his all neglected, be it ever so little.' Chamberlain was being told that his all did not rate the upper end of the Cabinet, that his ambitions ran ahead of the prime minister's esteem. Gladstone managed, if such a thing were possible, to make matters worse than they already were by proposing a £300 saving in the salary of Chamberlain's junior at the Local Government Board, the post he did take. The junior was that same henchman, Collings, whose motion had brought down the Tories. If Gladstone had been attempting by large and small offence to engineer Chamberlain's withdrawal, he would not have managed so well. The affronts were in fact wholly inadvertent, a tribute to the thickheadedness of which preoccupied genius is capable.

Chamberlain was finally given a department which he knew about, cared about and had plans for, plans which would be given second place in government business after Ireland. But he was now pure enemy looking for an excuse halfway consistent with what he had said before for getting out – for getting out and inflicting destruction upon Gladstone.

Having got everything wrong politically, Gladstone now embarked upon the most ambitious undertaking towards Ireland since the Act of Union itself and, by melancholy irony, the greatest before the treaty which would create the Irish state. He was working alone, confiding sometimes in Spencer and Morley, who would be chief secretary, but to a high degree working (and evaluating his thinking) without contact. There would be Tory (and Tory historians') charges of bad faith and *volte face*, also of extreme and revolutionary measures. In fact Gladstone, however close with his plans, would go to great lengths to reassure both the fearful and interested parties. The mix of Home Rule and land reform he would advocate in two separate acts was designed to conciliate moderate conservative opinion.

He would, in March, propose an assembly avoiding the word 'Parliament'; he would leave everything to do with the military and with foreign policy in Westminster (or imperial) hands. And the assembly itself, under the Crown, was also to wholly replace Irish representation in Westminster. This was an earlier (and drastic) attempt to deal with what we call the West Lothian Question. In fact, Gladstone would vacillate on this issue and come back to an Irish presence in Westminster. But the idea of being rid of Irish disruption – 'Stop their bills, sir, that's the policy' – was one of the selling points of Home Rule, the main reason that Sir William Harcourt for one cheerfully supported it. It was an imperfect state of affairs and Gladstone would be drawn late in the day to the notion of a Standing Committee of Irish assemblymen, lords and Westminster MPs to provide a sort of running commentary on matters reserved from the Irish Assembly by the act. The objective, as with so much else, was to balance real autonomy with an assertion of a shared British imperial connection.

As for the composition of the assembly, more could hardly have been done to reassure the established, owning and apprehensive classes. There would be two Houses, or 'Orders', as Gladstone called them. The Lower Order would be made up of 204 members elected under the existing franchise widened throughout the UK by that 1884 Reform Act which Hartington had so much disliked. The Upper Order was to have 103 members, 75 of whom would be elected on a single roll and 28 of whom would be Irish peers, those representative Irish peers whose membership of the House of Lords would now cease. There would be a property qualification for voting for this body – £200 annual income or £4,000 free of debt (in modern terms respectively £10,000 and £200,000). This was steeper and more restrictive than anything in England and slightly reminiscent of those multiple electoral rolls with which British ministers and white settlers played about in Africa during the 1960s.

With his Upper Order of peers and property qualifications, Gladstone was tilting against instant democracy and responding to Froudian talk about 'the intelligent part of the electorate'. Cartoon Paddy, the low Milesian of Froude's and Thomas Carlyle's understanding, was to be constitutionally confined by an upper house, which, given Gladstone's own tribulations with the Lords, had distinct ironies. Herbert Gladstone's Hawarden Kite speaks of 'the forces of intelligence, the wealth and interests of every class of the population' as those which would 'assert themselves; and the members returned to Parliament in Dublin will be very different in all respects to those who represent Ireland now.'[8]

The proposals perhaps also reflected that interesting streak of conservatism present in both Parnell and Gladstone, something invisible to Queen Victoria and Lord Salisbury. Gladstone, for all that he grew genuinely more radical as he grew older and did back the masses against the classes, tended to expect his own spirit of downward obligation and duty to be reflected in the dominant classes. Parnell of Avondale, the cricketing Protestant squire, in a like spirit believed that other Protestant squires would follow him. Oliver Cromwell, not a happy source in the Irish context, had nevertheless expressed sentiments which encapsulate such thinking: 'A nobleman, gentleman, a yeoman; that is a good thing.'

Gladstone, and more discreetly Parnell, were concerned not to have an Irish Parliament which was the Land League in legislative form; and very importantly, both men looked back to Henry Grattan. Grattan, driving the Dublin Parliament of 1782, was a wonder from the old times, the inspirational leader of a privileged group moving that group in a false dawn before the European Enlightenment was dissolved in terror and reaction – moving it against privilege. Parnell and Gladstone were Grattan-like figures themselves, but they grossly overestimated the tolerance of light and experiment among the beleaguered owners of land and attenders at evensong in the south and west of Ireland. All opposition to Home Rule was to be based on pessimism, Housman's 'sure foundation of despair'. The impossibility of what would a century later be called power-sharing, the certainty of change meaning decay, were to be the props of resistance – in Parliament, among southern landowners and above all in Ulster.

Yet again Gladstone sought – and Parnell endorsed him in the effort – to propitiate the fearful. The Irish Assembly was excluded, not only, reasonably enough, from defence and foreign policy matters, including treaty-making; it was also barred from making religious endowments, while the non-denominational character of national schools was specifically guaranteed. (Thirty years of resistance to Home Rule would produce a republic which Roman Catholic influence would dedicate in high constitutional form to 'the Most Holy Trinity'!)

For those who argued against an Irish police force excessively Irish, the transfer of police responsibility was to be staggered, with both the Dublin Metropolitan force and the Royal Irish Constabulary left in imperial hands for two years longer. The financial settlement which Gladstone would offer Ireland was initially a measure of both optimism and breadth of view. He was much influenced by the economist Robert Giffen, who had argued convincingly that Ireland paid twice as much in all British taxes as she ought to. 'Ireland, while constituting only a twentieth part of of the United Kingdom in resources, nevertheless pays a tenth or eleventh of the taxes. Ireland ought to pay about £3,500,000 and it pays nearly £7,000,000.'[9] Giffen also pointed out that the advantage to the exchequer thus gained was nearly all blown, not least through military impositions in Ireland. 'Actually it is beyond question, we lose as government nearly £3,000,000 while taxing Ireland over £3,000,000 more than it ought to be taxed.'

Gladstone proposed that Ireland should contribute a fifteenth of total imperial expenditure in taxes, a good deal more than Giffen's numbers implied she should. On the other hand, the Irish revenue would not lose the duty on goods collected in Ireland but consumed in Britain. This amounted to about £1,400,000, largely from spirits, beer and tobacco. There were serious doubts that Gladstone was correct in his calculations. Thomas Sexton, one of Parnell's lieutenants, would later argue that an Irish treasury would have a deficit to make up on these terms of £850,000 which would have to come from direct taxes. And a tax on land values raised to meet it without hitting the citizen would have been vetoed by the putative upper chamber with its landed interest.

The non-counting of revenue for alcohol and tobacco manufactured in Ireland was the by-blow of a late decision to insist upon imperial control of customs and excise in order to guarantee a continued single market between the two islands. Harcourt, solicitous for the Irish on this occasion, would with hindsight criticise the decision on the grounds that any British reduction of those duties – automatically applying in Ireland – would reduce Irish revenue disproportionately. If, however, excise revenues went up, they would oblige an Irish administration required to balance its budget to make cuts. As it had no control over indirect taxes, this could only mean reductions in taxes levied directly, benefiting the well-to-do at the expense of poorer people paying more for beer and tobacco. A pint of plain, to adopt Flann O'Brien, would be your only man for ensuring that it was the rich what got the pleasure.

If the problem of Ireland was a perpetual mirroring of politics and land, Gladstone, in providing for one, was certain that he had to move on the other. Actually, he intended more than that, though the Land Bill would be marked by the characteristic Gladstonian yoking of frugality and vision. He saw land reform as the means to end the running jacquerie of peasant menace against agents, new tenants and livestock. Irish agricultural product prices had fallen again in 1885–6, precisely what had triggered violent assaults after 1878–9. Something had to be done for the social order of Ireland. 'That is the first, the greatest, the most sacred and the most necessary aim of every government that knows its duty.'[10] As he wrote to Harcourt, 'I am morally certain that it is only by exerting *to the utmost* our financial strength (not mainly by expenditure but as credit) on behalf of Ireland, that we can hope to sustain the burden of an adequate land measure.' And without it, 'We cannot either establish social order or face the question of Irish government.'[11]

The point of departure would be the same Robert Giffen who had provided figures on Irish overtaxation. Giffen saw Irish issues keenly and made crisply for root-and-branch solutions. In an article in *The Statist* generally attributed to him, he proposed buying out the Irish landlord, giving in return twenty years' worth of judicial rents in government stock. The land would then be given free to occupiers who would pay something between a third and two thirds of rent to the new local government authorities of Ireland. 'The plan,' he said briskly, 'is to throw the cost of local government in Ireland upon Irish resources exclusively, and to give the Irish people the rents of the country for the purpose of conducting it'. The conflict between landlord and tenant would thus be at an end. 'We need no longer fear that if we give Ireland Home Rule the property of the landlords would be confiscated.'[12]

The devil lay in the numbers. Giffen offered a figure, £8,000,000* as the whole rent of Ireland settled judicially, and

---

* All sums of money require for conversion to rough modern values to be multiplied by fifty.

proposed paying for twenty years of this with £160,000,000 of government stock, something which would cost the British treasury £4.8 million annually. And, said Giffen, as we were already spending £4 million a year 'on law, prisons, police education and such matters',[13] we would have a bargain. Further, the tenants, paying together a figure between £4 and £5 million against the old £8 million, would be major beneficiaries, though as even fair judicial rents had taken no account of agricultural depression and recent falling product prices, this was simple realism. The bottom line was that very many tenants were in no position to pay even judicial rents after such a price fall.

The implications were political and organic. The new Irish authority would be collecting the rents protected by a police force which pretty obviously had to be under that Irish authority. Responsibility would be shifted, and with it the means to exercise it. With money coming from that rent charge rather than from a treasury subsidy, the Irish authority would have feet of its own to stand on. They would be £800,000 to the good on the transaction, but given Giffen's earlier point about long-term overtaxation, that was no great impropriety. Giffen was seeking to transform the whole situation and help autonomous Ireland, through British good offices, to meet the long grief of the tenant farmer's forever recurring despair. As for the landlord, he would, to amend Oscar Wilde, be relieved of a position while being provided with the means of keeping it up. Gladstone admired the grand sweep, but here his financial prudence got the better of him. Giffen had talked of a total of £160 million; the figure discussed among ministers was £120 million. Gladstone wasn't willing to go for compulsory purchase and suggested in a memo of 20 March setting aside a figure of £60 million. It need not be the last word if the scheme went well, but it would conciliate moderate and alarmed opinion.

More than many things in the combined programme of

reform, the Land Acts provoked rational rather than prejudiced opposition and Gladstone's caution was criticised by
Spencer. Earl Spencer, despite coming from the jittery and
armigerous wing of the party, was a radical on Ireland
by reason, after four years in the viceroyalty, of knowing
a great deal about it. Spencer had been ready to think
big and was disappointed. 'The bill as originally intended
will carry an idea of thoroughness which the new proposal
would not do . . .' But finally Gladstone brought down the
figure even further to £50 million. What he had in mind for
the tenant was something altogether more agreeable to the
treasury. His elaborate plans involved the purchase of net
rental only, producing a much smaller fall in rent payments
by the tenants.

Gladstone would be reproached by Sir James Caird, the
agricultural economist and earlier proclaimer of 'high farming' – scientific, high-investment, high-yield farming (Ireland
had altogether too much 'low' farming). The 'strong farmers',
a sixth of agricultural landholders, said Caird, paid two thirds
of all rent. The remaining five sixths paid one third, and they
were dirt poor. 'If the present prices of agricultural produce
continue to decline, I should fear that from the land held by
the large body of poor farmers in Ireland, any economical
rent has for the present disappeared. A purchase of it would
therefore be certain loss.'

But to rational and prejudiced criticism must be added a
third sort combining both – Chamberlain's criticism. The
president of the Local Government Board wanted an excuse
for resigning. In the *Fortnightly Review* he placed in February
1886 an article written under the pseudonym 'A Radical'.
(The device was to be echoed ninety years later, probably
by admiring design, by that other difficult Midlander, Enoch
Powell, with his series of *Times* articles bylined 'A Conservative'.) Chamberlain's piece tended in a very unradical
direction, expressing fear that a Dublin Parliament would at
once acquire control of all internal affairs and that contrary

to Gladstone's thinking, Irish MPs would have to remain in Westminster obstructing business. An independent, sovereign Ireland would raise a conscript army and we should have to follow. The Canadian model would not do because Canada was effectively independent.

It was poor stuff for a man of Chamberlain's intellectual resources. And his positive suggestions were no better: putting Parnell in a government and setting him to solve the land question or, alternatively, total inactivity on the grounds that Parnell would alienate the English (or Birmingham?) working class and thus cease to matter, were absurdly Anglo-centric ideas, not to say rather childish. His final call – for suspension of Irish representation at Westminster with the Speaker acting as a sort of dictator – might have come from Froude.

But Chamberlain would get his blow home and devise his own departure before argument on the size of contribution had started. He picked his fight at an early Cabinet meeting. Information was due to Cabinet ministers. Gladstone, who at this early stage, 13 March, with the government only six weeks in office, had kept his cards not so much close to his chest as in their packet, spelled out his plans for land purchase under the Land Act. Chamberlain demanded to know if monies would be paid to a full part of the United Kingdom or to a prospective independent nation. Gladstone said that he believed there would be an Irish legislative authority, his own prior conclusion. This provided Chamberlain with the handle he wanted, and accompanied by Sir George Trevelyan, he forthwith resigned, nominally over the land scheme. It was no more a tantrum than the resignation on-camera of Michael Heseltine exactly a century later. It was the sort of firing on a fort which starts a war.

However, hostilities were delayed for a couple of weeks by colleagues who persuaded both to defer departure till the other half of the package, the Home Rule plans, was made public. Once Gladstone had set out his broad resolution for Parliament, Chamberlain, always given to the hectoring approach, addressed to the prime minister a questionnaire. Would Irish representation at Westminster cease? Would the Irish Parliament have power of taxation including excise? Would the judiciary and the magistrature be vested in the Irish authority? Would the Irish Parliament have authority for everything not specifically excluded in the act or only as statute-authorised? The answer to all these questions was of course yes, and Chamberlain and Trevelyan went.

In discussing Chamberlain's relations with Gladstone, reasons and arguments, though they proliferate, are of secondary and cosmetic importance. Chamberlain could quote his old speeches against 'separation' together with his readiness to talk coercion going as far back as 1881. 'If nationalism means separation, I for one am prepared to resist it. I see in it the probability of, almost the certainty of, dangerous complications and an antagonism which would be injurious to the interests of the larger country and fatal to the smaller. Sooner than yield on this point, I would govern Ireland by force to the end of the chapter.'[14]

The more bloodthirsty right-wing commentators like George Saintsbury would soon start to talk of Gladstonian Home Rule as 'repeal' (of the union). But it was not repeal of the union, nor separation, simply a form of Irish autonomy more extensive and further from Westminster than the one Chamberlain had proposed in 1884. The move forward was Gladstone's, not his. Gladstone and Spencer had frustrated him, the prime minister was visibly staying and not going, the happy assumption of fifteen months before, and conflict had soured into enmity.

As Harcourt told Gladstone, 'You will be deceived if you think that Chamberlain is to be conciliated on any terms. He has no thought but of war to the knife.'[15] Anthony Mundella, president of the Board of Trade and a man with the same radical provincial background (Nottingham for Birmingham), wrote: 'He hates Gladstone. He has no sense of gratitude or loyalty.'[16] And Chamberlain himself, speaking to

Dilke, said flatly, 'The retention of the Irish members is only with me, the flag that covers other objections.' The principle other objection was Gladstone.

Meanwhile, he concentrated his fire upon the Land Act, ironically for his negative and conservative purpose, taking advantage of Gladstone's financial stringency.

> This scheme, while contemplating only a trifling reduction in the judicial rents fixed before the recent fall in prices, would commit the British taxpayer to tremendous obligations, accompanied in my opinion with serious risk of ultimate loss.
>
> The greater part of the land of Ireland would be handed over to a new Irish elective authority who would thus be at once the landlords and the delegates of the Irish tenants. I fear that these two capacities would be found inconsistent and that the tenants unable or unwilling to pay the rents demanded would speedily elect an authority pledged to give them relief and to seek to recoup itself by an early repudiation of what would be described as 'the English tribute'.[17]

The argument which hung upon this transaction cut both ways. In terms of the long tribulation of the small Irish farmer, wretchedly poor and placed by free-market food prices in a glutted market on a descending escalator, rent cuts had to be as heavy as Giffen wanted, both for humane purposes and in order to leave Ireland stable. Without them she could be satisfactorily governed neither by a struggling Irish executive nor by the policemen and soldiers of the next Crimes Act-presenting chief secretary. Chamberlain's rhetoric was municipal, suggestive not of 'A Radical' but 'A Ratepayer, Edgbaston'. Though in fairness, he had argued for the reduction of judicial rents at once by . . . twenty eight per cent.[18]

For the moment, Chamberlain had stymied Land Reform.

Gladstone, though he had every intention of bringing it back after Home Rule legislation, dropped the bill. And municipal populist objections played well in late Victorian Britain.

John Morley caught this tone of anxious self-pity satirically: 'Vivid pictures were drawn of a train of railway trucks two miles long, loaded with millions of bright sovereigns, all travelling from the British son of toil to the pocket of the idle Irish Landlord.' It was a tone which would recur.

4

Red Ruin

A virulent right-wing press is one of the jewels of the British system. The ability of the party of established order and convention to exist on a high, sparrow-killing note of rage would be more than demonstrated on this question with every attempt to achieve reform, by leader-writers and commentators in *Times*, *Telegraph* and *Morning Post*, not to mention publications like the *Northern Whig* of Belfast. There were also the journals of the day. The *Pall Mall Gazette*, as we have seen, solicited advance advertisement of government policy and criticised sympathetically; the *Saturday Review* was dedicatedly Tory and employed as its pronouncer on Home Rule and Ireland generally the literary critic George Saintsbury.

Saintsbury was a distinguished and very hard-working man of letters, author of a still readable history of English literature. He was moreover what in the Soviet Union would have been called a filthy formalist – someone admiring work strictly for its style. He could and did write approvingly of holders of radical and socialist sentiments if they wrote good enough prose. But in politics he was a ferocious fellow, not so much Tory as mugger, one whose notebooks, printed in the 1930s at the end of his very long life, doubted the actual imperative of keeping the needy alive. 'It takes guts to be as big a skunk as that,' George Orwell would comment. Saintsbury also believed in union and Empire in terms which made any amender of either an instant accredited traitor. As early as February in 1886, with detail on Home Rule still sketchy, he went for the throat, not of Gladstone but of his Irish Secretary, John Morley, also a litererary man and thus a congenial victim.

'Mr Morley has always been a consistent Jacobin ... Englishmen might naturally be surprised to see the Irish Secretary kissing the feet of the yahoos who follow Mr Parnell.' A swipe at the sinister Catholic influence came next. Morley 'appears like Gladstone between a brace of holy Bishops, the extremely reverend Drs Croke and Walsh'.*[1] But the sustained metaphor would be not Rome, but Paris: Paris 1793. 'It will not do of course to force the historical parallel between Mr Morley and Robespierre' – as, at a later date, it would not do to force the parallel between Aneurin Bevan and Stalin.

'We really do not know whether there is any reason for crediting them [Morley's sort of advanced Liberals] with dislike of the sanguinary consistency in deeds as well as words that marks their spiritual ancestors.' And besides, they were mixed up with the Irish National Party. 'At any rate their alliance with a party double-dyed in blood and outrage as the party of Mr Parnell does not show any very great squeamishness.'

Saintsbury appreciates Chamberlain's divergence from the Jacobins and makes a passing guess of great prescience. 'If Mr Chamberlain could get over his middle-class hatred of the nobility and gentry and his inborn hatred of the Church of England, we might yet see him a staunch Conservative.' It was up to the Liberals to react. 'It is now a question

* Thomas Croke, Archbishop of Cashel, and William Walsh, Archbishop of Dublin.

of how long the non-Jacobin portion of the Liberal Party
. . . will continue to act with the Jacobin portion and how
far Englishmen in general by sheer want of understanding,
prepare the way for a *conquête Jacobine*.'

Such a thing would not have happened in 1790s France,
of course 'if there had been no emigration and if the classes
representing property and intelligence in France had not
succumbed almost without conflict to the handful of fanatics
who were bent on destruction'.

There is a level, equally expressed hysteria in all this and
as Saintsbury grows more concrete, metaphor retreats into
earnest, crazed comparisons. He alludes to recent reverses
which had shaken imperial self-confidence. 'It is never safe
to prophesy anything of Englishmen after Majuba [Hill], the
Phoenix Park and Khartoum [death of General Gordon]. But
unless the corresponding class in England takes a fancy to
go to some new Coblentz, which is hardly conceivable, the
Jacobin conquest of England will be no such easy matter.'

Parallels between Ireland and recent colonial reverses which
had sent Queen Victoria into a state of pink indignation
with Gladstone were fashionable. The *Daily Telegraph* had
carried and the *Northern Whig* reproduced a letter from
the Ulster peer Lord Rossmore: 'The Gladstone England of
today, beaten as it was out of South Africa by a handful
of half-civilised Boers, is not the England to set the world
wondering that Ireland should also seek to put her aside,
the only difference being the greater cowardice of the Irish
mode of warfare.' Lord Rossmore then offered a taste of
an Ulster mode of thinking which would become familiar.
'What does Ireland want? Independence? Nonsense . . . She
wants the total removal from her shores of every Protestant
. . . They are just polite enough to want the landlords to go
first. Nobless oblige and the rest will soon follow and the
rebels will have their pretty green globe all to themselves,
fighting and all . . .' The thing to do, Lord Rossmore continued, was 'to say to Ireland, "Enough, you must be treated

like a naughty spoiled child. You have had too much holiday, your play disgusts me, all fire and blood, you must go to bed."' Who could deny, he asked, that mainly due to Mr Gladstone, party government and insane love of power was the curse of Britain? 'Do away with it and Ireland, I vouch, would be beneficially legislated for ... prosperous Ireland would dispense with the carrion agitators who live on the scanty fat of a lean land. Do away with party government and you would again allow the good old pluck of the British nation ... to reassert itself.'

He then addressed himself to Salisbury:

> If there are no patriots left any more, if Lord Salisbury is not one and should fail us now, the loyalists of Ireland must in very deed look to their own right arms. To the English I would say 'Disenfranchise Ireland if you are too frightened of the probable outcry of the handful of radicals returned to Parliament, then for pity's sake give us two Home Rules [Dublin and Belfast].' There is no use in the lion playing the sick sheep any longer. He must either roar to Ireland 'You will be disfranchised until you are sensible again' or bleat 'I am very weak and ill, please leave me alone, take what you want both of you.' And cowardly as the last sounds it would be less dirty than forcing a civil war upon this unfortunate country.[2]

The Tory Press was having its say across the early months of the year, blasting Gladstone and the Jacobin Morley as ministers struggled with the disenchantment of Hartington and the calculation and affront which drove Chamberlain. Chamberlain had caused withdrawal, for the interim, of the land bill. Aware of the threat, Gladstone made a succession of adjustments and was ready to offer a vote on the simple principle of Home Rule with the disputatious bill itself to be withdrawn and resubmitted in refined form later. This was the sort of tactic easier in the leisurely and talkative Victorian Commons, and on a momentous constitutional issue had something to be said for it.

Gladstone had not been skilful. The bill itself was sudden and imperious. The effects upon colleagues had not been worked out. Like Parnell himself, he had not begun to understand the extent of Ulster paranoia about religion nor her quasi-racism between one sort of Celt and another. But it was perhaps the measure of Gladstone's real earnest that the saving of face was subordinated to getting the principle of Home Rule accepted.

His speech at first reading – not something we do these days – was outstanding. Colonel Waring, the Ulsterman who followed him, called it a 'marvellous performance and extraordinary piece of eloquence'. It was also enormous: three and a half hours, Castroic length, though only the twelfth-longest of his career.[3] But if Gladstone's length is odd to us, his view of peoples, aliens, foreigners, Paddies, was in tune with the best of our age – not correctness so much as goodwill, wider faith in the human spirit. The contempt for, or patronage of, Irishmen on general offer in the following pages does not occur. If laws had been rejected by the Irishman, that was because 'the laws by which he is governed do not present themselves to him as they do to us in England or Scotland with a native and congenial aspect'.[4] There was local patriotism, itself a good thing. It could with care and sympathy 'be meshed with wider causes, the Empire and mankind itself.'

The language of Gladstone and his supporters in the second reading, held on and off over twelve days in May and June, also fell short of the Jacobin style. Gladstone himself stressed the example of Canada. He would quote the words of Charles Gavan Duffy, the young Irelander transported in 1849 to

Australia, where he had risen to the premiership of Victoria, the status of Sir Charles and had had influence in both parties, notably with Lord Carnarvon. Gladstone met the argument that Ireland could not be trusted, would not be loyal and therefore should not have Home Rule. 'Canada,' he said quoting Duffy, 'did not get Home Rule because she was loyal and friendly, but she has become loyal and friendly because she has got Home Rule.' The quotation would be a motif of his speech and indeed encapsulated the rationale of a policy of conciliation. Home Rule was 'something much higher than a concession, it is a grand reformation and improvement'. And it was essential, for 'social order is not broken up in Ireland, it is undermined, it is sapped and by universal consent, it imperatively requires to be dealt with', but there needed to be 'restoration of the social order by the removal not merely of the symptoms but of the cause of the mischief'.

'We want,' he added, 'not to drive discontent underground, but to abolish Irish discontent, bag and baggage.' This was his theme. The oppressive soldiery of the Turkish sultan, 'the bashi bazooks and bimbashes carrying out the Bulgarian atrocities', he had said six years before to enormous political and onomatopoeic effect, 'should be cleared out, bag and baggage'. And by social order, Gladstone was invoking the role of the governing classes. He looked for 'the minority representing wealth, landed interest, position and intelligence, with peace restored to Ireland, returning to their occupations and exercising their previous social influence'. It was neither a realistic hope from the Ascendancy nor the customary idiom of Jean-Paul Marat.

Gladstone by May was very familiar with the extreme language of opponents and their newspapers and observed that 'the Tory Party have announced their policy – repression – 26th of January!' Despite this allusion to Salisbury's acceptance of a Coercion Bill on that date, Gladstone minimised partisanship and generally tried to rise to the occasion.

'When this government was formed, it was formed on the principle of looking for some method of dealing with Ireland otherwise than by the method of coercion.'[5] The message was profoundly pacific: the abolition of Irish discontent, Ireland given the chance of Canada, to become friendly and loyal *because* she had Home Rule, at the least ambitious, something better than coercion.

He was faced with many reponses – anxious self-justification from defectors, legalistic disputations from lawyers and the virulence of Ulstermen. Speaking later in the debate his erstwhile attorney general, Henry James,[6] invoked poetry, first to excuse his defection:

> Spared to lift his hand against that king
> Who made him knight

(The customary adornment of a law officer had made James Sir Henry.) But regard for his leader (and himself) did not keep him from orotund dissent (and more poetry – Tennyson's 'Guinevere' this time). He spoke for several columns about assurance, not apparent to him in the bill, that Westminster was still to have supremacy as embodied in the Act of Union. And he invoked the minorities, the Protestants:

> Suppose some man prominent among his fellows should affect the imagination, so easily affected, of the Irish people, should earn their gratitude and gain their confidence and should then appeal to the mass of the people against the people who represent the social position and power and intelligence of the country [that phrase of class self-regard endlessly recurs], representing them as having been oppressors and opponents of every true reform, what would then become of these social influences? They would be swept away as easily as the acrobat sweeps away the flimsy paper from before the hoop through which he jumps.'

Two paths had been open to him, said James, one of them membership of the government where 'it is possible a word or two of welcome might have fallen on my ear. I should too have had the privilege – to me the great privilege – of following – with however an unequal step – a leader whose later triumphs, if I am not permitted to say I have shared, at least I have been allowed to witness.' But Sir Henry had to look where this path led, and 'as far as my erring perception goes, I can discover that it leads to nothing except confusion and chaos: "Red ruin and the breaking up of laws".'

But although James spoke throughout like most people's unfair image of a lawyer, he made one point which was to crop up again. He had just patronisingly alluded to men who 'made one claim for Ireland, which was that she should be a nation'. Parnell immediately interjected: 'She is a nation.'

'But,' said James, 'under this bill, her Legislature will be brought lower than that of any Province of any colony of the Crown when Ireland will have no Flag, no Army, no Navy, when she cannot deal with her foreign affairs or with her trade and commerce, or even protect her Coast. I cannot believe that the Irish nation will accept this as a final settlement.'

It was to be a recurring paradox of debate that opponents of the bill called up the fear of separation and dully and repetitively described Home Rule as 'repeal' (of the union) while asking the Irish how they could ever accept such a paltry, subordinating compromise. Hartington had already used similar arguments. Had not Parnell spoken of 'severance of the last link' and said that 'no bounds were to be set to the aspirations of a nation'? Had he ever stopped advocating complete independence?

Gladstone argued, like Lord John Russell, from finality – and he was perfectly sincere in doing so – and of course Ireland with the powers involved in his version of Home Rule would not be the miserable colonial province of James's rhetoric. The words Hartington asked about – that no man has the right to set the bounds of a nation – are those inscribed upon Parnell's monument. And though they contradicted the docile and Gladstone-friendly contentment he was declaring at this time, they are a historic truth.

But the argument of hindsight was not available – that after thirty years of refusing major concession because they were too paltry not to excite demands for more, then in circumstances of two-way bitterness and violence – killing and being killed – more would indeed be demanded and finality would be reached. Repeal of the union would take place and most of Ireland achieve what should have come in the way of subsequent parliamentary accommodation.

Hartington, as a Whig, ought to have seen this. Such parliamentary pre-emption of storm had, after all, been a Whig glory, but his second reading speech, immediately following Gladstone, concerns only the terrible danger of experimenting.[7] 'My Rt Hon. friend [Gladstone] has said that the government are charged with experimenting upon this great question; and the definition he gave of experimenting in politics is of treating grave questions without grave causes . . . I should rather be inclined to define experimenting in politics as treating grave questions for grave causes but without grave and mature consideration.' For a man rejoicing in the soubriquet of 'Harty Tarty', who had lived as long as he had with Skittles Walters, a notable courtesan, before transferring to a duchess, Hartington was something of an old woman.

And as an Old Whig, he dived back into history to make against Gladstone the backward-directed argument that though some of the great men of Foxite Whiggery had opposed the 1801 Act of Union, 'Lord Grey lived to be one of the strongest advocates of the union and one of the strongest opponents of repeal.' And in the same spirit of immobility lit by precedent, he quoted Gladstone's cautious words to Isaac Butt's broad-brush Home Rule Motion 22 years before.

Gladstone had said then, in 1874, 'It is a dangerous and tricky system for Parliament to adopt – to encounter national dissatisfaction, if it really exists with the assurance . . . which may, perhaps conciliate the feeling of the people of Ireland for a moment and attract a passing breath of popularity, but which when the day of trial comes, may be found entirely to fail.' But Hartington's anxieties were the exact opposite of James' reproaches to the Irish for accepting so little. Ireland, with no flag, no army and no navy might, according to James, have been 'brought lower than any province of any colony under the Crown', but, thought Hartington, it was 'an error to think the unity of the Empire is maintained when it presents a united front in foreign policy or if it is represented by a united navy and army. We might be able to preserve the semblance of unity after this bill is passed; but as far as our internal position goes, I say that with the passing of this bill, the unity of the Empire will have disappeared.'

Basically, the Irish would smash everything up and the proper reaction was panic. 'We might find the principles recently preached by the Irish Land League and the Irish National League translated into legislation . . . then English- men would find a state of law relating to property, liberty and security of life which will be of an altogether different character to that prevailing in their country.'

It is a speech full of historic jitters. Hartington preached fear of consequences. In Gladstone's autonomous Ireland, no one would be safe. Landlords were being bought out; what about civil servants? What about jurymen? Or 'men who have acted as independent witnesses; men who in one capacity or another have made themselves obnoxious to what will become the dominant power in Ireland'? And ever and again, it looked back for the reassurance of precedent. Hartington quoted the fierce language Gladstone had used five years before at the height of rural violence as guidance for now. For the future 8th Duke of Devonshire, nothing had changed and nothing should be attempted.

'I see no reason simply because the party professing these

principles has acquired greater strength and possibly a greater claim to represent a larger number of the people of Ireland ... why we are to retire from that which my Rt Hon. friend has called a conflict between law on the one hand and sheer lawlessness on the other.'

Hartington had his answer from William O'Brien (esteemed by Conor Cruise O'Brien one of the best of Parnell's men, and editor of *United Ireland*). It had been 'a manly and a straightforward opposition' which the marquess had offered, but he had opposed every other recent reform, notably the extension of the franchise. As for past hard words quoted against Parnell and quotations showing that 'to a comparatively recent period the people of Ireland were not particularly affected towards English rule and that hard things were said',[8] O'Brien struck a rather English note regretting all this preoccupation with the past and history. 'I think if we were to go digging into the grave of the past we might possibly retort and retort even more succesfully, in raking up unpleasant memories.' What chance was there, said the firebrand editor avuncularly, 'of this great controversy ever being settled if we go over old battles and bandy about stale quotations over and over again?'

Chamberlain's position was already clear. At first reading he had come bearing the knife which he and Gladstone had sharpened together and a rather rueful defence of his own ideas. He had favoured a Central Council (which William O'Shea, his unsuitable intermediary with Parnell, said had been superseded by a better offer). It had been mooted in connection with a scheme for local government in Northern Ireland and 'I think it was a very good notion. But it has at the present moment one very grave defect – if Hon. members opposite were ever disposed to give it their support, they are no longer willing to do so; they reject it ... Heaven forfend that any English member should attempt to impose that benefit upon them.' Yet if this sounded querulous, Chamberlain did not make play of his Central Council idea.

It was, he said, 'only a very large solution which can at any future time be accepted as a solution to this vast question.'[9]

But he settled upon Gladstone's Canadian analogy and wide reference to colonial autonomy. The ties with the colonies were strong, but only on a base of sentiment and affection. It could be broken tomorrow if the Canadians wished to break it because it was entirely impractical to enforce it. Oddly, in the light of Tory extremist speeches with their certainties of the Irish absconding and the subsequent need to increase military estimates to meet the Irish military threat, Chamberlain felt that Parnell would be unhappy with such loose attachment. 'I think the Hon. member for Cork would hardly like to see a tie of that kind [Canadian freedom to come or go] substituted for that which at present exists.' And he cited Isaac Butt: 'Since the union the wars which had brought possessions to England had been carried on by the shedding of Irish blood . . . and Ireland had acquired with England partnership rights which it would be impossible to distribute and of which Ireland could only have her share by continuing to be represented in that House.'

He was making this rather tearful point strictly in order to pick his quarrel on this issue of parliamentary representation. Chamberlain's rationale – and it made its own sense within its own logic – was for a kind of federalism. Germany had done it, as had Italy, and there was the United States. Radical Joe was positioning himself to become Imperial Joe by way of the very advanced notion of federalism which could apply to the Empire. The solution, he thought, should be sought 'in some form of federation which would really maintain the imperial unity and which would at the same time conciliate the desire for a national local government which was felt so strongly by the constituents of honourable members opposite'. And at a bound, he was Municipal Joe again. He ended a polite speech with a quick snarl at personal critics. 'Sir, there are some persons, servile partisans who disgrace political life, who say that I have been guilty of treachery because I have resigned an office I can no longer hold with honour . . . What would they say if, holding the opinions that I do . . . I had remained on that bench with a lie upon my lips?'

Chamberlain had changed his mind for a combination of reasons in which pragmatic disagreement of a kind which could have been respected was mixed with personal dislike – 'I really hate him' – and affront – 'A secretary of state!' So the pious forms may be disregarded. Still, if Chamberlain had come to bury Caesar, he did so with some style, all the forms of civility and a case which was at any rate rational.

Not all cases were. Parliament was for most of the time a more civil and inhibited place than the press. George Saintsbury, writing two months earlier, had had none of Chamberlain's earnest alternative plans for improvement or Hartington's shilly-shallying ways of expressing himself about the Irish: 'It is perfectly childish and unworthy of any reasonable man to attempt to deny that the great majority of the lower classes and all but a small minority of the hierarchy are profoundly disloyal.'[10]

What was wanted was a spot of violence. 'The great doctrine that moral force means physical force in the background has been too much abandoned of late to the dangerous and destructive classes . . . The party of order hesitates more and more at replying the same way.'

As for Gladstone and his prospective Home Rule Bill, why, that was of no account: chance majorities in a single House of Parliament elected for long periods and on accidental issues have neither by the English constitution, nor in common sense, any right to turn the constitution topsy-turvy. The only right which can be claimed for such a proceeding is the right of *force majeure*, and one kind of *force majeure* is as good as another.'

The use of the constitution as a weapon against Parliament, itself widely thought of as a constitutional instrument, is interesting, especially when linked to the crying up of violence. We are so devoted to our sacred constitution, the argument goes, that a mere Parliament isn't a good enough form of legality. Anyway, never mind legality, what we want is *force majeure* and one form of *force majeure* is as good as another. The very vote was to be questioned. 'It is not rash to conclude that of the enomous abstentions in every province but Ulster, not 5 per cent were Parnellite abstentions. The party of surgeons' knives keeps its men in too good order.'

The steady, ambling hysteria found in Saintsbury sees Parnell and his people as indistinguishable from the Invincibles who murdered Lord Frederick. Such thinking wasn't confined to Saintsbury. A readiness to believe this and a hunger for non-existent evidence would soon cause *The Times* to print and proclaim forged letters. But then, to all that opinion of which Saintsbury was only a vivid overstatement, the possibility of things being improved by change – amended, compromised, taken clear away from past and potential violence by constitutional reform – was unthinkable and intolerable. 'There is no middle term,' shouted Saintsbury, 'and no one . . . who has the slightest pretensions to intelligence believes that there is a middle term.'

One listens to Saintsbury as to Froude and, as we shall see, to A.V. Dicey, and catches an approval of elected democracy which is highly provisional. The constitution was the shibboleth, the thing to be treated as first and last court of appeal. And behind the constitution was the mystical order of things, Conservatism defined hard.

For Gladstone, according to Saintsbury,

the game is simply that of reversing the processes and the results of fourteen hundred years. The making of England is to be exchanged for the unmaking of England, consolidation for disintegration, strengthening for weakening, the creation of chaos out of order. They do not propose no doubt to disunite this United Kingdom, to alienate and anarchise the English Empire [*sic* – Saintsbury is very free with 'England' as a synonym for

wider entities] out of pure wantonness. They think that
. . . certain things which they hate – the monarchy, the
aristocracy, the system of economic and social freedom,
the graduation of classes and of wealth, the maintenance
of public religion, are bound up with the Union and
the Empire; to strike at them, they are willing to strike
against any of these. Their desire is to reach that ideal
republic hitherto approached only distantly by France
and America . . . where vulgarity in every sense shall
reign supreme, where there shall be no distinction of
any kind, where there shall be *ni dieu ni maître*, nothing
but the blind idolatry and blind tyranny of the majority.
Those and those only who look up and down to this ideal
are convinced Home Rulers among Englishmen.[11]

Saintsbury's kind of tiring virulence had its echoes in
Parliament. Speaking on the same day as Gladstone at second
reading, Ashmead-Bartlett, Tory MP for Sheffield Eccleshall,
blazed away. Not only had Gladstone sprung Home Rule
upon the nation, but he was trying 'to light up the baleful fires
of class antagonism and of social hatred'. Gladstone would
find 'that there are millions of loyal and patriotic working
men as firmly determined to maintain national union as those
unfortunate persons disqualified by wealth and position from
giving judgment.' Anyway, what mattered for him was the
Empire which Home Rule threatened.

The imperial ascendancy of this country has been of
priceless advantage to the countries of and the peoples
where it has been exercised. The British race has been
the foremost agent in the civilisation of the world. It has
peopled vast countries; it has civilised continents; it has
led the van of constitutional progress and of well ordered
freedom. The British rule over those 250,000,000 of
alien population in India is the most marvellous example
of beneficent government – good for the rulers and,

beyond precedent and estimate, good for the ruled –
that the world can show.

[The bill] contains the seeds of civil war in Ireland.
It can, if passed, only lead to separation or to a deadly
struggle between Ireland and Great Britain. This bill
means repeal of the union. That is clear. It removes the
Irish members from the imperial Parliament and with
certain exceptions it transfers the control of of Irish
affairs from the imperial Parliament to a separate Irish
legislature. That is, the bill repeals the chief conditions of
the Act of Union. That union has been of great advantage
to Ireland. At the outset it raised Ireland out of the slough
of Jacobinism, anarchy and bloody rebellion into which
she had sunk under Grattan's Parliament. It has been
the cause of enormous development in her commercial
prosperity and in the material comfort of her people.[12]

Then again, there were restrictions in the bill with which
'the Irish Celtic Irishman with his many generous and attractive qualities would surely never be content.' Accordingly, 'this
Bill creates and places in the hands of those who have been the
avowed and recognised foes of British power a tremendous
lever for ultimate separation. Depend upon it, that lever, once
it is established, will be used ruthlessly and to the bitter end.'
Power in the new Parliament would go to the lawbreakers –
village tyrants, 'Boycotters and blackmailers who constitute
the agents and the power of the [Land] League. It is too probable that the darker and more dangerous Irish conspirators
across the Atlantic will really control the new Parliament.
Ireland will therefore be in a very brief space, organised and
guided by those unfriendly, perhaps by those bitterly hostile
to our race, creed, laws and form of government.'

Despite Gladstone's weakness, Ireland was not at present
a danger.

A rising would have no chance of success. It is not

improbable that even without British help, the loyalists might hold the island for the Empire against a rebel party. Let the British people consider calmly and in time what the existence of an armed Ireland close on their western shores, within 60 miles of their greatest sea port, will mean in these days of of rapid communications and of sudden political cataclysms . . . Let them reflect what an enormous increase in their military and naval preparations and in the imperial expenditure and in the burden upon British taxpayers, such a portentous danger must involve.

Then there was the matter of America with its Irish population. The bill

will influence their hopes and strengthen their agitation. The fiercer and more active spirits there desire to humble and even to destroy British power and British prosperity. They hate the British monarchy and British institutions. They wish to substitute an anarchical republic for the authority of the British Crown. I see in this bill a terrible leverage given to the foes of Great Britain and the fatal germs of quarrel and war with the great and kindred people across the Atlantic.

Meanwhile, what was wanted was a bit of stuff. The problem should be met with

the small amount of manly courage and vigour and resolute vigour which would suffice to settle it. How much better and more far-sighted to enforce the majesty of the British law in Ireland as in Great Britain. How infinitely more statesmanlike to teach Irish agitators that . . . we will never yield either to self-seeking ambitions or to the menaces of terrified ministers or of lawless conspirators the National Union and the imperial integrity of these realms.

It would not after all, be so difficult.

There is a population of 1,500,000 declared loyalists in Ireland. There are at the outside only 3,500,000 of separatists or rebels or whatever it is right to call them. Out of this 3,500,000 I believe that if the law were enforced and individual liberty firmly upheld by the government, not one half would ask for separation. Irish loyalists know what they have to expect . . . they would be fortunate indeed if they escaped with their lives. But Ulster and the loyalists of Ireland have other claims upon our respect and support. They are our garrison but they are more. They are the salt of Ireland. They pay four fifths of the Irish taxation received by the imperial exchequer . . . Without them Ireland would soon become a desert . . . Drive from Ireland the loyal and Protestant population, you not only inflict upon them a cruel injustice, but you ruin the whole of Ireland.

But for the Catholic element, disloyal or otherwise, there were shorter ways. What was wanted was emigration. Though many Irishmen might feel that they knew something about emigration. Where the soil was bad and the district overcrowded, then

a government plan for emigration is the best, if not the only cure. A tithe of the sum which the prime minister proposes to spend in breaking up the Empire would move many hundreds of thousands of half-starving persons to ample and fertile lands in the colonies where they might, with industry, flourish and be happy . . . but first and foremost, the authority of the law must be asserted.

It is the primal condition of all national progress and social amelioration and until the law prevails, all else will fail. Union is strength . . . Germany, Italy and the United States owe their success and their present grandeur to the principle of unification.

The Americans had 'poured out their lifeblood till victory crowned the the standard of union . . . I believe the people of England and Scotland will decide as did their brethren across the Atlantic in that momentous crisis.' If Gladstone had been president, why, 'the United States would have been split up into discordant and hostile principalities instead of being a great, free and compact people'.

Otherwise what was needed was force. Smith O'Brien's rebellion had been seen off and then 'Ireland enjoyed eighteen years of peaceful progress from 1850 to 1868', assisted by lots of useful emigration and famine, of course.

Then came the fatal policy of surrender and destruction invented by the present prime minister. Since the prime minister resumed power in 1880, all has gone to rack and ruin; and now we are confronted with revolution and disruption. The task is by no means so difficult as the craven fears and the puerile menaces of the Irish secretary would have us think. He would have the British government yield to the Jacobin revolution of the National League in order to escape the dark plots of the dynamitards. Was there ever such a policy of unworthy and pusillanimous gospel of surrender?

Someone had been reading Saintsbury.

Bartlett was a backbench nonentity but not an unrepresentative one. His leader, the 3rd Marquess of Salisbury, made his contribution outside Parliament at a public meeting in the St James's Hall on 15 May, something much better phrased, notably obscurantist and sensationally offensive. After invoking Pitt, Castlereagh, Canning and Peel, he declared that the maintenance of the Act of Union was the unbroken Tory tradition. 'I am there only as a humble instrument to hand over the burning torch to my successors (Cheers).' As for Gladstone,

> if we let him have his way, the destructive series of measures which he started sixteen years before will end in the disintegration and separation of the Empire (Cheers).
>
> We are to have confidence in the Irish people, confidence in everybody. If we did that, the course to the Bankruptcy Court will be short and easy (hear hear and laughter).
>
> Confidence depends on the people in whom you are to confide (Cheers). You would not confide free representative institutions to the Hottentots for example. Nor, going higher up the scale, would you confide them to the Oriental nations whom you are governing in India – though finer specimens of human character you will hardly find than some of those who belong to those nations (hear hear), but who are simply not suited to the particular kind of confidence of which I am speaking.
>
> And when you narrow it down, you will find that this which is called self-government, but which is really government by the majority, works admirably well when it is confided to people who are of Teutonic race, but that it does not work so well when people of other races are called upon to join in it (Cheers). Therefore repel with indignation anyone who asks you because we have confided with the British people and we find no harm in our confidence, that therefore we should confide in a people who differ from them in every respect, who differ from them in race, who differ from them in religion and

above all, differ in this – that they are deeply divided among themselves.

Well there is one other thing which has done service in this controversy and that is the word 'coercion' . . . my alternative policy that Parliament should enable England to govern Ireland (Loud Cheers).

£150 millions of money are to be spent by the government on the pacification of Ireland [The Land Bill]. I think I can point out to them a better way of spending the money than in buying the landlords out (Laughter) . . . I would point out to them that if they could only emigrate another million of the Irish people, they might do it for a great deal less than that sum (Laughter). They could set them up in a distant colony under conditions in which they would be certain to prosper . . . and if they did spend this money in conveying a large portion of the population of the Congested Districts to Manitoba, the result would be magical upon the condition of the Irish people.[13]

That was the policy. 'Apply that recipe honestly, consistently for twenty years, and at the end of that time, you will find that Ireland will be fit to accept any gifts in the way of local government or repeal of coercion laws that you may wish to give her.' That is usually referred to in historians' shorthand as 'twenty years of resolute government'. Indeed, in Salisbury's exact words, it was to be 'government that does not flinch'.[14]

We take perhaps too much care not to be guided by hindsight. Salisbury's St James's Hall speech was an expression of the sustained Conservative (and the majority English) view of Ireland. And it expressed at once racial contempt, derisive levity and belief in the sovereign merit of repression. In its light, Tory governments would handle Ireland, though in practice, Salisbury's nephew, Balfour, *would* buy landlords out. England under Salisbury's judgement was to govern

Ireland – or as much of it as remained after a grand, cost-effective removal of population to the open-air oubliette of the Canadian prairie. The yearning to repress would finally be consummated after 1916 by the Conservative and military rulers who lost Ireland, a consequence surely not apparent only in hindsight. And the last word on Salisbury came four years later – from Salisbury. 'Rightly or wrongly, I have not the slightest desire to satisfy the national aspirations of Ireland.'[15]

Argument was exhausted for this stage of the campaign. The reformers had spoken; so had the defectors, Chamberlain and Hartington; also the Irish themselves and, in full plumage, Conservative opinion. Defeat had always seemed a probability, though there was a flutter of optimism that the bill might scrape through. Justin McCarthy, Parnell's most elegant lieutenant, referred on 21 May in his speech, a gay, ironical affair which delicately sent up Salisbury for his Hottentots, to 'the improving and ripening prospects of the bill'.[16] But in practice, Salisbury's political instincts were being proved right. The defection of great names involved the defection of many followers. Darius Clayhanger was to be represented in the lobbies on 8 June. Lady Gwendolen Cecil, Salisbury's daughter and biographer, tells of the moment when

> the Unionist tellers appeared at the right of the row (still the indication of the winning side) and the victors sprang to their feet, mounting on the benches, waving hats and order papers, and broke into a roar of cheers which rose and fell through long minutes of uncontrollable liberation. There was no question as to the spontaneity any more than that of the answering shout of triumph which came from the crowd of Ulstermen who were waiting for the verdict outside and who gave final expression to their relief by seizing upon Lord Hartington as he issued from the chamber and carrying him shoulder high round the Central Lobby.[17]

Salisbury, cool even for his era and social station, did not trouble with the Lords gallery, but impressed Lady Gwendolen by such animation in one 'disdainful as he habitually was of unnecessary emotion' by sitting up at Hatfield. The result was sent by telegram, 'for which one of his sons waited at the post office, disturbing the slumbers of the little town with his cheers as he ran up the hill with it at three in the morning'. In terms of pure this-worldly politics, Salisbury had every reason to congratulate himself. The fears he had expressed to Lord Bath when two-party co-operation was offered, fear of a repetition of the party splits created by reform and abolition of the Corn Laws, had long lifted and that fate now descended upon the Liberals and Gladstone.

The bill had been rejected by 341 members to 311. And if from those 311 supporting votes one subtracts 84 Irish nationalists, Gladstone had retained from his election total of 333 Liberal colleagues only 229. A mere ten of the defectors abstained. The rest, led by Chamberlain, Hartington, Trevelyan, Bright, Goschen, James and Collings, went into the Tory lobby. Liberal Unionism had been created.

There was no option for Gladstone but dissolution and an election. Dissolution, but not resignation, for Gladstone had minuted himself: 'My Conclusion is that a Dissolution is formidable, but resignation would mean abandonment of the *cause*.'[18] What followed was an electoral defeat which reduced the Liberals from their nominal 333 seats to 193. In a Parliament of roughly the same size as today's – 670 against the present 660 – this left the Liberals a little above the Conservative performance of 1 May 1997, and in the country seats from a previous vote of 1.1 million votes, they were reduced to 534,000. The defeat, as Gladstone himself wrote, 'is a smash'.[19]

Salisbury had done less well in narrow Conservative terms than might have been expected, holding 316 seats with 73 Liberal Unionists. The Irish stood where they did and no one knew what support the Liberal Unionists would give him outside the Home Rule issue. The Cabinet agreed without demur upon resignation. The Queen, with her usual satisfaction at dispensing with Gladstone, did not demur and Liberal government and a further attempt at Home Rule were delayed for another seven years.

Salisbury had opened up for his party a twenty-year period of domination, interrupted only for a second unsuccessful stab at Home Rule. In a longer perspective, a brilliant victory had been won for the Conservatives, entrenching them in commitments against Home Rule and for Ulster which would finally procure from the unflinching hands of other resolute men a compromise by violence and an unequivocal defeat for the United Kingdom.

As for Gladstone, he had been called every imaginable name – by Randolph Churchill, by Saintsbury, by Queen Victoria. To W.H. Lecky, the constitutionalist, he was 'an honest man with a dishonest mind', and a modern school of Conservative historians is devoted to finding his bad motives. But perhaps the best judgement came not long after this defeat from a member of his Cabinet.

Henry Campbell-Bannerman was secretary for war. As such he was in correspondence with Garnet Wolseley, the general for whom fellow Ulstermen cherished unconstitutional hopes, and Wolseley – who would write of 'the arch-traitor Gladstone' and had indeed snarled in private against the prime minister. A diary entry in 1885, before Home Rule, alluding only to his land legislation, prays: 'May he suffer in the next world for having taught the Irish to steal and for having endeavoured to persuade the people of England that it was a righteous thing to be insulted and wronged as a nation.'

Wolseley had criticised Gladstone to Campbell-Bannerman, whose reply answers the arguments just entertained and estimates the man as well as any.

Surely you do not take for gospel all the rubbish that does duty on platforms about the disintegration of the

Empire and so forth? That is meant only for the ground-lings. No one surely believes that to give the Irish the management of their own affairs will break up the Empire – if so, what a rotten structure that venerable structure must be in!

And then as to Mr Gladstone. I have never been a toady and worshipper of his. I never had much to do with him or much opportunity of intimately observing him till the last two years. But I am bound to say that the nearer I have come to him and the more behind the scenes I have got, the higher has been my respect and admiration for him. As to this last effort on his part – so far from serving his vanity and self-interest, he knew and feared from the first that the chances were enormously against success, that he risked power and position and party strength in advocating the new Irish policy; but he believed it to be the right policy and worth the risk and he believes this still.[20]

He did.

5

Roaring at Ballymena – and Belfast

Parallel with the general Conservative and Liberal Unionist resistance to Home Rule there ran a specific campaign, native and visiting, in Ulster. It was generally more extreme, founded in the unplumbable hatreds of proximate peoples. But across the three decades in which Home Rule and then independence were debated, it would always be disputable who, betwixt Tories and Ulstermen, was using whom, who serving whose purpose.

Parnell and Gladstone both profoundly misread Ulster. They had read about the radical Belfast of a hundred years before. Parnell had an unprofitable estate in County Wicklow, hard pressed then, today probably the Surrey of the Republic. A man with a dash of scepticism leading a party preponderantly Catholic, he had no notion of the close-packed particularist identity which exaltant Calvinism and a strong economy had bestowed.

The Ulster reaction – in its newspapers, on its pulpits and platforms – would be to translate Home Rule into repeal of the union, proclaim 'loyalty' to Crown and nation and enter into a Faustian pact, of a two-way kind, with the Conservative Party. Lord Rossmore's letter to the *Daily Telegraph*, the one calling for Ulster to be allowed to use her own good right arm, has already been quoted. But Rossmore, an Ulster landowner, rabid as he was, did not stir anxiety as much as the great text-pounding political minister of the day, Dr Richard Kane, who was also grand master of the Orange Order.

Gladstone was not yet prime minister again when Kane laid about him on 3 January 1886. 'Irish loyalists find it difficult to believe that any statesman who is not a traitor to his sovereign could propose to purchase a short tenure of power by playing into the hands of the avowed enemies of the Queen and of the British race.' The language of loyalism regularly inclined to menace and was given to crude hints of physical force. 'Irish loyalists to the number of a million and a half,' said Kane, were 'determined to stand by the union, and if it is repealed or so far as their liberties are concerned as good as repealed, they are determined, God helping them, to defend their rights and liberties another way . . .'

More attractive than Kane, as who would not be, was Edward Saunderson, army officer retired, County Cavan landowner, yachtsman, amateur caricaturist and MP for Armagh. But Saunderson also talked about armed resistance and was the author of a pamphlet called 'Two Irelands: Loyalty versus Treason'. He was determined to restore Orangeism as a force. Founded in 1795, the Orange Order had been a lower- and lower-middle-class organisation and there was some suspicion of Saunderson as a landlord, but he proved anything but aloof. The demotic politics which Gladstone had initiated with the Midlothian campaign of 1880 was spreading, and Saunderson took to it with gusto. 'My throat has not got over roaring at Ballymena,'[1] he wrote.

His energetic involvement with the Orange lodges had begun earlier in the decade as a reaction to the Land League and nationalist politics. While still Liberal MP for Cavan, he joined the Orange Order in 1882, the year of Phoenix Park, at the height of Land League intimidation. He gave his reasons at a major rally. He had become an Orangeman because the state of the country for the past two years had been simply unbearable. The very foundations of society had been shaken and were about to crumble into the dust . . . There was only one answer: an organisation not afraid to face and cope with it, and that was the Orange organisation; and he determined, by God's help, not to allow one day unnecessarily to elapse before he joined that body.

When Parnell, Biggar and their crew went into Parliament and said they represented Ireland, they well knew they never spoke a word in the name of the Irish Orangemen . . . They came over to Ulster and told the Orangemen that their sole object was to secure for the tenant farmers fair play and no favour . . . in Connaught and Cork it was 'Ireland for the Irish' and 'out with the English garrison'. Who were the English garrison? They were the Protestants of the north. They tried to seduce the Orangemen but, thank God, they have not succeeded in doing so.

He called for uniforms and for the arming of men: 'The Orange society should be made a disciplined society. In Cavan the Orangemen as a rule were armed, but they did not know know to use their arms and they should be taught to do so . . . If England in a moment of infatuation determined to establish Home Rule . . . they would take up arms and know the reason why.'[2]

Saunderson, though he would later oppose the establishment of a Catholic University in Northern Ireland, was comparatively eirenic about religion. Not so the Reverend Kane.

The reason I cannot be a Liberal is that I believe Mr Gladstone and his party put power into the hands of the enemies of my religion. The Ballot Act, as I told my friends before it passed, would give the power to the priests in the larger part of Ireland . . . If the priests have the power, who is their leader? Surely the Pope; and of course we know that obedience is an ordained virtue of function to the RC religion. Then the priests return the MPs, the MPs obey the priests, the priests get their instruction from their bishops, the bishops from their head in Rome . . . If I am right then a foreign power has a part in the councils of our nation. Should this be so?'[3]

But if Parnell and Gladstone couldn't focus Ulster, Ulster was entirely incapable of comprehending all Ireland. A piece in the *Northern Whig*, once a Liberal paper, speaks in January 1886 of 'the small minority of the population of the UK who have handed over their interests to Mr Parnell'. Such people had 'no right on any ground to insist on a fundamental change in the existing form of British government. Of the 36 million people who inhabit these islands, between 32 and 33 million are satisfied with the present constitution at least in so far as it consists of one imperial legislature.'

'A hundred years from now,' says the author, William Jeans, 'the vast majority of the Irish people will find in the connection with this country the great source of their freedom and prosperity and will laugh at the "patriots" who proclaim separation as the great avenue to national welfare.'[4]

Essentially, Ulster spokesmen dived deep into British identity as a refuge from the Catholic majority in Ireland. They sometimes speak of themselves as Irish – Saunderson does all the time – but they juggle the words 'British' and 'English' at will and in their exaltant identification with British or English interests and greatness are, ironically, more Catholic than the Pope. But fear, projected back to the cherished events of 1641 and forward to what the Catholics would do if they got their hands on Ulster property, was general. There were rumours that priests were already raffling Protestant-owned properties which would be seized and appropriated after Home Rule 'to drive the successors of the planters and the colonists out of the country and then to take possession of the lands they occupy in Ulster.' This was believed by the *Londonderry Sentinel* as surely as it was mocked in the *Derry Standard*. 'Not a bit of proof has been shown that it has not been taking place.'[5]

Fear of Catholicism was central. Huntley McCarthy, nationalist MP for Newry, had written in exalted terms (and back-to-front quotation) about new dawns and the church 'that has for so long guided the nation through darkness and the shadow of the valley of death[sic] will exercise its loftiest duty as the guardian of a regenerated race.'[6] The *Belfast News-Letter* would respond in February 1886: 'The aim of the Home Rulers is not merely an Irish Parliament, but a universal religion. The Protestants of the country must be forced to submit to 'the Church'. Mr McCarthy has been incautious enough to reveal the truth, and we trust that his paper may be widely read by English Protestants.'[7]

A very good sense of the Ulster Protestant mood may be divined from an astute analysis made by the historian James Loughlin of specific loyalist speeches. He looks at thirty orations reported in the *Belfast News-Letter*, delivered between 6 January and 18 June 1886 – speeches by Saunderson, the Earl of Erne, the Reverend Kane, E.W. de Cobain MP, Lord Ernest Hamilton and others – in order to quantify the comparative incidence of certain fixed themes. Pragmatic arguments rate low. The superior resources of Westminster over any Irish Parliament to pay for the regeneration of the Irish economy occurs five times. The likelihood of Ulster incurring heavier taxes for the rest of the island only four. 'Betrayal of Ulster loyalists' rates nine references, nationalist lack of respect for law and order turns up seventeen times. But the proposition that Home Rule would deprive loyalists of their imperial heritage and lower their status in the world occurs twenty-five times. And 'Under Home Rule, nationalists and the Roman Catholic priests who largely control them would persecute the Protestant and loyal community' was a proposition visited by orators on twenty-seven occasions. A final computation, not made by Loughlin, is that of his thirty speeches, while four were made by titled men, and two by identifiable army officers, *fifteen* were made by Protestant ministers of religion. A fair point could be made by moderate Protestants about Catholic theocracy – and it could be made back.

With Saunderson talking armed resistance, Kane denouncing 'the enemies of my religion', talk of the Pope as 'a foreign power taking part in our councils' and the *Londonderry Sentinel* running an article entitled 'The Irish St Bartholomew',[8] which recited supposed details of Catholic massacres of Protestants during the events of 1641, Ulster was ripe for rant. She would get it in the person of Lord Randolph Henry Churchill, Conservative member for Paddington, founder of the 'Fourth Party' and a minister in the short-lived Salisbury government of 1885.

Immature, arrogant, already sick almost certainly with syphilis, and emotionally disordered, Churchill has had a kindly press benefiting from the natural benevolence of his first biographer, Robert Rhodes James, and the revisionist historian's instinct in Roy Foster to extend cricketing fairness to unionists. But although a case can be made for Churchill being rather less inconsistent than the record of his earlier sympathetic dabbling in Irish conciliation first suggests, inconsistency is not the important charge. His speech to constituents in Paddington made the *Pall Mall Gazette* – pro-Gladstone but critical of the Home Rule bill – wonder aloud if he ought not to be prosecuted for sedition. H.M. Hyndman of the Social Democratic Federation and his associates were being prosecuted over the recent Trafalgar Square riots. Obviously, added the *Pall Mall*, he should not be pursued, on the common-sense grounds of doing him no favours. But incitement it was; indeed he was preaching 'the doctrine of the sacred right of insurrection'. But then, 'after his seven months of sobriety [in office] Lord Randolph needs a political debauch . . . preaching a doctrine of war.' His speech was 'a negation of the fundamental postulates of civilisation'.[9]

The speech which provoked such contempt is punctuated (in the *Pall Mall*'s own reports) with 'cheers', 'loud cheers' and 'cries of 'never'. And in conclusion the reporter noted: 'Loud and continuous cheering as his Lordship resumed his seat having spoken for just over two hours.' Such a reaction makes Mrs Thatcher at Blackpool look a little anaemic. So does his text. 'Mr Gladstone,' Churchill said in Paddington, 'obviously intends to establish in Dublin an Irish Parliament. He intends to effect the dissolution of the unity of the United Kingdom.' Gladstone had said this was a policy of peace, but 'by Heaven, gentlemen, it is a policy of civil war and imminent civil war.' Gladstone, he said, 'strongly mistakes or altogether dangerously underrates the history, the traditions and the power of the Protestants of Ireland.'

He went on to tell his listeners that as Englishmen they were 'bound to the Protestants of Ireland by every conceivable tie'. And in a statement of shattering candour, he proclaimed that these same Protestants of Ireland 'in a national crisis such as this, are *the only nation which is known to the English people* [my italics].' Better known at any rate than Lord Randolph's history, for he told Paddington Conservatives: 'During 680 years the Protestants of Ireland have held Ireland mainly for the benefit of England.' (The English Reformation had taken place 350 years earlier and the earliest plantation settler arrived in fact at the start of the seventeenth century, 280 years previously.) The Protestants, he continued,

> are at one with England, with the English people, at one with you in race and religion. They are essentially like the English people, a dominant and imperial caste, and it is only Mr Gladstone – it is only the insanity which is engendered by a monstrous combination of verbosity and senility – it is only Mr Gladstone who could imagine for a moment that the Protestants of Ireland would yield obedience to the laws, would recognise the powers and would satisfy the demands of a Parliament in Dublin,

a Parliament in which Mr Parnell would be the chief speaker and Archbishop Walsh chief priest.

Lord Randolph paused and then looked to the near future. 'I go in a few days to Belfast.' He would take his own message and the sentiments of 'this important constituency' with him.

I believe moreover that there will be hundreds of thousands of English hearts – aye and English hands – who when the moment of trial comes when the Protestants of Ireland are called upon . . . to give in the most practical and convincing form a demonstration and proof of their loyalty to the English throne, I believe there will be found hundreds and thousands of hearts and hands who will be beside them, around them, behind them and who will be of opinion that before the unity of this united Empire is forever shattered, before the sun of the British Empire shall commence to set, a blow will have to be struck and a blow will be struck – the sound of which shall go into all lands and the echoes of which shall reverberate to the uttermost corners of the earth.[10]

Churchill's own motives were complicated and not entirely rational. He had manoeuvred in Catholic circles entered in Dublin during his father's time as a Liberal Tory viceroy. His friend Gerald Fitzgibbon had an excellent line to the same Archbishop Walsh who is abused as chief priest. He had made a name in the previous Parliament by censuring Gladstone's viceroy, Spencer, over the Maamtrasna affair, a controversial Irish criminal case. He had never been a Home Ruler, but he had credentials as a man responsive to Catholic interests. On the other hand, he had acquired, through his wife, relations of diehard Protestant conviction who may have influenced a man easily influenced. He was friends with Henry Labouchère and in close confederacy with Joseph Chamberlain, Gladstone's enemy who talked of Liberal defections on a scale even greater than would be realised.

Above all, Churchill was a man who needed to proclaim cynicism. His later remark about playing the Ulster card and hoping it was the ace, not the deuce, fed his own fantasy of himself as a worldly and cunning politician. And in the same way, he was drawn to extremes. His Tory democracy looked left-wing and generous against the background of Salisbury's stodgy cunning on behalf of the status quo. But Tory democracy could be addressed to the prejudices of working-class voters, and anti-Catholic prejudice was very prevalent here, especially in Lancashire with its resented, poor, job-taking Irish immigrant population. Churchill would make another virulent speech in Manchester – and being anti-Catholic in Manchester in the 1880s was like being anti-Semitic in Vienna. But a conversation he had held with the Tory viceroy, Lord Carnarvon, in December shows him talking softly and dreaming excess. 'His present plan,' wrote Carnarvon, 'is to give a conciliatory *non possumus* to Home Rule, then if successful to proceed with procedure rules which will spend five or six weeks during which time he expects outrages and outbreaks, not to fill my place, but to govern by Lords Justice and then when things grow bad, send out Wolseley.'[11] General Sir Garnet Wolseley, conqueror of Kabul and a notable blimp, was to deal with County Kerry. But by 22 February 1886, a conciliatory *non possumus* had become altogether too milk-and-water. Lifted by his first speech, Churchill would now go to Belfast, to make an anti-Semitic speech in Munich.

Having disposed of Gladstone there with the customary Conservative canard that he meant to break up the union, Churchill demanded to know 'to what extent we [in England] can rely on the resolution of Ireland (cries of "to the death"). For Ulstermen should know that 'in this great crisis' they were 'the first line of defence, the second line of defence and the last line of defence'. It rested with his listeners whether they remained 'an integral portion of this great Empire, sharing in all its glory, partaking of its strength, benefiting by all its wealth and helping to maintain its burdens'.

The alternative to make the flesh creep was an Ireland which had become 'a focus and a centre of foreign intrigue and deadly conspiracy directed against a dominion with which I believe is indissolubly connected the happiness not only of the Western world, but the Eastern world'. The issue to Ulstermen meant everything.

It means religion, liberty and I should say when I think of the days of 1641, it means possibly to you all that is worth living for. To me as an Englishman, the issue of this struggle seems without doubt to involve the fate of the British Empire. If we cannot hold Ireland, why obviously we cannot hold India. If we cannot hold supremacy over our colonies, how may we govern this country? Commerce is founded on dominion. British commerce and British dominion must stand together.

Having swollen to the imperial theme, Churchill turned back to the domestic matter of the Ballot Act. This, enacted in 1872, he had not opposed (he had been twenty-three at the time). Unfortunately, in Ireland the ballot had done unforseen harm. 'We never intended in Parliament that the franchise should be extended so that the Irish people might demand a parliament in Dublin . . .' He turned to Parnell. 'I deny the right of Mr Parnell . . . to use the franchise to destroy the British Empire or for the purpose of ruining and scattering or driving into exile perhaps a million of those persons who for 200 years have helped the British Empire in its danger.' (Someone had put Lord Randolph right about dates). 'My Lords and gentlemen,' he continued, '. . . there is no doubt that a public minister at the present time is meditating a deadly blow at the union. Who is to help him? . . . Parnell.'

Parnell was pledged to gain freedom for his country. 'And

on what title did they base their wicked claim? Did they base it on action in the field as Italians, Greeks, Bulgarians and Montenegrins do?' In the orator's tedious way, Churchill asked the high-aspiring question and returned the scornful, anti-climactic answer: 'Mr Parnell's claim is based upon parliamentary action!'

As for the Parnellites, what motivated them was clear. 'The forces Mr Parnell directs emanate from the basest prejudices of class and sect – forces which are kept together by appeals to covetousness and greed and by terms which are held out to them of the acquisition of property by plunder, violence and fraud.' (Cheers.) Churchill turned to his audience. 'We are to call upon the citizens of this great and wealthy city to submit themselves to the power of, and to obey, laws which are framed and promulgated by miscreants such as these. But that is the inevitable result of a parliament in College Green [the proposed site in Dublin].'

Churchill was notoriously erratic, the result, possibly, of his illness, but since he had recently described his Protestant audience as the only nation England recognised in Ireland and added that they were a fellow imperial caste, an appeal to Catholic goodwill fits this oration only as brass neck or absentmindedness. But he did just that. 'I appeal to the loyal Catholics of Ireland to show which side they are on. I call on them to stand forth publicly in favour of that Empire and that legislative union in which they and this country have enjoyed more toleration and more perfect liberty than they and their community have enjoyed in any country in the world.'[12]

Churchill had spoken of 'toleration and more perfect liberty' for Catholics in February. There was low-level violence immediately afterwards, and when, on 4 June, a Catholic allegedly told a fellow shipyard worker that after Home Rule Protestants like him would not find work, a group of Catholic workers was attacked and one of them drowned. Rioting – Protestant-led and directed at Catholic life and property, killing forty victims – broke out generally and

continued on and off for the rest of the summer, finally
ending on 19 September. Thirty public houses were destroyed,
twenty-eight of them Catholic-owned. Eloquently, the 3,000
people thrown out of their homes would rely for relief upon
a 'committee of Catholic gentlemen headed by a bishop'.[13]

As the riots began, Viscount Cole called upon Protestants to
refuse employment to Catholics. During the riots a Protestant
MP, E.W.S. de Cobain, was accused of spreading the rumour
that Catholic policemen were to be drafted into Belfast from
the south by chief secretary Morley to shoot Protestants.[14] In
the trials which followed the riots, Protestant juries refused
conviction despite directions from the bench. In another case,
after a jury had refused conviction, local magistrates frustrated attempts by the attorney general to obtain a retrial.

But as Lord Randolph had said, continuing his Belfast
address, 'I would not hesitate in such unfavourable circumstances to cherish my hopes for the salvation of the nation
and the security of the United Kingdom to the efforts of
the people of Ireland, especially the people of Ulster.' (Loud
cheering.) 'For nearly 200 years now your motto and your
watchword has been "No surrender".' (Employed allegedly
during the Siege of Londonderry in 1690, that phrase would
occasionally be heard again.) 'For nearly 200 years now you
have kept alight the lamp of civil and religious liberty and the
flame has been kept alive from generation to generation.' He
now proceded to simple incitement.

> I ask you most solemnly – are those memories dead
> or alive? Because the time is approaching when you
> must show whether these ceremonies and forms which
> are practised in the Orange lodges are really living
> forms or only idle and meaningless ceremonies . . . The
> time is probably approaching when you will have to
> demonstrate this faith in a practical manner, when you
> will possibly have to show that the path of honour and
> safety is still mapped out for you and still illuminated

by the light of day ... No potential changes such as the repeal of the union, no change so gigantic, could be accomplished by the mere passing of a law. The history of the United States should teach us another lesson and if it should turn out ... that if the British nation was so apostate to its duties as to hand over the loyalists of Ulster to the dominion of a Parliament in Dublin which must of necessity be a foreign and alien assembly, if it stands with the design of providence to place upon you and your fellow loyalists so heavy a trial, then gentlemen, I will not hesitate to say and tell you, to tell you most truly, that in that dark hour, there will be found waiting for you hands in England willing to cast in their lot with you.

Having effectively incited the Ulster Protestants to military resistance, and compared an Ireland seeking Home Rule with the American slave south, Churchill concluded an evening of seditious bathos with a verse quotation:

> The combat deepens, on ye brave
> Who rush to glory or the grave
> Brave union, all thy banners wave
> And charge with all thy chivalry.

The lines are taken, mostly, from Thomas Campbell's 'The Battle of Hohenlinden', except that by a ghostly anterior irony, Winston Churchill's delirious father substituted 'Brave union', apt for a homicidal Belfast mob, for Campbell's actual words, 'Wave, Munich'!

The press heard Churchill's speech. *The Times*, oilily right-wing then as frequently since, reckoned to see in Lord Randolph, 'a spirit with which English statesmen and Irish separatists will have to reckon'. 'Vigorous and eloquent', Lord Randolph's speech 'took of necessity something of a sectarian colour. This, though regrettable, was inevitable.'

Adjusting to its best archdeacon's homiletics, *The Times* remarked that 'there are memories in Ulster to which Lord Randolph's eloquence appealed which it would not be wise to awaken except in the most urgent necessity, but which stand in need of no speeches from English politicians to call them into passionate life should it appear there was the remotest prospect of a negotiation . . . handing over Irish affairs to be administered by the nominees of Mr Parnell and Archbishop Walsh.'[15]

On the other side of the Irish Sea, the *Freeman's Journal* of Dublin (mainline nationalist) observed that though Churchill was dangerous, 'He presents a very pitiful specimen of English statemanship. In the Orange lodges he has begun to kindle the curse of fierce and relentless sectarian and religious strife.'[16] Back in London, the *Standard*'s comment was terse and probably wrong. 'Lord Randolph misjudged the intelligence of Belfast.' And among British politicians he was congratulated by Salisbury for 'his adroitness in avoiding giving offence to the Catholics'![17]

Churchill spoke to a specific constituency in Ulster. The representative voice of that constituency was Edward Saunderson, and Saunderson said: 'As long as the loyalists have a right hand to strike, these men shall never rule over us.' He also talked about another Battle of the Boyne.[18] William Johnston, a more unpleasant figure than the blustering Saunderson, offered the audience at the rally as troops to fight in a Protestant army.[19] As Carnarvon had remarked in a letter a year earlier, 'The Orangemen seem to me to be sometimes demented.'[20]

Churchill, with his background of access to Catholic and moderate nationalist opinion; Churchill, who had supported major educational reforms in Ireland, who had been menaced with threats of violence by the Reverend Mr Kane, was indeed playing the Orange card. The Tory Party had not been implacably opposed to all forms of co-operation with nationalism, still less bigotedly anti-Catholic. Carnarvon's overtures were part of an older approach. Hicks Beach had always represented attentive moderation (and would briefly do so again when the Tories returned to office). In practice, the demotic style of Paddington and Belfast, the direct appeal to an aboriginal Ulster Protestant prejudice, established the basis of official Tory thinking on Ulster for the next thirty years.

But Chuchill's father-in-law, Leonard Jerome, was to comment: 'I was startled at first and thought he was wrong; but as usual, his mistakes turn out to be the right thing after all; I hate religion in politics, but I have no doubt that in the present instance it is justifiable.'[21] Churchill's speech would be deplored for its tone by sound men, but more calmly, Salisbury would echo it. The Conservatives were nibbling the apple of discord and developing a taste for it.

Churchill would make a final Irish speech in Manchester on 3 March, defending himself from 'envenomed' attacks on his political honesty, denying any possibility that Conservatives might have contemplated Home Rule, and asserting himself a Protestant deliverer. Since Parliament, he said, 'was now in the hands of Irish repealers and Scotch radicals', the unhappy Whigs like Hartington and James should come across and join a new, 'essentially English' party to take on what he called 'the separatists'.[22]

Churchill's livid and offensive language, very different to the ponderous civilities of Henry James, were the product partly of his erratic nature, partly of his appeal via 'Tory democracy' to a working-class Lancashire audience flammable with anti-Irish and anti-Catholic feeling. The time of Alderman Salvidge's Protestant Tory rule of Liverpool was not far ahead. And a later voice consonant with Lord Randolph's in the final Home Rule crisis would be that of Frederick Edwin Smith, who inherited Lancashire Protestant prejudices from his lay preacher grandfather as surely as he would share Randolph's cynical, self-destructive urge to glitter. Like so many great leaders, Churchill would be captive to the enthusiasms of his followers. Saunderson and Johnson talked armed resistance; Churchill, according to Saunderson, had asked, 'What force we could raise if it came to civil war?'[23]

The idea (and the bombast) of armed resistance became serious subjects in Belfast. 'The words "Resist, Resist" were on the lips, not merely of Orangemen, but of Liberals, of those who by their profession were men of peace, merchants, manufacturers, bankers, medical men and even clergymen,' said Thomas MacKnight, editor of the *Northern Whig*.[24] The idea that Field-Marshal Wolseley 'All Sir Garnet', descendant of an Enniskillen soldier who had led troops at the Boyne in 1690, might take up the leadership of armed resistance had serious currency.

There are continental parallels. General Georges Boulanger on his black horse would shortly be touted throughout France by the rabid (and ironically Catholic) right as the military saviour to turn Parliaments out. In six years' time, during the second Home Rule crisis, we shall see Lord Wolseley assuring the commander-in-chief, the Duke of Cambridge, that Ulster Protestants 'will fight *à outrance*', though his reaction to the prospect of further Belfast riots was 'swift descent upon and coercion of Ulster'.[25]

Here and now the *Pall Mall Gazette* had its information about muster rolls of over 70,000 men and maps for areas of operations. It also had a list of fifty-one prominent persons – MPs, landowners and gentry – directly involved. Cobain, the MP thought to have spread the stories about John Morley sending southern Irish policemen north to shoot loyalists, talked a two-stage form of resistance. No members would be sent to a College Green Parliament and Ulster would pay no taxes. But if this complete ignoral failed, 'if an attempt is made to compel us to submit, our passive resistance will become active, and you will see that the 120,000 who are already enrolled will be but the advance guard of the force which will rally round the standard of the empire.'[26]

The language of Ulster Protestants was based on fear and

sectarianism, but there was also an echo of Lord Randolph declaring that the English recognised only one nation in Ireland. Another prominent unionist, Colonel Waring, said that he did not think the English and Scots would desert 'their own flesh and blood'.[27] The call from Rhodesia in the 1960s, much endorsed on the Tory right, would be 'kith and kin'.

The racial distinction was made on both sides of the divide. Michael Davitt, one of the bitterest of all nationalists, had dismissed the Ulstermen as alien settlers, not Celts. The *Belfast News-Letter* responded: 'We have every reason to be thankful . . . that Ulstermen are not Celts and not being so, why should they be subject to a government of the worst class of Celts?'[28] Froude's view of races, itself part of the post-Darwinian racism spreading through Europe, had been echoed by Lord Randolph and had occasional echoes among some nationalists like Michael Davitt.* It would make an important adjunct to the pure religious identity of Ulster Protestants and would snarl through the years which followed.

Without denying for a moment that nationalism had its bigots and triumphalists, it is worth recalling the words used by Parnell in his second reading speech on 7 June. Having accepted the Gladstone bill as a final settlement, he preferred that version to Grattan's Parliament because it provided an executive answerable to the Irish Parliament. But Ulster must come in – 'We cannot give up a single Irishman.' Her presence would reduce religious discrimination. He invoked 'the many liberal nationalists who do not altogether share the views of the Roman Catholic Church in regard to education.'[29] It would not be possible for the Catholic hierarchy to abuse its power in such a diverse Ireland.

The idea of a separate Ulster would leave out the 400,000 other Protestants of the island, of whom Parnell himself was

---

* Yet when an outburst of localised anti-Semitism occurred in Limerick, Davitt spoke up forthrightly against it.

one. The Protestants were doubtfully the majority in historic nine-county Ulster, and if they confined themselves to any more north-eastern stronghold, they would be abandoning many Irish Protestants. 'The best form of government,' he said 'should be the resultant of what forces are in that country.'[30]

By the time of the first reading, Randolph Churchill would be using moderate language. As his biographer put it, his performance then, on 12 April, was 'for him astonishingly muted'. It was confined to technical points, 'praised Gladstone kindly and gave Morley full credit for sincerity'.[31] But Churchill's resilings, emotional swings and calculations hardly matter. He had called up the ancestral fears of the fifteen ministers of religion, asserted Ulster's special relationship with Britain, exalted Protestant command politics and made sure that, far from being one of the forces making the best form of government for Ireland, Ulster would understand by the word 'force' one thing only: guns in the hands of militias proclaiming resistance.

Ulster was what it was; Churchill did not make it so, but he indicated to a generation of unfastidious Tory politicians that the politics of fear and communal enmity could be played to great metropolitan advantage. He indicated to Ulster Protestants that talk of arms, then later, the acquisition of arms, would be smiled through by one major party. And more than any other British politician, he indicated the street as a venue for politics, and violent menace as a strategic device. He was a sick man, but he imparted sickness to his party.

6

Tragedy Before Legislation

Ireland after 1886 involves three lines of development. The rule, after a brief hiatus, of Arthur Balfour, harsh and authoritarian, but with significant reforms worked in, was followed by the perfect tragedy of Charles Parnell, all of it centred in the courts. He would be brought to splendid and celebratory triumph in the libel case, then shattered by the divorce action, the whole thing an Ibsen-like drama progressing in months from *The Master Builder* to *An Enemy of the People*. The last part of the development in these seven years concerns the mind and intentions of William Ewart Gladstone who, in 1893, would return to what he saw as his great task.

A.J. Balfour, whose nickname had been the sexual slur of 'Pretty Fanny', soon swapped it in Ireland, where he went as Salisbury's chief secretary, for 'Bloody Balfour'. Balfour was a better than highly intelligent man and in more acute form than his uncle Salisbury a cynical and melancholy politician. Quickly succeeding the brief interim of Hicks Beach, not a natural for repression and whose sight was failing, Balfour, thirty-eight years old, beneficiary of literal nepotism, Cambridge aesthete and inquirer into philosophy, was dismissed by one Irish member as 'a more than usually mild member of the mild race of curates'.[1]

A stumbling speech when he introduced his Crimes Act prolonged the illusion, but he showed his purpose by giving full support to the divisional chief magistrate for Cork, who had ordered the police to fire on a rioting crowd in the southern coastal town of Youghal. The coercion which Balfour introduced, backed by an attorney general, Peter O'Brien, known for his skill in adjusting juries as 'Peter the Packer', produced in its first months over a hundred prosecutions and made its mark bitterly at Mitchelstown in County Tipperary. Evictions from the estate of a Lady Kingston had been met with resistance organised by William O'Brien and John Dillon for the Land League (now the National League). In the riot which followed on 9 September 1887, police opened fire, killing three people. Privately Balfour thought the police had blundered; publicly he was unrelenting and consequently damned and applauded in the expected places.

For Edward Carson, a young Dublin Protestant barrister to whom Dublin Castle was beginning to give prosecution briefs, 'It was Mitchelstown that made us certain that we had a man at last'.[2] William O'Brien, whom he had jailed, called him 'a perfumed Captain Moonlight'. Gladstone, who had cherished some affection for Balfour, identifed in his classic left-wing protester's way a public crime with a slogan. 'Remember Mitchelstown' became his set short dismissal of Tory policy in Ireland.

Balfour carried on his conquest insouciantly with the prosecution and imprisonment of Irish nationalist MPs, remarking coolly and aloud at a house party about the risk of John Dillon in his weak state of health dying in prison. In Ireland, Balfour was harsh, cold and directed to the point of restoring order at the necessary high price. 'To allow the latter to win,' he said, speaking of the nationalists, 'is simply to give up civilisation.' The resources of civilisation were being briskly utilised. Yet Balfour had no affection for and no illusions about ascendancy landlords, and in 1890 he would find money, serious money – £33 million, £1.65 billion at current values – as guarantee for tenants' land purchase. He also had the courage and imagination to do what chief secretaries did not generally do: set out for the impoverished west and show his face in County Galway and County Mayo.

In the west, in Catholic southern Ireland generally, he mixed hard-edged repression with intelligent reforms which implied long-term retreat. His whole conduct, practical and useful but autocratic, meshed with his formal philosophy, and Balfour was a respectable academic moral philosopher. 'Mankind,' he held, was 'poor indeed in any inbred inclination to the unselfishness necessary to the wellbeing of the society in which he lives.'[3] The virtue of religious faith, he came close to saying in *The Foundations of Belief*, was that it sustained authority – a comfortable conclusion for the heir to lowland acres, an East Indian fortune and family ties with Hatfield House. From divine crowd-control to fusilades at Youghal and Mitchelstown was a small step unflinchingly accomplished.

And however flexible and far-sighted he might be in the south, Balfour would demonstrate at the end of his stewardship exactly that comfortable sterility in accepting and encouraging Ulster prejudice and self-love which would confine Conservative thinking for the indefinite future.

Home Rule means that you are to be put under the heel of a majority which, if greater than you in numbers, is most undoubtedly inferior to you in political knowledge and experience. It means that the whole patronage of Ulster is to be handed over to a hostile majority in Dublin. You, the wealthy, the orderly, the industrious, the enterprising portion of Ireland, are to supply the money for that part of Ireland which is less orderly, less industrious, less enterprising and less law-abiding.[4]

The words went in like nails into a coffin lid. The quickest mind in Tory politics was giving himself over, after serious experience of Ireland, to that favourite Gladstonian term of scorn, negation. Coercion was the keynote, and Balfour prided himself on its 'vigorous' working. 'The result is satisfactory,' he wrote, convinced by a memorandum from a tax inspector touring the south of Ireland that many Catholics who had previously avoided commitment now supported the government.

But his period in office, widely applauded, contained, like most pragmatic mixes, vast paradox. As a rising young Liberal, R.S. Haldane remarked of land purchase, 'The more landlords are bought out, the less will be the difficulty when the time comes for Home Rule.'[5] This was a logic contrary to anything an intelligent Tory like Balfour could acknowledge. He did things in the short term with coercion which relieved the backbench itch, and he talked the supremacist language of Ulster *to* Ulster, if not quite as vulgarly as a Saturday Reviewer. But the implication of his land purchase policy, actually more liberal than Gladstone's because it involved less treasury supervision, had only one implication in the south: that Protestant landowners should accept the deal offered and go. What among white Rhodesians in the 1970s would be called 'taking the gap' was a procedure facilitated in Ireland quite as much by Conservative as by Liberal administrations. Balfour had coped brilliantly with the interim, but had confirmed the ultimate resolution of Ireland by force, demography, more force and exhaustion.

While Balfour was running Ireland, Parnell was providing some of the greatest theatre in modern history. His biographer, the great Irish historian F.S.L. Lyons, heads his chapters on the *Times* libels and the divorce case respectively 'Apotheosis' and 'Crash'. Conservative opinion, asked by Gladstone to accept constitutional accommodations with the member for Cork, looked at the spectrum of league activities – demonstration, remonstrance, non-payment of rent, boycott of services, intimidation of new full-rent tenants and violence, including occasional murder – and was inclined to roll the lot into a ball and lay it at the feet of Charles Parnell. For good measure, it wanted to believe that Parnell had winked at, approved of, or had a hand in the Phoenix Park murders.

The delicious notion that the prejudice of club and dinner table might also be true was particularly alluring to *The Times*. That newspaper, as rabidly Tory in substance as it was grandly magisterial in pose, had been Parnell's inveterate enemy.* On 18 April 1887, the paper published a letter in an unknown hand but bearing what was claimed to be Parnell's signature, dated 15 May 1882, which stated that 'to denounce the murders was the only course open to us. To do that was plainly our best policy,' and adding: 'Though I regret the accident of Lord F. Cavendish's death, I cannot refuse to admit that Burke got no more than his deserts.'[6] Parnell at once condemned this as a 'felonious and barefaced forgery'.[7]

Publication, ardently sought by the editor, Buckle, biographer of Disraeli, had been delayed by doubts as to authenticity, not least those of Sir Henry James, the former Liberal law officer who had seen 'Red ruin' in Home Rule. The outcome was a special commission created by the Salisbury government, two at least of whose ministers had come very close to collusion with Buckle. The commission was to inquire into the far wider issue of 'Irish crimes', and its composition – three judges of identified unionist convictions – would have done credit to Peter the Packer.

The gap between the libel and its investigation was one of almost two years. The proceedings of the court took fifty days. Parnell was thus the longstanding object of deadly allegations and then effectively put on trial less for his honour than for his civilised standing. But it was a trial which would blaze into triumph. On its fiftieth day, Richard Pigott, who had

* The letter had been offered to W.T. Stead of the *Pall Mall Gazette*, who would not touch it.

supplied *The Times* with its sensational copy, fled the cross-examination of Sir Charles Russell and a likely committal for perjury, went to Spain and, in a room of the Hotel Embajadores in Madrid, shot himself. Pigott the forger had created Parnell the hero.

And the hero was followed down the Strand from the law courts by a cheering crowd. Going over to the Commons, he was met with a standing ovation (from Liberal and Irish members). It was led by Gladstone, and Parnell's conduct impressed a Conservative witness, the solicitor general, Sir Edward Clarke. 'It might have disturbed the balance of mind of a smaller man. He took no notice of it whatever.'[8]

'Apotheosis' means a turning into a god. In Ireland Parnell was that already, but now it seemed to be happening in England. And, as Lyons points out, Parnell used the brief intervention he made then and there in the Commons to build a bridge to English opinion. His brief speech on this visit to Parliament took a soft line beautifully judged for moderate, small 'c' conservative opinion: 'It is legitimate and right that we, being the smaller country, should endeavour to conciliate you in every possible way, and yield to you and agree to such safeguards as you think necessary and desirable for your own interests (cheers) . . . I am convinced that our people, knowing that England, Scotland and Wales have for the first time turned the ear of reason to the solution of the question, will steadily resist every incitement to disorder, to turbulence and to crime.'[9]

Now was the time to consolidate the Liberal Party goodwill which had spread beyond Gladstone's commitments. Given normal political developments, the Liberals would be back and in candid coalition with the Irish, while the Irish leader was now viewed quite differently in Britain. Home Rule, peacefully achieved by consent, looked viable. Parnell spoke, with Morley in the chair, to enthusiastic Liberals gathering at St James's Hall, where Lord Salisbury had talked of Hottentots. 'We are on the eve of a great popular upheaval and movement which will not subside until you have enabled your great leader to carry through the legislature of the Empire a measure which will give to Ireland all legitimate control over her own future, her own interests and her own welfare, without any shadow of harm or ill to your greater interests.'[10]

The commission itself, investigating both Phoenix Park and connections between the Irish Party and agrarian crime, would comprehensively absolve Parnell from all suspicion of compliance in or approval of them, of conspiracy to bring about complete Irish independence or of directly inciting other, stronger countryside actions than boycotting. But in the wider, rather Scottish style which this single-instance court permitted itself, verdicts of 'not proven' were forthcoming over association with Irish American organisations which did promote crime, while Michael Davitt's Fenian past and undoubted American extremist connections were aired. But this had little impact. What mattered was Phoenix Park, and *The Times* would settle a libel action out of court for £5,000, endure much wider financial loss and suffer a crucifixion on its own and every other paper's pages.

Politically, Parnell, now the guest of a delighted Gladstone at Hawarden, could afford the submissive Empire-respecting tone of his St James's Hall speech. To the enemies of Home Rule, they must have read like civilities before conquest. And since Balfour's hard-handed campaign *had* effectively contained and blunted the league's efforts in the field, a balance had been struck, the sort of drawn conflict from which settlements most readily come. As for Parnell, he had at this time, as Roy Jenkins observes, Nelson Mandela status.

Unfortunately, in the course of giving evidence to the commission, Captain William O'Shea, formerly MP for Galway, spoke of having respected Parnell until a specific time in the previous June. The matter was not pursued, but behind it lay the events precipitating what Lyons calls 'the crash'.

For most of the decade, Parnell had been the lover of Katharine,* William O'Shea's wife. Late twentieth-century

---

* Katharine or Katy, never Kitty, a ubiquitous error.

opinion with its 'partners' would find little to condemn in the unregularised monogamy between the separated and deeply unhappy wife of a preposterous scoundrel and a man singlemindedly devoted to her.

There is material for a dozen bad novels in the Katharine –Parnell relationship, and material probably for a good one. They were two fraught, eccentric people clutching lovingly and a little desperately to one another. There was for a start, a good choice of villains – not only O'Shea, a moustache-twirling clown, a Catholic Irishman with notions of English gentry status who despised Catholic Irishmen, but also his erstwhile contact and intermediary, Joseph Chamberlain, widely suspected of putting O'Shea up to the divorce petition. Finally there were the bishops, the Catholic Irish bishops memorably denounced by Simon Dedalus in *Portrait of the Artist*: Croke of Cashel, who threw a bust of Parnell out of his palace, and the Bishop of Ardagh, who would speak of no man being false to God and friendship being true to his country, 'especially that country being Catholic Ireland'.

Friendship for O'Shea had been a judicious mixture of complaisance, parasitism and muted blackmail. But Victorian morality, which could cope with anything it had not been officially told, had viewed Hartington's two, sequent long-running liaisons without distress and accepted a Prince of Wales whose assortment of mistresses would, at his coronation, be packed like chocolates into a pew known as the 'loose box', fell like a public stoning upon Parnell – and upon Home Rule.

With better luck and management, Parnell's case, made sympathetically and with his allies standing firm and where possible mute, need not have been a disaster. But the very urgency of this sincere lover to make Katharine his wife left him in the court without sharp counsel to deal with the version according to William O'Shea, wronged husband and betrayed friend, and to anecdotes not necessarily true in which Parnell was portrayed as the furtive lover in a

Feydeau farce climbing out of windows and down fire escapes in order to come in through doors. 'What's the use, we want the divorce,' said Parnell to Katharine, who was more alert to the risk.[11]

The other half of the problem rested with Gladstone and the Liberal Party. British Liberalism was heavily Nonconformist in its religious make-up. Given the heavy cloud of latent opprobrium so often replacing charity between counter-triumphalist churches, English and Welsh Protestant Nonconformists had a decent record. They had struggled to overcome their dislike of Roman Catholicism – understandable with the Vatican, in resentful mourning for temporal powers taken by the Italian state, then at its most ultramontane and imperious – and had recognised the profound injustice of the Irish condition and given Gladstone vigorous backing.

But Nonconformity could get on to quite as high a horse about adultery as any Cardinal archbishop. The St James's Hall was booked yet again for an Irish Night. The Reverend Hugh Price Hughes, who sounds like the Neil Kinnock of Welsh Methodism, put it with due elaboration: 'We love Ireland. We passionately desire her wellbeing, but our first obedience and our higher devotion must be to God. We have sacrified much for Ireland. She is entitled to many sacrifices at our hands. But there is one thing we will never sacrifice, and that is our religion . . . any politician who is the acknowledged enemy of God and social purity can, under no circumstances, be the true friend and rightful leader of men.'[12]

Whatever Irishmen's love and sacrifice for Ireland, said Dr Hughes, if they continued with 'an adulterer of Mr Parnell's type . . . so obscene a race . . . would obviously be unfit for anything except a military despotism'.[13] We have bugging microphones, cameras and tabloid newspapers; the Victorians had pulpits.

In the view of Sir William Harcourt, Gladstone's clever, difficult henchman, secular opinion was quite as weighty. After a major meeting in Sheffield at which he and John Morley had exercised discretion and listened to rank-and-file opinion, he believed that opinion to be 'absolutely unanimous and extremely strong' that Parnell could not remain leader without wrecking the Liberal–Irish alliance. He told Gladstone: 'Nonconformists are the backbone of our party, and their judgement in this matter is unhesitating and decisive.'

Jenkins favours the view of Francis Birrell, son of the Augustine Birrell who would have his own tribulations in Ireland, that the Liberal leadership – high church Gladstone, agnostic Morley and unchurchy Harcourt – simply did not understand Nonconformity, which liked to fulminate and roll its drum, but lacked the bitter inveteracy to keep up the rhetorical hatred. 'A Lloyd George or even a John Bright,' thought young Birrell in his much later study, 'might have taken the bluster at its proper value.'[14]

Sheffield told Morley and Harcourt what to think and they put pressure on Gladstone. But the biggest problem derived from the logistical difficulty of talking quietly in private to Parnell. For a public man he was intermittently reclusive and it was enormously hard to get hold of him. What ensued was a letter from Gladstone to Morley for Parnell to see, which was given to an Irish member, Justin McCarthy, to pass on to Parnell. Since the message, actually phrased by Morley and inserted against Gladstone's better judgement, was that Parnell's 'continuance as leader would render my retention of the leadership of the Liberal Party, based as it has been mainly upon the prosecution of the Irish cause, almost a nullity', Parnell's reaction, after initial calm, was a vast explosion of anger against Gladstone himself.

The blazing quarrel in which Parnell anathematised Gladstone represented simple tragedy. For the Liberal leader in the toils of his party's prejudices had let words be used which in no way represented his feelings about Parnell. He thought him simply the greatest man he knew. What might at a private meeting have been astute and acceptable advice to stand back temporarily from the blast of spontaneous self-righteousness

came through in Morley's fussily imperious words as a
dropping, and a sanctimonious dropping at that.

Parnell's rage turned Gladstone into the 'unrivalled sophist'
and the idea of a deal with the British state about which
he had so lately been reverentially enthusiastic was dead.
But Parnell's own leadership was dying. The motives of
his party were complex. Few of them wanted to end the
Liberal ties which had brought everyone so close to triumph,
and those with the clerical cringe deferred to the thump-
ings of the bishops. And then Parnell, for all his hypnotic
grandeur, his speakings and his silences, had withdrawn in
recent years from ordinary jog-along commerce with his party
colleagues.

We know now what the autopsy revealed: that since 1887
Parnell had been suffering from severe kidney illness. On top
of that he had been preoccupied with fighting and winning
the *Times* libel, which had been, to party and cause, worth
any number of public meetings in County Longford. He was
also preoccupied, humanly enough, with Katharine, whom
he simply wanted to marry and live with openly. But astonishingly, it had been four years since he had spoken in the
Ireland he was striving to liberate. His party, in perfect
turmoil, was driven to an act of slaying its god. Motives
which spread cross-spectrum from a reasonable concern to
keep up the Liberal connection, through the effects of clerical
coercion, to simple exasperation with the grand impossibility
of the man himself, succeeded in bringing about the six-day
private committee-room debate of 1–6 December 1890 which
ended in a majority of his party's rejection and the consequent
division of that party. The young John Redmond remarked
during the debate that in effect, Gladstone was the master of
their party. 'And who,' asked Tim Healy famously, 'is to be
the mistress of the party?'

Had they known it, the party need not have bothered to
split, nor the bishops to have denounced. Parnell had not
long to live, but obliging his enemies and the requirements

of tragedy, he brought events forward. Plunging into activity in Ireland, fighting and losing by-elections for what was now only his faction, he finally stood in the rain to address a crowd on the Roscommon-Galway border, mislaid a change of clothes and compounded kidney disease with pneumonia. Returning to England, he found himself intolerably cold, and, saying 'Kiss me, sweet wyfie, and I will try to sleep a little,' he died in his sleep – dying, as he had lived, perverse, wilful and magnificent, more like a Hardy hero than a Victorian politician.

'Romantic Ireland's dead and gone,' said Yeats. 'It's with O'Leary in the grave.' With every respect to John O'Leary, from the grave of Charles Parnell romantic Ireland flourished as never before, and the practical Ireland which had to be put together without him was an anticlimactic cause. Not, though, to Gladstone, who, when he had spoken of his life's work, had meant his life's work.

7

Preparing and Bringing in the Bill

Between the ages of seventy-seven and eighty-three, Gladstone had concentrated his purpose for the next attempt at Home Rule. To some of his own colleagues he was obsessed. Harcourt was cynical and hostile to the Irish; fortunately even more hostile – from abstract principle and love of a fight – to the Tories. Morley was privately patronising about Gladstone himself and contemptuous of the 'racial instinct in the pure Celt', which explained the 'deliberate squalor in which he elects to live'. Rosebery, a swell and a paradigm of overrated aristocratic conceit, remained limply and insultingly indifferent in the languorous style he cultivated.

Such burdens notwithstanding, the government which Gladstone formed in 1892 with a thin Liberal–Irish majority was, in terms of work done, an almost brilliant affair. Across the two years of his last premiership, district and parish councils were created, the school-leaving age raised, the hours of railwaymen limited, the labour department of the Board of Trade (later the Ministry of Labour) established, the factory inspectorate strengthened and a major coal dispute settled amicably.[1]

But for Gladstone the purpose of this government was

Home Rule. As long as Parnell lived and was unassailed by the divorce courts and the men of God, Home Rule, even with its friends in opposition, had been an immensely powerful prospect. Given the sheer volition of the idea and two men for whom the word 'charismatic' was not rhetorical, good election results should have produced the sort of legislation which the Lords would think twice about defying. And had they done so, that resistance would have anticipated the constitutional crisis of sixteen years later. But given the fit of morality, the death and the split, Home Rule, when a Liberal–Irish majority did address it in 1893, was an act of will against the odds.

But if Gladstone was resolute enough in his purpose, he was altogether too resolute in his thinking. The idea that Ulster was different, had to be handled as a place or community with its own (ferocious) identity, remained inimical to him, as it had been to Parnell, and as it would remain to Parnell's ultimate, later successor, Redmond. United Ireland, to the mildest nationalists – and Redmond was as Anglophile and obliging an Irish leader as could be imagined – was a sort of Diana of the Ephesians, insistence upon it a guiding mantra. And Gladstone had his own historically instructed certainties on this matter.

Ulster, he knew, had played a part in late eighteenth-century reform politics at the time of Grattan; had supplied his own (and Parnell's) sort of aristocratic and professional opposition to the old ascendancy regime and even armed resistance under Henry Joy McCracken. This could not have ceased to be the case, and the sort of people who attended Orange rallies and wrote sulphurous letters to the *Northern Whig* could only be a destructive minority wholly unrepresentative of true Ulster opinion. Speaking with an Ulster delegation on 23 March 1893, Gladstone told them that they constituted 'the disunion . . . which constitutes the real obstacle'. Indeed, Parnell, before he died, had made a speech at the Ulster Hall rather more conciliatory to Ulster Protestants than anything

Gladstone felt like saying: 'Until the religious prejudices of the minority, whether reasonable or unreasonable, are conciliated ... Ireland can never enjoy perfect freedom; Ireland can never be united.'[2] But then, in Ulster unreasonable religious prejudices were laid like linoleum.

An Ulster Liberal Unionist tried in a letter to explain to Gladstone the developments of a hundred years, the effects of free trade with the mainland, the meeting of all grievances, freehold tenure of what had been leasehold land – all the things which proverbially make for a comfortable Conservatism better not disturbed. Given the recurring and ardently believed word 'superiority', which Ulstermen and their English Unionist friends brutally reiterated in relation to the Catholic rest of Ireland, a state of mind existed which Gladstone not only did not understand, but never afforded recognition. He thought that there was a Protestant Ulster lying to the humane and listening side of Orangeism; perhaps there was, but it did not show.

And it was given no encouragement to show by the Conservative leader. Salisbury, speaking to a monster meeting of the Primrose League at Covent Garden Theatre, said that Parliament had no right to sell the people of Ulster into slavery. He did not believe, he said, in the unrestricted power of parliaments any more than he did in the unrestricted power of kings. James II had stepped outside the limits of the spirit of the constitution, and they knew how the people of Ulster met him. If a similar abuse of power should ever again occur, he did not believe the people of Ulster had lost their sturdy love of freedom nor their detestation of arbitrary power.[3]

In polite form, Ulster's sturdy love of freedom expressed itself in the convention, 12,000 strong with 150,000 in the streets outside, soberly rejecting Home Rule in advance and undertaking non-co-operation with any government on College Green, Dublin. The Duke of Abercorn proclaimed: 'Men of the north, once more I say we will not have Home

Rule'.[4] Thomas Sinclair, a prominent Ulster Liberal Unionist, conjured up the prospect of British coercion of Ulster.

> We are children of the revolution of 1688 and, cost what it may, we will have nothing to do with a Dublin Parliament. If it ever be set up, we shall simply ignore its existence. Its acts will be but as waste paper; the police will find our barracks preoccupied with our own constabulary; its judges will sit in empty court houses. The early efforts of its executive will be spent in devising means to deal with a passive resistance to its taxation co-extensive with loyal Ulster.[5]

In the election, as the wife of a unionist candidate acknowledged in a letter, seats were won back between elections by unionists through the discreet movement of population into marginal seats. 'Working men . . . who quietly took the matter into own hand [sic] and, at any cost to themselves, moved into each house that fell vacant in our debatable land and at last by their determination converted the minority of 1886 into the solid unionist majority of 1892.'[6] The Northern Ireland administrations of Lords Craigavon and Brookeborough would have recognised one form of the gerrymander which they would very nigh perfect.

But then, with clerical diktat dominating nationalist politics – and a police survey reckoned that 129 branches of the 153 making up the Irish National Federation (anti-Parnell and now dominant) were controlled by the clergy – Ulster Protestant goodwill was even less to be expected than in 1886. 'The rule of Mr Parnell,' said the *Belfast News-Letter*, 'is now the rule of the priest.'[7] The two parts of Ireland had a way of fulfilling each other's paranoia.

On the optimistic side, in most other respects Gladstone returned to Home Rule with an open mind ready and happy to consult with the Irish members. A committee made up of himself, Morley, James Bryce, Sir Henry Campbell-Bannerman,

Spencer and the lord chancellor, Herschell, was created on 21 November 1892. Meetings had been taking place across the year with the dominant non-Parnell faction of the Irish and had underlined the need for a better financial settlement than in 1886 and the removal of any external body examining the legitimacy of Irish parliamentary acts. An essential channel of communication was set up between Morley and John Dillon, nationalism's most effective parliamentarian, and the level-headed Thomas Sexton, the party's financial expert.

The mood was excellent, and optimism was increased, not least through the early efforts of Edward Blake, a Canadian lawyer and legislator of Irish extraction and an expert on colonial legislatures, on whose advice the proposed assemblies were slimmed from the 1886 figures of 204 and 103 to respectively 100 and 48, and a representative group of (public-spirited) Irish peers was to be incorporated in the Upper House. The restraint exercised by that Upper House was to be a delaying power, not a veto. The coming preoccupation of a Liberal government yet unborn was dallied with here in microcosm.

On the financial front, the government recognised that it had overestimated Ireland's tax base, which should be seen as a twentieth, not a fifteenth, of the United Kingdom total. Apart from small sums, such as the £15,000 (three quarters of a million at current values) found miscounted and reallocated as Irish revenue, and a much larger sum, £680,000 (£30 million), transferred as past overtaxation, the main change was to drop the 1886 scheme for crediting Ireland with taxes paid in Ireland on beer and spirits consumed in Britain as too tricky for collection. Dubiously, it was discovered that Irish civil expenses and charges connected with revenue collection balanced exactly with revenues from beer and spirits and should substitute for it – they didn't, but it was a handy start. Meanwhile, a rebate of a third of the cost of maintaining the police would supposedly give the Irish treasury a working balance.[8]

Attempts by Sexton to raise more generous terms in the light of Ireland's poverty and diminishing population were furiously slapped down by Gladstone in high treasury terms. In fact, the money allowed would not have permitted this incontestably poor country to maintain her current level of expenditure. She was required in classic terms to retrench. And as the civil expenses and drink revenues turned out *not* to miraculously balance after all, the scheme looked too baroque for its own good.

Sir William Harcourt who, despite his truculent style, often talked sense, would have preferred a round sum from the British exchequer plus an extra provision to provide a balance. But the change which excited most derision and indignation from unionists was that from exclusion of all the Irish from Westminster, 1886 style, to inclusion of them all. The point was not one of principle and was reached in rather haphazard fashion, but it gave unionists a handle to turn.

However, the arguments through the usual channels between the government and its Irish allies were serenity itself compared with the debate on the floor of the Commons. Complaints in our own time at rowdiness among MPs ignore history. Mr Dennis Skinner is a *preux chevalier* by the standards of 1893. The bitterness of the parliamentary contest – protracted, and marked by continuous obstruction, Irish style, from the Conservatives! which finally developed into a physical fight on the floor involving forty hon. members – was ugly. Manic and unhinged opposition occurred recently during the Maastricht legislation, but even the grim element gathered under the Union Jack for that conflict abstained from football-terrace violence.

The fight, not surprisingly, was provoked by Chamberlain, for ever resentful of his victim. It occurred during the guillotine debate of 27 July. By an elegant irony, the guillotine, which had been devised a few years earlier as a way of frustrating Irish obstruction, was now used upon Conservatives who had not been too proud to resort to the methods of Joe Biggar. Chamberlain, whose instinct for distilling disagreement into malevolence was unexampled, had compared Gladstone with Herod, not on the grounds of innocents slaughtered, but for the deference, 'the slavish adulation', shown to him by Liberal and Irish followers. T.P. O'Connor, Irish nationalist member for a Liverpool constituency, followed the unparliamentary term 'Herod' with another scriptural allusion – 'Judas'. At which point the goal-end stuff began, not on the Millwall terrace, but around the Speaker's table.

Such a climax, 'the Catastrophe', as Gladstone called it, highlighted the bitterness of the whole parliamentary encounter. Nine nights were given to the second reading, which passed on 21 April; the committee stage took up fifty-three days; the middle weeks of August were given over to the report stage – August! – and when third reading passed on 1 September, eighty-two sittings had been more or less given over to the bill.

An impression of parliamentary progress may be derived from the account given by the furiously Tory and grindingly partisan *Blackwood's*. That Edinburgh-based publication had been on hand to deplore all reform of anything since the 1820s and knew its duty. The report appeared under the suitable title, 'The Struggle for the Union', and first of all touched on the prelegislative demonstrations in a style somewhere between *Pravda* and the *Eatanswill Gazette*.

Mr Balfour's visit to Ireland and the splendid reception afforded him by the loyal minority was in itself an episode of historic importance and full of the highest promise that the doom of Home Rule agitation will be speedily and promptly pronounced. Speaking to the men who are marked out as the victims of Mr Gladstone's policy of dismemberment . . . and it was no artificial outburst of enthusiasm which greeted his stirring words when he said . . . 'I do not think that any rational or sober man will say that what is justifiable against a tyrannical king may not, under certain circumstances, be justifiable against a tyrannical majority.'

'Ulster,' said *Blackwood's*, clearing its throat, was 'preparing herself for the worst; and the men who Mr Balfour addressed were those who are already drilling and arming to safeguard if the fatal necessity is imposed on them, their rights and freedom as citizens of the British Empire.'[9]

As for the second reading, Gladstone's view of the question was marked by

the same narrowness of opinion that has been the most prominent feature of his treatment of the subject since he first became converted to Home Rule as the panacea for Irish disaffection. The bill and nothing but the bill is to be that charm that is to secure peace, prosperity and contentment in Ireland, to stop the operations of American Fenianism, to make Irish socialism content with its humble own, to teach humility and meakness to a hierarchy and clergy grasping to place their feet on the necks of all who are not of their own faith.

Gladstone had praised the Grattan Parliament, but that 'was composed of men who from their class, their character and their faith supplied the best possibility of their loyalty to Great Britain. The Home Rule will necessarily put all power in Ireland into the hands of men who have acquired their present influence solely by their professions of hostility to England and their denunciation of the Saxon.'

Gladstone, arguing that the 'incorporating union' he offered would lead to better ties to the mainland, had mentioned Catalonia, where 'some relic of ancient self-government offered a species of resistance to the French invasion'. This was epigrammatically disposed of by Colonel Saunderson's advice to 'remember Ballinamuck', where the Irish 'Patriots' and their French allies had surrendered to the yeomanry in the Year of Rebellion.

Blackwood's simply adored Joseph Chamberlain. 'His great speech on the third night of the debate wherein the hollowness of the pretences on which Home Rule had been brought forward, the temporary character of the arrangement, the absurdity of the fiscal provisions and their injustice to the British taxpayer and the danger to the honour and existence of the country were all set forth in the tersest and most telling terms.'

The magazine conceded the talents of young Asquith (Gladstone's imaginative choice as home secretary), only because they were 'instructive as showing to how little account even forensic ability and talent could turn so bad a brief. Had Mr Asquith been addressing an open jury instead of a packed one, he must have sat down with the conviction that his case was lost.' Goschen, for the unionists, had delivered an

> exposure of the futility of the 'safeguards' to which the government points as its conclusive answer to all the apprehensions of the minority of the gerryman-dered second chamber of the paper supremacy left to the imperial chamber and of the improbability of the two parliaments working without the most disastrous friction and collision . . . He pointed out with a force which swept all Mr Asquith's special pleading away, the consequences that might arise . . . from the the interfer-ence of the Irish government with the detention in this country of Irish criminals convicted of treason-felony, or as dynamitards. 'Is the dealing with crime,' asked Mr Goschen, 'to be left unhampered by the Irish Executive and the Irish legislature?'

Lord Randolph Churchill, who had earlier memorably 'forgotten Goschen', was reported next by *Blackwood's.*

'He displayed so complete and masterly a grasp of its details coupled with such fresh and original handling, that his speech produced an impression second to none during the present debate.'* In fact Churchill was rational on this occasion and rather mild. 'Lord Randolph Churchill holds that as the British imperial Parliament is deprived by this bill of all personal control over the members of the Irish executive and deprived too of all direct or indirect control over supply, rating and taxing and the disposal of revenue by the Irish government, it is thereby deprived of the two great organs by which a parliamentary supremacy can be maintained and vindicated.' He had then argued that 'nowhere else is there a constitution which has placed the legislature in a position "so limited, so questionable and with such subservient jurisdiction."'

As for the Irish members, said *Blackwood's*, 'a change has come over the spirit of the party, as if the weight of Irish office was already oppressing that buoyancy and native ardour which is so dear to the House of Commons . . . They will loyally accept the measure – in the meantime – and fight for as much as they can get out of the Saxon taxpayer when the bill goes into committee.'[11]

Blackwood's reported Balfour's summing-up with relish. He 'pointed out that the enormous preponderance of the English nation in population, wealth and in power, forbade the idea of a British federation. He also denounced the creeping hypocrisy which throws upon this country and this country alone all the responsibility of Ireland's ills.'

He also addressed himself to 'the Celtic race'.

If you pass this bill, Great Britain loses these men

---

* Churchill, who was dying of syphilis, had been intermittently incoherent for some time, and Henry James, now a Liberal Unionist and sympathetic, wrote of a contribution a year later, 'R.C. terrible.' *The Times* correspondent thought that: 'nothing more tragical has been seen in the House of Commons in our generation'.[10]

for certain. I do not mean necessarily by separation, although I think that will ensue, but because every member of the Celtic population will look to the assembly in Ireland and they will regard the imperial Parliament as a foreign and defeated body and as one from which even greater concessions can be forced by legitimate or illegitimate means. You will condemn them to drink at the bitter, narrow and polluted stream of purely Irish history, and forbid them to touch that which I desire them to partake of and which they may partake of if only they have patience. If you choose in your madness to commit the great political crime and if you choose to make yourselves responsible for this irreparable national disaster, then indeed all hopes of a peaceful and a united Ireland will vanish and will vanish for ever.

After that splendid burst of percussion and brass, *Blackwood's* dismissed the anticlimax of Mr Gladstone. He, if not 'losing his powers, is at least neglecting his opportunities . . . he was content to retire into the lobby with his mechanical majority of forty-three.' In committee 'the docility of Mr Gladstone's followers will be stretched to a tension which nothing but a miracle can keep from snapping. Moreover Gladstonians are not likely to view with indifference the rising tide of unionism which is now surging all over the country.' They could 'force the bill through the House of Commons,' the resources of the constitution will not then have been exhausted . . . it will have to be submitted to the British nation . . . with all its crude, degrading and irrational details.'

Blackwood's complained bitterly by committee stage at the oppression of the proceedings. 'Not merely is the plague attacking the very roots of the parliamentary constitution, but it is tainting the whole life of the House of Commons.' The Tories wasted all the time they could and Gladstone saw no reason to make elaborate returns to delaying tactics. *Blackwood's* agreed with Chamberlain that the opposition faced a conspiracy of silence. They had a sounder point saying that Gladstone's hint about excluding Ulster would unite Parnellites and anti-Parnellites against the bill. But with McKnight's bleak, null response to Gladstone's invitation to propose a separate Ulster scheme, he had other reasons for not starting down that road.

In ways familiar a hundred years later, *Blackwood's* was much preoccupied by supremacy, British parliamentary supremacy, which the Tories claimed was not guaranteed. Henry James, for the Liberal Unionists, had sought to insert: 'The supreme power and authority of the Parliament of the United Kingdom of Great Britain and Ireland shall remain unaffected and undiminished over all persons matters and things within the Queen's dominions.' Balfour wished 'the religion embodied in the words "supremacy of Parliament" to be a real religion.' Gladstone had tried to meet James with a clause to be inserted at the end. James accepted, but *Blackwood's* was not satisfied.

> It is not enough to concede the supremacy in principle; it must be secured in practice and made distinctly operative with respect to every provision of the bill. On the groups of clauses dealing with the executive powers in Ireland, the financial relations between the two countries, the exchequer, the viceroy and the veto, the same question of imperial supremacy must be fought over and over again unless the government distinctly states . . . the means by which it can be effectively exercised when need arises for its intervention.[12]

Blackwood's stood ready for 'every legitimate tactic that can be made available for putting an end to this unprincipled measure', and they were again overjoyed with Chamberlain – 'able to throw himself into the struggle with a zeal and a devotedness that mark him out as *par excellence* the champion of the union.' By contrast the Tory rank and file lacked keenness and slacked. *Blackwood's* found it 'unpleasant to to have to confess that many members of the opposition have already failed in their duty to the country in the divisions on the first two clauses', in the process conceding to Gladstone 'solid majorities'. Whatever their 'disgust', Conservative MPs 'should be in their place to emphasise by their votes the indignation and abhorrence with which the measure has filled the minds of the majority of Great Britain'.[13]

Supremacy and sovereignty were what mattered, and *Blackwood's* trusted that 'the mind of even the average Gladstonian member will be able to grasp the fact that the Irish majority are to be made the virtual arbiters of the imperial Parliament and that there is an intention to plunder the British taxpayer in the interests of Home Rule government'.

Blackwood's also had a succinct view about what the hereditary House should do. They should reject the Home Rule Bill without debate! 'Here is a bill which violates the fundamental character of its own chamber, the equality of all its members on the floor of the House.' (Irish peers were to be excluded from the debate of non-Irish matters). Accordingly the Lords were 'under no obligation to discuss the subject of Home Rule at all.'[14] Having taken this mediaevalist, 'by my halydon' view of a transcendental Upper House never to be violated by amendment, *Blackwood's* revealed an ingenious if implausible scheme.

Gladstone, they thought, was likely to urge the case of 'peers versus people' in any election. So, startlingly, the high, peremptory hand of the Lords would be a defence against such a charge. For 'if the peers declining to express their own opinion of the principle of Home Rule until the sense of the country has been taken regarding it, summarily throw out the bill on account of the unconstitutional innovation which it introduces into their own House, no reasonable blame can attach to such a decision.' It couldn't? Unluckily for Gladstone, their lordships ignored this invitation to show their house in Iolanthe mode and did their rejecting in seemly form after debate, however perfunctory and uninstructive.

Blackwood's, like many unionists across the entire struggle, could slip lightly from high Castilian style to populism. It was perhaps learning from its new hero, Joseph Chamberlain. 'The agitation that is being maintained thoughout the country – and 'the crowds raised by the campaign' indicated that 'the British people has made up its mind regarding the unconstitutional and dangerous character of the measure'.

As for Gladstone, he 'is contending with a power stronger than his own – stronger than the Irish Party who are dragging him to ruin and dishonour.' Their lordships would be acting 'on strictly constitutional grounds and consistent with a majority of the British electorate which has for a time been swamped by the host of Irish agitators'. The choice of words is interesting. The people, aroused by a successful agitation, would redress a situation which had been distorted by Irish agitators. Clearly some agitators were more equal than others.

Blackwood's, of course, wanted more than rejection this time. Home Rule should be ruled out for good. Had not Lord Salisbury put it very well on 24 May, saying that he could see in Home Rule 'only unnumbered calamities and terrible degradations', not to say 'a black and irreparable stain upon the fame of England'? And Salisbury had said that at issue were 'not merely the rejection of the present measures, but a final and decided resolution against breaking up of the Empire by the concession of Home Rule to Ireland'.[15] Such insistence upon a foreclosing argument on Ireland demonstrates as much panic as arrogance.

In reality the Lords gave the bill four days of debate, from 5 to 8 September 1893, before arriving at its preordained rejection. The Duke of Argyll would take up twenty-two columns of *Hansard* to proclaim that he knew of 'no government in the history of the kingdom which has been so corrupt as this government. There is nothing that has not been put up to auction – the auction of a few votes . . . a permanent fountain of corruption planted in the hearts of the people and the customs of the country.' For his part he had been lately

in a part of Scotland whence we can look down upon the hills of Antrim. We can see the colour of the fields and in the sunset we can see the light upon the windows of the cabins of the people. This is the country . . . which the greatest English statesman tells us must be governed as we govern the Antipodes. Was there ever such folly? I agree with Thomas Carlyle when he said in his own picturesque style, 'England, Scotland and Ireland are one by the ground plan of the world.'[16]

Lord Londonderry, having asserted that the leaders of the Nationalist Party, 'these men who have maintained their system of intimidation and crime, will occupy the fore-most places in the new Parliament', and observing 'that the Ethiopian cannot change his skin', he launched a general charge of betrayal at the government. 'You have betrayed the landlords of Ireland . . . you have betrayed the Protestants of Ireland . . . you have betrayed Trinity College, you have betrayed the police and you have betrayed the civil servants.' But Ulster was something different. Ulster 'will not submit for one moment to place her neck beneath the yoke of Mr Dillon and Mr O'Brien.' Ulster, continued Londonderry, 'has never bragged or boasted.' Ministerial cries of 'Oh!'[17]

'When?'

Kimberley, for the governnment, was succinct. 'Continu-ally. They never stop.'

'Ulster has never bragged,' repeated Londonderry, before spending three quarters of Column 279 of *Hansard* listing tonnage in Belfast Harbour, the growth of the linen trade and comparative estate prices in Antrim and Tyrone. Quite reasonably, Lord Selborne argued that there could be no finality in legislation like this. All the Irish leaders had been on the record wanting more, and they would come back for more, and he projected recurring conflict between the two parliaments and the courts.

But Selborne concluded with one of those assertions of England's duty which surface in such debates. The bill had been passed 'by a majority of Irish members in the Commons against a majority of the representatives of Great Britain; and if there is to be any duty, the shrinking or retreating from which would be an act of the most abject meanness and cowardice, it is the duty of giving to the British people an opportunity of saying whether, upon this subject, they agree with the majority of their own representatives or not'.[18]

The Bishop of Ripon said: 'We all know the Irishmen; the finest gentlemen in the world; loved for their simplicity, their charming expressions and individuality, their honesty, hospitality and fascinating indolence. I do not mean to say that they are idle; but I must say that out of all the races of the world they have rather a strong talent that way.' There was, however, 'enough generosity and enough appreciation in the minds of Irishmen everywhere to know that there was nothing which we would not be ready to grant them in satisfaction of their legitimate aspirations so long as we keep whole that union and Empire which is so priceless to us and so indispensable to them.'[19] The Earl of Morley* spoke up for the function of the House of Lords in this affair. In the absence of a distinction between fundamental laws and ordinary legislation

a very heavy responsibility rested on their lordships. They are asked to try an experiment which they could not undo. That experiment involves surrender to the disloyal; it involves betrayal of the loyal. It involves

---

* Not to be confused with John Morley, Gladstone's lieutenant, who, as Viscount Morley, features heavily in later chapters.

dangers to the Empire and to the constitution . . . Every effort would be made to discredit their lordships' House . . . but unless the flame of patriotism burned low in this country, unless our generation was oblivious of its great imperial and constitutional traditions, I for one feel little doubt that the verdict of the country will support the vote your lordships' House is going to give and will, with scorn and indignation, reject this dangerous and unjust measure.[20]

The last word on the unionist side lay with Salisbury. And for Salisbury, active dislike of the Catholic Irish vied with conservative prudentiality. The special commission into Parnell and crimes, though packed (by Salisbury) with Conservative judges, might have acquitted the Nationalist Party of any actual criminal act from the *Times* libel downwards, but it had said that 'the respondents did not denounce the system of intimidation which led to crime and outrage, but persisted in it with knowledge of its effects . . . The bill has not just passed the Commons with Irish support. It is a bill which has not only been passed by a south Irish majority, not only been passed by men elected by carefully watched illiterates, not ony passed under the orders of Archbishop Walsh, but passed by men on whom this criminal brand has been placed by three of the highest judges. Is not Ulster right to be afraid?'
Salisbury was concerned for military defence.

Give over Ireland to your enemies, to those who hate you. Let the ordinary government of Ireland be conducted by those who are hostile to you . . . then all those harbours of this country would be at the mercy of the enemy who attacked you and unless you undertake the task of reconquering Ireland and shattering by mere military force the structure you are now so painfully building up, you would have no security from the sympathy which the Irish in command of their own harbours could give to the navies or privateers or cruisers by whom your trade might be threatened.

After quoting extensively from Macaulay at his most paroxysmal, Salisbury continued, concluding on a high note of stridency.

The repeal of the union we regard as fatal to the Empire and we will not consent to it . . . even though another Bonaparte should pitch camp in sight of Dover Castle, never till all has been staked and lost, never till the four quarters of the world have been convulsed by the last struggle of the great English people for their place among the nations.

If England withdraws her mandate; if England tells us she wishes that this horror should be consummated, I agree that a different state of things will have arisen. I believe that to be impossible, and that as long as England is true to herself now or any future occasion, if you allow this atrocious, this mean, this treacherous revolution to pass, you will be untrue to the duty which has descended to you from a splendid ancestry, you will be untrue to the trust that has been bequeathed to you from the past, you will be untrue to the Empire of England.[21]

The House of Lords was not, of course, untrue to England. As *Hansard* puts it, 'Their Lordships divided: Contents 41: Not-Contents 419.' The premiership, crusade and the political life of Gladstone were effectively ended; Home Rule was put aside for ever until the next time. But before that next time, another revolution would have signally changed the House of Lords itself.

8

A Belligerent Civilisation:
A.V. Dicey and Other Thinkers

*B*lackwood's did not have the idea of the referendum to
themselves. For A.V. Dicey, Vinerian professor of law,
it followed from everything he believed.

> The electors again must be made to feel that it is the
> essential principle of Home Rule, the setting up of
> an Irish government and an Irish Parliament to which
> unionists are opposed. The least appearance of con-
> cession to Home Rulers, or any action which gives
> increased currency to the delusion, certainly cherished
> by some moderate Gladstonians, that Home Rule can
> be identified with or cut down to extended local self-
> government, will be fatal to the cause of unionism.[1]

The underlying rationale of the absolutist stand of Dicey
was a shrilly exalted notion of the United Kingdom as it stood
– triumphalism spiked with fear. *A Leap in the Dark*, his
pamphlet of 1893 from which this and immediate quotations
come, is full of it. 'The difference between unionist and
separatist remains, but it has merged in the wider difference
between constitutionalists.'

'The people of England must again be warned that errors in policy or acts of injustice may snatch from us the power of determining a political controversy at the ballot box instead of on the battlefield.'

And, most fervent of all, 'We stand on the brink of a precipice . . . we are asked to leave an arduous but well-known road and to spring down an unfathomed ravine filled with rocks on any one of which we may be dashed to pieces. Blind leaders are leading a blind people and our blind leaders, some of whom care more for radical supremacy in England than imperial supremacy in Ireland, are, like many other men of our time, the slaves of phrases such as "Trust in the people" which pass muster for principles. If the blind lead the blind, what wonder if they tumble over a precipice?'

Dicey, contemplating federalism with distaste, looked to Switzerland. He marked: 'The struggle measured by centuries through which at last the Protestant and progressive cantons of Switzerland asserted their rightful supremacy over the Catholic and unprogressive cantons of Switzerland.' He also, interestingly, observed 'the weakness of Prussia when not more than thirty years back she could hardly maintain her rights and her dignity against Austria.' Belief in the Protestant and progressive all-rightness of Prussia derives from the Thomas Carlyle who had perceived England, Scotland and Ireland as 'one in the ground plan of the world'.

At the end of such musing lay thoughts about what should be done, thoughts about violent, illegal action. 'The artificial supremacy of Ireland, or of a faction supported by Irish votes, will not last long. If the new constitution prove intolerable to Engand, it will not be borne, it will be overthrown or evaded.' Dicey expressed hand-wringing fears lest 'weak concession at the present moment will at such crisis be found to have contained among its other perils the danger lest England, when she re-asserts her power in Ireland, should not re-assert her justice.' There is something about this which suggests not so much port and walnuts at an Oxford high table as the serious talk of an officers' mess near Buenos Aires.

So far did Dicey's fever, with its hints at putsch and illegality, run ahead of a lawyer's mind that by half lifting a skirt to violence against 'legal oppression', he was justifying the most violent fringe of the Land League. His flirtatious nod to force if it could claim to be resisting oppression is an invitation which for the last three decades of the twentieth century has been taken up against the lives of passing citizenry by the IRA.

The entire Dicey tone is that of a man alerting victims against their destroyers. 'The people must be told, as they may be told with absolute truth, that the fate of England is in question, and that nothing but the efforts of every unionist throughout the land can save the country from destruction.' Such tearfulness at the fate of England is best taken together with the economic estimate advising Gladstone (probably optimistically), as he prepared the financial clauses of the bill, that Ireland's taxable worth was not, as supposed, a fifteenth of Britain's, but a twentieth.

The idea that an identifiable part of the UK might reasonably wish for and seek any form of devolution threatened the sacred structure and, as Dicey slipped into saying, did an injustice to England. The logic of his position is an English veto on the wishes of Ireland (or Scotland or Wales) seeking a measure of autonomy. It wouldn't do for the Irish to have 'a petty, paltry, peddling legislature which dare hardly call itself a Parliament and is officially designated say as a national council, combined with some faint imitation of a Cabinet, called say a committee'.

This might disappoint Home Rulers, 'but it would afford them the means of gaining their end'. Such a concession would mean 'the destruction of unionism'. Plaintiveness from strength is hard to take, but Dicey thought the English beleaguered. Fortunately, the constitutional lawyer had an idea for securing an England standing on a precipice and facing destruction by mild concession.

'The policy of unionism,' he said 'has always relied upon appeal to the nation.' So when the House of Lords came to reject the Bill 'as a matter not so much of right as of obvious duty,' something more than the likely dissolution of Parliament and election might follow. This something more would be direct appeal to the electors by way of a referendum.

For the unelected Lords to frustrate a majority of the Commons, even one elected when Liberal disposition towards Home Rule was perfectly clear, was fine by Dicey – more than fine: it was their duty. 'Their lordships should take steps which can easily be imagined for providing that the rejection of the bill shall entail a dissolution.' But suppose Gladstone had the impudence then to win an election and send up another Commons-approved Home Rule Bill? 'My own conviction which has been well laid before the public, is that the Lords would do well if they appended to any Home Rule which they were prepared to accept, a clause which might make its coming into force depend upon its within a limited time, receiving the approval of a majority of the electors both of Great Britain and Ireland.'

The role of the referendum as a last resort of reaction would be illustrated in Switzerland, where it kept women from the exercise of a vote long after every other developed country. It would, as we shall see, become during the budget crisis an incessant cawing from that superior rookery, the House of Lords. And in our own time, a multimillionaire resident on another continent, also invoking 'the nation', created a mushroom party and injected millions into securing a referendum on the complex and technical question of European Monetary Union. Dicey had his own reasoning. 'At a time when the true danger is that sections or classes should arrogate to themselves authority which belongs to the state, it is an advantage to bring into prominence the sovereignty of the nation.' The delicate progress from general apprehension about democracy to a readiness to use it in the highly coloured form of populism is impressive.

The hereditary peers who should bring this about did not of course constitute a class arrogating state power to itself, and the consequences of a mainland vote against Home Rule and an Irish vote in favour were not afforded the condescension of attention. The supremacy of the Protestant and progressive canton would presumably have been asserted and Ireland dismissed to its kennel by as much coercion as the safety of England required.

Dicey had written the last word of English self-preoccupied supremacism and he would be widely read, quoted and influential on the unionist side. But his arguments as they coloured Conservative English thinking did not stop at the referendum. The question of 'at what point legal oppression justifies armed resistance' would in due course be put outside England. Colonel Saunderson and his drilling Ulster Protestants had already indicated it by way of menacing charade. But in his funeral oration for an old Fenian in 1915, Patrick Pearse, a newer sort of nationalist disdaining the long grief of the parliamentary route, would give a perfectly consistent answer. 'Life springs from death, and from the graves of patriotic men and women spring living nations. We may make mistakes in the beginning and shoot the wrong people, but bloodshed,' said Pearse, contemplating a resistance to legal oppression which he would actually make at the Dublin General Post Office a year later, 'is a cleansing and sanctifying thing.'[2] Dicey's version of the same thing, armed resistance – the concluding section of his pamphlet – is entitled 'The Path of Safety'!

Dicey was an odd character, spindly, undersized, so deficient in physical control that his tutor later recalled tying his tie for him before his finals. But his standing as an academic lawyer was remarkable.

The law abounds in names which attach themselves to

sections of it in Siamese conjunction: *Megarry on Torts*, for example, or the scholarly volume which conjures up thoughts of Anna Karenina, *Tolstoy on Divorce*. The Constitution being what it was to the Victorians, a hallowed thing given a capital letter and handfuls of incense, any major study of it would have been accorded reverence. Dicey on the Constitution, more precisely Dicey's *Laws of the Constitution*, would become a public monument, an Albert memorial among law books, and its author a sage.

The Victorians revered law; judges in their scarlet and prejudice were few and godlike. W.S. Gilbert, himself a member of the bar, in having the lord chancellor in *Iolanthe* say: 'The Law is the embodiment of everything that's wonderful and excellent/And I, me Lords, embody the law', had his tongue clenched between his professional teeth. It was what lord chancellors thought anyway. As we shall see, Lord Halsbury, while resisting any infringement of House of Lords' privilege, would show that statutes of Edward I could and would be bandied about and listened to with deep respect as reasons for doing entirely absurd things in the reign of Edward VII.

So the Law was wonderful and excellent, and Dicey was an academic lawyer, *the* academic lawyer, holder of the Vinerian chair at Oxford. In some sense he was the keeper of the Law. He had his own copy of the Tablets and was reckoned to hold his tutorials a little below the summit of the mountain. He was, altogether more doubtfully, supposed to be disinterested and objective. The fact that, like his equally fervent brother Edward, Albert Dicey had credentials, however faint, as a Liberal of sorts, only added to the credit of his proclamation of some of the most unstrung, emotionally airborne and frantic opinions ever uttered by a don in either of the ancient universities. Edward would speak of himself as 'a malcontent Liberal'; Albert was more like a god who felt let down by the Liberals. The extent of Dicey's objectivity was that, unlike Froude or indeed Salisbury, he was not against the Irish as

Irish. He does not, in his three pamphlets written across the three-bill controversy, talk about the unfitness of the Irish to perform simple tasks, describe Roman Catholicism as a conspiracy against England's greatness or talk about 'the Paddies'.

Dicey's fever was theoretical. He was, even at fifty-one, when the first bill was brought in, elderly and fussed. He was a curator, and in the way of curators, clucking with anxiety. The Constitution was a tender and beautiful thing, in Oscar Wilde's phrase 'touch it and the bloom is gone'. Even Chamberlain's plans for Ireland, involving as they did extensive growth of local government, were dangerous meddling and quite unacceptable. Anything which interfered with the ice-cave perfection of a Constitution which had stood perfectly still while Dicey wrote about it was dangerous, a calamity against which he must urge the unionists of the Kingdom to prepare themselves. Oddly, in all of this, Dicey was a Liberal at one remove. He was speaking the language of the Whigs, certain that in 1688 a near optimum had been achieved which the act of 1832 had made absolute.

Our age is accustomed to political dons, sounders off who, qualified by being remotely connected with education, pronunce on sex, God and the environment without drawing breath. The late Professor A.J. Ayer was a good case in point, as ready with copy for any telephoning journalist as the most desperate backbencher. But such people are a kind of cabaret. Dicey spoke before the majesty of academe had been diluted with chat. He was strong magic. The furious partisanship of what he actually said, its lack of any elasticity or reservation, merely reinforced its quality as judgement, investing it with declaratory finality. Conservative politicians nodded and quoted and rolled their knuckles on the table. The union, and in recent years the Empire, had higher claims which the Irish, alas, disputed. 'The Empire,' he would write, 'meant for many peoples of the world what the Kingdom had signified for the peoples of the United Kingdom' – always excepting the Irish. 'I must except the feelings of three fourths of the Irish people at home or abroad who, not from a sense of right and wrong . . . but for reasons which need not here be enumerated, are always upon the side of any nation, tribe or people with which England is at war.'[3]

There is something schizophrenic about Dicey. He wasn't a brute. He lacked malice or racial contempt, but held that we should be prepared for last-line defence as if the Irish were the Goths and England Rome. The gates to the imperial city should be manned by their lordships – advised, of course, by Dicey. Moreover, panic was to be joined by ingenuity. The Lords' chief defensive weapon against menacing foreigners would be that foreign instrument the referendum. It was all very unConservative, tradition protected by the newfangled. But that referendum would speak for England. Irishmen thought differently and had other loyalties, he would not concede them the right to separate enjoyment of them. They were in conflict with English wishes, and that was enough. Dicey is that oddest of things, a *regretful* supremacist.

For the union to Dicey had sacramental magic, such magic that ultimately, twenty-five years on, Ulstermen importing German rifles could not be condemned.

> Moral resistance . . . will from a constitutional point of view be fully justified. I do not even assert that it may not be rightly carried by Ulstermen to extreme lengths . . . I will not give, because I have not found, any certain opinion as to the right course to be pursued should the British electorate sanction the monstrous iniquity. What are the limits within which the tyranny either of a king or of a democracy justifies civil war is not an inquiry on which I will enter.[4]

Dicey and Patrick Pearse were sisters under the skin.

Ferdinand Mount, in his refined and elegant *The British Constitution Now*, argues convincingly that Dicey is the ancestor of those English nationalists to whom the idea of overlapping sovereignty with the European Union is also a monstrous iniquity. They also recall strangled atrocitarian cries, right down to the referendum campaign of 1997, against the shocking notion of Scottish devolution.

Home Rule implied a federal treatment of Ireland. Dicey had very briefly, in correspondence with James Bryce, fellow academic and tepid Home Ruler, accepted this as an unwelcome possibility. 'If it were possible and in accordance with English habits, I should have first a plebiscite with the simple question of an independent Parliament for Ireland or not. Were there a vote in its favour I would then have a constitutional convention to draw up a constitution fairly carrying out this popular vote, and the constitution itself I would then submit to the people, aye or no.'[5]

But such flexibility did not last. It was in conflict with Dicey's governing passion: sovereignty. Irish Home Rule must necessarily lead to a general federation of Britain which must lead to the downfall of the sovereignty of Parliament. 'Turn the UK into a federal state and parliamentary government as we know it is at an end.'[6] The words come from *A Leap in the Dark*, but in their clenched certainty, they sound curiously as if they had been uttered by Enoch Powell.

A civil war called up against that sovereign Parliament, if it departed from the union structure he extolled, might – he could not quite say – be justified. And in fairness to the man who knew that Irishmen could be very difficult, full Irish separation and statehood were acknowledged as that extreme solution which should be preferred. By a bleak irony, Dicey would die aged eighty-seven in 1922 with Irish statehood accomplished.

But although his passionate intensity and the lurid ideas expressed in soft language seem slightly unhinged to a contemporary reader, Dicey was part of a wider school of intellectuals resolved against Home Rule. Many of them thought of themselves as Liberals, and to hear them is to understand the Victorian proliferation of sub-Liberal castes – Liberal Unionists, Liberal Imperialists and so on. They were diverse, these critics, learned but fearfully apprehensive men and those to whom scornful use of the word 'sentimentality' and in particular 'Gladstonian sentimentality' came easily. Sir James FitzJames Stephen was a special case in his savagery. Stephen, jurist and uncle of Virginia Woolf, knew and was ready to say what Empire was:

> essentially an absolute government founded not on consent but on conquest. It does not represent the native principles of government, nor can it do so until it represents heathenism and barbarism. It represents a belligerent civilisation and no anomaly can be so striking or so dangerous as its administration by men who, being at the head of a government founded on conquest, implying at every point the superiority of the conquering race, of their ideas, of their institutions, their opinions and their principles and having no justification for its existence except that superiority, shrink from the open, uncompromising, straightforward assertion of it.[7]

This is *verismo* imperialism. To the contemporary mind Sir James sounds like Goering with syntax. Consistent in the exclusion of all sensibility toward the conquered, he is the unblinking proclaimer of the role of force and believer in the natural superiority of the coloniser. 'A belligerent civilisation' is a striking phrase. And for people like him, including those less brutal, Home Rule was the coming about of something they had long feared, and 'sentimental' Gladstone the ultimate betrayer. Stephen would write in 1885, a year before Home Rule was launched, 'It is intolerable. England seems have become a huge Gladstone with a conscience like the liver of a Strasbourg goose.'[8] For the many such old Liberals Gladstone, even before Home Rule, was an appeaser, truckling to socialism and to 'democracy', a tricky new word often used with bristling disapproval. The 1867 Reform Act, seen from here as a natural progression coming not before time, had been a sort of abdominal operation to many, and the act of 1884 which enfranchised the urban workman the inevitable terminal complication. Stephen speaks in 1886, the year of the first Home Rule Bill, of 'a tyrannical democracy which will change the whole face of society and destroy all that I love and respect in our institutions. I can only turn away from it in disgust.'[9]

As for Gladstone himself, to Stephen he was 'a wretched old man turning lunatic'. Not that Stephen was changing his style. He had reacted to the French Revolution of 1848 with 'fierce unqualified hatred for the revolution and revolutionists; feelings of the most bitter contempt and indignation against those who feared them, truckled to them or failed to fight them wheresoever they could and as long as they could; feelings of zeal against all popular aspirations and in favour of all established institutions whatever their various defects or harshnesses (which however, I wished to alter slowly or moderately).' By way of *envoi* he favoured grapeshot in the street and the execution of the retiring King, Louis Philippe, for not having used it.[10] And responding to the 1863 New York riots against the military draft, J.F. Stephen's brother, Leslie, father of Virginia Woolf and founder of the *Dictionary of National Biography*, commented: 'Some volleys got the brutes under, but there should have been a really good massacre.'[11]

The ferocities of the Stephen brothers represent the special effects of disaffected liberalism at an extreme, but the wider mood in Oxford and Cambridge was strongly negative. Henry Sidgwick, one of the subtlest of the old Liberals and a very different man from Stephen, logged his diary with observations of opinion in his college, Trinity, Cambridge. 'July 5 1886 unionists gaining slowly but steadily. Dined in Hall and was surprised to find the great preponderance of unionist sentiment among the Trinity Fellows, a body always, since

I have known Trinity, predominantly Liberal'.[12] The highest figure claimed at Oxford for dons supporting Home Rule was forty-three. Yet in the 1878 contest for the university seat, 288 dons had voted Liberal.[13]

The old Liberals were an elect body, highly educated and socially placed, making judgements from a viewpoint elevated above the the scrambling depths whose occupants they viewed inexpertly with as much fear as disdain. Writing in *The Times* in January 1886, Stephen questioned:

> If socialism and Jacobinism are unchained in Ireland, how long will they take to pass into England? How many English, Scots and Welsh farmers are there who will fail to see why they should pay rent any more than Irish farmers? Many English debtors will find it difficult to see the distinction between one debt and another, between the non-payment of rent and the non-payment of rent? In short, if the general question, 'why should you be rich and I be poor?' be answered as to Irishmen by saying 'it is a great shame and you shall have a distribution of property'; will not the same question arise in a terrible form in England?[14]

Sidgwick, much milder but reluctantly coming down on this issue with the strong party, saw Home Rule as 'putting a premium . . . on a combination of political and agrarian agitation'. The temperate and uncomfortable opposition of Sidgwick is important as a form of swing or floating vote. He had not regressed very far from Liberalism and would live to speak scornfully of the Boer War and the accompanying jingoism, but his temporary loss signified more perhaps than the chunterings of Stephen about a nervous mood towards democratic ventures which was catching on.

'Democracy,' said W.E.H. Lecky – harder than Sidgwick, saner than Stephen – 'pushed to its full consequences, places the whole property of the country in the hands of the poorest

classes giving them unlimited powers of helping themselves.'
As for what was happening in Ireland, it could only bring
about 'the permanent lowering of the character of public men
and the moral tone of public life'.[15]

In his Liberal day Lecky had written admiringly of Grattan
and the 1782 Dublin Parliament, but Lecky was a small Irish
proprietor himself and his ideal seems to have been an Ireland
run not by England or the masses, but by proprietors. The
roughness and want of genteel character among Irish MPs
was an unquantifiable factor in the revulsion of middle- and
upper-middle-class opinion against Home Rule. Parnell might
impress Gladstone and Asquith as a great man, Thomas Sexton might possess a sound financial head, Justin McCarthy
might be an elegant and polished writer, Tim Healy a wit;
the Irish MPs were yet a lower order of men who induced
fastidiousness. If England was going to the dogs, these were
the dogs.

The very idea of self-government for such a people was
repugnant. A.V. Dicey's brother Edward put it briskly:

> My own conviction is that the real bane of Ireland is
> the possession of parliamentary institutions which the
> character of her people, the stage of her civilisation, the
> condition of *our* national existence render her unfit to
> employ with advantage to herself or others. My own
> belief is that in the interests of Ireland and the United
> Kingdom, the only statesmanlike course is to deprive
> her for a time of parliamentary representation in fact
> if not in name, and to govern her as a crown colony
> till her people have become fit to enjoy political liberty
> without abusing it.

That comes from *Plea of a Malcontent Liberal*, which Edward
Dicey published in 1886, a title with general application to
this entire group of writers and academics. George Brodrick,
warden of Merton, put it more gently and with a rare hint

of past English fault: 'A peasantry whose minds have been dwarfed . . . by the effect of the penal laws could not govern itself and carry out the programme of land and educational reform necessary to modernise the country.'[16]

As to how Ireland was to be ruled, Gladstone, of course, had taken up and quoted in Parliament the maxim of Charles Gavan Duffy that Canada had not been given freedom because of her loyalty. Having been given freedom, she was loyal. But Canada was made up of English and Scots plus a minority of subordinable French. Its autonomy was natural and the native peoples were no part of such freedoms. By contrast, wrote George Campbell in the *New Edinburgh Review*,

> Ireland is a colony which we have only partly colonised, and in which the natives have been neither exterminated nor thoroughly assimilated and we have the race difficulties . . . familiar in other countries. In Canada and New Zealand the colonists far outnumber the French, Red Indian, Esquimaux and Maoris. Ireland is in a position more analagous to that of the South African colonies in which only British authority prevents collision between a colonist minority and a native majority.[17]

Ireland was complicated as an issue by comparison with other territories: Canada was misleadingly happy and India both a natural object of force and prospective follower of a dreadful Irish example. She was complicated also by the social implications which concessions to lower and demanding elements could inflict upon the mainland.

Because Ireland could be seen as a piece of union, or indeed a colony – and despite the official Conservative rhetoric, these ex-Liberals spoke far more candidly about her status – she was a danger. Concession and deal-making meant loss of face and risky example within the Empire. Indeed, the Liberal viceroy of India himself, Lord Dufferin, commented on the threat during the first Home Rule crisis. 'I cannot help asking myself how long an autocratic government like that of India . . . will be able to stand the strain implied by the importation en bloc from England, or rather from Ireland, of the perfected machinery of modern democratic agitation.'[18]

Dufferin, having the job he did, had reason to be anxious on a practical level, though that anxiety complicated his relations with a then moderate enough Indian nationalism. But for imperialists at home, a pragmatic holding together of the territory in hand was not really the issue. They inclined to an English triumphalism which Empire had exalted and which Gladstone's 'sentimentalism' threatened.

A true imperialist like Stephen, favouring short ways, was not deterred by the institutions of the Liberal state. What Ireland needed was force. If they applied it, they 'might govern it without conspicuous effort, so that it would never trouble anybody any more. This of course is quite inconsistent with parliamentary government and trial by jury, but are they, after all, so beneficial and glorious?'[19] The distinction between yearning backwards to predemocratic thinking and anticipating later ideas about vigour and force is more interesting than wide.

Discussion of Ireland here was recurringly England-centred, expressing a selfishness given tone by patriotism. Edward Dicey would speak of 'the condition of *our* national existence'. An England which did not preserve the union, itself a sort of proto-empire, would not be a dominant nation. Commanding the Irish was not just good for the Irish, it was essential for England. The question, wrote A.C. Sellar, a contributor to the *Edinburgh Review* in 1886, 'is whether England is to continue a dominant nation'.[20] (There is a pre-echo here of that other Sellar who, with R.J. Yeatman, wrote in *1066 and All That* about England being 'top nation'.) The language would be echoed by Lord Randolph in Paddington telling the Protestants of the north that they were 'like us, a dominant and imperial caste'. In the view of Lecky, 'a great and ancient nation is obliged to acquiesce in its own disintegration whenever a portion of its people can be persuaded to desire a separate political existence'.[21]

There was a clear sympathy between such elder and discontented Liberal academics and Salisbury, who had some claims to intellectual status himself and who had said as far back as 1872, 'Ireland must be kept, like India, at all hazards, by persuasion if possible, if not, by force.'[22] Into all such preoccupations with England's interest as debenture-holder in the union and Empire, with the natives as last consideration, one other early twentieth-century comparison must come. Salisbury had, after all, told his St James's Hall audience in 1886 that representative government was not offered to Hottentots. Crude racial talk was rife in those days and an American scholar, Lionel Curtis Jr, has devoted a book to malign English perceptions of the Irish. Was academic opposition also based on racism?

That prejudice did not universally fit. The historian Edward Freeman did not care for 'those great black apes' the negroes, and notoriously remarked, 'What a grand country America would be if every Irishman would kill a negro and be hanged for it.'* But Freeman was a Home Ruler, if for the unGladstonian reason of 'getting rid of the paddies' from Westminster. And anyway, Freeman reckoned that the Irishman, with all his faults, was still one of us: 'He is Aryan; he is European; he is capable of being assimilated by other branches of the European stock.'[23]

Goldwin Smith, another academic busily resisting Home Rule with the best of them – though he wrote of the Irish as the weaker race in relation to stronger England – also spoke a language which, after so much bombast, comes as civilised and a relief. He thought that race distinctions were more matters of circumstance than congenital. And

---

* Disraeli had famously said: 'All is race, there is no other truth,' and Freeman in turn had described him in another context as 'The Jew in his drunken insolence.'

'that which is not congenital is probably not indelible, so that less favoured races, placed under happier circumstances, may in time be brought to the level of the most favoured, and nothing warrants inhuman pride of race.'[24] In fairness, Dicey, for all his febrile and obsessive 'England in peril' talk, was honourable on this, concerned to keep racial taunts out of the argument.

The intellectual unionists knew of course that Gladstone could and did turn on them with charges of following 'the doctrine of the natural inferiority of a race' if that card was played. But it would probably be fair to say that the old Liberal academics, for all their agitation and moral coarseness, were not crude racists. Their spectrum ran from administrative fears of what came next in an empire if anything were conceded in Ireland, via preoccupation with the English interest and a primitive Hobbesian belief in conflict and conquest, to a final extreme contempt for and fear of the democracy of recent legislation. They feared that, by making concessions to Ireland, they would cause other lesser groups 'to help themselves'. Though they were negative, narrow, apocalyptical and often brutal, these thinkers, their broad prejudices did not extend to any elaborate theory of race.

But *realpolitik* flavoured with hysteria is quite enough to be getting on with.

9

Mr Gladstone and the Ulstermen

While legislation proceeded, Ulster reacted. The response of the north had many spokesmen, but for the period of the second Home Rule Bill one of them makes the case plainly enough. Thomas MacKnight was as down-to-earth a spokesman for Ulster as might have been found. Originally a Liberal, the longstanding editor of the *Northern Whig*, still officially a Liberal-supporting paper in Belfast, MacKnight would not have been thought of as an extremist. And as the necessary follower of his readers' letters over three decades, he had a fair claim to know something about Ulster opinion. His summing-up three years after the second Home Rule Bill was one of geological non-compliance. 'I have more than once said, and I deliberately repeat, that the unionists of Ulster would rather be governed by a foreign, a German army, whose headquarters might be Dublin, than by such an Irish legislature and ministry the Home Rule Bills proposed to establish.'

The German officers, thought MacKnight, would at least be impartial. 'But there would not be anything impartial in an Irish Home Rule Parliament and government. They would represent a political and social triumph over their fellow countrymen, whom the nationalist majority so thoroughly hate, and against whom they would be only too ready to raise the cry of *vae victis.*'[1]

The Ulster Protestants made (and still make) great play of their loyalism, using the word like punctuation, but in the ever-recurring Ulster rage at supposed betrayal, loyalism did not have to mean loyalty. MacKnight quoted another unionist:

> I am a loyal man. I am a Liberal as my fathers were, but rather than submit to an Irish Home Rule Parliament and government, I would prefer absolute separation and would do everything I could to bring about such a result. If we were thus abandoned by a government and Parliament bound to protect us, I would become one of the most bitter and irreconcilable enemies of Great Britain and of everything British. There is scarcely anything I would shrink from to show my detestation and scorn of such shameful surrender of the loyal to the disloyal. I would not hesitate to join an Irish Fenian Republic at once.

After the 1893 bill passed the Commons, wrote MacKnight, a nationalist paper in Belfast had rejoiced that slaves were now the masters; and we knew 'what use slaves made of their newly acquired freedom, especially when they found their former masters left in their power'.[2] 'Slaves' is an important word. There is something in what MacKnight quotes and asserts which suggests that sense of hopeless difference existing between European settlers and Africans in a former colony or the white-black divide in the American south. The Catholic Irish were – must be – an inferior people, absolutely and categorically inferior, primitive, peasant, not like us. MacKnight did not fear the Catholic hierarchy as themselves seeking to persecute, but 'the Catholic clergy, including the bishops, except in the matter of education, are driven on from below'.

In Tipperary a few years earlier, a woman suspected of being a witch had been burned, demonstrating 'what depth of ignorance and prejudice exists among the peasants who under Home Rule would have so many votes for an Irish Parliament'. He quoted a Presbyterian clergyman: 'It could not have occurred among our people under any circumstances.'[3]

That racial and confessional scorn was gleefully relayed by the reporter of the virulent *Birmingham Gazette*. He describes an Ulster politician who 'bore a Scottish name and had the incisive argumentative style of the typical Ulsterman': "Yes there is a party of ascendancy. The Protestants are distinctly the party of ascendancy. They have the ascendancy which ability and education and industry will always have over incapacity and ignorance and laziness."' Flax would grow better in the south than the north, but

> they won't be bothered with flax which wants no end of of attention. Why if they grew flax, they'd have to work almost every day. And nobody who knows Irishmen, real Keltic [*sic*] Irishmen, ever expects them to do that, or anything like it. I've been in India and I deliberately say that I prefer the Hindoo to the Southern Irishman for industry and reliability. These people who are too lazy to wash themselves expect their condition to be improved by a Home Rule Parliament. Can anything be more unreasonable or more unlikely? And because there are more of them, their wishes are to be taken into account and the opinions and wishes of men of whom each one is worth a hundred are to be disregarded. Where is the English sense of the fitness of things?[4]

'Ireland is a distinct entity,' quoted MacKnight ironically. 'Now this is just what Ireland is not. There are in Ireland two distinct entities, if not more.' He then argued from fear. If the Ulster Protestants had been 'as tyranical and incapable of improvement as the Turks were in Bulgaria . . . it would still be a gross breach of faith in a British government and a British Parliament to hand them over to an Irish domestic legislature and administration by which . . . their attachment to Great Britain and the British Crown would be regarded as criminal and their very virtues treated as crimes.'

The Turks had refused to have anything to do with new governments in former Turkish provinces and had emigrated in great numbers. So would the Protestants. 'To subject the unionists of the north of Ireland to the necessity of either becoming rebels or of leaving the country in which they, like their fathers, have done and are doing a great and civilising work would be shameful.' There was a constitutional doctrine to their stand, said MacKnight. Ulstermen believed that they were 'asserting the same cause of freedom as the Long Parliament did against Charles I, as their ancestors did against James II and as the American colonists did against George III'.[5]

As for giving a Parliament to the Irish, everything would break down. 'Ireland would be too small for the Irish. Then would come true what was said of the Wars of the Roses after France was given up by the English.'[6]

MacKnight himself was much taken with a connection between Scotland and Northern Ireland. He devotes pages to urging the case for a tunnel from Portpatrick to Donaghadee, no further apart, he says, than Dover and Calais. This project was 'not for separation, division or dismemberment in any sense. It was for not only a political, moral and social union which may be said virtually to exist on the basis of equal laws; but also for a physical union between the two islands.'[7]

In 1887, when MacKnight was invited to meet Gladstone, he pursued this enthusiasm and records the reaction. 'In introducing your Home Rule Bill, Mr Gladstone, you stated that the 60 miles of sea rolling between the two countries increased the difficulties of governing Ireland. If you come to the coast of Down near Belfast, you will find that there are only 20 miles of sea between Scotland and Ireland; and if you go further up the coast of Antrim, you will see that Ulster is only separated by 11 nautical miles from Scotland.'

'Ah! Have another cup of tea.'[8]

But if Gladstone's response on the question of the shortness of the distance between Scotland and Ulster was sociably negative, MacKnight depicts himself at the same teatime encounter briskly dismissing any thought of that separate Ulster autonomy which over the next twenty-eight years might have saved everyone so much labour.

'Introducing the bill,' said Gladstone, 'I stated I was willing to consider any plan for a separate government in Ulster or even a part of Ulster. I am still ready to consider any scheme your friends can suggest. There will be some difficulty, I know, in inducing certain parties to consent to such a proposal, but I have no doubt we can carry it. Let the Ulster unionists think over a plan.' At that time, replied MacKnight, he did not think 'even the Liberal Unionists would take that question into consideration. They consider that, the constituencies having been appealed to on it, and by a large majority having declared against Home Rule, the question is for some time at least, settled.'

But MacKnight records raising Gladstone's suggestion with friends at the Ulster Reform Club, now a haunt of Liberal Unionists. 'They now said, "It is no part of our business to form any plan for the future of Ulster to render it easier to carry an Irish Home Rule Bill. We are decidedly opposed to any such measure. We are not going to make Mr Gladstone's task easier. We wish to remain as we are; but if we are driven into the last ditch and have to make a choice between the two evils, we shall prefer absolute separation from Great Britain to any Irish Home Rule Bill.'

'In their opposition to Home Rule,' he adds, 'the people were and are terribly in earnest.'[9]

That earnestness took different forms. Sinclair and MacKnight, as Liberal Unionists, were content with what would be called a Quaker rebellion, passive resistance in the face of any

Dublin government – Quaker in its rejection of violence and its understanding of the role of money. A Dublin government, it was reckoned, simply would not be able to afford to collect taxation which had been refused. This way the British army would be kept out of the action. The earnestness of some of the Presbyterian clergy was more alarming. Lord Kimberley, for the government, would quote the Reverend Leslie Carter of Armagh. 'They, the Protestants of the north, would march to the House of Commons and compel their enemies to be silent while their representatives were speaking. If [Michael] Barrett was executed for blowing up a prison, the time might not be far distant when for attempting to blow up our venerable Protestant constitution, Gladstone and his co-conspirators might be hanging as high as Haman.'[10]

But serious thinking concerned tax. As St Loe Strachey, editor of the *Spectator*, put it, 'The Ulstermen would of course refuse to pay a tax levied in Dublin, and then the Dublin Parliament would be face to face with a strike against taxes in which every merchant of wealth and position in Belfast and Derry and every landlord in the north would be engaged.'[11]

Talk of armed resistance existed of course. Colonel Saunderson was always good for hot-headed bluster and there existed another group, 'Young Ulster' under F.H. Crawford, which also made military gestures. But broadly, resistance by violence was not expected. Rentoul, the member for East Down who had first mooted the convention, said that he 'never met anyone who regarded that statement – "We will not have Home Rule" – as committing us to civil war or war against Great Britain in any contingency whatever . . . Lord Randolph Churchill's statement "Ulster will fight and Ulster will be right", though quoted with great frequency, was, so far as I know, never regarded seriously by even the keenest unionists. It was merely used as a political catchword.'[12] If the Ulstermen had both a hard notion of their own identity and a vaunting sense of superiority over the Catholic Irishmen around them, they did not want for English encouragement. The *Birmingham Daily Gazette* reporter let fly with a volley of uncomplicated prejudice which would have done credit to the Mississippi Delta. Visiting Protestant Armagh, he says in awe:

> Look around the shopkeepers' signs in Tipperary or Tuam and note the names. Ruane, Magrath, Maguire. O'Doherty, O'Brien, O'Flanagan, O'Shaughnessy and so in saecula saeculorum. In Newry you see a striking change, Duncan, Boyd, Wylie, MacAlister, Campbell, McClelland, McAteer and so on greet you in all directions. You are in one of the colonies. The breed is different. You are among the men who make railways, construct bridges, invent engines, bore tunnels, make canals, build ships and sail them over unknown seas. You are among the people who have the instincts of achievement, of enterprise, of invention, of command, who depend for themselves, who shift for themselves and believe in self-help rather than querulous complaints . . . The Westport people have endless quarries of hard blue marble which they are too lazy or too ignorant or both to cut. The Ulster breed would have quarried, polished, exported a mountain or two long since. The universal verdict of employers of labour proves that a northern Irishman is worth two from any any other point of the compass, will actually perform double the amount of work, and is besides incomparably superior in brains and general reliability.[13]

Reflecting on this rapture today, when economic decline long ante-dating the political breakdown in Northern Ireland has made that province limp behind the rest of Britain, his lines read poignantly. No part of the UK has been in receipt of as much public money raised from general revenue to prop up business, make work or maintain a carousel of service employment as superior, harder-working Ulster with its better brains and enterprising nature. And of course the decline *isn't* her fault. But in 1893, economics, morality and comparative religion were heavily intertwined; so was racial theory taken neat.

This attitude underlines the heroic originality of Gladstone. He was attempting to give Ireland self-government in the teeth of such prejudice, which was present in his own Cabinet, as well as facing a House of Lords almost certain to reject any bill, from a mix of cynicism and the good-faith nullity of orthodox Conservatism. Meanwhile, the superiority complex of Ulster Protestantism either preached the present danger from a Dublin Parliament or excluded any idea of self-government for herself in parallel with such an assembly.

Gladstone was trying to make reforms when the violence of the Land League fringe provided an alibi for the conflation of Irish autonomy with rural intimidation. And he was toiling in the false glow of imperial self-congratulation, disgracefully suggesting that something was badly wrong and saying so between royal jubilees! Ultimately, the bill was certain of passing the Commons and of being blocked in the Lords. Balfour, the former chief secretary and future prime minister, would wind up the debate on 1 September conceding that it would carry. But he was sure that there was 'not a single man who feels the force of parliamentary tradition who does not look back upon this session with regret as the moment in our parliamentary life when we can distinctly trace and note the beginning of a decadence, and when it became clear for the first time that this House is not in the future to be what has been in the past.'[14] There is a hint there of 'Chard Whitlow', Henry Reed's Eliot parody: 'As we get older we do not get any younger.'

For Balfour there was 'but one body of men in the whole country who have reason to congratulate themselves upon the part you are compelling them to play – that is the House of Lords.' Balfour is always thought of as sophisticate and

Cambridge soul, a languid and cerebral politician doing what made practical short-term party sense without delusive belief in the orthodoxies of the Conservative bourgeoisie. But he could put on that act very well. The man who said that he would as lief take advice from his valet as from party conference could, when he turned on Gladstone, sound like anyone's valet. 'I say that by your insane action you have done more than a hundred Tory governments to demonstrate the necessity for the House of Lords and the part it may play as the bulwark of the interests and greatness of the Empire.'

A.J. Balfour had very little in common with Colonel Edward Saunderson, the Boanerges of Ulster, but an admiration for their lordships was an exception. 'The bill would be beaten in another place, and why?' asked Saunderson. 'Because in the House of Lords there is not a Catholic majority. It is only because the government have a Catholic majority here that they have brought in the Home Rule Bill.' Saunderson and Balfour had one other conclusion in common: that life was better under the union. During the previous fifty years, said Saunderson 'the record of England's dealing with Ireland is one of which any great nation might be proud . . . The people of Ireland are infinitely more prosperous, better fed and better educated than they were.' But hadn't large numbers emigrated? The diminution of population is no test of decreased prosperity. Population has decreased because the people, being more educated, have learned that there are more countries in which they can live and thrive.'[15] The education of Ireland was perhaps most effective in the years immediately after 1845.

Balfour, a little later in the same debate, remarked, 'I think any man who chooses to examine with impartial eyes any contemporary account of the conditions of the peasantry of Ireland in the beginning, middle and end of the last century will see that an incomparable improvement in their lot has been has been effected in the last ninety-three years of the union as contrasted with the corresponding class in England

and Scotland.' (Visiting the west of Ireland fifteen years later, Augustine Birrell would write: 'I was at Galway the other night. Oh Lord! The melancholy of it was overwhelming. Belmullet was a pleasure beside it. Galway and the workhouse at Clifden will never quit my memory.'[16]

In this summing-up speech, Balfour expressed a great part of the mood which sustained resistance to Home Rule. Apart from a heroic account of Ireland's comfortable prosperity across the century of the famine, skipping the agrarian depression which in the late seventies had created rural violence and a migration that had taken out a vast tract of the population, he strikes and holds to the proud achievement of England, an Anglocentric viewpoint verging on the sublime.

The vote that evening was directed to Ireland, which he did not wish to have autonomy. But the Irish MPs, elected under the terms of union, had had the impudence to vote. Accordingly,

> every elector knows and must know that in the management of his affairs will mingle the voices of eighty irresponsible members from Ireland; of eighty gentlemen not belonging in the full sense to our political system, not bound by our traditions, not looking forward to the same object; and every elector will know that in order that he may obtain a questionable privilege, he must give up everything that his fathers cherished, everything he was taught to revere, and that he must throw upon himself a perfectly unnecessary burden of taxation . . .
>
> Never again [he told the government] can you come before the constituencies of the country and with all the mist of ingenious rhetoric pretend to them that you want to give to Ireland everything she wants and subtract from Great Britain nothing that she cherishes . . . Every elector will now know what the grant of Home Rule involves to him – a diminution in the security and unity of the Empire, a diminution to the

safety of those in Ireland to whom his honour is so
deeply pledged.[17]

The mixture of rhapsody and self-pity is not attractive, but
the insistence upon retaining Ireland in spite of her irresponsible, not-one-of-us alienness, on account of imperial loss
of face if she went, speaks a marvellous self-preoccupation.
Roy Jenkins' description of Salisbury as a cynical pessimist
applies well enough to his nephew, but needs the addition of
something that Victorian Tories had in full without knowing
the word or commonly recognising the quality – *chutzpah*,
defined in the *Concise Oxford Dictionary* as 'shameless
audacity'.

PART II

The Liberals, The Budget, The Parliament Act

10

'We Are in for a Great Time'

An idea exists of the British aristocracy as absentmindedly benevolent, one reinforced by the picture painted by P.G. Wodehouse of Lord Emsworth, besotted owner of the prize pig Empress of Blandings. Lord Emsworth, affable but harassed, is mentioned as being a Conservative. He is an invention of the 1920s, and it is difficult to imagine him a dozen years earlier on terms of agreement with the Duke of Bedford, who said in a letter to Lord Willoughby de Broke, whose National Service Bill proposed compulsory military training for the middle and upper classes, 'I don't think it would be prudent for me to speak in support of arming and training the classes against the masses. I am strongly in favour of so doing, I quite admit.'[1]

The same Willoughby de Broke, Richard Greville Verney, 19th Baron of a creation of 1491, would respond in 1913 to legislation to create Irish Home Rule with the establishment of the 'British League', and, speaking to the House of Lords, would say that what decent men would 'wish to see is this matter fought to a finish. They would sooner see it fought to a finish in a General Election, but if that means of settlement is denied to us, then we must fall back on the only other means at our disposal.'[2]

And earlier in that year, another peer, Lord Saltoun, also speaking of military resistance, wrote: 'We cannot be guilty of civil war because we are maintaining the Constitution of the United Kingdom & Ireland as by law established and it is they who seek to destroy that constitution who will be guilty of civil war. A curious one it will be. Civil wars up to this date have been against the Supreme Authority The King. This, if it comes, will be on our side for The King & Constitution and against the government of the Country.'[3]

The final struggle for Irish Home Rule would be the last of all the crises of England before the First World War. It represented Conservative opinion at its most irrational and blazingly enraged, but it followed closely on the great defeat of the Conservative Party and the landed interest with the passing on 10 August 1911 of the Parliament Act, which effectively ended the Lords' veto on legislation. This was done after the threat had been made clear, with agonisingly extracted royal endorsement, that the alternative was the creation at a single stroke of 500 pro-government peers to enact this bill, swamp the House and lower the tone.

This humiliation would inflame the extreme vehemence which Tories would show towards Home Rule over the next three years. But for many Conservatives it was a sufficient climax in their own embittered, excluded state since the last demoralised days of the Balfour government, which had ended ahead of electoral defeat in 1905. The Tory grief of the intervening years, expressed in rage and, at the extreme, in proto-fascist dabblings, would be part of a pattern. Its weave took in a number of strands, not just Ireland and the House of Lords, but the remote and, to the English, pragmatic-seeming issue of Welsh disestablishment and the large, lost cause of economic protectionism, otherwise, and in very large type, Tariff Reform.

When Joseph Chamberlain crossed by way of Liberal Unionism to the Tory Party, he brought with him great talents, grinding willpower and a perfect genius for division.

An earlier, grander David Owen, he joined nothing he did not come close to destroying.

The Tory Party, having been split on the initiative of Disraeli and Lord George Cavendish-Bentinck in 1846 over the Corn Laws, had long reconciled itself to free trade. When, across the seventies, the combination of opened-up north American prairies and five years of freakishly bad weather had drastically reduced price and product volume, with wheat falling from an average price of around 50 shillings a quarter weight to 17s 4d, Disraeli, ironically prime minister at that time, had had no answer except cynical submission. The industrial advantages of free trade and the domination of urban interests over rural made fidelity to the rhetoric by which he had risen unthinkable. Rural depression was to be endured; the working population, long on the move to the towns, went in a final wave, while to the owners of land, having made their own adjustments – reducing estates, sacking staff and shifting further into equity and bond markets – the issue seemed resolved.

But Chamberlain, as a Birmingham screw manufacturer remote from the concerns of either Lord Willoughby de Broke or Lord Emsworth, had become in his Conservative incarnation an imperialist before all other things. He was the supporter in South Africa of Milner, Rhodes and Jameson, the embarrassed defender of Chinese indentured labour, a conniver at the Jameson raid and a party to instigating the Boer War. Chamberlain on protection had no defensive purpose. Piqued at the removal of a temporary duty while he had been away in South Africa, he made his Birmingham speech in favour of what he called 'Tariff Reform' in May 1903, a year after Arthur Balfour had succeeded his uncle, Lord Salisbury, as prime minister. A fervent admirer, Leopold Amery, would compare it with the nailing of ninety-five theses to the church door in Wittenberg by Luther. The effect on the Conservative Party would be closer to that of the Counter-Reformation.

Chamberlain wanted protection partly because German

competition now threatened industrial goods and partly as an imperialist measure. He had been colonial secretary for eight years and believed in a forward policy of British self-assertion. A tariff wall, once erected, was something behind which friends and allies could be invited. The imperial preference he demanded would admit the white dominion states into material advantage from their ties with the motherland. Greater autonomy already existed for those white settlements than had been envisaged for Ireland under any Home Rule bill, but the new de facto union of self-interest would make the Empire into a species of superstate. The thought occurs that a consistent Conservative, having accepted Tariff Reform, would have offered it to Ireland while endorsing Home Rule as a combination of policies which might do for the neighbour island what it was intended to do for New Zealand. But the notion of treating Ireland in a way mistakable for friendly remained repugnant.

As for Chamberlain, with his customary regard for the fragilities of politics, he resigned four months after making the speech. What had been done for the Liberal Party in 1886 could be done for the Tories seventeen years later. The impact on the Conservative Party of this stand was not unlike the destructive effect of anti-Europeanism in our own time. And without pushing analogies too far, when trade is not the central issue of Euroscepticism, there is a kinship between the emotional appeal of both ideas. But the political effect was to split the Tories. The free trade chancellor, Charles Ritchie, departed and Balfour himself was left straddling a party in which Tariff Reform became furiously popular with a right wing soon to be liberated from any remaining restraints by defeat.

Of all party leaders, Balfour was least equipped for rough politics. A respectable second-line philosopher and author of *A Defence of Philosophic Doubt*, he was also, as a Cecil (through his mother, Salisbury's sister), rather better than a second-line aristocrat. He tended to look at the Conservative

Party and its virulent enthusiasms with understandable distaste. Despite the hard-handed and creative policy he had
followed as chief secretary in Ireland, with his own party he
would show no appetite for a fight. The view of Sir Edward
Hamilton, a senior treasury civil servant, was that on free
trade, Balfour was 'rotten'.[4]

In fact he stood somewhere between agnosticism and compliance. Deferring to a stronger personality, he succeeded
in alienating his free trade ministers without keeping or
controlling Chamberlain who, he agreed, should resign, but
for the purpose of 'educating the country' on Tariff Reform.
He kept this deal a secret from the Cabinet with a post-dated
promise of bringing official Conservatism behind that policy.
Then, in Cabinet, he picked a fight with the free-traders
provoking resignations. He had already lost his chancellor,
Ritchie; Lord Balfour of Burleigh and Lord George Hamilton
followed, with Chamberlain functioning as a licensed critic
of free trade while that same policy was being proclaimed
as the official line. Balfour had begun by running from the
right without acknowledging the retreat and making a show
of courage by abusing the weaker side. The divisions in the
party would also cost him the reluctant resignation of the
grandest grandee of Whiggery, the Duke of Devonshire (the
Hartington of the 1886 crisis) and, from his backbenches, an
ardent young free-trader, Winston Churchill who, in March
1904, crossed the floor to join the Liberals. Managerialism
had been preferred to a clear stand, something acknowledged
as respectable politics. But on Tariff Reform, as subsequently
on the Lords veto, what Balfour would really offer was his
own teasing style of contemptuous inertia – what might
fairly be called mis-managerialism. It was to be the dominant
pattern of the vicious-tempered years of opposition.

Devonshire was replaced by the outstandingly incompetent
Marquess of Londonderry, whose civil servants advised that
he should never be given two memos at the same time since
he was liable to confuse them. Devonshire set up the Free

Food League, a middle-of-the-road group, to resist Chamberlain's busy protectionist campaign, and Balfour found himself speaking from its platform. In due course, Free Food candidates would be opposing protectionist Tories at by-elections. He had even managed to alienate his own family, the Cecils, in varying degrees free-traders and out of all sympathy with Chamberlain.

The descent of Avernus was swift enough. Chamberlain set out on a massive nationwide campaign for his own brand of imperialism whose higher food prices made it effectively a tax targeted on the poor, something the Liberals delightedly underlined. For the split in the Tory party had been chosen on a subject perfectly suited to the healing of all Liberal wounds. On free trade all Liberals were at one and they vigorously returned Chamberlain's campaign. Margot Asquith describes her husband coming into her bedroom with a copy of *The Times* reporting Chamberlain's Birmingham speech and saying, 'Wonderful news today, and it is only a question of time when we shall sweep this country.'[5] And Campbell-Bannerman wrote to his local party chairman: 'This reckless escapade of Joe's is the great event of our time. It is playing Old Harry with all party relations . . . We are in for a great time.'

The next crisis ironically derived from the absence of Chamberlain. A proposal to use Chinese bound to labour in South Africa – whom the Liberals would inexplicably call 'Chinese slaves' – was something which Chamberlain as colonial secretary had been too shrewd to accept from Alfred Milner, high commissioner in that country. Milner was the new, decisive, unpleasant sort of man for whom Chinese indentured labour, liable to suffer corporal punishment at the hands of overseers, was as distinguishable from slavery as it was acceptable. Chamberlain's affable, inferior replacement, Lyttleton, accepted the idea (as, instructively, did Edward VII). The group of Liberals around Asquith, the Liberal Imperialists, had also been squared, but the Nonconformist conscience responded to any sophisticated tolerance of such things by throwing up.

Campbell-Bannerman, the Liberal leader and a man out of all sympathy with imperialism, hit the right note early and kept on hitting it. Outraged and saying so, he was described as 'coming down on Balfour like an eagle on a sparrow.'[6] Resistance to Tariff Reform had united the Liberals. Chinese indentured labour set their leader, long trammelled by his right wing, free as a genuine radical able to rouse the public. Chinese labour rapidly became an intolerable embarrassment to a Conservative government charged at once with undermining white workers and treating yellow ones as helots. From South Africa Milner wrote to Lyttleton: 'I regard the opposition frankly as wreckers . . . and inside information given to them simply would be material supplied to the Powers of Darkness.'[7] But as Balfour himself commented on the right to inflict floggings, it was 'an amazing blunder which seems to violate every canon of international morality, of law and of policy'. A disgusted and returned Milner would be a serious player, not just over Ireland but as a caller to world war and defender of their lordships' rights.

But the Balfour government could get into trouble for doing things which to posterity look creditable. A crisis in Ireland over devolutionary proposals from the senior civil servant Sir Anthony MacDonnell overwhelmed and destroyed the graceful and enervated chief secretary, George Wyndham. Conservative paranoia on Catholics, Irishmen and the threat to the sacred union on this occasion took on a distinct colouring of 'the enemies within'. Wyndham, highly strung and drinking, had not apparently taken notice of his official's proposals or not remembered them. Then, these modest ideas having provoked much talk of 'insidious cliques', he collapsed into nervous breakdown and, as the saying goes, had to be let go. A limited scheme of devolution, even if based on MacDonnell's touchingly unlikely belief in the reasonableness of Irish landowners, was something too dangerously fairminded for any Conservative administration of the day to acknowledge having contemplated.

The government, making successive misjudgements, unresolved on its central economic policy and split wide open, had become something of a ship of death. Balfour, like his uncle, thought in party terms. Where Salisbury had ruled out Home Rule from its inception, irrespective of any good it might do Ireland, because of the political harm which the great nineteenth-century reforms had inflicted on the Tory Party, Balfour told his friend Evan Charteris that 'the two greatest villains in political history are Sir Robert Peel and Gladstone, because both of them broke up their parties'.[8]

In his own case, his party was breaking up very nicely even as its leader was avoiding the provocation of leading it. He continued, elegant, intelligent, surrounded by personal admirers, but performing rather than directing. The Liberal veteran John Morley would quote Cromwell at Balfour, showing the same impatience with which Leopold Amery would cite him to Neville Chamberlain in 1940. 'Oh, Sir Harry Vane, thou with thy subtle casuistries and abstruse hair-splittings, thou art other than a good one, I think. The Lord deliver me from Sir Harry Vane.'[9]

It was not God but Balfour himself who did the delivering. In the words of a biographer, 'The government tottered on until December.'[10] Tariff Reform plagued him. Chamberlain was lobbying for full-scale commitment to his protectionist scheme while Morley, for the Liberals, was demanding in Parliament a summary 'on a sheet of notepaper' of Balfour's own position. To this demand, only impenetrable generalities could be returned. The idea of running a two-in-hand policy – a party neutral on protection combined with a faction fully blessed to campaign for it – collapsed, as it was always going to collapse.

He had moreover the uncomfortable support of a right-wing press heavily committed to Tariff Reform and short on

sympathy for Balfour himself. As a friendly journalist wrote
to him,

> The ardent spirits of the Tariff Reformers are disloyal
> to *you*. There is not a Tory amongst them: Leo Maxse,
> Garvin, Amery, Gwynne, Goldman are all radicals inocu-
> lated with fiscalitis. Douglas Straight, who edits the old
> rag the *PMG* [*Pall Mall Gazette*] does not know what he
> is . . . but his young men are of that persuasion, and the
> *Globe* is Orange and leans to Chamberlain because he
> is more anti-Irish than you are. So that all the Unionist
> papers are for the time engaged in denigrating you in the
> interest of Radical-Fiscal-Reform-Unionism. And mark
> my words, this rotten crusade will be developing with
> increasing malignancy *till* the Election.'[11]

Balfour was reduced to that saddest of all political under-
takings, an appeal for party unity. He made it in Newcastle at
the National Union's Conference, forerunner of today's Party
Conference. A week later, Chamberlain, in Bristol, demanded
an election to be fought on a full protectionist platform. On
4 December, Balfour resigned.

The idea was prevalent that Balfour was the subtlest of
politicians, an assumption that behind such vagueness some
cunning design must lurk. Perhaps, given past differences
between Campbell-Bannerman and his Liberal Imperialist
colleagues, accelerated Cabinet-making before an election
would create an exploitable wound. But inadvertently, he
did express another, even more subtle notion. Balfour did
not wait for defeat in the Commons, still less call an election
to face it in the country. He had suffered defeat in his
own party and by making way for an election called by
Campbell-Bannerman in the worst possible circumstances
for the Tories, he effectively dissolved *them*.

The futility of Balfour's relations with his own party was
caught by Campbell-Bannerman in his Albert Hall speech.

The government had 'run away . . . in the murky midnight of December', and this was typical of a leader preoccupied with tactics. 'Tactics! Tactics! Ladies and gentlemen, the country is tired of their tactics . . . they have lived for some years on nothing but tactics and now they have died of tactics.'[12]

The outcome in a contest counted over ten days was, as always in such contests, one registered in slow motion, but it was a smash in slow motion. The first result, on 12 January, was a Liberal gain in Ipswich. The next day thirty-five declarations came in a rush, and from these Liberals and Labour had gained twenty seats. Balfour himself went down in East Manchester by 2,000 votes while the floor-crossing free-trader Churchill was elected at the other end of the city as a Liberal. Lyttleton, Bonar Law, Lord Hugh Cecil and Balfour's brother Gerald were all defeated. There would finally be 377 Liberals in the Commons, 132 Conservatives, 83 Irish nationalists, 53 Labour members and 25 Liberal Unionists. No fewer than 229 seats were won by the Liberals and their allies and Conservative membership fell from 369 to 157 (25 of them Liberal Unionists), actually, even with this increment, eight seats fewer than the Tories would hold in the disastrous General Election of 1997. On top of which the Tories divided between 102 supporters of protection, 16 free traders, 36 who accepted Balfour's own halfway house on tariffs, and 3 undecided.

The Conservative Party (in those days more commonly called Unionist to assert its position over Ireland), having quarrelled irresponsibly and split, but having also held office without a break for ten years, had been as outstandingly hubristic as it was now savagely humiliated. But its conduct over the next few years of opposition would be marked less by humility than by a sort of triumphalism in exile. Balfour's own private comment in a note to Lady Salisbury had a sublimity in its unwillingness to accept personal or party blame. It was all the doing of revolutionaries, it seems. 'If I read the signs aright, what has happened has nothing to do with any of the things we have been squabbling over in the last few years. C-B [Campbell-Bannerman] is a mere cork dancing on a torrent which he cannot control, and what is going on here is a faint echo of the same movement which has produced massacres in St Petersburg, riots in Vienna and Socialist processions in Berlin.'[13]

This was a cast of mind – arrogant, unperceiving and taking easy refuge in the paranoid style – which would characterise Conservative conduct in opposition, and in particular its behaviour over and inside the House of Lords. But Balfour, for all his sophistication and despite the enmity roused against him in the far-right reaches of his party, *was* arrogant and unperceiving. As for paranoia, it was to have its full festive day as the conflict between Lords and Commons mounted. Ultimately Balfour, the man of charm and intellect, on affable terms with the Liberal chancellor and future prime minister, Asquith, would take the irresponsible demagogic course, putting his aristocratic associate Lansdowne into a position of confrontation which Lansdowne himself, in some ways a sounder man, might well not have chosen. A Tory Party removed from office in a wave of popular contempt was fundamentally unabashed. It had, after all, been defeated only in a contest concerning the Lower House.

II

'Mr C-B Forgets the Danger of Increasing the Power of the H of C'

The issue which would in the next four years come to explosive conclusion had been many years in growing. The unreformed House of Lords had acceded in 1832 to the ending of an unreformed House of Commons. It had next accepted, in a shrewd or abashed way, the spate of early reform legislation which followed in the Reform Parliament. Its own actual Conservatism was itself an innovation, the result of waves of ennoblements – 140 in seventeen years imposed by Pitt upon the formerly Whig Upper House.[1]

After a vicious burst of vetoing in the late thirties – during which English and Irish Corporations Bills and an Irish Tithes Bill were all blocked – it became relatively quiescent, with the pressure easing mid-century (apart from in rejection in 1860 of Gladstone's Paper Duty Bill). It did so largely because of a coming together of Whig and Peelite peers. But their lordships drifted rightwards in the democratic decades after the second Reform Act as land legislation and Home Rule affected their own interests. The term 'domestic legislation' could, for an owner of acres in County Clare, be entirely literal.

The second Reform Act was of course passed in 1867 on a Conservative initiative – Disraeli's catching the Whig dogs bathing and stealing their clothes – but the subversive and unmanly Ballot Act, a Liberal measure, of five years later, had twice been thrown out, abolition of army commission purchase was defeated and the Irish Land Bill of 1884 seriously held up. Their lordships were to be denied satisfaction over Home Rule in 1886, Chamberlain having shot their fox in the Commons, but their rejection of the second Home Rule Bill in 1893 was by 419 votes to 41, the largest majority ever recorded in the Upper House, something accomplished, as we have seen, after long but perfunctory debate and a fit of derisive giggling.

Liberal discontent with this state of affairs was crystalising. So immoderately moderate a man as Lord Rosebery would, in his Bradford speech of 1894, hint at a move to end 'an intolerable situation', and he spoke of the next election being fought on the conduct of the Lords, something involving 'a great national danger'.[2] The assumption of the Lords that they not only might, but should reject bills proposed by elected governments, bills which had figured in election programmes, would give one eminent personage no problems at all.

Queen Victoria's imperfect understanding of the role of a constitutional monarch had let her nominate Rosebery to the prime ministership without consulting the retiring but detested Gladstone. She now revolted in horror at such radicalism coming from her nominee. She wrote to, of all people, Salisbury, leader of the Tory opposition, complaining that her prime minister's remarks were 'mischievous in the highest degree' and, she must add, 'disloyal'. 'Is the Unionist Party ready for a dissolution now?' she asked, incredibly. As it happened, the minister currently shivering in the Balmoral cold of a castle which the impervious Queen declined to heat was Campbell-Bannerman.

The then secretary for war conveyed in a letter to his wife the mood and style of Victoria's late court. 'Carrington says Archie [Rosebery]'s speech fell like a bombshell among them: all the Alec Yorkes and others were loudmouthed in denouncing it; treason, revolution etc. etc. The ignorant set, not to know it was sure to come! Then he says all this has such an effect on the Q to whom it was conveyed – "everyone thinks so & so", "all the gentlemen at lunch were saying so & so" – "the gentlemen"! what is their opinion worth?'

Campbell-Bannerman, through the medium of Arthur Bigge, the Queen's private secretary, sent her a memorandum stressing the effects of a democratic franchise upon Commons–Lords conflicts, the unrepresentative nature of recent very large Lords majorities against Liberal legislation and the prospect of recurring conflict hardening into deadlock. Campbell-Bannerman noted the main points of Victoria's reply.

> Mr C-B forgets the danger of increasing the power of the H of C and having no force to resist the subversive measures of the so-called Liberals but better called destructives. Could never agree to taking from the Lo. their power to alter or reject measures – this might be obtained from a president but not from her. Thinks it cruel that after her long reign at her age she shd be obliged to refuse her assent to proposals of her ministers where it would be her greatest pleasure to support them.

As Bigge remarked to Campbell-Bannerman, 'You must remember what the Queen is, how apart she is and, above all, who her grandfather was.'[3]

Victorian and Edwardian politics were an incestuous affair, with the participants moving largely in the same social throng. The prejudices of a very Tory court were not so different from those of Conservative politicians, academics and journalists. More people than Queen Victoria in this Lords-sanctifying, paranoid-about-Ireland era seem to have been the grandchildren of George III. George Wyndham, whose apathetic indifference over the MacDonnell initiative in Ireland would make him so suspect to other Tories, nevertheless spoke for the social order tapering from Lords to court when he looked back. But, in a menacing style, he also glanced ahead to twentieth-century preoccupations. He had looked at 'the fat, fair expanse of English fields with their smouldering girdle of chimneys around the fair horizon. And I have sworn that they shall not be sucked like eggs by the weasels of pure finance.' Wyndham's father had asked him 'never to marry an American, a Jewess or an heiress, but an English lady'.[4]

Lord Willoughby de Broke, the Warwickshire squire who would be centrally engaged in the Lords' resistance, quoted a more attractive conversation between his father and mother about the menace of radicalism as embodied by John Bright. Would the revolution come then, she asked? 'Not yet,' replied the 18th Baron with equable prescience, 'but it will come probably some day; they won't cut off our heads; the whole thing will be done by act of Parliament.'[5] Willoughby quoted with approval Disraeli's words at the Crystal Palace in 1872. 'The tone and tendency of liberalism could no longer be concealed. It was to destroy the institutions of the country under the name of reform and to make war on the manners and customs of the people under the pretext of progress.'[6]

The Duke of Northumberland would put it more candidly. 'There has never been a period . . . when masses of men . . . have been persuaded that it is good that they should be compelled to work for a daily wage while others should not. Our ancestors were wise enough to see this and kept the political power of the state in the hands of those who had property. We have destroyed their systems and placed political power in the hands of the multitude. We must take the consequences.'[7] And the Earl of Meath, in a Malthusian vein, had warned in 1899 that the increase in population would cause the expanding group of the poor 'driven to desperation and beguiled by the honeyed words of socialists and anarchists, to endeavour to improve their miserable lot by the general destruction of society.'

Moreover, Lord Meath had for a long time been as clear as Queen Victoria on the threat from a subversive Commons: 'A single omnipotent popular assembly . . . might by a bare majority take an irretrievable step . . . entailing widespread misery, even shaking, if not destroying, the foundations of the social fabric.'[8]

The mood of such peers which, from a vantage point a hundred years on, looks notably self-pitying and emotionally fraught, also fitted with the general malaise of the Tory Party as a whole. The Tories at this time, divided by Tariff Reform, were superficially in agreement about the anxious splendour of an imperial role from which that protectionist drive had come and comfortably concurred that Irish Home Rule was a Gladstonian evil which only actively disloyal, unBritish elements would seek to revive.

But distrust of their leaders over Ireland ran deep, especially for those with something to lose. In 1903, with Balfour in Downing Street, Lord Muskerry wrote:

'For some time I have been wondering what has become of the Conservative Party. Past governments who claim to be Conservative have been anything but Conservative as regards their Irish policy.' The trouble lay in those Irish land reforms involving extensive land purchase which had been pursued by Balfour with Salisbury's support since the eighties and renewed by Wyndham in his early, effective phase as chief secretary. This, thought Muskerry, had involved 'great cowardice on the part of successive governments, who have prostituted their sense of justice to the outcry of agitators and for the purpose of gaining a few votes or disarming opposition in the House of Commons.'[9]

Another Irish landowner, Viscount Templetown, had asked if socialism was to be 'the watchword of the Unionist Party'.[10] Lord Muskerry owned 15,000 acres in Wexford, Limerick, Tipperary, Carlow, Waterford, Kilkenny and Cork. Lord Templetown had 29,000 in Antrim and Monaghan. But the particularist resentments of superabundantly interested parties mingled easily with the general discounts of the Conservative and Unionist Party. The *Globe*, a London-based newspaper, was, as we have seen in the words of that letter to Balfour, 'Orange, and leans to Chamberlain because he is more anti-Irish than you are'.[11]

The politics of the budget, Lords resistance and the Parliament Bill were wrapped like honeysuckle and bindweed around the internal quarrels of the Tory Party and with the anti-Balfourism which would soon surface. One major charm of the unreformed House of Lords was its function as a roadblock, guaranteeing an unreformed Ireland. Tariff Reform, the whole idea of an Empire politically and economically served by a protectionist drawbridge let down for 'the dominions' and kept up against the Americans and Europeans, obviously appealed to the owners of land who had seen agricultural product prices fall hideously since the mid-seventies.

It meshed well with aggressive nationalism, that pre-First World War mixed mood of bristling antagonism, anxiety and militarism. Lord Selborne, successor to Milner as pro-consul in South Africa, fervent protectionist and close friend of Lady Bathurst, proprietor of the *Morning Post*, was an embodiment of this strand of Conservatism. 'The social system,' said Selborne, 'is out of joint.' It was, he thought, 'the duty of the peers to save the constitution from immediate overthrow.'[12] And it would be Lady Bathurst who, in 1910, at the height of the Lords crisis, would write privately to her editor, H.A. Gwynne, 'I want to say boldly, we have done with such leaders. They have been the bane and ruin of the Unionist Party for ten years . . . no amount of brilliant speeches will atone for cowardice, indecision and utter lack of principle.'[13] This was the ferocious right in opposition which a Liberal Government was certain to provoke and with which Balfour, 'utterly discredited' as Lady Bathurst would also call him in 1910, had to co-exist.

There was an element of hysteria about their unwillingness

to contemplate gradualism as being gradual, never mind inevitable. It was a state of mind cast in the embers of triumphalism. The high and easy dominance of mid-Victorian Britain was over. Germany loomed, the working class lowered, the economy failed to sparkle. Social revolution, the destruction of fabrics held dear and the overthrow of society, not to mention Society, were all readily envisaged. Lord Malmesbury talked about socialism, 'narcotic-like,' having 'drugged the spirit of patriotism into forced slumber' with the effect of 'destroying our national defences and warping the strength of the nation'.[14] The excited talk of 'communism' which, far across the century, would attach in American Republican rhetoric to any incremental social adjustment, was paralleled by fretful Edwardian Tories with similar talk about the French Revolution and Jacobinism.

Not everything which came from these Conservative peers was simple reaction, an intense desire to hang on to what they had and take pot shots with a 12-bore at outsiders eyeing the pheasants or the cucumber frames. Eugenics, the notion of engineering the species by selective breeding and the genetic phasing out of the 'unfit', was an unhealthily fashionable notion of the day and had its friends among Fabians and other ruthless reformers. Winston Churchill, so often a genial and enjoyable troublemaker at this time, had been fascinated by the idea and would be creditably restrained by Home Office civil servants from promoting it.

But the rurally based, foxhunting, cattle-raising aristocracy found the stud notion of society particularly to their taste. The Duke of Bedford had a busy adviser, Arnold White, who made the very modern observation that 'race improvement today is not a question of philosophy but existence . . . if the first law of life is self-preservation, England must choose between state suicide and race improvement.'[15] And Willoughby de Broke, despite harbouring a sense of humour uncommon among this rather whimpering set – his Warwickshire estate being 'too close to Birmingham to be agreeable to a peer' – was also capable of talking in this unamiable vein. A friend of Saleeby, founder of the Eugenics Society, he linked biological selection with other right-wing notions of the day to assemble this package: 'Breeding from the best stocks and bringing to maturity the greatest possible number of mentally and physically sound men and women, reared among healthy surroundings, in the ideals of religion and patriotism, equipped with a trade education, protected by a tariff from unfair foreign competition, trained to bear arms.' Interestingly, though, belief in eugenics made Willoughby a supporter of women's suffrage. This would, he said, provide the nation with 'the effective advice of the mothers of the future race'.[16]

The time would come when it would be possible to write patronisingly about the absurdity of the diehard peers. It would be explained that they were the victims of economic forces, chiefly the collapse thirty years earlier in agricultural prices, and marginalised by inevitable democratic extension of the franchise. Lord Curzon would make a cruel little speech about Willoughby in the reformed House of Lords in 1920. 'He still remains, a magnificent relic of the old guard, but the backwoods in which my noble friend ranged at the head of a formidable band some years ago are now relatively deserted, and his picturesque figure is seen stalking, consoled only by Lord Farnham, amid the scenes that were once those of his adventures and triumphs.'[17]

But perfect hindsight is a poor guide to a past era, and Curzon, for all his intelligence and involvement with practical government, had at one time shared the sentiments of the diehards. The Conservative opposition of 1906 onward was dominated by an alliance of such peers and their resentments significantly combined with the new, efficient, imperial outlook of Chamberlain and Milner. There was nothing quaint about Milner, the 'British race patriot', administering South Africa in circumstances of emergency congenial to his undisguised contempt for democracy anywhere. And the Birmingham against which Willoughby had railed was now making war on free trade in the interests of its own anxious manufacturers and coupling it with strident talk of Empire. Triumphalism and anxiety resentfully coalesced. As a cocktail this was serious politics.

And for over a decade, that coalition was utterly triumphant within the party. A letter to Lansdowne after the post-election Tory Party meeting on 15 February 1906 puts it very plainly. 'I am afraid it has been a capitulation. Joe was able to say that he had surrendered nothing, that A.J.B. agreed with him, and that the result was official policy; and amid the resounding cheers of Tariff Reformers, A.J.B. said nothing.'[18] As for the role of the lords militant, there is an ironic contrast between Curzon's complacent contempt and the words of Balfour immediately after electoral defeat, when he spoke openly about using the Lords as a means of continuing the Tory fight.

For a clever man, Balfour could say very foolish things. Consulting with the more circumspect Lansdowne, he anticipated a Lords versus Commons conflict but made assumptions about the weakness and divisions of the Liberals which he had no grounds for making.

I conjecture that the government's method of carrying on their legislative work will be this: they will bring in bills in a much more extreme form than the moderate members of their Cabinet probably approve: the moderate members will trust to the House of Lords cutting out or modifying the most outrageous provisions: the left wing of the Cabinet, on the other hand, while looking forward to the same result, will be consoled for the anticipated mutilation of their measures by the reflection that they will be gradually accumulating a case against the Upper House and that they will be able to appeal at the next election for a mandate to modify its constitution.

This scheme is an ingenious one, and it will be our business to defeat it as far as we can. I do not think the House of Lords will be able to escape the duty of making serious modifications in important government measures, but if this is done with caution and tact, I do not believe that they will do themselves any harm.

On the contrary, as the rejection of the Home Rule Bill undoubtedly strengthened their position, I think it quite possible that your House may come out of the ordeal strengthened rather than weakened by the inevitable difficulties of the next few years.[19]

This is bleakly typical of Balfour: splendidly perceptive up to a point, but underinformed about his opponents and looking wilfully on a bright side that didn't exist. He overestimates the distinctions between moderates and radicals in the government (though the antics of Grey and Haldane in their intrigue against Campbell-Bannerman had given him reasonable excuse for this). He fairly enough appreciates that many Liberals would be alerted to the opportunity of wreaking the sort of revenge on their lordships' House which would be satisfyingly permanent. What he failed to see was that this glint in the eye was not confined to extremists and dangerous subversives, about whom Edward VII, like Victoria before him and George V afterwards, would make resentful noises in letters to his prime minister – 'Mr Lloyd George has made another indecent attack on the House of Lords . . . the King says nothing will induce him to go to Cardiff unless Mr Lloyd George learns how to behave with propriety as a Cabinet minister holding an important office.'[20] Balfour and both kings were to find the Liberals distressingly united.

The issues which had divided them – the Boer War and the personality of Lord Rosebery – had been resolved. Chamberlain's war had been 'won' in circumstances of incompetence topped off with brutality, but Campbell-Bannerman would make the peace. As for Rosebery, that fastidious peer existed in sulky retreat and private grandeur somewhere between the parties and as far from influence as calamitous misjudgement could take him. The Liberals, meanwhile, were as comfortably together on the House of Lords as they were on free trade and indeed Home Rule.

But Balfour was far more importantly wrongheaded in drawing comfort from the precedent of the Lords' rejection of Home Rule in 1893. Not only had volumes of water passed under bridges in the intervening thirteen years, but the Lords had got away with that contemptuous veto over an unhappy, divided Cabinet at the end of Gladstone's last ministry, one sustained by a modest majority and ill placed to retaliate. Now, in 1906, with his landslide victory, Campbell-Bannerman had a majority clear of 200 and his successor, the 'moderate' Asquith, who would readily share a cab with Balfour returning from a dinner party to the Commons, would in due course prove himself quietly ready, through two elections and endless royal snivelling, to impose 500 new creations on an upper House convinced that nothing had happened since 1893.

Balfour was doing what he would do for the next four years: rationalising a situation in which his own party was split, while an increasingly unconstitutional and irrational right wing called the shots. And Balfour, as Campbell-Bannerman was to remark dismissively, was not the man for clarity or firm stands. 'The Rt Hon. gentleman is like the Bourbons. He has learned nothing. He comes back to the House of Commons with the same airy graces – the same subtle dialectics – and the same light and frivolous way of dealing with great questions. He little knows the temper of the new House of Commons if he thinks those methods will prevail here.' The questions Balfour had raised, he added, were 'utterly futile, nonsensical and misleading. They are invented by the Rt Hon. gentleman for the purpose of occupying time in this debate. I say, enough of this foolery . . . move your amendments and let us get to business.'[21]

This was no new attitude for the prime minister. At the height of Balfour's reputation Campbell-Bannerman had not believed in him. With policy directed by Chamberlain and continuing even after his stroke, to be commanded by the Chamberlain faction, and with the Lords the only available weapon – and one whose capacity for exploding when used he gaily disregarded – Balfour would come to take on a great question in a light and frivolous way. He would end with most of his party not believing in him.

12

'The Real Discussion . . . Must Be Elsewhere'

The House of Lords began the new Parliament in a mood of quarrel-picking and party-political defiance. No figure associated with the previous government had been more controversial than Alfred Milner, the central command administrator of South Africa. (It had been Milner's Chinese labourers and their employers' right to flog them which had raised – along with a quota of opposition opportunism – the Nonconformist conscience (and every other kind of conscience) against the Conservative government and had, heroically, moved Balfour to unease.)

Milner, now ennobled, made a maiden speech in the Lords and devoted most of it to a snarling assault on the 'pro-Boer' Liberal conciliation policy now being successfully put through. He believed it to be a policy that the public 'should have spat out of their mouths'.[1] Reaction to this included a backbench Liberal motion censuring Milner over the flogging of labourers which, to save Milner's name, was mildly amended by the government front bench. The amendment was introduced, in terms more coolly dismissive than those of the original motion, by the under-secretary to the Colonial Office, Winston Churchill. 'Lord Milner has gone from South

Africa probably for ever. The public knows him no more. Having exercised great authority . . . he now exercises no authority . . . Having disposed of events which have shaped the course of history, he is now unable to deflect in the smallest degree the policy of the day . . . Lord Milner has ceased to be a factor in public life.'[2]

There was much outrage at such cheek. Lord Halifax, applauded by Northcliffe's *Times* which, in proprietory mode, called it an 'expression of the abiding wishes of the country', introduced a resolution of grateful thanks to Milner, which was carried in the Lords by 170 votes to 35. Any deficiency of ill will between the Houses of Parliament was being earnestly made up.

Meanwhile, for a party which had been beaten further into the ground than the Conservatives of 1997, the opposition proved quite as truculent as the Upper House. When an Education Bill was brought forward to offset the sectarian guarantee of subsidised Anglican privilege which Balfour himself had put through in 1902, Conservatives broke into a startling display of piety. A minority of godly peers were disposed in that direction anyway. 'Politics,' said Lord Halifax, Milner's admirer, 'are a delusion, and I am quite convinced that to have a vocation to be a monk is the happiest lot in life.'[3] But the bill, like most education bills of that sectarian era, was about religion anyway. And in any case, so long as the House of Lords continued unreformed, delusive politics had its uses. The bill was lacerated beyond saving.

And delusive politics had its uses not just in the Lords. The president of the Board of Education in charge of that bill was Augustine Birrell, a specialist in short straws for whom the tribulations of Ireland would soon be reserved. 'I have,' he said, 'freely consorted all my life with Catholics, Roman and Anglican, with ardent evangelical churchmen, with Nonconformists of every shade, with modernists, agnostics and atheists, but never have I drawn my breath in so irreligious and ignorant an atmosphere as that of the House of Commons when debating religion.'[4] Balfour, the author of that book on doubt, was especially active. During the late phase, when an attempt was made to rescue the bill after Lords mutilation, he was particularly malevolent. Birrell again:

> Hate 'my' bill he undoubtedly did. It seemed to stink in his philosophical nostrils . . . He blocked all the roads that might have led to settlement. We had a private conference on the bill in Lord Crewe's house in Curzon Street, which the Archbishop of Canterbury attended . . . I was bent on securing the attendance of the Duke of Devonshire [the Hartington of old days], with whom I had several interesting interviews and who I knew was anxious that, if possible, the bill in some shape should pass. The Duke was willing to come. But Mr Balfour was determined to keep him out, and was able to get his own way and to put in his place Lord Cawdor (who had been his fag at Eton).

The dispute itself belonged even more to its time than the Lords veto. As Birrell, writing in 1933, remarked, 'Hardly any of the speeches made for or against the bill could possibly be made today.'[5]

It was possible for Balfour to say smoothly after three grinding months in committee, 'I think most of us have begun to feel that the real discussion . . . must be elsewhere.'[6] This was a pregnant and astonishing remark. The Conservatives had gone down in a landslide in the country six months earlier, the bill had passed the Commons by a majority of 200, but 'the real discussion . . . must be elsewhere'. By November, in the form of wrecking amendments, it had suffered 'elsewhere' the martyrdom of St Sebastian.

The charge which Balfour made in his correspondence with Lansdowne – that the radical elements of the Liberal Party yearned to pick a peers-versus-people quarrel – could be made quite as well against him. He had done everything he could to sabotage a compromise. But Balfour was a weak man in a weak position. After the 15 February meeting which submitted to Tariff Reform, St Loe Strachey, editor of the right-wing *Spectator*, congratulated Leo Maxse, editor of the very right-wing *National Review* (who would later become Balfour's open and abusive enemy): 'The Balfour climb-down is a great triumph for the Nat.'[7]

His mind made up for him on protection by Chamberlain, Balfour needed a victory – any victory, however temporary and provocative – in the overall war. Religious teaching in schools seemed as good a pretext as any for striking the necessary tremendous attitude. Balfour's hard line ran great risks. When he spoke in the Commons debate on 12 December he was particularly arrogant and defiant. 'His own party,' wrote Sir Almeric Fitzroy, 'were evidently taken by surprise, and though they responded ... by some perfunctory cheers, I am told that never, even in the failing days of his ministry, did he encounter so much latent antagonism in the House of Commons.'[8] He was playing the Lords card early, and playing in both a sectarian and politically partisan way. He was also sailing close to the point at which abuse of the veto would provoke action to end that veto. Lloyd George was being given every occasion to make speeches which would upset people in Buckingham Palace. He did so in Oxford by asking whether the country 'was to be governed by the King and peers or by the King and his people.'[9]

But if Balfour felt able to call up the peerage over the Education Bill, no such resistance was offered when it came to trades union rights. One of the excellent selection of *Punch* cartoons in Lord Newton's life of Lansdowne shows that marquess, in dress armour and Tudor costume, having already killed a marauder called 'Education Bill', confronting another called 'Trades Disputes Bill'. Lansdowne's sword is pointed diplomatically downwards. '*I* bar your way? My dear fellow! Why, you've made a mistake.'[10] The mace carried by 'Trade Disputes Bill' is marked 'Mandate'. But it is doubtful that this was the deciding factor. The bill was, after all, a far more radical affair than the Liberal law officers or Asquith had intended. All had advised that the restrictions placed on unions by the verdict in the Taff Vale case of 1900 (something which had been directly responsible for the creation of the Labour Party by way of the Labour Representation Committee) could be handled by making exemptions to the law of agency as it applied to unions.

The Labour Party wanted simple immunity and had friends like John Burns arguing for it in Cabinet, but the lawyers seemed to have won. Labour accordingly had a separate bill, apparently without hope, while ministerial legislation on modest lines went ahead. Yet while this government bill was actually being introduced on the floor of the Commons, Campbell-Bannerman simply changed his mind. According to Newton, a temperate Tory and not gratuitously unfair, 'Thereupon the prime minister, with remarkable cynicism, threw over his attorney-general and adapted the bill of the Labour Party.'[11] 'Cynicism' was almost always the wrong word to apply to Campbell-Bannerman who, on impulse, was doing the radical pro-employee thing which came naturally. And since he was prime minister, he was, like Pope Leo X, enjoying the fact.

The powers now given to organised labour to strike with immunity in tort were ones which responsible and unextreme Conservative opposition, noble or otherwise, could have resisted in good conscience and with a reasoned case. They didn't. Lansdowne, as leader of the Lords, was left, as so often, holding a tricky baby, but he used language which, if followed and applied to the general conduct of the Lords under a reforming administration, would surely have preserved its prerogatives.

> We are passing through a period when it is necessary for this House to move with very great caution. Conflicts and controversies may be inevitable but let us at any

rate so far as we are able to, be sure that when we join issue, we do so upon ground which is as favourable as possible to us ourselves. In this case I believe the ground would be unfavourable to this House and I believe the juncture is one which, even if we were to win for the moment, our victory would be fruitless in the end.

He would therefore not vote against the bill. It conferred excessive privileges, dangerous privileges on a single class, and was likely to embitter the industrial life of the country. 'But I hold also that it is useless for us, situated as we are, to oppose this measure.'[12]

Newton, noting the phrase 'on favourable ground' and being scrupulous, thought his subject as cynical as Campbell-Bannerman. It might be fairer to say that he was being candid about the interests of his House and that such rational calculation was something both Lords and Tories could have done with. He was anyway stating a temperamental truth – cynicism didn't come into it. If the two men were left to themselves, C-B was as instinctively radical as Lansdowne was inherently cautious.

Much more significant is the fact that the Lords, the institutional House, not given a lead to attack by the Conservative and Unionist Party, did not attack. The famous jibe of Lloyd George, 'Mr Balfour's poodle', was never more apt than during their lordships' rest period of statesmanship. The dog which did not bark in the night, Sherlock Holmes had indicated, had recognised its master. The quiet poodle was very eloquent.

Campbell-Bannerman would set out his own view plainly in the Commons debate of June 1907 after the education debacle, and it was a view of Balfour personally: 'I cannot conceive of Sir Robert Peel or Mr Disraeli treating the House of Commons as the Rt Hon. Gentleman has treated it. Nor do I think there is any instance in which when the leaders of the opposition, they committed what I can only call the treachery of openly calling in the other House to override this House.' Balfour's conduct had made one thing clear. 'It has left no room for doubt, if it had ever existed before, that the second chamber is being utilised as a mere annexe of the Unionist Party . . . One begins to doubt – in fact I certainly doubt – whether he or his party have ever finally accepted representative institutions.'

As for the remedies which the Tory press was now urging: 'The referendum or the plebiscite, or some other way of getting behind the backs of the electors themselves, such as was advised by both the first and third Napoleon . . . there is no course open but to recognise ungrudgingly the authority which resides in this House'.

The debate of June 1907, though it moved to no conclusion, told the Lords and the Tory leadership, which used the Upper House as an annexe, what government ministers thought and, by extension, what they might do. Winston Churchill described the General Election of 1906 as 'the most vehement expression of public opinion which this generation had any knowledge of; and that expression of public force was countered by . . . by the most arbitrary and uncompromising assertion of aristocratic privilege'. This was something done by a House at once 'one-sided, hereditary, unpurged, irresponsible, absentee'.[13]

Lloyd George, affronted most by the treatment of his fellow Nonconformists over the Education Bill, then made his poodle remark about the Lords, and it is worth quoting at greater length. The House of Lords was 'no mastiff', but 'the Rt Hon. gentleman's poodle; it fetches and carries for him, barks at and bites anybody he sets it on to.'[14] However the court might be offended, it is hard to see that as anything but a canine variant of Campbell-Bannerman's 'annexe' and an equally fair description.

A notable member of the Upper House, giving an insider's account of its doings, would frankly admit as much. The House of Lords was there, proclaimed to be a vital part of the constitution – in excitable moments to *be* the constitution. But its chief component, the majority of Conservative peers – what had come to be seen as a *natural* majority of Conservative peers – was regularly given directions. Willoughby de Broke, nothing if not a candid man, provides a description of what was to happen in 1908, after Campbell-Bannerman's death, during the preparatory lead-up to a further Lords assault on the government programme and the rejection of yet another piece of Liberal legislation, the brewer-offending Licensing Bill.

That defeat, he says, 'must have been very galling to the Liberal government, particularly in view of the manner in which it was carried out.' The actual decision to stop the bill had been made in the town home of Lord Lansdowne. 'We common or garden peers knew nothing of this conclave; but we do know that we were invited to a meeting of Unionists held in the drawing room of this historic house where, after a somewhat perfunctory debate, we agreed to reject the measure when it came before us at Westminster and then adjourned for a good luncheon at the Carlton Club.' Just think of that meeting at Lansdowne House from the point of view of an earnest young Liberal who took himself seriously. His party, at one time despised and rejected of men and driven into the wilderness for twenty years, was now invested with all the patronage and power that was said by Bagehot to accrue to a brand-new, thumping majority in the House of Commons. One of his pet projects – long overdue – is translated into actual performance. And yet a great nobleman living at the heart of Mayfair causes a few letters to be written to his brother noblemen in the country, summoning them to take private counsel with him under his own roof where, after a desultory conversation lasting less than an hour, it is agreed to turn down a proposal that has occupied the Liberal Party for something like a quarter of a century. The thing could not have taken place anywhere except in England.

'The meeting itself was great fun. Some of us who had

never spoken in the House of Lords [Willoughby himself had, before translation, been a Unionist MP for five years], and who had never been consulted about anything outside our own counties, met each other fresh from the hunting field and were able to compare notes about the past season and to discuss the possible winners of the spring handicaps.'

One peer, Lord Lytton, had defended the bill. 'But the backwoodsmen who had mostly breakfasted at cockcrow in order to catch the early train to London were in no mood to listen to any tampering with the liquor traffic.' Balfour wanted this veto cast in this House of Parliament and was content to have it agreed to in this way. But even Willoughby de Broke, who would soon make his name as the energetic whip organising resistance to the Parliament Bill, the diehard dying hardest, speaks of 'an unnecessary humiliation of the government . . . also a tactical blunder from the point of view of the hereditary peerage.'[15]

Willoughby's view of the likely provocative effect is worth contrasting with Balfour's judgement. As we have seen, the former prime minister had told Lansdowne in 1906 that if the Lords made 'serious modifications' to Commons legislation 'with caution and tact' they would be all right. 'On the contrary, as the rejection of the Home Rule Bill doubtless strengthened their position, I think it quite possible that your House may come out of the ordeal strengthened rather than weakened by the inevitable difficulties of the next few years.' Willoughby, the naïve Warwickshire squire, says: 'The country Tories began to think that the day of reckoning would be indefinitely postponed and hugged themselves with joy at the thought that they had got a House of Lords'. But the Liberals had been put in a position which compelled them to make a decision. 'Anything that they could do to relieve the situation would seem to admit defeat . . . they might resign, they might submit . . .' Drawing a metaphor from chess, he said: 'They might castle behind a temporary acquiescence; and let everybody know if the Liberal Party caught the Lords once upon the hip, they would feed fat the ancient grudge they bore them.'

But, he added, shifting briskly to the more apt bare-knuckle ring, 'to admit the power of the House of Lords to compel the government either to resign or dissolve Parliament was the one thing the Liberal party could not do.' It was 'the equivalent of lying down on the sawdust until such time as they were counted out by the timekeeper.' Long debate and election on Lords reform wouldn't help the government; people just weren't interested enough. 'To deliver a lecture on the constitution is an almost certain way of boring a British audience.' Accordingly, 'Liberal thinking was revealed in a popular budget which . . . would be certain to bring into the firing line those vested interests of which the hereditary peerage was the principal trustee, and so make it easier to mobilise all the government forces for a direct engagement with the House of Lords.'[16]

Lord Willoughby de Broke was of course writing with hindsight, but the hard-edged clarity of his account stands in embarrassing contrast with Balfour's damning letter to Lansdowne. For all his gifts and reputation, Balfour was not just frivolous, he was lazy, and in opposition he resorted to the improvisatory mode of the lazy. He would indeed be later pressed and hounded by the Tory right, Willoughby strenuous among them. But the hounding would come after 500 men 'drawn at random from the ranks of the unemployed' had been led first up the hill, then down it.

Since that 'meeting at a great nobleman's house' could command a veto on legislation, and since, where Lansdowne's better judgement prevailed, they could as readily be stood down from resistance to the Trades Disputes Act, it was open to Balfour to think through consequences and use that power of command to avoid suicidal provocation. 'With caution and tact,' he had said, throwing the words after his advocacy of war. 'Caution and tact' didn't fit with an opposition leader's need to cut a fighting figure, and anyway they needed concentrated attention. Balfour had been praised too often for his own good for effortless brilliance. After 1906 he managed in a sustained way to be effortlessly (and steadily) wrong. Laziness and an itch to score points prevailed with the leader of the opposition; and he, in Housman's phrase, 'to the hill of his undoing, pursued his way'.

13

Lord Roehampton Strains a Vocal Cord

It had been supposed by Tories that when the dying Campbell-Bannerman went they would be dealing with their own notion of a civilised Liberal. He could not perhaps be another Rosebery, one of their own permanently appalled by the revolutionary excesses of the party he had once led. Still, Asquith – bridge-player, diner-out, dragged not unwillingly into society by his vivid and well-connected wife – might be altogether more comfortable. He had, after all, been a Liberal Imperialist and a member of the failed conspiracy to send Sir Henry upstairs.

But Asquith would prove a disappointment to Conservative wellwishers. There was, for all the bland grace and conventionality, a streak of stubbornness there which, once he had been persuaded to a radical purpose – the budget, the Parliament Bill, Home Rule – would cause him, patiently and with annoying politeness, to stick to it. And Asquith understood very well the central fallacy of Rosebery, that a reforming party could ever be led by a moderate pushing moderation out of sight. He recognised that Campbell-Bannerman, whom he acknowledged having underrated, had, despite frustrations from their lordships, been hugely successful with his own party by cutting gladly with its radical grain.

197

The *National Review* saw it the other way round. In an article of 1910 signed 'Observer', it looked back at his past soundness: 'When the troops in the Featherstone riots fired on a disorderly mob, he resolutely upheld the cause of law and order.' But after two years of his premiership, he stood 'invited to destroy the whole machinery of government as a means of stirring up odium against the House of Lords, and to scuttle the ship of which he is captain.' Ten years before, he 'would have met such proposals with ridicule and indignation. But will he meet them in the same temper today after his long list of abject surrender to the demagogues? *Facilis descensus Averni*, and he seems powerless to act like a man.'[1]

The point they missed, and which some historical accounts also miss, is one peculiarly bitter to Tariff Reform Tories. One thing was certain and immutable about Asquith: he was a down-the-line, committed free-trader. He held Tariff Reform in perfect contempt as a species of revolt against gravity. And as chancellor of the exchequer, he had made the distinction between earned and unearned income, which meant quite plainly that the rich would pay more. It was Gladstonian finance carried on and further. It was intended to blunt the revenue side of the Tariff Reform argument by bringing in more money from a new source and putting the Tories in the position of having thereafter to defend a shift from taxes on the rents and rewards of rich men for a flat tax on food.

The land survey which featured in the 1909 budget was part of the same thing. The idea of that budget as a delinquent inspiration of Lloyd George on a frolic of his own misses the truth: the cleverness of Asquith and the conflict between free trade and protection which runs through Edwardian politics like a great waterway. Asquith was to become prime minister because he was the ablest man in a senior position. His ability lay in a celerity of mind that let him cut through work at great speed without apparent effort. Cultivated and literate in ways unimaginable in any modern, vibrant prime minister, he had Balfour's own quality of the Oxonian star, but he was better-natured and, despite a weakness for wine and whisky, a more reliable doer of the job. The debility of easygoing first-rateness was there, however, very well put by a friend of mine who compared him with the cricketer David Gower – perfect style, beautiful to watch, achieving quite a lot, but somehow leaving one slightly disappointed.

Asquith, as both appointment on merit and man needing to balance the rest of the ticket, overfulfilled the Cabinet's quota of radical credentials by appointing in his own place at the exchequer the man who had shocked the King as he would shock his successor, and whom Charles Whibley would characterise in *Blackwood's* as 'the cad in politics', David Lloyd George. It would, of course, in eight years' time, be an appointment he would regret, but they worked together happily enough and long enough to distress their lordships. And Lloyd George at Number 11 would be fruitfully engaged in finding the money to pay for a notably radical Asquithian measure, old-age pensions.

Cabinet approval of the budget was a lengthy affair lasting through fourteen meetings from mid-March, six weeks ahead of budget day, to 29 April. Lloyd George was emphatic that Asquith had been his chief ally in having such a contentious budget accepted. Increasingly, the purpose of the Liberal government was social, and one piece of legislation which had gone through had been the provision of old-age pensions. Despite being denounced by Whibley, in the same breath as he deplored the reprieve of a condemned man as a piece of contemptible sentimentality, old-age pensions had not been stopped in the Lords for the good reason that they had formed part of Asquith's 1908 budget and had been judged privileged by the Speaker. The convention, standing for 200 years and supposedly a binding one, was that the Lords did not intervene in budgets. Lord Rosebery, owner *inter alia* of Mentmore in the Chilterns, Dalmeney in Scotland, The Durdans, Barnbogle Castle, the yacht *Zaida*, a couple of villas near Naples, 138 Berkeley Square and several racehorses, had thought the idea of paying out 5 shillings a week, £13 a year, to those who had reached the age of seventy 'so prodigal of expenditure as likely to undermine the whole fabric of the Empire'.

The idea of such pensions had been mooted seriously for the first time in 1895 with the Royal Commission on the Aged Poor – not many euphemisms for the Victorians – which had rejected them. The majority report had dismissed any plan at all on the grounds of 'the financial and economic difficulties involved', while a minority report favoured pensions sustained by private insurance contributions. King Edward, then Prince of Wales, had been a conscientious member of the commission and, as his biographer puts it, 'addressed many shrewd questions to witnesses; was most affable to his working-class colleagues, Henry Broadhurst MP and Joseph Arch MP; and doodled Union Jacks at odd moments with the aid of red and blue pencils'.[3]

Only one member of the commission, Broadhurst, advocated non-contributory pensions as of right. The Prince, we are told, 'was eager to see suffering relieved, but he equated socialist remedies with revolution. He feared the risk of damage to the organic structure of a hierarchical society which he regarded as divinely ordained, and the unforeseen bitterness of the controversy aroused by the inquiry inhibited him from expressing or endorsing publicly any view.'[4]

Augustine Birrell, travelling as chief secretary in the west of Ireland, recorded less inhibition at the other end of the transaction from old people 'in their rain-sodden cabins, with the shadow of potato failures and other disasters always before them in the years before the Pensions Act passed. The wonderful, incredible pensions, bringing in 10 shillings every week, every Friday morning, as regularly as the rising sun, for the old couples in the chimney corner of every cabin in the west. It was a stupefying stroke of good fortune.'[5]

The Lords, doing what it could for the fabric of Empire, had tried to amend the proposals. But that Speaker's ruling, prevented them, something which Lansdowne, in a memorandum, characterised as the 'bitter experience of the manner in which His Majesty's Government treated amendments inserted by the House of Lords'.[6] But the pensions (and the dreadnoughts for which Conservatives had been clamouring), had to be paid for. And the budget of 1909 was the means to do it.

In practical terms, it involved increased taxes on alcohol, tobacco, motor cars and petrol, a marked increase in death duties and the introduction of a new impost on the highest incomes, supertax. There were also taxes on land: 20 per cent on the unearned increment of land value; a duty, set at a halfpenny in the 240-pence pound, on the value of undeveloped land; a reversion duty on the benefits to lessors at the end of a lease and a shilling in the pound duty on mining royalties. And there was provision for undertaking a sub-Domesday Book, a survey and valuation of all land in Britain.

While drink and tobacco taxes would be staples of the treasury for ever, it would seem, the land element was not a particularly good fiscal policy, costing too much for the modest revenue raised. However, the permanent secretary to the treasury, Sir George Murray, was unnecessarily defeatist in spectacular fashion when he referred in a letter to Asquith to 'the petrol tax, which I believe will be quite unworkable'. But in terms of smoking a social class out of graceful seclusion and into a sustained burst of self-parody, the budget worked rather well.

Hilaire Belloc, at this time Liberal MP for Salford South, caught the peers' response nicely:

> During the late election, Lord
> Roehampton strained a vocal chord [*sic*]
> From shouting very loud and high,

To lots and lots of people why
The Budget in his opin-
-Ion should not be allowed to win.[7]

Not quite everyone in the Conservative and landowning camp
was quite so fraught. Given that, according to Lloyd George,
Lords Derby, Sefton and Salisbury between them drew at that
time £354,000 a year from Liverpool rents alone, this was a
very reasonable approach, but it was nice to have a sense
of proportion flashing, however briefly, over a Conservative
horizon.

The peers, as great landowners were in focus; they had
been singled out and they were screaming. In fact the heaviest
charges fell upon urban land, of which many men who talked
foxhounds owned a good deal. But the distinction between
acres and slums or suburbs was not much made in the general
outrage.

Lord Rosebery who, like Roehampton, was only an earl,
called it 'not a budget but a revolution, a social and
political revolution of the first magnitude.'[8] Lord Sherborne
announced his intention of cutting estate expenditure.
'Supertaxation', he announced, required 'super-economy'.[9]
The Earl of Onslow, a modern, not to say prophetic
peer, said that he would have to dismiss all labourers
directly employed and instead hire more cheaply on contract.[10] And reaction was not confined to such suburbs
of aristocracy. Actual dukes entered the field, Rutland
condemning Liberal ministers as 'piratical tatterdemal-
ions',[11] Buccleuch famously cancelling his £1 subscription
to a local football club, while Beaufort genially wished
that he could put Lloyd George and the equally combative
radical Winston Churchill 'in the middle of twenty couple
of doghounds'.[12]

There was also some snarling at the beneficiaries. Lord
Halsbury, of whom much was to be heard later, said: 'It
means of course that everyone who has nothing and deserves

to have nothing because he would not work, has a right to take away something from his neighbour who has something because he has worked, while the other has been idle and lazy.'[13]

The Times, not able to manage such bangs, achieved in its next-day leader an authentic whimper. Conceding, 'Let it be granted that however hardly it may be used, that class remains very well off,' the editorialist added rather pitifully, 'Is it wise in the general interest or in the interest of the poor themselves to tax these well-to-do people into embarrassment and discouragement?' Lloyd George, it went on, making a primitive stab at the multiplier effect, 'talks of waging war on poverty, but that is never to be wisely waged by unjust actions upon those whose custom prevents a worse poverty than we know and whose brains and capital count for at least as much as their sinews'. And *The Times* was shocked at the one-sided concessions to the grasping poor. 'Unless men exempt from income tax either smoke or drink, they do not pay a single penny toward making up a deficit mainly due to a pension scheme of which they reap the whole benefit. The doctrine of the social ransom has never been carried quite so far.'[14]

This was, of course, another age. Those poor not making the slightest contribution to an old-age pension scheme of which they were to reap the whole benefit appeared in cameo form in the same paper on 17 April, when the case came up before a magistrate of 'Arthur Hudson, said to be of excellent character, keeping his father and mother too ill to work, charged with stealing a nightdress from Messrs Stapler of London Wall'. Hudson died in Brixton Prison after an operation there for appendicitis, preventing the disclosure of further particulars which, it was understood, would have led to dismissal of the charges. Hudson's mother was in the deepest distress both mentally and physically. The magistrate, Sir Vezey Strong, directed a sum of £2 to be handed to her from the Poor Box.'[15]

On a lighter note, another instructive gathering on the social landscape of 1909 were the most prominent martyrs to the doctrine of social ransom, the dukes. Their graces were held up to the curious by a contemporary advertisement appearing at the same time as the budget. The *Strand* magazine advertised on 1 November: 'Dukes: who they are – what they are – and how they acquired their estates. With photographs of all 27 wearers of the strawberry leaves'. But an era fascinated by strawberry leaves had not yet come to terms with the motor car. *The Times* reported that 'Dudley Bruton, said to be connected with the Army Ballooning Depot at Farnborough, was charged with driving a motor car at a speed greater than 20 miles per hour.'[16]

Among the earliest reactions were those voiced through the Primrose League, at that time a major Conservative institution, a combination of adoring middle-class chorus and football supporters' club which held on 7 May its conference, or 'Grand Habitation', at the Caxton Hall, that temple of left-wing causes – as odd a venue as Biarritz for the ceremonial appointment of a British prime minister. The chairman, Sir Robert Gresley, having dilated on 'our Empire threatened by a weak and parsimonious admiralty and by the weakness of the administration in Ireland', observed that, 'everywhere they saw the self-same example of maudlin sentimentality and gross incapacity coupled with a good deal of spite and malice (hear hear)'.

Sir Robert looked backwards and forwards – to the Education Bill, and to House of Lords reform. 'Our ancient institutions are under attack.' He invoked an interesting concept, 'the property of God', which was 'no longer sacred' (a reference to Welsh disestablishment, then painfully under consideration), 'our historic Church, the House of Lords, the ownership of land, a man's right to choose religious instruction for his children, all these are singled out for attack and no institution, however venerable, no assembly, however historic, no right, however elementary and natural, is to be spared in the radical party's miserable schemes of public plunder (cheers)'. On the motion of Lord Desborough and the Duke of Norfolk, it was agreed to confer on Sir Robert the Order of the Conservative Star (fifth grade). 'Proceedings concluded with the singing of the National Anthem.'[17]

This was the mood, both ducal and rank and file, to which Balfour had to address his fire when, 'after the usual procession to the platform by champion banners followed by members of Grand Council, a march by Mendelssohn played on the organ and the National Anthem sung by Mme La Mer . . . and presentation by Miss Balfour of the champion banners, gold banner to Croydon Habitation, blue to Saffron Walden and red to Bedford', he spoke to the league at the Albert Hall the next day. 'The budget' he said, represented

the strange, unexampled, inconsistent and grossly unjust method of taxation which the government means to impose on the country. The government has obtained its ill-gotten majority (hear hear) in small degree on prom-ises of economy, retrenchment and diminished national expenditure – we have had that government increasing recklessly by leaps and bounds the expenditure of the country . . . While they have been priding themselves on giving the great masses of our fellow countrymen some new boon in the way of expenditure, they have been at the same time recovering mainly from these very classes some of the expenditure which might well have been used to achieve their grand objects.[18]

Not that everyone was instantly animated on the subject. The *National Review*, in 'Episodes of the Month', its regu-lar introductory account of recent events, devoted twenty-seven pages to foreign affairs: the Kaiser's note to St Peters-burg, an attack on 'our anti-patriots', a denunciation of the *Manchester Guardian* and *Westminster Gazette* (owned by a man with a German-sounding name, Alfred Mond), 'who divide their time between encouraging foreign Powers, especially hostile Powers, to augment their armaments, and keeping down our armaments'. There were also castigations of 'a purblind admiralty', which was not building enough dreadnoughts. Only after all this did the *National Review* get round to three and a half pages of perfunctory abuse of the budget, 'a huge hotch-potch of suggestions collected from Tom, Dick and Harry'. Even then the *National*'s first instinct was to denounce Lloyd George's very North Walian taxes on drink. 'After raiding the Sinking Fund and plundering the well-to-do classes by every imaginable device, he was compelled to find the balance by increasing the already exorbitant duties on tobacco and whisky.'[19]

Such casualness is interesting, for the *National Review*, together with the *Observer* and the *Spectator* (despite that paper's discreditable resistance to Tariff Reform), would lead the shouting in the streets when the budget, now relegated to the late pages, had become the foundation for ending the House of Lords veto. The *National*'s editor and proprietor, Leopold Maxse, despite a name readily mistakable for Viennese Jewish, came from a Somerset gentry family, the son and brother of generals, and was given to unengaging asides about aliens. 'It is to be Ireland for the Irish, Wales for the Welsh, Scotland for the Scotch and England for the Aliens,' he would later write.[20] The enpurpled opinions of the *National Review*, which he had bought in 1894, usefully illustrate the wide preoccupation of opposition opinion at this time.

This was a war party journal furiously concerned with the building of eight dreadnoughts – 'We want eight and we won't wait.' (Churchill and Lloyd George, who had argued successfully in Cabinet to keep the dreadnoughts to four, were referred to simply as 'the traitors'.) Its second enthusiasm was compulsory military service. It carried advertisements for the National Service League, which would 'secure the place and safety of the Country and the Empire and improve the moral and physical condition of the people by bringing about the adoption of Universal Military Training for Home Defence'. It would, said the advertisement, 'Strengthen the national fibre and the sense of civic duty by bringing all men into relation with national ideals though personal training during youth'.[21]

The *National* was also a keen advocate of Chamberlain's notion of a great Empire behind the walls of a protective tariff. A regular feature in the paper was a report from Empire countries, headed, with Balkan truculence, 'Greater Britain'. The *National* pushed Tory attitudes to extremes; it was boorish and abusive in its patriotism after the style of a stage colonel retired to Upper Slaughter. Highly alert to the virulent nationalism about in the Kaiser's Germany, its own tirades must have made reassuringly warlike reading in the circles of Tirpitz and Schlieffen: 'The creation of a German Navy of the same standard as the German Army involves the destruction of British Sea-power and the downfall of the British Empire which, from the German standpoint, blocks the way.' Any hesitation about a massive building of warships was 'what we have described, and shall continue to describe as "treason in high places".'[22] Ironically, the war with Germany, when it came, would be fought on land and measured by the millions dead, while naval conflict could be summed up in the drawn Battle of Jutland and the observation of Admiral Beattie, 'There's something wrong with our bloody ships today, Chatfield.' The *Review* was, however, dismissive of air power – 'imaginary movements of mythical airships'.[23]

Maxse felt uncomplicated hatred for the politicians and newspapers of the pacific, socially reforming kind. Asquith and his 'government of windbags and weekenders' deserved no civilities. 'Very few of them care a brass farthing what happens to the nation so long as they continue to draw their salaries and are allowed to posture as "responsible statesmen".' Winston Churchill, in addition to being a 'traitor', was 'the pot boy'; also 'the soul of disloyalty' and 'a determined adventurer'. With the aid of 'Mr Lloyd George, Mr L. V. Harcourt and other traitors' he had limited the number of dreadnoughts to four.[24]

The thickheaded intolerance involved here was impressive. Churchill was a traitor because, as a free-trade Tory, he had crossed the floor in opposition to the Conservative shift to Tariff Reform. Yet the *National* in the same edition opposed toleration of any free-trade Conservative candidate – 'Worse than an ordinary Radical Member, because an open enemy sitting on the other side of the House is less harmful than a nominal friend on our side who on the main question would work with the enemy.'[25]

When the *National* finally came round to giving the budget full attention and advocating the course of inflamed resistance which would lead to the ditch, it would do so in the high, paranoid spirit of Upper Slaughter, but also in a context. The budget embodied social irrelevances – sentimentality towards the poor, animus against the traditional base of society – the actions of a government unwilling to build a big navy or go for national service. It was also doing something disagreeable to Tariff Reformers – finding new, unthought-of taxes with which to pay for both old-age pensions and at any rate four dreadnoughts.

Tariff Reform rested on two planks: assertion of Greater Britain against the foreigner and additional sources of revenue. By a combination of cheerful party prejudice and fiscal ingenuity, Lloyd George was taxing two Tory redoubts, the brewers and the landowners, balancing the budget and practising free trade at the same time. He was enabling the Liberals to preach against dear food while committing the economy to the foothills of social security. The budget rolled up into one four-and-a-half-hour speech almost all the horrors an Edwardian Conservative could think of.

The idea of this evil package being resisted in the Lords was not, during the summer months immediately after its delivery, considered realistic politics. Balfour had used the Lords against legislation within the conventions while talking of 'caution and tact', and Lansdowne had made his crisp assessement of the need not to provoke Labour over the historically important Trades Dispute Bill. But by its June number, the *National* was already thinking ahead. And as with Conservative argument against Irish Home Rule, it resorted at once to the constitution, or as Conservatives of that era tended to call it in breathless awe, 'the Constitution'. 'Should the House of Lords tamely submit to this imposition, it acquiesces in its own annihilation. It will, so to speak, be knocked out of the Constitution and the nation will have no use for such a Second Chamber.'

There was a chance that the budget might fail anyway. Maxse hopefully cited 'shrewd people' who thought that 'Mr Lloyd George is such an ignoramus and that his Budget is so impossible that much of it will collapse of its own weight, burying its author beneath its ruins.' The House of Lords should keep their powder dry for the moment in the hope that 'the Radical Party' (a wearying Tory tag for the Liberals since late Gladstone) 'in their efforts to knock the Lords out of the Constitution, will only knock themselves out of office and afford the hereditary enemies of the people an opportunity of re-asserting legislative rights which have only been allowed to sink into desuetude owing to the supineness of one House and the effrontery of the other'.[26]

The *National* was also reflecting on Rosebery's published letter of 22 June, the one which had said, 'This is not a budget, but a revolution.' Rosebery was looking to the Lords at this time and had mused about the democratic mandate. The budget, he had said, 'would be effected, if it is effected, without the participation of the country, without the country indeed having the least pretence of voice in the matter. It will be carried over the heads of the people by a majority of the House of Commons without the faintest desire or attempt to ascertain the views of the people on the vast changes projected.' Indeed, 'British citizens will have no more control of them than if they were Tartars or Lapps.' Rosebery saw 'vast flaws in the constitution, and that the absolute rule of a party in power differs very little from that absolute rule of an individual, which is what we used to call despotism'.[27] Or, as Lord Hailsham would later put it – during a Labour government – 'elected dictatorship'.

The *National* wanted Rosebery to act. That lethargic and peevish peer was 'a man of authority who can make himself heard, while as a Peer he can give effect to his opinions. If he chose, he could "hold up" almost any government. He could speedily destroy Mr Asquith and Co., to whom he owes no obligation whatsoever since the four vice-presidents of the [Liberal Imperialist] Liberal League deserted their President in order to take office under Sir Henry Campbell-Bannerman.' It might, conceded Maxse, have been a long time since Rosebery had actually *done* anything, but if he were willing 'to take his coat off and work against the wreckers', the effect would be enormous. Rosebery 'could impose his own terms on a discredited Cabinet, who are terrified lest the Peers should touch the Budget and force a dissolution, while on their side, many Peers who detest the Budget are terrified of a General Election held on the specific issue of their powers and privileges'.[28]

What Maxse really wanted was a strong man for England, which he agreed Rosebery was not. He quoted Owen Seaman of *Punch*, who in turn had quoted Tennyson:

> Ah God for a man with heart, head, hand . . .
> Aristocrat, democrat, autocrat – one
> Who can rule . . .

Seaman had added:

> But where's the courage bold to say 'You *must!*
> There lies your duty; follow where I lead;
> Else I resign my trust!'[29]

Go back and shame us into living deeds,
For here at home, in speeches deftly spun,
We talk and talk of England's needs,
And nothing's ever done.

In fairness, Seaman's long, smug editorship of *Punch*, just begun in 1906, had not yet shifted the paper to the complacent right. He did not impinge on that lamented publication's ability to deride the attitudes about to be struck by lords and Tories.

But the idea had its sympathetic ears. Resisting a budget approved by a mere majority of the Commons through a display of aristocratic powers not invoked since the second decade of the eighteenth century would at least be something done.

14

'No More Tactics!'

The Commons duly debated the budget and proceeded to committee. It would take forty-two parliamentary days, which included a good many nights, with Lloyd George as floor manager. ('A very little man overwhelmed by a very big job is always a pitiful spectacle,' wrote Maxse at his most wish-fulfilling.[1]) But the prime minister himself from time to time would go down from Downing Street to conclude things, putting in an hour or so before breakfast.[2] There would also be procedural moves in July to hasten the lagging bill through. But for all this toil, what happened in the Commons, given the vast government majority, though it mattered, lacked excitement.

The idea of a Lords' rejection looked at this expectant stage rather like Peter Pan's description of death as 'an awfully big adventure'. The question was how adventurous were the Lords, and how ready to risk dying? Lansdowne spoke by way of broad hint and distinct possibility on 16 July at the Tory Associations' annual dinner: 'I do not think that when the time comes, the House of Lords is at all likely to proclaim that it has no responsibility for this bill and that because it is mixed up with the financial affairs of the nation, we are obliged to swallow it whole and without hesitation. That to my mind would be not only a mistake but an unconstitutional proposition.'

Claiming, as politicians at their most baroque often do, to be arguing only from common sense, Lansdowne considered it

> unthinkable that either under the theory or the practice of the constitution, in a country with two legislative chambers, it could be left to the absolute discretion of one of those chambers to impose on the nation any burden, however monstrous and intolerable, any taxation, however inequitable in its incidence, any financial system, however subversive of society; and I believe that to be specially true when one bears in mind, as we must, that this government cannot claim to have received on the occasion of the last General Election any kind or sort of mandate from the country to deal with this vast financial revolution.'[3]

It was vague but menacing, an indication of what the Lords could do and an indication that they would do something. It called for an answer and received one – unofficial, to be distanced from and clarified, but prophetic – from the 'pot boy' adventurer, Winston Churchill, now president of the Board of Trade. The bill, said Churchill, ought to leave the Commons 'in its final form. No amendments, no excisions, no modifying or mutilating will be agreed to by us.' Churchill had either misread Lansdowne or read a misprint and taken a refusal 'to swallow the budget without wincing'[4] to one committed to not 'mincing'. So, he said, 'We will stand no mincing and unless Lord Lansdowne and his landlordly friends choose to eat their own mince again, Parliament will be dissolved and we shall come to you in a moment of high consequence for every cause for which Liberalism has ever fought.'[5]

Asquith was angry and rebuked Churchill for purporting to

speak on behalf of the government, 'something quite indefensible and altogether inconsistent with Cabinet responsibility and ministerial cohesion'. He would never have spoken so bluntly and his own public response raised the tone and blurred the option. It was, he told the Commons, 'clearly impossible for His Majesty's ministers to state now what advice they would feel it their duty to tender to the King as to the exercise of the prerogative of dissolution in hypothetical circumstances which may never occur'. The implications remained, but Asquith seemed to be pushing them into grass not only long, but abstract. Churchill had not spoken, he insisted, of 'an immediate dissolution, but all that he intended to convey was that a constitutional conflict between the two Houses must ultimately be settled by an appeal to the country'.[6]

For a dedicated bridge-player this was a bad case of pulling a face over an unhelpful hand. The manoeuvres to be conducted between Houses and parties over what proved to be a two-year struggle turned upon expectations of the other side's real intentions. And bluff fiercely put up is especially in order where any calling of bluff can and must be met. If at this point Asquith sounds rather like Edward Heath talking about the miners in the early seventies, he was to follow soft words with dogged purpose. He might wisely have invested that purpose with a hard edge from the start. Asquith, a gentlemanly Liberal and personal friend of Balfour, probably at this time believed in the possibility of modest accommodations, but for the best achievement of these, withdrawal of weaponry was not wise.

The hairy primitives of the *National* knew retreat when they saw it. 'This statement,' tromboned Maxse, 'confirmed the view we expressed last month, that the House of Commons is far more afraid of the House of Lords, as it has every reason to be, than is the House of Lords of the House of Commons. The Peers are indeed masters of the situation, as the Premier recognises in proclaiming the doctrine that the House of Lords cannot dictate a dissolution.' Maxse also seized on Asquith's words to the Liberal Eighty Club against 'the precipitate pursuit of unpractical ideals'. This, the editor added, 'was interpreted by optimists as foreshadowing the abandonment of the more preposterous portions of the Finance Bill'.[7]

Asquith at this time was being nagged by the King through the royal secretary, Knollys, who was 'continually obliged to complain of certain of your colleagues'.[8] But, in fairness, he also had a tactic of his own with which Churchill was colliding. Asquith wanted to smother Tories and Lords with their own upper-case Constitutional rhetoric by suggesting that rejection was ridiculous, unthinkable, indeed 'revolutionary'. 'Amendment by the House of Lords,' he said in Birmingham, 'is out of the question. Rejection by the House of Lords is equally out of the question. That way revolution lies.'[9]

For Liberal ends he was using Tory language with its shudder of anxiety. But in dealing with the febrile Tory Party of 1909, which read *Observer* and *National Review*, *Globe* and *Morning Post*, and at the head of which so temperate a man as Lansdowne could talk of a finance bill as 'subversive of society', such an appeal to their own interior reason was doubtful tactics. Asquith faced counter-revolutionary hysteria in need of a hard slap. He would come good as the struggle deepened, but at this stage he lacked the ringmaster's instinct and, nibbled by heraldic lions, treated his whip as a hypothesis. Lansdowne might not be wincing, but Asquith certainly looked to be.

Accordingly the *National Review* drew conclusions. Maxse proceeded to misread the situation in ways which give a rationale to the actual coming conduct of more ostensibly sensible figures. Asquith, he judged, was

powerless to translate words into action or of exercising any control over his 'wild men'. From our point of view, the situation leaves nothing to be desired. For the worse the Budget, the greater the triumph of the House of Lords, the greater the set-back to the House of Commons which of late years has got too big for its boots, and the greater the radical smash, which promises to be unparalleled. On the other hand, any attempt to moderate the budget would simply disintegrate the Radical rump. The one and only thing upon which the Cabinet are unanimous and determined is to postpone the dreaded day of dissolution which would probably involve the extinction of two thirds of the 'record majority' besides depriving Ministers of their posts, to say nothing of their emoluments. The duty of the Opposition is as clear as the noonday sun – to fight this Budget to the last gasp in Parliament, to keep Tariff Reform in the forefront in the constituencies and *coûte que coûte* to force a dissolution at the earliest possible moment, so that the issue between the Parties and the Houses may be submitted to the only competent tribunal.

Having explained how easily it would all be accomplished, Maxse went gaily on in his next paragraph to discuss the composition of 'the next Unionist Cabinet' – no more of the vacillating old gang![10]

Churchill was not, of course, the only Liberal minister making provocative speeches. Lloyd George, at Limehouse on 30 July, made history with his elegant antagonisms and a good deal of kitsch. '"Won't you give them something towards keeping them out of the workhouse?" they scowl at us, and we say, "Only a halfpenny, just a copper." They say "You thieves!"' Actually, despite the offence it gave, most of the Limehouse speech is a closely reasoned defence of budget policy. Lloyd George describes the land around Limehouse itself, mostly marsh and worth very little, before a great Liberal idea hit it.

The commerce and the trade of London increased under

free trade, the tonnage of your shipping went up by hundreds of thousands of tons and by millions; labour was attracted from all parts of the country to cope with all the trade and business which was done here . . . the population overflowed . . . All that land became valuable building land and land which used to be rented at £32 or £33 an acre, £3,000 an acre, £6,000 an acre, £8,000 an acre. Who created that increment? Who made that golden swamp? Was it the landlord? Was it his energy? Was it his brains? . . . It was purely the combined efforts of all people engaged in the trade and commerce of the port of London – trader, merchant, shipowner, dock labourer, workman – everybody except the landowners . . . In future those landlords will have to contribute to the taxations of the country on the basis of the real value – only one halfpenny in the pound! Only one halfpenny! And that is what all the howling is about.

Then there was his increment. If land went up in value in the future, the community would get 20 per cent of that increment. Northumberland County Council had wanted a small plot to build a school on. They had approached the Duke of Northumberland, a noted landowner, and 'What did he demand? Nine hundred pounds an acre! All we say is if it is worth £900, let him pay taxes on £900!'[11]

This rather gay and mocking performance provoked King Edward, the dukes and the press. The King, who was much preoccupied at this time with resisting the viceroy, Minto, who was pressing for the appointment of a Hindu lawyer, Satyendra Prassano Sinha, to membership of the viceroy's council – 'fraught with the utmost danger to the maintenance of the Indian Empire under British rule' – was deeply offended. He sent a letter to Asquith to be read to Cabinet against the Limehouse speech. It was, he said, 'full of false statements, of socialism in its most insidious form and of virulent abuse against one particular class, which can only have the effect of setting "class" against "class", and of stirring up the worst passions in its audience. It is hardly necessary to allude to its gross vulgarity.'[12]

That Limehouse speech lit the blue touchpaper for King, dukes and Tory press, but a later speech, in Newcastle on 9 October, was both more biting and seriously combative about the constitutional question. The Tories wanted their dreadnoughts, but 'a fully equipped duke costs as much as two dreadnoughts; and they are just as great a terror and they last longer.' Then came the question of Lords' rejection, the proposal of 'the more featherheaded' of the Tory peers.

> But this is the great constitutional party, and if there is one thing more than another better established about the British constitution it is this: that the Commons and the Commons alone have the complete control of supply and ways and means; and what our fathers established through centuries of struggle and strife – even bloodshed – we are not going to be traitors to.
>
> Let them realise what they are doing. They are forcing a revolution. But the Lords may decree a revolution which the people will direct. If they begin, issues will be raised which they little dream of, questions will be asked which are now whispered in humble voices.

One question in particular would be asked: 'Should 500 men, ordinary men chosen accidentally from among the unemployed, override the judgement . . . of millions of people who are engaged in the industry which makes the wealth of the country?' And Lloyd George concluded by declining from this cool but highly pertinent impudence to an error-of-taste, sobbing tenor conclusion about refreshing 'the parched lips of the multitude who have been treading the dusty road along which the people have marched through the dark ages which are now emerging into the light'.[13]

*   *   *

The language of debate was getting rougher all round. Garvin of the *Observer* referred to the government as 'the Plunderbund', and this insult was tossed from hand to hand in right-wing publications, while the *Spectator* took to referring to Lloyd George by the name of the mediaeval peasant leader Jack Cade. Lansdowne, the pupil of Jowett, was more complex and more ironic. 'There is a particular kind of gull, particularly voracious and unscrupulous, which does not fish for himself, but hovers about and swoops down upon the other bird, and makes him let go his mackerel or herring . . . I am told that the name of that bird is a word derived from the Greek which literally translated means "swooping robber bird".'[14]

The summer of 1909 had been a season for orations: Churchill at Edinburgh then at Leicester; famously Lloyd George at Limehouse and Newcastle; Asquith at Bingley Hall near Birmingham in September; Balfour at the same venue in October; Lansdowne to his associations dinner; and Lord Rosebery defending the dukes as 'a poor but honest class'. Lloyd George, though, had been doing more than making speeches. His disquisition on the great lords turning him and Asquith from their door had ended with a sentence directed at the Tory press. 'And they turn their dogs on to us, and you can hear their bark every morning.'[15] But he was perfectly happy to tickle the tummy of such a hound – or to slip a dog biscuit to a press lord.

Understanding the importance of the press and the impressionability of many of the men who owned it, Lloyd George had turned his compelling charm (which, incidentally, had reduced King Edward after his outrage at Limehouse into agreement about the 'foolish and *mean* speeches and sayings' of 'great landowners and capitalists'), upon Alfred Harmsworth, 1st Lord Northcliffe, the owner of *The Times* and the *Daily Mail*. Giving generously of his time, and consulting Northcliffe about the draft of the Development of Roads Bill, in which he knew him to be very interested, for his perusal and use as a scoop, Lloyd George made a marked impression. *The Times* and the *Mail* were quickly noted as beginning to wobble.

It became necessary for J.L. Garvin, editor of the *Observer* and adviser to Northcliffe, for whom, at this point, 'the whole tone of *The Times* and *Daily Mail* seems . . . utterly disastrous', to conduct his wayward employer to Balfour for lunch and an interview. Balfour seemed amused by the fervent Garvin's 'violent general onslaught on the iniquities of the measure, prospects of its fatal effect on the Empire, the Constitution and the Party if it were allowed to pass, the duty of the H. of Lords & so forth. All this was of no use to poor Northcliffe, who wanted "sense" (as we called it at Eton) for leading articles, not general expositions of policy.'[16]

The *Mail* and, more gradually, *The Times* would be got back into the Tory laager (though Buckle at *The Times* independently opposed Lords' rejection). It was Garvin who appears to have done the work. And the image here of Balfour and his aides, the *roi fainéant* and the new fierce middle classes with their curious enthusiasms,* is wonderfully illuminating. Balfour had made that remark about as readily taking advice from his valet as from a party conference, but in a sense, Garvin *was* his valet. And he was being listened to. Balfour would be borne along by the opinions and energies of the party he happened to be leading. He was ironic, supercilious, not quite participating – and they noticed.

Lord Robert Cecil, distanced by his serious free-trade convictions from the leadership group, would have said earlier something which Balfour could never have avowed, but it echoes the Etonian amusement. 'If the Unionist Party were free from Tariff Reform and the middle classes – in which I include the Chamberlains, Bonar Law, Milner *et hoc genus omne* – we should get on all right.'[17] For all the noise coming from the dukes about their narrow personal interest, this sort of virulent fighting Conservatism depended on middle-class people from Chamberlain outwards for its will. Garvin, the son of an unprivileged Irish Catholic family, was something else: the romantic convert, in this case to the world view of Joseph Chamberlain.

Although Lansdowne had fired one barrel, his commitment to resisting the budget was awaited and Lansdowne was getting advice. Lord St Aldwyn, the former Hicks Beach, contemplated amendment of the budget rather than rejection – just as much against the convention on money bills, but 'it would throw the onus of the loss of the budget on the Commons, and would, I think, avoid that loss and save their own dignity by sending up a new bill without the obnoxious clauses which of course we should pass.' Yet having run over that idea, he concluded: 'I own that my House of Commons feeling on finance is against it, and I think the right and the wise course is to pass the budget as it comes.'[18] A group of peers – James of Hereford (the Gladstonian lawyer who had seen 'Red ruin' in Home Rule), Balfour of Burleigh, Cromer, the indignant Onslow and Lytton – took the same view.

Lytton put it astutely. The government were putting about the notion that they desired to tax the luxuries and super-fluities of the rich whereas the opposition proposed to tax the necessaries of life of the poor. It was untrue, but it was believed. Accordingly, the government had recovered some ground, enough to be 'returned with a sufficient majority to re-enact the budget and to remain in office another five years.

This would be bad enough, but it would be still worse if they obtained – as they must inevitably try to obtain – power to curtail the veto of the House of Lords.'[19] One couldn't have read the actual events yet to unfold more sharply than that, but the unfortunate Lord Lytton, only thirty-two at the time, was the peer who had argued at Lansdowne's townhouse gathering in favour of accepting the Licensing Bill. It was probably this rejection which had persuaded Asquith that moderation was wasted on the House of Lords; it had provoked his observation at the end of 1908 that Lords' obstruction was 'the dominant issue in politics'. Lytton had been right and disregarded then; he was right and about to be disregarded again.

If Asquith's tolerant 'you know you can't do that' line was to succeed, the rational advice of people like Lytton had to carry with their own side. The reason it didn't was that the Tory Party was in too bad a way to face anything except a fight. Tariff Reform, which divided the party then in very much the way Europe would divide it in the 1990s, made sensible tactical manoeuvre exceptionally difficult. The people who wrote furious articles about Lloyd George as cad and the budget as a combination of felony and socialism also demanded Tariff Reform to the dogmatic letter. Willoughby de Broke, quite typically, was a zealous campaigner for Tariff Reform and future zealot against Home Rule.

It wasn't a good thing merely for native agricultural producers like himself, it was the only thing the working class 'really cared about', and he went about the country preaching it to them. He was to be particularly exalted by his experience of Lancashire, a county which, despite its cotton mills, retained under the Derbys creditable elements of the feudal spirit. 'It was an honour to talk to them . . . Many of these good people, moreover, sprang from families who had lived in Lancashire for generations; they were proud of their ancestors and were by no means averse to hearing about the hereditary principle.'[20]

Lansdowne was only too well aware that almost all the moderating advice he was receiving came from men who were still free-traders or who had tepid feelings towards protection, and that virtually all the calls to arms derived from supporters of the Chamberlain panacea. But Lansdowne's biographer, Lord Newton, reported the rejectionist pressure from all sides. 'Unionist MPs were almost unanimous, Tariff

Reformers were eager to seize the chance of testing the opinion of the country; wire-pullers reported that the budget was already losing popularity ... some simpleminded peers were convinced that as the action of the Lords in throwing out Home Rule in 1893 had been approved, similar approval would be forthcoming in 1909.'[21]

There was a mood in the party, in its press and activist ranks, that caution and tactics were part of a wider decadence in respect of which both Balfour and Lansdowne were highly suspect. As Willoughby would much later write to his friend, Maxse, 'The British Constitution ... is the only thing the Conservative Electors understood ... First principles and again First principles are what we must preach ... No more tactics.'[22] 'No more tactics' already described the dominant mentality in Tory politics weighing upon Balfour and Lansdowne. Ultra-imperialism, taxes on foreign goods (and a desire to build naval ships and instigate national military service) meshed together with rejection of a budget which stymied all that by raising revenue not from foreign, continental exporters but from native landowners. All the threads were woven together in the making of the diehards who were soon to dominate Tory politics.

Resistance to the budget came very close in the mind of Balfour to being a diversionary issue, a foreign war to rally the party/nation. His own indulgent biographer, Egremont, says flatly, 'Balfour, desperate to draw his party together, decided upon rejection by the Lords because he believed, in the face of the Liberal onslaught, there was no other way to enter the next election united. Rejection would provide the much-needed standard around which the faithful could gather, fiscal quarrels at last forgotten.'[23] As so often with Balfour, the impression is of improvisation followed by rationalisation. He was a man retreating up a flight of stairs leading only to the roof from which he would be flung. But for the all-important present, it made sense to retreat.

Since the impossible and the absurd were clearly going to happen, Asquith would have to revise his thinking. A Cabinet on 8 September investigated the likely consequences of rejection and, in practice, Asquith found himself saying responsibly to the King in September what Churchill had indefensibly said to the Edinburgh meeting in July. 'Such an action on the part of the House of Lords ought to be followed by an accleration of the register, so as to secure at the earliest possible possible moment, an appeal to the country.'[24] What Asquith did *not* want was a dissolution forced by the Lords.

The King was also getting advice. Cawdor, the Tory peer who had access to him as a guest at Balmoral in early October, told Edward that the peers had a constitutional duty to provoke an election since this wasn't a budget, but a major piece of social legislation wrapped up in a financial document. The King was also being encouraged at this time to play broker. Viscount Esher, the Pooh Bah of court politics upon whose malicious intellect royalty relied, sent a short, simple memorandum to the King setting out the precedents of Victoria's mediation in 1869 on the Irish Church Bill and the reform legislation of 1884. But on these two occasions, the prime minister (Gladstone each time) had not formally claimed that the Lords was actually exceeding its conventional powers.

The instinct of courtiers was to protect the equanimity of the King. Francis Knollys, his secretary, himself a member of the Lords, told Esher that he was 'filled with dismay' at the decision of Balfour and Lansdowne to reject. 'They appear totally to ignore the effect it will probably have on the Crown, and the position the King will be placed in.'[25] Esher, who was fireproofed against the obsessions of rural peers and Tariff Reformers, had the consequences as coolly measured as had Lytton. 'The whole situation too perilously resembles that of 1640 for my taste. The idea is that the General Election will practically destroy the Liberal majority.

The whole thing is a political gamble. It may yet turn out a political blunder . . . I think the end will be, not perhaps yet, a complete constitutional change – at the expense of the House of Lords.'[26]

By the time King Edward came to talk to Asquith on 6 October, he and his advisers favoured an attempt to buy off the Lords and Tory leadership. They should be told that if they passed the budget, then they would get an election. Asquith believed that such an offer would not attract the Tories since it involved an election *after* public retreat, while they would hope to do better in a rather later contest. It also meant, though Asquith wasn't going to say this, a major concession to the Lords' constitutional case. The implication would be that if they were against something strongly enough, there ought to be a General Election. That was a pitch for entrenched (and enhanced) Lords authority by way of convention, something no democratically elected statesman thinking ahead could contemplate. Accordingly, the King's message to Balfour and Lansdowne when he saw them on 12 October was an unsweetened appeal to persuade the Lords to pass the budget. They were anxious not to seem under pressure from the King, who would not be meeting them without the approval of Asquith, who would be entitled to know what they said.[27] They took the message stiffly and without comment.

In fact, as Asquith also knew – through his friend Carrington, who in turn was a friend of the restraining Tory Onslow – a private meeting of peers on 28 September had already recommended throwing out the budget. As for Balfour, he was taking the advice of his valet. Garvin had appealed in print on 8 August for Balfour to follow Asquith to Birmingham and commit himself *inter alia* to Tariff Reform, the alternative to the budget as a form of revenue-raising. From early August onwards, Balfour, or his adjutant, Sandars, had been in steady touch with Garvin, who had a flattering recollection of events. 'From the beginning of August Mr Balfour's mind was made up . . . After the Limehouse speech Mr Balfour's decision and dexterity were the master influences upon the situation from first to last.' The Birmingham speech put the question of 'socialism' – as excitable Conservatives saw Lloyd George's scatter of incremental taxes – in conflict with Tariff Reform. Leopold Amery, a representative right-winger, put it succinctly. 'On the whole [Balfour] is doing thundering well.'[28]

To do thundering well Balfour had to follow, not lead. Valet power was now deferred to. In making the key obsession of the right his own central ploy in debate, he was retreating into assault. Accordingly Lords' rejection was assented to. Balfour was a man happiest being gracefully tactical, but Willoughby's thinking – 'No more tactics' – was taking over.

15

'Time Has Touched It with His Finger'

The seemingly interminable Commons session of 1909 ended after a ten-day report stage on 4 November with the Finance Bill carrying against Austen Chamberlain's motion by 379 to 149. The budget had passed the Commons after seventy parliamentary days, including 42 days in committee and 554 divisions, in which Lloyd George had voted in 462 and Asquith 420, in a year without a recess.[1] The ball was now bouncing dangerously in another court into which Lansdowne promised he would shortly move: 'That this House is not justified in giving its assent to the bill until it has been submitted to the judgement of the country.'

On 2 November, the Lords reading commenced with Lansdowne beginning as Conservatives meant to go on – in the seventeenth century. 'If this bill is to pass into law, he said, 'it must be enacted "by the King's most excellent Majesty, by and with the advice and consent of the Lords Spiritual and Temporal". Is that some musty anachronism? I think not.' Lansdowne quoted Oliver Cromwell who, under the Commonwealth, had set up a mini-House of Lords to prevent 'an omnipotent House of Commons – the horridest arbitrariness that ever existed in the world.'

And he quoted a Commons argument of 1689: '"As the

Kings and Queens by the Constitution and laws of Parliament
are to take all or leave all in such gifts, grants and presents
from the Commons, and cannot take part and leave part, so
are the Lords to pass all or reject all without diminution or
alteration." There you have clearly and distinctly placed on
record the right of this House to reject a bill of this kind.'
Lansdowne went on to say that 'if that right was necessary
in the seventeenth century, it has become indispensable to
us today.' Governments, especially reform governments, had
become too fond of 'tacking', that is attaching to a sacrosanct
money bill clauses which ought to have had a separate
and Lords-vulnerable existence. The Lords had rejected a
Licensing Bill in 1908. But with the licensing provisions of
the budget, they faced 'an equally cynical invasion of your
lordships' rights and privileges' – legislation 'more crushing
in its severity than the bill of 1908, with which you had the
right to deal, and you are told that you are precluded from
dealing with it because it is bound up in the cover of a Finance
Bill. I ask your lordships, what self-respecting second chamber
would tolerate such treatment?'

Lansdowne then contemplated the increased death duties,
comparing the state's intrusion to tax at death with Islamic
law. He quoted a French commentator who had described
the British budget as 'a reversion to the theory which prevails
in Musulman countries where the sovereign is the sole proprietor of all property and private individuals have to be grateful
to him for any portion of that property which he permits
them, not to own, but to enjoy without any permanent
enjoyment, or the right to transmit it to their heirs.'

As for land taxes, they offered 'an almost unlimited opportunity for what I am afraid I must call predatory taxation'.
Lloyd George had talked about a halfpenny in the pound for
undeveloped land duty. But Lansdowne had a vision of a new
monster, the junior civil servant, 'the young man at £500 a
year'. If that young man 'or the department that he chooses to
serve, chooses to discover that your uninteresting acres have

a potential value for some remote purpose, your halfpenny in the pound becomes not a halfpenny but 3 shillings, 4 shillings or 5 shillings'.

Lansdowne could cheerfully take on Lloyd George, but he was also obliged to drop incense at the new Conservative altar of Tariff Reform, where he was at best an occasional communicant. The budget, he said, was 'a confession that you have virtually exhausted the possibilities of a financial system based upon free imports . . . staunch free-traders are beginning to realise that our singlehanded struggle in favour of free trade can no longer be maintained with any prospect of success'. With splendid insouciance, Lansdowne, a marquess with much of south-western Ireland in fee in addition to the sort of English estates which merit the word 'rolling', made a memorable observation. 'People,' he said, 'are asking themselves whether, after all, cheapness is everything.'

He concluded by facing up to the crisis inherent in rejection of the budget. There would not of course be a breakdown in tax-collection; doubtless the lord chancellor had 'a nice little scheme for tiding over any temporary difficulties which may arise'. That would not of course be resisted. Assistance we shall give 'loyally and do our best to mitigate any inconvenience that may possibly be experienced'. The episode would be no more than 'a temporary chaos', so much more preferable to 'the permanent dislocation and permanent chaos' which would arise from passing the budget.

But on the larger constitutional conflict, Lansdowne sounds stoical, not to say fatalistic. They had been told 'long before this budget could even have been thought of by its authors that the question of curtailment of the rights of the House of Lords was to be the dominant issue at the next election'. The question thus was, 'Shall we stand better or shall we stand worse when the struggle comes if we shirk our responsibility now?' What would the Lords gain 'by refusing to act upon our undoubted rights in regard to this bill?' By rejecting the budget, the Lords would do their duty by 'those who look to you as the guardians of their greatest constitutional right, the right to be consulted when fundamental political changes are contemplated by the government of the day'. The Lords had no right 'to give your indispensable consent until you have been assured by the people of the country that they desire it to pass into law'.[2]

This all reads very high and dry, but in some respects Lansdowne intended to convey in a casual tone his usual pragmatic self. The Lords had certain rights as presently defined. It was worth pitching things high, because the public might endorse those rights and give an adverse vote to the originators of the budget. In aristocratic terms, he implied, this was not plunging at Monte, more like a flutter at a point-to-point.

As coolly as he could, Lansdowne invoked those past threats and present intentions by the Liberals to make House of Lords authority a major issue. They were threatened. 'We are told to think well of the consequences to this House. That is conveyed to us in various tones, sometimes full of solicitude, and sometimes minatory and violent. It is in effect intimated to us that as the penalty of rejecting this bill we are to expect an attempt to deprive this House of its constitutional right of dealing with money bills . . . I am not greatly alarmed by these threats.' Yet he would move from this blithe remark to assert that, facing 'the coming struggle', the Lords should make a stand. He had spoken both lightly and fatalistically, skilfully giving himself two reasons for doing the wrong thing.

For the government, Loreburn, the lord chancellor, replied. Loreburn, Robert Reid, was a Scottish radical, dear to Campbell-Bannerman and far from the tentative or Whiggish position which found the budget an imposition. He was also brisk. The licensing clauses were variations of tax; they belonged in a budget. Tacking had been defined in a standing order old enough to impress any traditionalist. 'The annexing of any clause . . . to a bill of supply which is foreign to and different from the matter of the said bill

... is unparliamentary and tends to the destruction of the constitution of this government.' What in the budget then offended? Land tax and valuation related as much as licensing directly to taxation.

Otherwise everything was a matter of common sense. Four of the six years normally served by a government in those days under the Septennial Act were up. If people didn't like the government, they would soon enough be able to get rid of it without any constitutional crisis. The Lords had used much of that time in destroying Commons legislation. The Licensing Act, whose demise at 'the private house of a great nobleman' had struck even Willoughby de Broke as irksome to a Liberal, Loreburn picturesquely described as 'perishing by the stiletto in Berkeley Square'.

So now the House of Lords was going to 'destroy the Finance Bill of 1909 and to refuse supplies'. Loreburn was specific: 'It is in my opinion impossible that any Liberal government should ever again bear the heavy burden of office unless it is secured against a repetition of the treatment such as our measures have had to undergo for the last four years.' If the government lost the election, it would only be the beginning of a conflict. If they won, 'I hope we shall not flinch from that which we will have to follow'.[3]

The tradition of antiquarian allusion and remote precedent was more than maintained by Halsbury, a former Conservative lord chancellor. Halsbury was a very old man, eighty-six, though in sprightly and vengeful health, and his speech divided between small points of law of the deepest-buried kind and the instinct to bandy no nuance but to interpret every government proposal in terms of unadorned apocalypse.

We were indeed violating the constitution by adding extra business to the Finance Bill. The practice, he said, had been for any bill needing supply which had 'anything in it considered to be alien' to be out of order. A bill containing malt tax and tobacco duties had arisen long since and 'the then chancellor, in vindication of the privileges of this House, moved that it be disagreed with and rejected because it contained multifarious matter'. And this had taken place 'as late as 1807'! Lord Halsbury himself had been born early in the reign of George IV.

Halsbury also invoked his classical studies against the fighting style of Lloyd George and Churchill by recalling that in Athens there had been two altars, to Impudence and to Insult; a number of government speeches might have 'formed appropriate offerings on these two altars'. For the most part, though, he was expressing huff. The Lords had rights, that was certain; as for the government, they were troublemakers. Ministers had told the Lords 'that it is time to make the dukes pay'. A minister was using such language 'for the purpose apparently of setting the poor against the rich, at all events for making a sort of attack on those who are very well off and inciting the people to aid and assist him in "making the rich men pay", to use his own phrase.' Halsbury bridled: 'Is that the language to be used by an English statesman speaking of such an important question . . . as the accounts of the year?' Threats of curtailed powers (which in Halsbury's mouth became 'We will abolish you' did not deter him. If he were supposed 'to be actuated one way or another because I was threatened with extinction and made to suppose that I would be deprived of all my privileges, I would not value a seat in a House which would yield to such a paltry apprehension'.[4] Not for nothing would Halsbury become the adornment, toast and table decoration of those for whom death in a ditch would be a guiding principle.

The bishops were to prove broadly amenable to the budget, but Bristol, having advantageously contrasted the comparative antiquity of bishoprics and peerages and claimed 'a spiritual heredity', quoted the form of prayer used in the Lords, 'the uniting and knitting together of the hearts of all persons and estates within the realm in true Christian love and charity one toward the other', and found the Liberals deficient in such qualities. 'On the other hand,' said the lord bishop, 'we know who is the real author of this bill.' He meant Lloyd George. 'Not to say a word about his parliamentary utterances, I only ask your lordships to consider his speeches out of Parliament, and particularly one delivered near my old charge when I was in Stepney [Limehouse], made in certain language and with evident motive.' Well, if the bill could be judged – and it could – on that speech, 'there is nothing in the world for this House to do but to pass the amendment of the noble marquess.'

The bishop, heckled by the Liberal Lord Sheffield, was determined in an interminable baroque way that 'while earnestly desirous to do everything I can for the amelioration of the conditions of the poor and of the working classes . . . my vote shall be given for making it as sure as we can make it that those whom the amendment trusts, whom those who are against it will not trust – namely the people of this country – shall have the chance to express their opinions distinctly for or against these proposals.'[5]

Another bishop, Birmingham, with different priorities, would observe sadly that it was impossible 'to live in one of our great cities without becoming conscious of the fact that for the great body of the workers, our country is not a good place to live in at the present moment'. As for the tax on unearned increment on land in and about towns, 'Those who have been taught the political economy of John Stuart Mill have been expecting to see this tax in England for a great many years.' And quoting the story of the sailor who destroyed the barometer indicating stormy weather, the bishop spoke of 'a not very highly developed revolutionary spirit . . . that will rejoice if your lordships accept the amendment of the noble marquess.'[6]

The most candid Tory intervention of the first day came from Willoughby de Broke, not yet the acknowledged Carnot of Reaction, but, as always, gaily truculent and quite funny. The feeling had been, he said, that lesser peers should pipe

down. It had not been 'considered during the platform campaign, that it is good form for anyone under the rank of a marquess to talk about his own affairs. I belong to that equally
struggling but still more deserving class of the barons.'

In Willoughby, real charm and a lightness of touch, which
suggested that he might occasionally see an opposing point of
view, went with a quiet and insistent paranoia. Recent Liberal
administrations had 'produced in me a complete object lesson
of the wealthy class that they have tried to destroy in this
country without any assistance from this budget at all'.
Willoughby had reached 'the sincere and honest conviction
that the vast majority of the thinking people in this country
look to the House of Lords to save them from the tyranny
of that small knot of Cabinet ministers who have managed
somehow to gain mastery over their colleagues and to get
control of the House of Commons'.

Having spoken of Asquith, Crewe and Runciman in terms
appropriate to contemporary Russian goings-on in Zurich,
Willoughby told a tale of the South African war. A soldier had
'begged a man on the other side to spare his life and he would
give him all his money. The other man took the money away
from this unfortunate man who was on the ground, and then
he shot him. That is exactly what will happen to us. We shall
not receive any more lenient treatment from the radical party,
and those who wish to abolish the House of Lords will not
change their attitude in the future, however amenable we may
be at the present moment'. Like all extremists, Willoughby
had a dedicated belief in the extremism of other people.

The Lords for the moment would get 'a bowdlerised version' of the budget, but the intentions of the radical government were clear: 'to set up a single-chamber government in
this country'. Their lordships, said Willoughby, would be
told all about the chaos likely to follow if they rejected. This
possibility he met with a disarming innocence. 'The blood
of this budget will have to be on the heads of its authors.
They have called all the trouble . . . if the budget is killed, as

I honestly believe it will be by the people,' the government would only have themselves to blame. And anyway, he added, they hadn't supported the budget 'like men who have confidence in it'. Part of Willoughby's reasoning process was an ability to credit opponents with opposite motives. At one point he talks about a longstanding radical (meaning Liberal) intention to impose 'swingeing taxation' as a provocation to the Lords; then, suddenly, he shifts to charging them with faintheartedness.

Meanwhile, his denunciation of the use of closure in the Commons allowed no credit for government forbearance. 'They have taken into their hands in the House of Commons every single sort of weapon that they could find or forge in order to pass this bill through that House.' This had been the budget with 554 divisions over seventy days and no summer recess; *chutzpah* could ask no more.

In parenthesis, Willoughby made what might be called a lateral attack on the other rich – finance capitalists. He would criticise the budget, he said, 'because it leaves untouched so many rich people who deserve to be taxed and whom I admit it is very difficult to get at . . . a growing class of rich people in this country who have a position of freedom with a lack of responsibility . . . whom I for one should like to get hold of . . . They have been created and flourish under a system of free imports and it is only by taxing the luxuries of these people that you will get at them at all.'

It was an instructive insight into the impulses behind Tariff Reform. The other and more luxuriantly rich, the creatures of free trade, were 'a class not particularly productive considering the small amount of interest they take in public life', men who 'could be got at in the interest of the taxpayer'. Willoughby does not mention that many of them were Jews or other foreigners – George Wyndham and Hilaire Belloc were saying that. Being rather better humoured, he observes only that '£28,000,000 worth of luxuries come into this country for use, absolutely free, which these people enjoy', and that while new taxes had been imposed on the beer, tobacco and spirits enjoyed by working men, 'I may mention that the taxation on champagne is not increased at all'.

Willoughby was speaking the language of lateral class war. He had 18,000 thousand acres, the land which, as Oscar Wilde said, gave one position and prevented one from keeping it up. New money owned something better. Willoughby was, at one and the same time, denouncing 'socialism' in the form of taxes falling on his friends, while calling for it in the case of 'men who could be got at in the interests of the taxpayer' – the new class of those rich disposing of and acquiring wealth more advantageously. Social history is being recorded here.

But for all that, the government, in Willoughby's eyes, had 'surrendered to the forces of socialism'. Had not Asquith said that 'there were certain sums of money which would be far more fruitfully and much better employed if they were taken away from the individual and given over to the state and spent on things which might be thought for the good of the state'? He ended by quoting from a parody of Tennyson's 'Locksley Hall':

> Saw the landlords yield their acres after centuries of
>   wrongs
> Cotton lords turn gentlemen in patriotic throngs
> Queen, religion, State abandoned, and the flags of party
>   furled
> In the Government of Cobden and the dotage of the
>   world . . .[7]

On the second day's debate the internal griefs of the Conservative Party had an airing in a speech by the tentative moderate Cromer, one of those earlier advising Lansdowne against the rejectionist path. Cromer was concerned about the threat of war and the fact that the country was facing that threat with lengthy argument, 'which may not improbably cripple us to a certain extent in the event of any great national emergency arising'.

As for the emergency facing the Conservative Party, Cromer complained of the 'somewhat shortsighted and, as I think, vindictive policy which has been adopted towards unionist free-traders by a few extreme sections of the Tariff Reform party.' But the core of Cromer's case, expressed in tortuous and agonised debating chamber prose, was that the Liberals would punish the peers. 'And, my lords, it cannot, I think, be doubted that the result of throwing out this bill will be to produce acute and prolonged dissensions, for it will almost oblige even the most moderate members of the Liberal Party to engage in a ceaseless agitation in order to secure a material alteration, not merely in the composition but the functions of the second chamber.'[8] Cromer was scared and almost said so.

The Duke of Marlborough, after early intimations of globalisation – 'Capital is leaving the country' – struck a high Castilian tone. 'We exercise these rights not for ourselves but for the people.' And, he argued, the Lords were the object of assault and 'language of peculiar vindictiveness and remarkable abuse unparalleled so far as I am aware in our political controversies' all motivated 'by a desire to strike at those whose existence is a bar to the dominion of the demagogue'. And from such heights, his Grace, suffused in periodic purple, soared upward.

> The present relations between Lords and Commons are in themselves a monument to the sagacity of the British people. Their adjustment has been perfected by the genius of great men. That subtle and delicate equipoise has been preserved practically unchanged during centuries by the statecraft of leading men in either House, so that today it bears something of that mysterious sanctity which time alone can give. It is as with the abbey within whose shadow we deliberate. Inspired architects planned

its noble outline, its solid walls, its flowering buttresses and its dominating towers. Zealous masons laboured to transmute the architectural vision into the reality of solid stone. But not all the splendour of the initial conception nor the patient services of its builders could suffice to have won for the abbey the place which it holds in our hearts today. Time has touched it with his finger, and to his ineffable touch it owes its ultimate consecration.'

With a final flutter, his Grace returned to a note of resonating bathos. 'So I say it is with the relations between the two Houses of Parliament in the vital matter of finance.'

Lords and Commons arrangements over raising of revenue also had their ineffable side: 'they too have been slowly upreared in the passage of centuries. They too have been hallowed by tradition.' Yet this government, 'acting through the Lower House, are prepared to lay rude and irreverent hands upon a political fabric which has been the admiration of the civilised world. This magnificent monument, this unique expression of the temperament of our people is to be shattered at the bidding of a demagogue from Wales.' As for Crewe, Liberal leader in the Lords, the Duke recognised a 'self-constituted mute at the obsequies of the British constitution.[9]

From the Liberal benches Earl Russell engaged in a measure of intellectual slumming. This was Francis, elder brother of Bertrand and a man hardly less radical than the hero of the Campaign for Nuclear Disarmament. He was very cool about dreadnoughts and rearmament generally. 'There is to my mind nothing reasonable in nations behaving themselves as if they were two armed desperados sitting on a bench each waiting to see which would make the first move.' As for taxation, broadly, he was for it. Death duties might cause people like himself some inconvenience, 'but I must say I contemplate death duties for a millionaire with great satisfaction'. There was talk about such duties 'interfering with people providing for their families'. But then, 'There is some difference between providing for them in the sense of keeping them out of the workhouse and leaving them a million diminished by 15 per cent.'

As for rejection: 'Your lordships have been told that that course is not illegal; and no more it is.' They had been told it was unconstitutional, but on constitutional adjustment, their lordships were missing the point of their own jewel. He was no friend of written constitutions. In America, legal interpretation was to the letter and sterile. The unwritten British constitution rested upon convention. It was 'limited and guarded by custom . . . which has hitherto proved sufficient to meet the strains which have been put upon it'.

But who was flying against custom and convention? Why, their lordships, at this moment.

> Your lordships are seeking to destroy, and assuming the right to destroy, the work of an arduous year and the work of a large and representative majority in the elected and representative house which has admittedly the right to deal with finance, and it seems to me . . . that you are destroying very lightheartedly and without having fully considered the consequences.
>
> You say you are not afraid of the consequences. Well, I should hope not. The aristocrats in the Reign of Terror were not afraid of the guillotine, but the knife fell none the less.

Russell had fewer inhibitions against scornful argument than a Liberal minister, and less need to reserve his position. The Lords it was who were making a revolution, putting an end to the understanding upon which two-house government had rested. Whatever happened in the next election, quite soon now they were going to be rendered powerless, and he wasn't sorry. 'From my point of view, this House has always been in favour of reaction . . . It has delayed measures of reform of every character . . . its history is a record of interference with the course of progress.'

But the Lords were playing their hand as reactionaries very badly. The lucid Cambridge knife sliced fine – and was turned. 'If any useful check has been exercised in the past, your lordships will not have the chance of exercising it again . . . You are playing into the hands of those whom you say you are afraid of – the democracy – and giving it the opportunity it has long wanted.' Russell aimed a valedictory boot. 'I shall rejoice to see the veto of this House swept away. To my mind that is the only good thing we can hope for from the amendment which has been put before us.'[10]

After a final pre-dinner speech from sensible, disregarded Lytton, one of so much lament and regret that it recalled the falling sevenths of that melancholy Tory Sir Edward Elgar, a grumbling Lord Londonderry rose at the resumption to complain that he might not be speaking to such an empty House if more time was allocated to dinner. The bill was 'absolutely unconstitutional' and not only that, it was unjust, being 'vindictive towards a certain class of the community who are hostile to His Majesty's government'. And this was being done on purpose. 'It is not to collect revenue from the tax they propose to impose on land, but simply for the purpose of nationalising the land in future.'

Londonderry, who was most upset by the land survey and valuation set up by the budget, had read an article by Lloyd George, a very mild article talking about local authorities making use of the valuation figure if they wanted to buy land for development. The man to, whom, in his junior ministerial days, civil servants had been warned never to give two state papers at once as he would confuse them, was quite clear, clearer certainly than his syntax. 'To my mind the land clauses of this Finance Bill are, in effect simply this: how can we get rid of the landowners?'

Londonderry, who owned large tracts of the Durham coalfield, also spoke for several columns on the iniquity of taxes on mineral weath, something which would gravely affect miners and steelworkers. A pamphlet he had read argued: 'If a rich man has to pay an extra £50 a year for income tax he would have £50 less to spend on the multifarious industries that minister directly or indirectly to his comfort. The people he was employing are thrown out of work.' He, Londonderry, lived in the north of England, where there was grave unemployment. Given the intrusion of the state, capital would flee 'and naturally all those great industries must languish'.[11]

For the government, Lord Beauchamp pointed out that resistance to the budget was not merely a negation, a defensive act, it also proclaimed quite new powers for the House of Lords. Logically, rejection would imply the expectation that government and Commons would humbly come back with a list of taxes they knew did not offend the Lords, 'an action to make this House supreme in financial affairs and give the House of Lords the power of the purse'. Did their lordships really think that the Commons 'would appear at the bar of the House of Lords next week cap in hand and on bended knee and ask your lordships to be good enough to pass a budget which will commend itself to your lordships?'

Beauchamp regretted the absence of that moderate and restraining Tory St Aldwyn. It was, as we have seen, St Aldwyn who had excused himself from amending the budget on the grounds of 'House of Commons prejudices about finance'. Beauchamp was as ready as any Tory to quote English history with a flourish, and he had the advantage of living at a time when legislators might reasonably be expected to have heard of it. He thought that 'no more momentous or far-reaching step has been taken in the history of this country since Charles I raised his standard at Nottingham'. As for the present, he was not threatening anyone, merely saying that in the unanimous opinion of his party, 'This House with its past record, with its present constitution and with its powers as they exist at present is unworthy and incapable of guiding the destinies of a great and mighty Empire.'[12] Which, as non-threats go, went very well. Their lordships then adjourned their second day of debate, as one must here. Sherlock Holmes spoke of a three-pipe problem; rejection of the 1909 budget involves a three-chapter debate.

16

A Noble Utterance – a Balaklava Utterance

The fourth Marquess of Salisbury was a lesser figure than his father, but 'Jem', as the family called him, was a gentler kind of Conservative than the norm of this time. His right-wingness was of the anxious rather than the enraged sort. He was, for a start, a free-trader and, like his more vivid brothers, Lords Robert and Hugh, out of sympathy with Chamberlain's mob appeal of physical-force imperialism and protectionism. The Cecils were not enamoured, either, with 'Tum-Tum', the overweight King of England with his finger-clicking requirements in country houses and reverent devotion to his own comfort. In Mr Kenneth Rose's phrase, they thought him 'trivial of mind and deficient in morals',[1] and Jem observed that the monarch 'with all his little peculiarities about ribbons and tailoring . . . seems to have an intelligence which was stunted by these things early in life'.[2]

Salisbury was a loser by the budget but philosophical about it. As his sister Gwendolen wrote, 'It will cost Jem an extra £3,000 a year, but as he observes, he is very rich and I don't think it need make any catastrophical change in his life.'[3] It

243

was nice to see a sense of proportion flash, however briefly, over a noble horizon. But Salisbury was in earnest about the 'horrid arbitrariness' of single-chamber government. And like so many Conservatives, he was convinced of a determination to obtain it by tacking. The government were not taking on a great constitutional issue by way of the budget, he argued. They were determined to override the House of Lords generally. Having been amended on the Licensing Bill (amended out of sight), they had now brought it back in the budget.

Salisbury quoted from Winston Churchill, who had mocked, 'I say to our brewing friends, when they are gathered round the flowing bowl drinking the health of the House of Lords, cheering for an assembly which boasts that it will defy the will of the masses of the people, let them remember that budgets are beyond the control of the House of Lords.' It all amounted to the Commons saying that 'the Lords might not amend or reject any bill which the Commons insist upon'. Salisbury turned to Russell and his readiness to sweep away the Lords' powers. 'Lord Russell, with all his ability was, if he will allow me to say so, the victim of one or two fads . . . If he had his way . . . and the power of your lordships' House to reject any bill is thereby destroyed, he will have to put up with all the fads which come from the House of Commons.'

Salisbury, like most Conservatives of his time, though probably more sincerely, invoked 'the people'. (The term appears so often and with such awe in so many Conservative and noble speeches of the Edwardian era that it is difficult to recall the outrage which greeted the original toast to 'our sovereign lady, the people'.) Salisbury favoured an appeal from lords to people and believed that it was the function of lords to speak *for* the people. He gave as his illustration the Education Bill of 1906. But for the Lords' action, it would have been passed into law. But the people had not wanted it. 'When they had recognised that the awful spectre of secular education was standing at the gate . . . they began to think that these stupid Conservatives and those simple religious men were in the right of it.'⁴ In accomplishing that popular wish, it was the Lords who had served their masters.

Salisbury, though by no means simple, was a religious man, but he was reiterating a standard Conservative assertion (or rationalistion) that a subtle sympathy existed between people and peers – and that licensing public houses and defending sectarian education demonstrated it. (Animated by such demotic impulses, he would between the wars be a dupe of the so-called Oxford Movement, or Buchmanism, though he would be shocked by the American huckster's admiration for Hitler). The populist claim came from a party which, notwithstanding Disraeli's canny footwork in 1867, had resisted two out of three major enfranchisements of 'the people'. Meanwhile, the awful spectre of secular education has settled down in front of the fire, guest of a Conservative minister of education, R.A. Butler. What Salisbury was really expressing was a doctrine of resistible reform: whatever did not command massive demonstrable public clamour was not legitimate and could reasonably be knocked on the head by a hereditary chamber. Spasms of public conservatism and troughs of public inertia validated all resistance to change.

But it was quite wrong for political radicals to stir up feelings among 'the people'. He reproached the Bishop of Birmingham for having supported public pressure. The bishop 'practically says to the people, "You have got covetous desires; gratify them; have a readjustment of wealth by means of taxation."' Putting aside the imperfect propriety of a man owning a great tranche of Liverpool calling anyone else covetous, Salisbury was treating the opinion of 'the people' as a piece of variable political geometry invocable at convenience. It was a doctrine which could not (quite) speak its name.

Rosebery, once Liberal prime minister, once the owner of a Derby winner, a man at the same time irresolute and petulant, but a good mind for all that, had once also, fifteen years before, levelly criticised Lords' interference, thus affronting Queen Victoria. Rosebery detested the budget with all the feelings of a rich man contemplating taxation. 'The budget has done incalculable mischief . . . no longer is the country the strong-box and the safe of Europe'. Instead, 'We find every avenue of commercial enterprise blocked up because the chancellor of the exchequer stops the way . . . Ships crossing the Atlantic are carrying stocks and bonds as ballast in order that they might be got away from the jurisdiction of Her Majesty's government . . . the measure has spread over the country like one great pervading miasma or fog, the diseases of want of confidence and want of credit.' In the middle of this keening at the deathbed of the 3-per-cents, Rosebery reminded listeners of overlooked complexities by striking a sudden note of agreement with Russell on the subject of armaments. 'In the time of those who are young, we shall see bankruptcy produced by the insane competition of armaments which is now eating out the hearts of the people.'

And for all his City of London official mourning, Rosebery was clean against dying in ditches, or anywhere else. 'I cannot, I think, be more hostile to the budget than I am, but I am not willing to link the fortunes of the second chamber with opposition to the budget.' Lansdowne's motion of rejection would have been all right if Britain had had referendums; they didn't, they had General Elections. And 'General Elections, whatever else their merits may be, are not conducted in a Palace of Truth'.

There was a streak of anxious apprehension about Rosebery. Unlike Willoughby, less sensitive, poorer, he was not capable of striding about Lancashire and finding staunch skilled men with a good opinion of the hereditary principle. He had a highly alarmed notion of opinion beyond the Villa Rosebery at Posilippo. There existed 'a considerable body of opinion which is extremely hostile to the existence of this house. We must all be aware . . . that the hereditary constitution of this House does lend itself to effective, even if it be unjust, satire.' And then again, their lordships had been sturdily resisting previous attempts at reform, notably his own. Accordingly, 'I do apprehend the result of an appeal to the country on an unreformed hereditary second chamber mixed up with the promises of the budget.'

Rosebery's prudential instincts warned him against the Samurai impulse of his brethren. 'My lords, I think you are playing for too heavy a stake on this occasion.' In opposing 'an iniquitous and dangerous measure' they were risking 'the very existence of a second chamber'. And he coolly analysed the ululations coming from warriors. 'There has been talk of damning the consequences. That is a noble utterance – a Balaklava utterance. Nothing more intrepid could be said.' But intrepidity was not enough. The consequences were not to the individual but to the state – and they were enormous. It would be sensible to weigh them several times.

Rosebery then put his finger on the true strength of the House of Lords: the subtle, unquantifiable strength of what it *might* do, the strength of latency. And this required pulling back from always doing exactly what it believed in. For 'the House of Lords exercises enormous power without always voting on its convictions, and the power that it exercises was never so valuable or so much wanted as now'. Patiently, Rosebery reminded the peers that they did not want Irish Home Rule and had so far been able to stop it. John Redmond, who knew a thing or two about that, had said, ' "The only remaining obstacle to Home Rule is the House of Lords." Are you going to weaken that barrier?'

In his own words, Rosebery would have desired a 'less heroic policy'. There was heavy unemployment, the budget would be unpopular in practice. And in the election which duly came, there would be an anti-socialist majority of some size. If he had had his way, there would also have been by then a reformed second chamber, something 'achieved in the best and, in the non-party sense, the most conservative interests of this United Kingdom'.

But that, he acknowledged, wasn't going to happen, so

he would not support rejection and 'stake all my hopes of [the Lords'] future utility and reform on the precarious and tumultuous chances involved as they will be with many other irrelevant and scarcely honest issues – the tumultuous hazards of a General Election'.[5] General Elections filled Rosebery with fastidious distaste, and what he found distasteful he was not prepared to gamble on. For all his self-importance and streak of absurdity, Rosebery had contributed wisdom to the debate.

The next speaker was Milner – Milner of South Africa, a man everlastingly referred to by historians as a pro-consul. The title was Roman, and Milner, a hero to people who wanted heroes, had Roman qualities. Indeed, there was something about him of those generals, successful or otherwise, men of will and presence commanding troops in a grim corner of fourth-century Thrace or Britain, who, in the decadence of the Empire, took it on themselves to seize the throne. He had been undermined in South Africa by Liberal opposition, denounced by a demagogue from Wales and dismissed as forgotten and irrelevant by a demagogue from Blenheim. And Milner had no doubts about the rightness of resistance. The suggestion 'that in doing so we shall be transcending our powers and that because if we suspend this particular Finance Bill therefore we should make it a practice in treating similar bills with which we do not happen to agree, seems to me a patent absurdity'. Custom and convention being delicate, subtle things, Milner did not bother with them. 'We have always had this right. We have never exercised it. But we have always reserved to ourselves the right to exercise it.' They did so in order to be able to deal with an exceptional occasion. 'The exceptional occasion has now arisen. How exceptional it is, is constantly and vehemently pressed upon us by the author of this budget himself.' Milner avoiding uttering the name 'Lloyd George'. The chancellor 'never ceases to proclaim that it is not the immediate financial problem which he is so much concerned about as the social revolution which he is initiating'.

248

Milner, like *Blackwood's* and Willoughby, saw revolution in the doings of Lloyd George. The chancellor was 'otherwise than a friend to the institution of the private ownership of land. There are those behind him who avowedly are enemies to the private ownership of anything. If we wish to maintain that principle of private ownership, if we believe that the country is not prepared for the threatened gigantic change, we cannot shrink from the conflict which is now forced upon us.' He had heard Rosebery's arguments and respected them, but 'I must say that I think the course which he recommended would be deadly to the reputation of this House in the country.' This wasn't a normally bad budget, but 'an abnormally bad one'. If it was 'a measure having far-reaching consequences of a disastrous kind, how can we allow the country to suffer those disasters which we clearly foresee?'

Leaving all to 'a great faith that our action and the motives which prompted it will be fairly judged by our fellow countrymen',[6] Milner proclaimed rejection. He was a returned proconsul. He was not placed to become emperor – though he would soon be conniving at the sedition of armed Ulstermen – but unlike Rosebery, he was a man of action, and rejection was the course of action. And he truly hated Lloyd George.*

For Lord Hardinge, the budget had been 'cunningly devised as a vehicle for socialistic revolution'. It adopted 'the doctrines of the extreme Socialistic Party whilst it provides at the same time all the machinery that is necessary for carrying these doctrines into effect at any time hereafter'. The public were grateful to the Lords for having stopped Irish Home Rule –

---

* Milner proceeded later in the week to Glasgow and there contemplated 'an autocratic House of Commons' without their lordships' restraining wisdom, which might give itself perpetual power by abolishing the term of Parliament. This, ironically, the Commons would do in the Parliament Act when they replaced the seven-year term with a more answerable Parliament of five.

a public, as usual, exclusive of the Irish – and were equally happy at rejection of the Education and Licensing Bills. Anyway, the government 'persisted with that system falsely called free trade' which was the main cause of unemployment. The Lords would gain, not lose, popularity by rejecting the budget.[6]

The Earl of Mayo was concerned at Liberal profligacy. 'I will speak of only one measure, and that is the Old Age Pensions Act. I know in my country that is not a very economical measure, and the Liberals have had to pay for the experience of old-age pensions in Ireland.'[7] (Lord Mayo owned 15,000 acres in County Wicklow, County Dublin and Herefordshire.)

Carrington, president of the Board of Agriculture and close friend of Asquith, enjoyed himself to the extent of pointing out that 'there is such a person in existence as Mr Arthur Balfour', who was the leader of the Conservative Party and who had said that, given the need to raise money, there was no objection in principle to the income tax, super tax or the additional death duties. So would their lordships like to stick to their party's concerns, the liquor and land taxes. Carrington mused that over the period of the Salisbury government there had been something like six hours of parliamentary time given to discussing agriculture.

He quoted from a book written by the Duke of Bedford about the 23,000-acre Thorney Estate, recovered by draining the Bedford Level in the seventeenth century, but which in consequence of the agricultural depression had become unsaleable and the maker of a net loss. Government measures on valuation and development tax were everywhere being called ruinous. Walter Long, a leading Tory, had said that the budget was 'especially destructive to land'. Without claiming the credit as part of the pure bliss of Liberal government, he, Carrington, had recently bid for the Thorney Estate on behalf of the Crown – clearly, he added, the thin end of the wedge of land nationalisation. He had, quite rightly, been brushed aside as bidding too low and the unsaleable estate had gone for three quarters of a million.

That, in the 4 per cents, would bring in £330,000 a year, and of course it would be taxed at £1,500, which would go towards pensions and battleships. Yet here was Rosebery saying that Lloyd George had 'blocked every channel of enterprise and entirely destroyed the confidence of the country'.[8] Carrington, like Arnold Bennett's Denry Machin, was in the business of cheering every one up, also of agreeing with David Hume that there was 'a deal of ruin in a nation', something which a House of Lords wallowing in calamity, ruin and socialism preferred to disregard.

Lord Onslow was not cheered up. He saw a Finance Bill making 'rash and vast changes' of a kind that 'may destroy the slowly built-up fabric of our national credit, which may drive the accumulated savings of the people to other lands to provide employment for foreigners instead of for Englishmen, and which are designed to establish a system of land nationalisation that may corrupt the whole system of government and debase the people by making them dependent on those whom they have elected, instead of upon energy and enterprise.'[9] Edmund Burke had said that 'the virtue, spirit and essence of the House of Commons consisted in its being the express image of the nation'.

The government wasn't that, as it hadn't been at the time of the second Home Rule Bill, and the Lords stood between the nation and those 'rash and vast changes', land nationalisation and destruction of the whole fabric of credit.

The fourth day's debate was opened by Ashbourne. Like certain other Tory peers, he could not avoid a touch of scorn for Rosebery, willing to wound but afraid to strike. Lord Ashbourne took the simple, manly course – if you were against something, you stood up and fought against it. 'What is the use of this House of Lords having the strongest opinions about a bill if, when the time comes for action, it does nothing? What are we waiting for? If the House of Lords does not act now, will it ever act?'[10]

This was to be a recurring finale to many speeches. Having made their points about tax, or licensing, socialism, demagoguery, or, as with Lord Ashbourne, that this was a budget 'so enormously out of harmony with all previous action, so opposed to every budget that Mr Gladstone framed', they would conclude that unless they rejected it, they would lose all public standing. Like the girl doubtful about going to bed with a boy, they asked, 'Will you still respect me?' But unlike the girl, they sought respect through action. It was, though, a somewhat lemming-like action, with a long succession of lords reminding one another that they were doing their duty, defending the nation and/or the people, asserting rights which, if not used, had never been denied in principle, and generally cutting a figure.

They did so, of course, in response to a war speech by Lansdowne and the authorisation of Arthur Balfour: on similar instruction they had exercised precisely the rational self-interest Rosebery advised, over the Trade Disputes Act, something incomparably more radical than any part of Lloyd George's budget. But it was the way of the lords to gain respect and do their duty in group formation. In fact they look less like lemmings, which obey a gene, than the senior officer-commanded heavy dragoons in *Patience*: 'By the Right – Rapture!'

It took serious courage for a Conservative peer to resist such regimental thinking and to do so in uncompromising terms. But Balfour of Burleigh, a remote relation of the leader who had sacked him with other free-traders from the Cabinet as a sacrifice to Chamberlain, was equal to it. Like Rosebery, he was against the budget, though without visions of ruin or socialism, but even more than Rosebery he was against rejection. First, it was no good saying that a Lords right to challenge financial measure existed. There was a distinction between law and usage, and 200 years of usage had made it clear that whatever their notional rights, the Lords did not challenge budgets. They didn't control governments, either, and the two powers, both vested in the Commons, were closely related.

Equally, it wouldn't do to treat Lansdowne's motion of rejection and the election implicit in it as the calling of a referendum. Finance was different. Stop any other bill in the Lords, and the law harmlessly reverted to the *status quo ante*. Life didn't work that way for budgets. To stop them, you could challenge only by being ready 'to spoil and destroy the control of the other House of Parliament over the government'. To do that would be to make 'the most momentous change in the constitution as it has grown up which has been made in the whole history of that constitution'.

Balfour of Burleigh spelled out consequences: 'My lords, if you win, the victory can at most be a temporary one. If you lose you have altered and prejudiced the position, the power, the prestige, the usefulness of this House . . . If you win you are but beginning a conflict . . . You are remaking a conflict which has gone on from year to year and century to century until the House of Commons has attained the position . . . it enjoys by usage at the present time.'

Balfour was readier than most peers to take a step back and notice changes which had taken place in constitutional practice. Party management had reached a high point, making MPs less independent. (Living before Millbank paging, he had seen nothing.) The 'pernicious doctrine of the mandate' had increased. Accordingly, MPs sat *contra* Edmund Burke, more as delegates than representatives. Finally, parliamentary management through closure was far more intense than it had been. Balfour did not want to make party capital here. The Tories were engaged in all these things – as a free-trader aware of the harassment of free-trade Tory MPs, he was well placed to know that. On the parliamentary guillotine: 'I throw no stone. Both sides are responsible for it. The government of which I had the honour to be a member introduced it and increased it. It came to this: they were to have no second chamber ... no referendum because it will interfere with the power of the party organisation to get the legislation out of Parliament ... Members are not to have the legislation they want; they are to have what the party managers give them.'[11]

Balfour of Burleigh's advice to his party in the Lords not to take a false step and, as he put it, to recognise that the balance of Lords and Commons could survive only with Lords' restraint, owed much to his own minority position in the Tory Party. Free-traders, almost to a man, had urged Lansdowne not to reject. The party organisation leaned very hard on them. It was not perhaps an accident that the Joseph Chamberlain who had called up the dubious genie of Tariff Reform had thirty years earlier created the Birmingham Caucus, inventing machine politics as we know it, and as Edwardians were coming to know it. A free-trade Conservative was like Kipling's toad beneath the harrow which 'knows exactly where each tooth-point goes'. The antique chivalry of putting on armour to defend the ancient honour of a hereditary House was a shining, impossible anachronism, even in 1909, an era of only 6-horsepower machine politics.

Four days of debate use up a lot of argument, and their lordships, especially the great majority arguing rejection, had begun to grow stale. Their points about the ruin of the liquor trade, the movement of capital, iniquities put upon landowners, the awfulness of Lloyd George's and Churchill's rhetoric at Limehouse and Leicester, the threat of land nationalisation and of an inexactly defined socialism, along with quotations from Keir Hardie applauding 'first steps by the government' were stretched a long way, as was, of course, that detestable and much alluded to 'young man on £500 a year'. But they were beginning to perform circuits of debate.

But across 25, 26, 29 and 30 November some comments are worth recalling. Lord Faber would turn the remarks of

Winston Churchill about wider use of the unearned increment principle into the prospect of a capital gains tax – Willoughby the capitalist-basher would have liked that![12] The notably left-wing Bishop of Hereford, Dr John Percival, using very modern terminology, quoted Alfred Marshall, the economist, who had described the budget as 'a social welfare budget'. He also deplored the 'bloated' military estimates, called Tariff Reform 'gambling with the necessities of life', damned the liquor trade and told the Lords that if they chanced their arm with the public, they were liable to be told, 'Never again, never again, in this country, shall the fundamental liberties of the people be endangered by any privileged class.'[13]

From a different political angle Lord Lamington said that the aborigines of Australia were 'living strictly under a system of socialism. They suffer from two things – absence of religous beliefs and . . . absence of any knowledge of the rights of property'.[14] Lord Morley opened the fifth day for the government pointing out that Shelburne, Lansdowne's ancestor and an eighteenth-century prime minister, had said – in 1778 – that 'your lordships have a right to alter, to amend or to reject a money bill, and I say that this House is equally with the House of Commons representative of the people.' But then there were greater men than Shelburne, for example his man of intellect, that difficult Irishman Edmund Burke. Morley quoted Burke in Tory teeth. 'We are the sole representatives of the people. The Lords have no right to the disposition, in any sense, of the public purse.' That hadn't been seriously challenged in the previous 100 years.

Morley, who, as an academic, gets less of a good press than a reading of his contributions suggests, reverted to his experience as MP for a Newcastle constituency. The skilled artisans in the Elswick factories he had appealed to were not 'Reds'. But if their lordships feared the advent of 'socialism', was it wise of them to give such an impression of 'straining the constitution and straining it as champions of the rich against the poor'? Was credit going down and money leaving the country? Between 1898 and 1905, prime Conservative time, consols had fallen from 113 to eighty-nine, the Boer War playing its part as rearmament was probably now doing for both Britain and Germany.

The Lords, Morley thought, was taking an eccentric course, rather like the Fifth Monarchy men, the believers in a coming of the Fifth Monarchy of Christ and his Saints who had made a stir at the fringes of Commonwealth England. But what had been going on for the previous few days shouldn't be seen as just a brilliant stage play. 'It is the first step on a tremendous journey.' They would not think on going home 'that the curtain has fallen upon a completed drama. We shall all know in our hearts that the note has sounded for a very angry and perhaps prolonged battle.'[15]

Middleton, the Tory who followed, disagreed. Lords' rejection didn't compare with the Great Reform Bill, of which Eldon, highest, driest and sublimest of Tories, had said, 'With this Reform Bill in operation, the monarchy cannot exist, and it is totally incompatible with the existence of the British constitution.'[16] That quotation might be taken to mean no more than that elderly Conservative peers had overdone apocalypse before. But Middleton preferred the shock-horror stories from City men about falling credit and thought that if the Lords, 'the most independent assembly in the world', did not act, *that* would be the truly unprecedented course.

James of Hereford, whom we saw in 1886 wringing his hands and talking about 'Red ruin' as he left Gladstone over Home Rule, had not drifted, like many floor-crossers, into becoming an extremist of the new persuasion. He was a free-trader yet, and had advised Lansdowne against plunging here. He was plainer than anyone, invoking 'political training in old Whig principles; but clearly and distinctly, I submit the proposition and stand by the view that we have no competency to reject this budget'. Their lordships, said this former attorney-general, really must come to terms with convention. It was no good saying they had a legal right to reject. They probably had a legal right to vote in elections, but convention stopped them. Then there was 'tacking'. In his view, in the case of this budget, there wasn't any, but the rules for dealing with it were clear. The Lords would 'semi-judicially determine any "tacking" and we should reject the bill . . . But that question does not arise. You are not rejecting this bill on the grounds of tacking.' Then again, they must stop whispering among themselves that they were not really rejecting at all, only postponing. Any postponement was a rejection.

In merely political terms, James had been here before – as a Liberal. 'The House of Lords in 1884 threw out the franchise bill . . . and I was told off in very good company – the late John Bright and the late Duke of Devonshire – to do what we could in Lancashire. I can assure your lordships that it is very easy work to howl against this House.'[17]

Lord Ellenborough, inheritor of a noble and reactionary name from Regency times, complained that Lloyd George and Churchill, as opponents of the heaviest dreadnought-building, threatened the nation. If Lloyd George and his colleagues 'are returned to power, we shall have Lloyd George naval budgets for seven years longer. If that happened, then at the end of that time a great deal more than the House of Lords will have ceased to exist. Great Britain as we know it will have passed away and the inhabitants of these islands will have learned to submit to the dictation of foreign Powers [*sic*] under pain of starvation.'[18]

The succinct comment of Lord Reay, 'from the point of view of a Gladstonian Liberal', was that 'oligarchies are seldom destroyed and more frequently commit suicide'.[19] Lord Knaresborough, in an unpleasant little speech, was an exponent of the 'what use is the House of Lords if . . . ?' school. There were some 'who think it is unwise to carry this amendment, for fear that worse will follow. But what worse can follow?' He was sure that 'if you lose the power . . . to oppose finance bills of this character, then this House had better cease to exist. The state, the Empire and the individual can be ruined by so-called finance bills just as easily as in any other way.' Much better, thought Knaresborough, 'if history has to record the fall of this ancient house, let it record also that while it existed its members had the courage of their convictions and fell fighting gloriously in a just cause'. Knaresborough also, in a flash of spite, thought that their lordships 'might derive some cynical amusement from seeing the effect which the abolition of this House will have upon the group of very rich men supporting the government which they are so fond of boasting about'.[20] Not long before, one of these, Swaythling, the Jewish banker Samuel Montague, with, as he said, sixty-one years' experience of the City of London, had commended the budget and good-humouredly exploded the flight-of-capital theory upon which rested the school demanding rejection because of economic ruin.[21]

Lord Ampthill from the right wing of the Russell family, accused the government of 'assuming a policy of penal admin-istration'. The licensing clauses had been introduced into the budget in order to get even with the Lords and the licensed trade. Ampthill spoke at length about dreadnoughts and the government's response. 'What did they do? Did they seek to unite all classes in a patriotic determination to discharge that first and most human duty of all, the duty of self-preservation? My lords, they have done none of these things. On the contrary, they chose the very moment of national awakening . . . to provoke a bitter internal conflict, to stir up a class war, to embitter party animosity, all for the sake of their own party policy.'

He had a profound conviction 'that a measure advocated as the measure has been advocated cannot be a righteous measure. It has had to be recommended to the people by appeals to class prejudice, by gross personal attacks on individuals'. Ampthill thought that it was 'not the budget, but the policy of the budget, everything which is connoted in the budget, a budget which is the climax of and the outcome of years of radical policy, the policy which aims at abolition of the House of Lords'.[22]

The tone lacks comedy. It was not a Gilbertian number but a long whine. But then, so many noblemen that week seemed to be running a festival of self-pity.

17

Lord Curzon and the Old Man of the Sea

Very handily for researchers, the Liberal peer Lord Denman responded to Ampthill's talk of 'gross personal attacks on individuals' with a fair-sized anthology of gross personal attacks on individuals lately made by unionist figures. Having listed the excesses of the dukes already recounted, he quoted the Tory candidate for North Manchester, Hiram Howells: 'The Lancashire working men are sick of the selfish cry of "Property, property, property," and wish that somebody would give the dukes a hint, if they have not already done so, to put away their pocket handkerchiefs.'

He addressed himself to another victim of the budget, Sir Spencer Maryon-Wilson, who had announced that he would be obliged, if the land clauses in the budget passed, to sell the Rectory Field, Blackheath. Sir Spencer, incidentally, had lately instructed tenants communicating with him not to use the address 'Dear Sir' but to write 'Sir Baronet'. Anyway, it had recently been announced that 'Sir Spencer Maryon-Wilson has taken an estate of some 30,000 acres belonging to the Dowager Countess of Seafield for the shooting'. Then there was Sir Gray Humberstone d'Estoteville Skipwith, Bt, who had lately said that the lord advocate, Alexander Ure – another Tory hate figure – was 'one of the most unprincipled blackguards living', adding that Mr Lloyd George ought to have been shot and that if the budget passed, not only would he not help to resist an invasion of our shores, but he would actually welcome the invaders. If these seemed to be backwoods squires of no real political weight, what about Sir Alexander Acland-Hood, longstanding chief whip of the Conservative Party, who had said that 'all the members of the government had faces like sausages or suet puddings'?[1]

But back in the debate, once Clifford of Chudleigh said that the budget 'was purposely formed so as to lead to the nationalisation of land, so as to lead to the nationalisation of the liquor trade, so as to lead to the nationalisation of the railways, and so as to lead to the nationalisation of all sources of production',[2] the star of the last day was undoubtedly Curzon.

That superior person had guaranteed himself attention by delaying his entrance. Much had been said, observed the former viceroy, and there was much he would not linger on; that would be 'to flog the deadest of dead horses'. But this was to be Curzon in high Tory vein urging resistance. 'If you pass this budget into law, you will be setting a veritable Old Man of the Sea upon the shoulders, not of your lordships alone, but of all the respectable and reputable classes in the country.' No one intervened to ask Curzon how small salaried and waged men and their wives, living exemplary lives on means useless for supertax and death duties, came to be excluded from the conditions of respect and repute. But as one of Peacock's characters put it, '"Respectable" means rich and "decent" means poor.' The man who had said that 'gentlemen wear brown in the country', and 'ladies do not move' was often rather narrow in his categorisation.

No one took a high line quite so splendidly as Curzon, or for so long – twenty columns of *Hansard* – or in a fashion so arch and smirkingly Oxonian. He of course sympathised with the desire to ameliorate social evils, 'overcrowding, sweating, insanity, poverty and crime', but he could not accept the argument for agreeing the budget as being at any rate directed at good ends. 'My lords, I object to this argument not only because it is immoral. I object to it because it is unsound. I do not believe that at any time in history, poverty or the consequences attendant on poverty have ever been mitigated by taxation or the products of taxation.' The budget would not lead to creating 'a happier or more moral people'. Curzon feared that 'the principles upon which it rests must lead to a social demoralisation among the people'. But he 'greatly resented the implication that on this side of the House there is any indifference to these social questions'.

Curzon then dismissed the suggestion that the tax imposed was not actually so very heavy by alluding to the Roman Emperor Caracalla, who had imposed a 10 per cent tax and upped it to 20 per cent. Curzon, addicted to allusion, then switched from Ancient Rome to Israel and King David. Rosebery had argued that if a rejection and an election were denied, the natural unpopularity of the budget would shift the voters soon enough into creating 'an anti-socialist majority'. But that might be two years yet, said Curzon, 'two more years not merely under the miasma of this budget, but under the even more mephitic exhalations that might be expected to emanate from its successor or its two successors ... two more years of socialistic experiments, two more years of tampering with the Church ...' It was all like King David who, when rebuked by a higher power for making a census of his people, presumably with a view to increased taxation ... evaded the punishment 'which was to fall on himself and chose that which was to fall on his people'.

But then, Curzon didn't believe that any punishment would fall on this latterday Israel. The secret of his insouciance was a belief, as mistaken as it was comforting, that a government bluff would be called. He rested his case on the Lords challenge against Gladstone's paper duties in 1860. 'What happened? The House of Commons did then what I believe they are going to do now. They passed a number of resolutions affirming the privilege of the House of Commons ... But in the next year Mr Gladstone inaugurated a new financial era ... he embodied for the first time in a single bill all the measures which it had previously been the fashion to send up one by one.' The Tories had accepted that. 'But my point is that the House of Lords did not on that occasion surrender their rights ... they could not be extinguished by the vindictive act of a minister in the other House ... If now your lordships choose to revive them, they can only be extinguished by an overwhelming pronouncement on the part of the country.' So the lords would be acting within their rights. They acknowledged general Commons supremacy in ordinary finance. But 'we have the power and the duty, always enjoyed and frequently acted upon, to see that that right is not abused to carry through, under the guise of financial measures, policies or principles which have not been approved by the people.'

Curzon, for whom the word 'supercilious' is inadequate, believed that 'the country will be quite sufficiently intelligent to see where the real revolution lies'. The Liberal Party had been committed by the lord chancellor 'to destruction of the veto of this House and the subversion of the ancient balance and equipoise of our constitution'. Though willing to contemplate reform of the House, he hoped that people would make it clear that 'a second chamber shall not be a mere phantom, rendered equally impotent and ridiculous by the paralysis of its powers and scarcely worthy to deliberate if it could only delay'. But this reformed House should be like the present one, only more so, representing 'the stability, the character and the experience of the state and one which, like your lordships' House, will be independent and fearless and strong'.[3]

Courtney of Penwith, a Liberal, dragged the question back from the baroque pinnacles of Curzon to ask a low political point. There had been a survey of constituencies in *The Times*

– we were thirty-six years ahead of George Gallup's first political opinion polls, but the *Times* investigator was doing extraordinarily well. The indication was not for 'a victory for the opposition, but that perhaps the supporters of the opposition in the other House after the General Election will approach to something like equality with the avowed supporters of the government. There will, however, remain two independent bodies of members – the nationalists and the Labour Party.' Courtney became interrogative.

> Are you pleased at the suggestion that the nationalists and the Labour Party should hold the balance in that assembly? . . . The nationalists are not very fond of your lordships; and the Labour members, they do not feel any great respect for your lordships. Remember, however narrow may be the balance between the ministerialists and the opposition . . . the very first question raised there must be the question of the power of this House over the budget and the question of the relationship between these two Houses . . . This is the future you are very lightheartedly preparing to encounter.'[4]

It was a simple statement of what across the next twenty-one months was going to happen. Courtney, interestingly enough, had been described by Gladstone twenty years before as a 'lover of paradox, the advocate of women's franchise, minority votes, bi-metallism and the rest'.[5] But he was talking simple truth here.

Lord Montague of Beaulieu applied himself amiably to an index of enterprise. When a man founds a family or has aspirations to establish himself as a power in the land, the first thing he does is to take out a licence for armorial bearings. The number taken out had fallen – from 56,792 ten years before to 55,449 in 1907–8. Then again, 'As far as I can make out the number of game licences issued has seriously diminished. The number in 1908–9 was 73,885 as against 68,331 this year.' He would not weary the House, 'but the effect of this budget will be, I believe, to intensify and increase the poverty of some of the most worthy members of the community . . . and hit the small family and businessman.'[6]

Lord Denbigh, reverting to the money-fleeing-the-country line, quoted 'a friend of mine, a man who made a large fortune in the colonies', who, turning down a piece of good business in Britain said, 'Ever since Lloyd George laid it down that nobody is entitled to what he has got except the man who has not got it, I have sold every English investment except my land, and don't intend to buy any more.'[7] Lord Harris was convinced that an attack on the House of Lords was long-planned Liberal policy. 'This quarrel has been forced upon your lordships deliberately, coolly and calmly by His Majesty's ministers.' Campbell-Bannerman, in his Albert Hall speech, had said that what had been the pleasure-ground of the rich should be the treasure-ground of the poor. 'Why, one of the original intentions of the bill was to tax every pleasure-ground in the country, whether it belonged to the poor or the rich.'[8]

The eighty-year-old Lord Stanmore, a Gordon in spite of the suburban title, and a former governor of Trinidad, Mauritius, Fiji, New Zealand and Ceylon, described a tropical bee which 'deposits a spider for its grub to eat when it comes out of the egg . . . it injects a fluid into the spider which at once has the property of absolutely paralysing every faculty of the spider but at the same time keeping it alive. The fate of that spider is the fate which His Majesty's government intend for us.'[9] No one suggested to Lord Stanmore that the House of Lords, which, he said, he 'would rather see destroyed than degraded', was perhaps best seen as the indigestible part of the constitution.

Cawdor, friend of King Edward, said that 'the case began long ago. It has nothing to do with the budget; this declaration of war started some years back.' He quoted Campbell-Bannerman, who had stated that 'the power of the other

House to alter or reject bills passed by this House should be restricted by law so as to secure that within the limits of a single Parliament, the decision of the Commons should prevail'. He did not add, when talking about declarations of war, that Campbell-Bannerman had said this during the Commons debate following rejection of its Education Bill, hardly itself a pacific act. But Cawdor had a vivid notion of what would be involved: single-chamber government which would 'amount to a suspension of the Septennial Act and the establishment of the Rump Parliament again . . . I do not know how you would get rid of it without a revolution.'[10]

It was 30 November 1909. The debate was drawing to an exhausted close and the final words fell to Crewe, a gentlemanly, good-tempered, reassuring sort of Liberal, personally close to Asquith, but one who could be elegantly injurious. The result was known well enough. That, after all, was what the debate was really about. Their lordships could pass a contentious Liberal measure only by an act of conscious restraint, and they were accommodating only when Lansdowne asked. They were voting on Lansdowne's amendment of rejection, and would do so by a majority in hundreds.

Their lordships had accepted, 'grudgingly I am afraid, but still you have accepted the principle of old-age pensions'. Even under the contributory scheme they would have preferred, 'unless you were prepared to postpone the benefit of pensions for some forty or fifty years, you must at any rate raise in the present year a sum not much less than we are now asking the country to provide'. What was really at issue was that the Lords thought government methods of raising the money revolutionary, 'and you consider that that justifies a revolution on your part, and in order to meet that revolution, you are forming yourselves not into a Committee of Supply but into a Committe of Public Safety to refuse supplies.'

As to tacking, and the government's 'vindictive motives', Crewe said wearily that they were not tacking. They had a right, if a bill was rejected, to come back a different way. As for their motives, 'even if our minds are churning with the most hideous sentiments towards all respectable persons – such as millionaires, brewers and others – that has nothing whatever to do with "tacking".' And he had a little jab at Tariff Reform. What sort of taxes would be raised under it? There was Viscount Ridley, who 'is prepared to get it all out of the foreigner. Like Caesar Augustus, he is prepared to issue a decree that all the world should be taxed.' Lord Salisbury wanted to tax the rich on luxuries. But that wouldn't work through protection. Luxuries, with the exception of champagne, tended to be made in this country – racehorses, yachts, expensive motor cars, deer forests – 'what form of sumptuary laws the noble Marquess may have in mind to tax these luxuries, I do not know.'

But having mocked gaily, Crewe grew serious. He had come to the Lords in 1886 and had spent most of the intervening time in opposition. 'I can say with all honesty that I cannot recall a single case when I or my noble friends ... did the slightest good to himself or any human being by his attendance in the House ... I cannot recall a case when any amendment of substance to any of the bills of the then governments were modified at our instance.' Lansdowne should know that 'although I hope I do not underrate the value of the privileges of this House I cannot look upon them with exactly the same eyes as he does'.

In fact, the Lords were trying to expand their powers. 'For instance, I never heard before the plain statement made by Lord Curzon that it was a reasonable thing for this House to have the power of dissolving Parliament.' Things had changed for good. In the past the two Houses had 'jogged along together as acquaintances jog along who are not perhaps consumed by a burning affection for each other but are at the same time prepared to do business together'. But after that night, 'The two Houses, regarding them still as people, will barely be on speaking terms.' There was speculative talk, and there had been an unregarded report on Lords reform, but 'My lords, it is an unreformed House of Lords which is throwing out this budget . . . If you think that any of us on this side of the House welcome this crisis you are entirely mistaken, we are compelled to face it . . . after the action your lordships have thought fit to take tonight.' The government had to seek guarantees, 'if necessary, and if there be no other way, guarantees fenced about and guarded by the force of statute – guarantees which will prevent that indiscriminate destruction of our legislation of which your work tonight is the climax and the crown'.[11]

It was very soft-spoken and courteous, and there would be delays, hesitations and parlays along the road. But the logic of the situation was clear. What Crewe had indicated – statutory definition (and diminution) of the Lords – had to follow if they voted down the Finance Bill. They voted Contents 75, Not Contents 350.

18

Crocodile Shooting and its Difficulties

Francis Knollys, secretary to the King, put it most succinctly to Sir Almeric Fitzroy, clerk to the Privy Council. He observed 'very gravely and emphatically, that he thought the Lords mad'. The Commons, invited by Asquith, passed a resolution declaring that 'the action of the House of Lords in refusing to pass into law the financial provisions made by this House for the service of the year is a breach of the constitution and a usurpation of the rights of the Commons'.[1]

There was now one thing which a government could do and had to do – dissolve Parliament and seek new elections. The contest which followed would relate to the conduct of the Lords, though a good deal less than Liberals might have wished. It turned also on the budget itself. Conservatives, while not denying their Tariff Reform credentials, hardly popped corks or swung from the chandeliers on the topic for the very good reason that they had no illusion that it was a popular policy. The leadership was caught between a party captured by protectionist zealots and an electorate which suspected that food prices would go up. An adjustable scale of enthusiasm between the two markets made that leadership affirm Tariff Reform – very quietly.

The Irish, meanwhile, major losers by the spirits taxes

– a rare example of Welsh and Irish priorities clashing –
consoled themselves by thinking ahead to the possibilities of
Home Rule and the delectable circumstances of a government
not only friendly but minority. The biggest Unionist concern
was to suggest that the government wanted single-chamber
government, and much of the rhetoric of the Lords' Finance
Bill debate would be thriftily recycled. The Tories also fought
this election in the darkened sky of a coming storm. The term
'Tory press' had been a broad expression for some time.
The Morning Post, Standard and *National Review* were
all fighting the Liberals with hopes of defeating Balfour;
the *Glasgow Herald* and *Daily Dispatch* were for Balfour
but also for free trade; the *Daily Graphic* was split on the
issue. The Tory *Daily Express* was roundly abusive of the
Tory *Spectator* for its free-trade views. The *Morning Post*
in particular, under the virulent editorship of Fabian Ware
and the less moderate proprietorial hand of Lady Bathurst,
cut itself off from a piece of serious revenue by its politics.
Balfour's machine preferred to place advertisements in papers
friendlier to the leader of the Tory Party.[2]

The *Morning Post*, in the hands of Fifth Monarchy Tariff
Reformers, had a leader-writer, Richard Jebb, standing, with
his editor's full approval, at Marylebone East as an independent, specifically as a spoiler against the free-trading Lord
Robert Cecil. (Cecil withdrew from the contest, a moderate
protectionist won and Jebb came third.)[3] It was rather like
the 'Referendum' candidacies of 1997.

But for all the excursions, it was possible, then as now, for
a Tory manager to remark: 'Let me say how admirably our
party is served by the *Daily Mail*. It is the most potent auxili-
ary. Everyone reads it; it is a brief for all our speakers. Its arguments, its facts, its criticisms supply the best and most modern
ammunition.'[4] Jack Sandars, Balfour's adjutant, was able to
say that at a time when another Northcliffe paper, *The Times*,
was wobbling, 'giving prominence to Winston Churchill who
flatters and toadies to him in a sickening way'.[5]

The Liberal press – *Chronicle, News, Manchester Guardian* – were smaller in numbers but more solid, though they grumbled a good deal about the unwillingness of Asquith's Liberals to be as Liberal, not least about Home Rule, as they were. And Tory divisions gratified Lloyd George, who amused himself during the election by blaming the Tory press for the stand taken on the budget which had so undermined sensible Conservatives: 'All the weightiest papers on the Conservative side were against it, *The Times, Birmingham Post, Glasgow Herald, Spectator* and, I think, the *Yorkshire Post*,' while the *Observer*, edited by 'the Mad Mullah' J.L. Garvin, was the 'rabidest of the lot'. Meanwhile, said Lloyd George, the *Daily Mail*, after much dithering, 'came in at the last moment [and] placed at the disposal of the wreckers that passion for accuracy of statement which has been so dear to it'.[6]

Whatever their differences, the Conservative press managed some heavy ferocity against what the *Daily Telegraph* called 'the Yellow Parliament' elected in 1906 – elected through 'a policy of social bribes and imperial betrayal'. The *Telegraph* promised the 'temperate Christian tone we adopt against a bitter opponent'. 'No Englishman,' it proclaimed on 15 January 1910, by way of fanfare to Balfour's message to the country, 'with an ear to hear the trumpet call of patriotism, can fail to respond to the ringing summons of the Unionist leaders.'[7] That plural, 'leaders', was significant. The manifesto was joint and signed by Joseph Chamberlain. Paralysed since a stroke in 1906, Chamberlain still clung to the shoulders of Balfour like the Old Man of the Sea invoked by Curzon. But, as always, the *National Review* spoke for the raw right. Britain was 'in the hands of a needy, greedy gang of political adventurers, mostly lawyers', with 'scarcely a spark of patriotism among them', who were 'cynically indifferent to the future of these islands, while the word "Empire" never pollutes their lips'. It had no more respect for the moderates who claim the respect of decent folk to which they are no longer entitled since their abject surrender to a couple of blatant Demagogues [*sic*] who live only to injure public interests and to advance their own . . . One is a hysterical Welsh attorney with a positively insane hatred of England . . . totally unfit for office, whose chancellorship of the exchequer has probably cost this country some £200,000,000. The other is a renegade who only became a radical politician because he had failed to become a unionist minister.[8]

Reverting to that favourite topic a few pages into its copy, the *National* had another go at Lloyd George, speaking of 'the devilish temper of this foolish and foul-mouthed Demagogue' whose 'Machiavellian scheme for capturing the government and making England an appendage of Wales'[9] had miscarried. Abuse was not only directed at the two future wartime leaders of Britain. In furtherance of its campaign for more dreadnoughts, under the heading 'Treason in High Places', the *National* wondered 'how far aliens of the Brunner-Mond type who control and inspire influential radical newspapers which used at one time to do lip service to a Big Navy – worked for the relative weakening of Great Britain?'[10] The two ugly sisters Xenophobia and Paranoia enjoyed the rocking chair at the *National*, with even Lloyd George's Welshness counting as a moral defect. The *National* was extreme, but it was a full part of the Conservative family and its hatred for 'traitors' and 'aliens' (two future prime ministers and the creators of the British chemical industry) simply reflects the tearing, distressed and unhinged state into which so much Conservative opinion had brought itself.

Blackwood's, feeling oppressed by the 'social-radical' threat embodied by Lloyd George, which aspired to 'a world in which there will be no dukes', found comfort in a speech of Curzon's on 15 December stating that 'all civilisation has been the work of aristocracies'. The speech was made in Oldham, from which town civilisation derived the largest quantity of cotton yarn spun anywhere in the world, but one which was defective in the armigerous qualities.

Even so, Charles Whibley was comforted by the soundness of the lower orders, remarking in his best noble-superb manner: 'We are very well aware that among our peasantry and artisans are to be found the same sympathies and the same appreciation of the social order as animate those above them.' But looking ahead, *Blackwood's* feared that re-elected Liberals would forge ahead with Irish Home Rule. So the staunch yeoman should beware. 'We may however just remind the agricultural labourer that as Home Rule will certainly make Ireland poorer, the Irish peasantry will flock over to England in increasing numbers and lower the demand for native labour in every village in the kingdom.'

There was a hint of social concern in Balfour's speeches at this time and *Blackwood's* perfunctorily concurred. 'The Poor Law must be reconstructed and some better methods than state-organised schemes must be found for the relief of the unemployed.' This boiled down to Tariff Reform which kept out foreigners. The government was diverting 'the capital which under different conditions would provide for our own unemployed into German and American pockets'. Conservatives, in the election as in the Lords debate, made much of export of capital. 'The weakening of all those guarantees on which men are accustomed to rely who by dint of perseverance and self-denial hope to build up large private fortunes, is sapping the character of the English middle classes, the backbone of our population and the cradle of our wealth.'

And for *Blackwood's*, social sympathy was a crumb compared to the loaf of its concern for social discipline. The demagogues had got at the nation. 'The insidious doctrines of the demagogue have found their way to the ear of the soldier. In public houses, in tap-rooms, the author has heard the soldier openly discussing the shortcomings and quality of his officers ... In short, the understanding of the working classes has become honeycombed with lies – lies with the express purpose of reducing the influence of the the upper and middle classes'.

It was all the fault of the board schools, a lifelong obsession of Whibley's. 'Here the teachers, risen from the masses, taught individualism to the rising generation. National discipline, patriotism, *esprit de corps*, these things were not for the working man.' Demagogues and board school teachers 'have driven great wedges in, and are now preparing to complete the work of demolition by sawing through the trunk of the tree of state. In this process the chancellor of the exchequer has been top sawyer . . . he brought the board school influence into the forefront of the parliamentary battle. He carried the role of the kerbstone demagogue into the Cabinet . . . so that we have seen the electoral campaign of 1910 debauched by a display of unmannerly hyperbole that has no parallel in British politics.'[11]

Blackwood's was a general magazine stocked with stories, historical pieces and travelogues as well as political comment. This indictment was followed in the next (February) issue by articles entitled 'Muttra and its Sport' (sub-headed 'Hunting Wild Pig'), 'Tent-life in India' and, perhaps suitably for those enraged and frustrated by Lloyd George, 'Crocodile Shooting and its Difficulties'.[12]

For all these anxieties, and the demagoguery in which Conservative politicians and journalists also occasionally indulged, the General Election of December-January 1909–10 was not excessively exciting. Lansdowne at Plymouth, and Balfour in his City of London election address, spoke of the things they had been speaking of for some time: single-chamber government, the menace of socialism and, in muted fashion, Tariff Reform. Austen Chamberlain proclaimed by way of his manifesto that the Liberals were bent on destroying both the constitution and the Act of Union. There was also some talk (on both sides) about pushing Church disestablishment beyond Wales. The more virulent Tariff Reformers tried to extinguish free trade as a permitted opinion within the narrowing church of Conservatism. The campaign of Richard Jebb of the *Morning Post* was part of a movement, 'the Confederacy,' reaching up to Austen Chamberlain, Bonar Law and Jesse Collings, the Chamberlain henchman of 1886, and still henching, which set itself to split the vote against any free-trade Tory candidate.

Lloyd George's unmannerly hyperbole was directed towards a great tease of the upper class. 'Neither Ireland nor Wales can ever obtain its rights except by marching over the ruins of the House of Lords,' he said in Caernarvon before observing of those who complained about higher level taxes, 'Many wish that they had £3,000 on which to pay tax.' And he used this constituency occasion to reminisce about collecting wood for Uncle Lloyd's household in Llanystumdwy, recalling that after a great storm he always came back with an armful. 'We may be in for a winter of storms which will rock the forest, but when the storm clears there will be something brought within the reach of the people.'[13] Lloyd George was in his element. The 'unmannerly hyperbole' was deftly aimed at delighting his own people and driving the Tories mad.

Peers encountered rougher treatment from public meetings than, as it were, unadorned Conservatives. Acland-Hood, their chief whip, tried to tell Watchet that the budget was 'socialistic' and heard 'Rot!'. But that was nothing: any peer venturing from his moated grange to mix it with voters had a hard time. The Duke of Norfolk was received in Taunton with 'a rousing reception mingled with groans from a small section of the audience'. He was luckier than Lord Ampthill who, in Kettering, 'spoke amid considerable uproar and resumed his seat without completing his speech'. Lord Denbigh, who would later figure on the roll-call of diehards, tried roughing it at Finsbury Town Hall. He too 'spoke amid considerable uproar'. The chairman, appealing to the hecklers for order, described them as 'unEnglish and ungentlemanly'. When his Lordship – 3,000 acres in Flintshire and Leicestershire[14] –

protested that it was no crime to own land, a voice demanded, 'Where did you get it from?'

Nor was all the hostility unreasoning. When Denbigh suggested that the government planned to nationalise land, 'a voice at the back shouted, "That's not in the manifesto. You don't even know what's in it."' As *The Times* put it, 'Throughout the remainder of his speech Lord Denbigh was subjected to a continuous series of interruptions, the noise at the back of the hall becoming louder as he continued.'[15] Perhaps the hardest time of all was had by Lord Camperdown, who chose, heroically, to speak at Motherwell, where he was 'received with a stream of booing, hisses and cries of "Down with the Lords" and "Here he is, a real, live Lord." His Lordship, arguing against the land clauses, was received with cries of "Rot." Socialists, said Lord Camperdown, were more honest than Asquith and said they did not want a Second Chamber. A voice: "It's rotten," and amid great disorder, a resolution approving the Lords' decision was lost by a large majority.'

Lord Londonderry, who did get a hearing in West Hartlepool, as robust a place as Finsbury, said that the government had sold themselves to socialism and [Irish] nationalism. Their lordships were resisting 'ill-considered legislation being forced on the people by a tyrannical temporary majority'. After Asquith was done, 'any radical or liberal or socialist government' – he considered these to be synonymous – would be 'an absolutely despotic autocracy . . . it would be possible for a radical government to introduce measures for ruining and plundering any industry of which they did not approve'. It would be possible to impose taxation of Church property, plunder the licensed trade and plunder 'loyal and prosperous Ulster'.

Curzon's account of aristocracy to Oldham, described by *The Times* of 16 December as 'more courageous than politic', was 'a good deal interrupted and there was even something like disorder when he made those remarks [a quotation from Renan] to the effect that "all civilisation has been the work of aristocracies". However, 'the Liberals present were a small body and for the most part exercised a proper self-control.'[16]

Curzon was at his most superabundantly disdainful at the Oldham Empire and conceded no fault or flaw – Balliol made flesh. 'We members of the House of Lords have nothing to apologise for, nothing to extenuate, nothing to be ashamed of.' He was also very stylish, using at least one phrase which deserved permanence: 'We are not landgrabbers, blackmailers, thieves and poachers. We are merely the broken glass on the top of the wall to keep out the poachers who are the Radical Party.'

Having suggested that heredity ran beyond escutcheoned limits and that there were hereditary bankers, lawyers, soldiers, clergymen and doctors, 'and, I dare say, hereditary cotton spinners', Curzon contrasted the venality of the Commons with the moral elevation of his own House.

Members of the House of Lords by virtue of their composition are not exposed to all the temptations of popular election. I have been an MP and I know pretty well what they are. You have to keep a pretty stiff upper lip and a very firm back in order to resist them. In the House of Lords there is no danger of that . . . we are not threatened by gusts, we are not pestered by crotchet-mongers running around to force us to agree with their particular fads.

Then again, the Lords were a gallant crew. 'One hundred and eighty of our number served His Majesty in the regular army, twenty in the navy. I say nothing of the officers and governors (cheers) and ministers in our foreign possessions and colonies. I say nothing of diplomatists and ambassadors.' Lloyd George had complained that there were no sailors, pilots, miners, railway guards, weavers or spinners in the Lords. 'That is quite true, but then, neither are there any field marshals or great governors-general in the House of Commons. I would be delighted to see representatives of the working class in the House of Commons. For my own part, I am not in the least averse to seeing them in the House of Lords. But is it not clear that the place where they can properly sit is the House of Commons?'

Then, after remarking,' What cant it is, what insufferable hypocrisy it is to talk about an effete oligarchy into which you are perpetually pouring radical recruits', and regretting that radicals should 'vituperate us as a House of landlords when a great many of us do not own a single acre of land', he turned to the ideas of Ernest Renan. 'If for four centuries there had been a very widely extended franchise there would have been no change of dynasty, no toleration of dissent, not even an accurate calendar. The threshing machine, loom, spinning jenny and possibly the steam engine would have been forbidden.' (Not altogether nonsense if you worked in the Fleet Street of the 1970s.)

Nor were these omissions the only horrors which representative government could inflict. 'Without the restraint of a second chamber, a government could pass Home Rule, it could weaken to a disastrous extent the army and navy. It could disestablish the Church, it could enforce Woman Suffrage [sic] or even manhood suffrage and modify or even abolish the monarchy itself.'

Curzon had his largely Conservative audience with him. Lancashire, with its Protestant nativist strand, where the Earl of Derby was called King of Lancashire and Lord Sefton was hardly less influential further west, was disputed territory, not the radical geology of County Durham or urban Scotland. Curzon was able to end with a peroration of perorations. After refusing on behalf of the House of Lords to 'sink into being members of a paralysed and useless body', he turned to the British nation in all its grandeur.

This country of ours, its extended Empire, vast accumulated wealth, enormous trade, prodigious responsibilities
pressing upon it, mighty and glorious traditions in the
past, universal adhesion to caution, order and sobriety
and freedom – do they think that a country such as this
is going to dispense with all checks and all guarantees,
all criticism, all control? (Cries of 'No, no'.) Is it going
to hand over its destinies in the future to an unfettered
House of Commons?

He did not doubt that 'here, as throughout the country, the
answer you return to that question will be "No, no, a thousand
times no."' It was the sort of speech which could only have been
delivered before the First World War.

Oldham was well served in this election. It had already
heard Churchill speak of the Tory document as 'a manifesto
which makes so few things manifest . . . the flattest, plainest,
nakedest contradiction in terms ever recorded in the history
of a great party', and the overall Tory case, 'a weak, maudlin
whine of selfish riches'. But going on to Burnley, Churchill
replied to Curzon, who 'had treated a great public meeting to
a prize essay on the Middle Ages'. And perhaps with this in
mind, he reminded Burnley of Lansdowne's first reaction to
the old-age pensions legislation of 1908: 'A system to destroy
the thrift and wreck the self-respect of the working classes.'
(In this election, Conservative politicians, led by Balfour, were
giving furious assurances that if re-elected, they would treat
the old-age pension as sacred!)

Lloyd George, speaking to a gathering of Nonconformists
in the Queen's Hall on 17 December, continued to mock.
Since his audience suffered no apostolic guidance, he mocked
the bishops. Some of them had behaved very well during
the budget debate. 'Actually five out of the twenty-four
voted for taxes on the rich.' He mocked Curzon, 'who had
quoted a great agnostic writer with approval'. And, being
among believers, but still Lloyd George, he responded to

the aristocratic claim with pious kitsch, but spiked it with wit. He thought that civilisation, rather than being the work of aristocracies, went back to a certain carpenter and his disciples. Most of them were fishermen, and 'the heaviest swell among them was an exciseman'. Only Lloyd George could have got a joke out of St Matthew.

And he turned his scorn on aristocratic involvement with elections not so long since. In those days, it had been ' "Squire So-and-So is a Tory with 300 tenants. Put down 300 voters." Those men's convictions, in the jargon of lawyers, were "covenants which ran with the land." ' *The Times*, he said, 'talks about the House of Lords as a jury. All I say is, "We challenge the panel." ' [17]

The relationship between Lloyd George and the landed classes was summed up by Viscount Middleton in Northampton. He had 'never read a speech by Lloyd George which was not intended to create dissension and division'. Lloyd George 'talked to the poor man and set him against the rich, to the labourer and set him against his employer, to the free churchman and set him against the Church, to Irishmen to set their minds on separation'. Remarking on Lloyd George's 'want of self-respect, the language which characterised his ultimatum', Middleton wished he had been 'brought up differently'. [18]

Lord Middleton's concern about 'separation' was not gratuitous. John Redmond had chosen this moment to commit the Irish nationalists to Asquith by calling on the Irish vote on the mainland to support the Liberals. Redmond was being statesmanlike. For the budget, for spirituous rather than constitutional reasons, was not popular in Ireland, and Tim Healy and William O'Brien would withdraw, taking a dozen MPs with them to run as independent candidates. But Redmond's sacrifice conferred a favour not to be enjoyed without censure. Conservatives congregated around a favourite subject: the Irish threat.

A hint of the bitterness he would shortly expend on Ulster

'Ah. Have another cup of tea.'
W. E. Gladstone

'You would not confide free representative
institutions to Hottentots.'
The 3rd Marquess of Salisbury

Sore throat from roaring.
Colonel Saunderson.

'She *is* a nation.' Charles Parnell.

'A consistent Jacobin.' John Morley.

'Pretty Fanny' *and* 'Bloody Balfour'.
A.J. Balfour

DOOMED!

The Home Rule Bill is mugged by Salisbury and *(far right)* Hartington.

Above left: 'I notice an increasing exaltation of spirit.' Augustine Birrell.

Above right: 'If the wholesome methods of old were still in force, he would stand at the bar of the nation, an impeached and guilty minister.' H.H. Asquith.

Right: Lord Lansdowne surrounded by shot-down Liberal legislation.

STANDING FOR HIS TRADE PHOTOGRAPH (CHRISTMAS AND NEW YEAR SEASON, 1908-9).
(Lord L-nsd-wne.)

Above left: Roi Fainéant. Lord Rosebery.

Above right: 'I don't like him. I really hate him.' Joseph Chamberlain.

Left: Lansdowne waves through Campbell-Bannerman's trade-union legislation.

THE BETTER PART OF VALOUR.

LANSDOWNE. "*I* BAR YOUR WAY? MY DEAR FELLOW! WHY, YOU'VE GOT A MANDATE!"
TRADE DISPUTES BILL. "WELL, SO HAD MY FRIEND HERE."
LANSDOWNE. "AH! BUT NOT SUCH A BIG ONE!"

Right: Rosebery's compromise Lords Reform Bill at a private showing.

Below left: 'I say, enough of this foolery.' Sir Henry Campbell-Bannerman.

Below right: 'Stirring up the worst passions... gross vulgarity.' David Lloyd George.

THE PROBLEM PICTURE.

SCENE—*Selecting Committee's Room at the Peers' Royal Academy.*

LORD ROSEBERY. "THAT'S MINE. PRETTY GOOD, EH?"
LORD LANSDOWNE. "H'M, I CAN'T SAY I QUITE——"
LORD CURZON. "I'M SURE I COULD IMPROVE IT."
LORD HALSBURY. "TAKE IT AWAY!"

THE VETO GAME.

Mr. Asquith (to Lord Lansdowne). "WHILE YOU'RE THINKING OUT YOUR NEXT MOVE, I'LL JUST SEE TO A FEW LITTLE DOMESTIC DETAILS."

Above: Asquith, with his parliamentary majority, could play a long game.

Below: The Parliament Bill passed on a day when the temperature touched 95 degrees in the shade.

Perspiring Customer. "PH-H-H! BRING ME SOMETHING COOL."
Waitress. "YES, SIR. WOULD YOU LIKE AN ICE!"
Perspiring Customer. "NO, NO; SOMETHING COOLER THAN THAT."

THE OLD TROJAN.

LORD LANSDOWNE. "DON'T LUG THAT INFERNAL MACHINE INTO THE CITADEL. THE THING'S FULL OF ENEMIES."
LORD HALSBURY. "I KNOW. THAT'S WHERE MY HEROISM COMES IN."

Above left: The hereditary principle. Lord Willoughby de Broke.

Above right: Lord Halsbury did his best to let in the 500.

Right: Halsbury would fight anybody.

"A SORT OF" WELLINGTON.

LORD HALSBURY (*bursting with military tags*). "UP, LORDS, AND AT 'EM."
SCEPTICAL PEER. "AT WHOM?"
LORD HALSBURY. "WELL, I WANT TO DAMAGE THE GOVERNMENT FOR CHOICE; BUT ANYHOW DAMAGE SOMEBODY."

'A steadily regimented thing.' James Craig (Lord Craigavon).

'Come back to Erin.' Sir Edward Carson.

'Ireland for the Irish… England for the aliens.' Leo Maxse.

Holding Ireland for the Empire. Eoin MacNeill.

came from Bonar Law, speaking in Newcastle-on-Tyne. He knew what to fear. If the Lords lost their veto 'in the course of a single session and a half under the new system, then by means of the guillotine they would grant Home Rule to Ireland. The next step would be to disestablish the Church of England, then,' he added rather lamely, 'to pass a licensing bill in the name of temperance.'

He would be echoed by the resolution of a gathering of Scottish Liberal Unionists that 'since Mr Gladstone sold his party to Mr Parnell in 1886, there has been no such immoral transaction fraught with sudden disaster for the UK as the accord established between Asquith and Redmond. The loyal Protestants of Ulster are to be put under the heel of the disloyal Catholics of the south.'

The element of scare, popular with all parties and a particular favourite of the Conservative Party, flourished. The naval scare was neatly dovetailed with the Irish scare in a speech by Lord Cawdor in Leeds which, having compared the Liberals to Bulgarian revolutionaries (who had abolished the Bulgarian upper chamber), demanded how the establishment of a German naval base in Belfast could be prevented if Home Rule were granted.[19] That charge stood in interesting contrast to statements recorded in the first section of this study; statements made independently by the leading Ulstermen Craig and Crawford and, before them, Thomas MacKnight of the *Northern Whig*, that the German army would be welcome in Dublin in preference to a government of Catholics and nationalists.

But Ireland was a treat in store. The election had ranged across the budget proper, naval preparation and free trade versus protection. It had always been certain, given the ordinary wear and tear of a parliamentary term, and one badly frustrated, to heavily reduce an exceptionally large majority. As the results slowly trickled in across late January, it did so, giving the Conservatives 116 net gains over 1906 and bringing them to 273 against a Liberal total of 275.

The Tories had done well in England, where they now had a majority (239 to the government's 191) and, as Asquith put it, had achieved their greatest successes 'in the smaller boroughs and cathedral cities'. They were gainers in places such as Bath, Bedford, Cambridge, Colchester, Exeter, Gloucester, Kidderminster, Rochester, Salisbury and Warwick, and in rural home counties seats. They also had success in naval and shipyard towns like Devonport, Chatham and Portsmouth, beneficiaries of the naval scare and where there was a healthy self-interest in building more ships.

But they had had very little impact in industrial England. It was all very well for Tariff Reformers to seek the extermination of free-trade Conservative candidacies, but protection did them no favours in Lancashire and Yorkshire, where they scrambled only 6 gains, 3 of them non-industrial. To a degree Barchester swung Tory and Coketown stayed with the Liberals. Celtic Britain was unmoved by either their lordships' duty to the constitution or the threat to the union. The 82 Liberal seats provided in 1910 by Scotland and Wales, had been no more than 83 in 1906. On top of which the Liberals actually won 12 seats, including all those involved in by-elections, which had played their part in nerving Tory leadership and Lords for rejection and the great gamble.

In terms of actual parliamentary control, Labour, upon which the government could rely for everything that mattered, though down 11, commanded 40 seats, and among the Irish (including the O'Brien element) were 82 nationalists ready to accommodate constitutional *quid* for devolutionary *quo*. The working majority required for removing the Lords' veto was not the combined well and church door of 1906, but it would suffice.

19

Lord Crewe's Champagne

There was one election speech whose consequences outlasted a couple of days' impact and riposte. It was made by Asquith and, coming from that prudential and scrupulous statesman, was the more remarkable. In December 1909 he had spoken at a monster meeting at the Albert Hall to an all-male audience – something made necessary by the violent activities of suffragettes – saying that he and his colleagues would not 'submit again to the rebuffs and humiliation of the last four years. We shall not assume office, and we shall not hold office, unless we can secure the safeguards which experience shows to be necessary for the legislative utility and honour of the party of progress.'[1]

Churchill had already declared, while hurrying through Lancashire, that 'no Liberal government will at any future time bear the burden of office without securing guarantees that the reform [Lords' veto abolition] should be carried out.' And Lloyd George had told the National Liberal Club on 3 December that he would not wish to serve in a Liberal government 'unless full powers are accorded to it which will enable it to place on the statute book a measure ensuring that the House of Commons in future can carry ... Liberal and progressive measures in the course of a single

Parliament either with or without the sanction of the House of Lords.'[2]

Nobody was lying, but the optimism and uplift of all three speeches implied more than determination to see that such powers were obtained. By way of their immense confidence, they implied that guarantees, the King's guarantees for mass ennoblement to vote down the Lords' negative, had already been secured. They had not. Asquith, on meeting Parliament, had to announce the tribulation of Sisyphus: the rock had to be rolled up the same slope from the same bottom. He was, as Roy Jenkins remarks, probably exhausted. He also took an unnecessary knock from a rather blustering speech of Redmond's and from the independent assertions of a Labour Conference in February.

With the real options of the Irish and the natural sympathies of Labour seen in perspective, these were minor muscle-ripplings and not to be minded, but for some time Asquith seemed bowed by the prospect of not being able to govern. For an interim lassitude ruled. Altogether more upsetting had been the King's message through his secretary, Knollys: 'Not justified in creating new peers (say 300) until after a second General Election . . . thought you should know this now . . . The King regards the policy of your government as tantamount to the destruction of the House of Lords and he thinks that before a large creation of peers is embarked upon or threatened, the country should be acquainted with the particular project for accomplishing such destruction.'[3] The words – 'destruction', 'threatened' – hardly mask the royal hostility. And who from a position of neutrality uses the word 'tantamount'?

Most comment on the King's conduct has been indulgent. Put plainly, the head of the House of Hanover was not ready to back a re-elected majority of the Commons in destroying the veto of inheritors until it should painfully repeat across the country what it had just as painfully done. And such unwillingness rather implied a profound hope that it would fail to do so and fall. Certainly he wanted to see the back of the main reformers. He told Haldane – admittedly according to Haldane – 'This government may not last. I say nothing of some of my ministers, but I wish you may very long be my minister.'[4]

The best reading to be put on the King's action is that he favoured instead some form of Lords Reform. On the other hand, Asquith had been warned by Knollys a fortnight before the Albert Hall speech that the creation involved would be too heavy. And after the speech – on 15 December – Knollys again gave due warning of the need for a second election.

Asquith had to break the bad news to the Commons. He did so on 21 February. 'I tell the House quite frankly that I have received no such guarantee and that I have asked no such guarantee.' In rationalisation mode, he added that it would not do 'to ask in advance for a blank authority for an indefinite exercise of the royal prerogative in regard to a measure which has never been submitted to or approved by the House of Commons'.[5] That might be literally so, but Asquith had been hoping not to have to ask. He had looked for pennies dropping in the mind of the sovereign. The Liberals in the Commons were loyal to Asquith, but they were badly disappointed and a group of thirty went to him demanding concentration on the Lords veto. *Per contra*, both Grey and Haldane were instinctively drawn to schemes for reforming the Lords, the watering down of veto abolition with a sort of meliorism directed at the aristocracy.

Whibley in *Blackwood's* was troubled by no such subtleties. He had no difficulty in interpreting what had happened and producing a marvellous cascade of anti-logic. Asquith was the prisoner of Manchester; worse, he was the prisoner of the Manchester Catholics. (Asquith had pointed out that whatever else was achieved in this Parliament, it would not include Tariff Reform. Manchester and the rest of Lancashire, where the Tories had had hopes, had come down in the election for free trade.) 'Birmingham is nothing,' wrote *Blackwood's,*

> Liverpool is nothing, the English counties are nothing! Manchester has obeyed the command of Mr Asquith: her Catholics have listened to the sly promises of Home Rule and therefore she is the only governess of the British Empire! A majority of Englishmen supports the House of Lords, but a majority cast against Mr Asquith is nothing ... He has purchased Ireland for the moment with a half-believed promise of Home Rule. Therefore Ireland is competent to destroy the Constitution of England.[6]

Actually Asquith had a majority without the Irish, but it never seemed to strike unionist pronouncers that an Irish vote – against the Lords veto or for Home Rule – was the natural consequence of union, the Constitution with a capital C and everything that Conservatives held most dear, and that under union, it was valid.

'England is Conservative,' declared the same article. And an irresistible impression is created by most right-wing rhetoric of this era that what was really believed in was an English Empire of which contemptible Wales, unsound Scotland and loathesome Catholic Ireland were adjacent dependencies, unaccountably contiguous Fijis needing those colonial governors-general celebrated by Curzon to keep them in line.

But co-operation with the nationalists and Labour, however Whibley might denounce it as something 'as infamous as the Fox–North coalition', would, after an unnecessary bout of coyness and anxiety, be on. Redmond pronounced himself ready to give Lords reform legislation Irish support as long as the Liberals were committed to Home Rule, which they were.

Asquith had dithered in his tiredness and had told an audience at Oxford Town Hall on 18 March that 'the Ministry had hesitated whether they should go on', but that wobble over, he indicated that on they would go, and would set about passing the budget in form, ending the Lords' financial veto in law and limiting the Lords' legal restraint on general legislation to a delaying power. With the government finally collecting its will to act, legislation to bring in the deficient revenue, which would involve short but quite vicious debate, was begun on 29 March. It passed in all its forms by majorities around the hundred mark with Irish and Labour support and was finally given a third reading by a margin of ninety-three.

The Irish support, always inevitable given the balance of interests, was denounced by Balfour as a selling-out to the Irish. In fact, the only offer – more buy than sale – came from Lloyd George. That inveterate coalitionist tried to do a side deal on whiskey duties with the O'Brien faction, an instance of redundant flexibility since Redmond would not touch an offer worked through his Irish enemies which would reward O'Brien's business backers. After that third reading, on 27 April, the financial legislation went on the 29th to the Lords. After a three-hour debate, they approved the collecting of the taxes they had denounced across six days in November. Their point had, it was supposed, been made.

With this much accomplished and Asquith visibly bent on legislation, he rather than Lloyd George became the hate figure of right-wing Tories. It was left to *Blackwood's* to give its own definition of what had happened in its May 1910 number. The King, it said, had originally been kept out of the dispute. 'It has justly been esteemed an act of cowardice to involve in open discussion one who by the very terms of his office is unable to accept or contradict the statements of politicians. But at Mr Redmond's command, Mr Asquith has hastened to outrage the solemn traditions of his high office.' He was creating a precedent which 'will make the limited monarchy which has conferred so many blessings on Great Britain a manifest impossibility. He is driven headlong down the path to ruin ... Mr Asquith is attempting to initiate a revolution, compared to which the revolution of 1789 was moderate.'[7]

And it was being made 'not in answer to the demand of the people, but in abject obedience to one Irishman or rather to two Irishman. Mr Patrick Ford has found the money; Mr Redmond has supplied the force and the gang of men who once described themselves as Liberals cowers in terror beneath the Irish lash.' When they were through with all that, 'there would remain nothing for them to do but to suppress the Crown, which could not exist with a single-chamber constitution, and to abolish their own quinquennial act, that they might hold the seals of office until death or revolution overtook them'.[8]

Such rage was a kind of compliment, acknowledgement that Asquith in his jog-along way was serious. And he was. The ground was now clear for a Parliament Bill. The Cabinet, having at the instance of Grey and Haldane ranged around the option of alternative reform without the grief of dragging a promise of nominees out of the King, finally put up a preamble nodding towards 'a second chamber constituted on a popular instead of a hereditary basis'. But as this could not be brought about at present, they would offer instead 'such provision as in this act appears for restricting the existing powers of the House of Lords'.

There had to be some form of Lords response, and a cartoon in *Punch* at about this time shows Lansdowne in a long apron in the role of publican – landlord of 'The Peer's Head' – halfway up a ladder armed with whitewash bucket and brush. 'Say this House is badly conducted, do they? And mean to stop the licence? Ah, but they haven't seen my coat of whitewash yet. That ought to make 'em think twice.' The Bucket is marked 'Peers' Reform Bill'.[9]

It was an apt picture, and the idea that the Lords might by this sort of busy tinkering keep hold of the substance of their licence was far from nonsensical. Given the enormous reluctance of the Palace to dilute the nobility with multiple grocers and novelists (Thomas Hardy was pencilled in as a possibility), a show of goodwill might perfectly well be expected to work at least as a bid for a reconciliation agreement, leaving far more Upper House power than simpleminded Liberals had supposed when they voted. And to this end, Rosebery now busied himself. Having advised against pulling down the House during the budget debate – and having been roundly sniffed at for pusillanimity by the death-or-glory element, he would now (14 March) propose and the Lords inconclusively debate a scheme for Lords modification concentrating upon membership rather than powers. For all Rosebery's fussing good intentions, and the fact that his motion when debated was actually carried, the resonating voice belonged to Halsbury, the eighty-six-year-old ex-lord chancellor, who did not believe that it was 'possible to make an institution more consonant with our habits and more practically useful than the House of Lords is as at present constituted'. Rosebery's desire to keep the House in touch with the public was met glacially. 'I have heard over and over again repeated the words "to bring this House in touch with the opinions of the country". It is such a delightful thing to have a phrase which ends a sentence and appears to have some meaning.' Halsbury also reminded his brethren that 'by the twenty-fifth of Edward I it is enacted that no tax shall be imposed except with the goodwill of the archbishops, barons, earls and so on. That is still an existing Act of Parliament, be it remembered.'[10]

Willoughby de Broke, who followed Halsbury and shared with him the leadership of what might be called 'advanced reaction', defended heredity. 'Do not let us stultify ourselves by the negation of the principle of heredity. Are we to tell the country either that we consider ourselves unworthy sons of our fathers or incapable of begetting a suitable posterity? I have been brought up in the midst of stockbreeding of all kinds all my life, and I am prepared to defend the hereditary principle in that or any other animal, whether the principle is applied to peers or whether it is applied to foxhounds.'[11]

Asquith, recovered from his exhaustion and having deluded himself once that the Palace would oblige him with guarantees, set out his position this time in terms when, on 14 April he introduced the bill: 'If the Lords fail to accept our policy . . . we shall then either resign our offices or recommend a dissolution of Parliament. And let me add this: that in no case would we recommend dissolution except under such conditions as will secure that in the new Parliament the judgement of the people as expressed in the election will be carried into law.'[12] This was a quite deliberate painting into a corner directed as much at the King and his advisers as at their lordships. It was saying plainly that there would be no climb-down, no compromise, only the finishing of what the Lords had themselves begun.

The Conservatives, their judgement inflamed, began to contemplate royal refusal of guarantees after a second election and a Unionist minority government *without supply*. The chief muser on such lines was Austen Chamberlain, with Balfour listening sympathetically. If denied money to govern by 'the radicals', could they get by with a loan from Lord Rothschild, or would a bridging loan from the Bank of England see them through to another election? And what if the Unionists still lost the contest? If the Liberal working majority was reduced, might it not be argued that not enough had been done to justify the creation of peers?[13]

This was fairly desperate thinking. The government had its numbers in the Commons now and no amount of mouthing about infamy and sell-outs invalidated Irish and Labour votes cast for the resolutions of what was, after all, His Majesty's government. As for His Majesty, it was one thing to drag feet and discourage guarantees after one election, but after two, advised by the realistic Knollys, Edward would surely not fulfil Austen's fevered hypothesis? We were never quite to know, for on 6 May, with the Cabinet on holiday and Asquith in the Bay of Biscay making for the Mediterranean, a radio message informed the prime minister that the King was ill. The next day, as Asquith headed back for Plymouth, he was told by radio by the new King, George V, that his father was dead. Edward's death, brought on by a bronchial condition caught on a trip to Sandringham, would be charged to the government. Sir Almeric Fitzroy, clerk of the Council, observed that 'some Tories of the baser sort are disposed to attribute the King's death to the unscrupulous tactics of ministers, and you are gravely told that the King's visit to Sandringham was due to the want of some vent for his anxieties after his interview with the prime minister.' The blame, said Sir Almeric, 'rested solely with his medical attendants for not reacting to the King's blotched face and other obvious symptoms'. One of these occurred at a reception for Moore, the prime minister of Western Australia. A Colonial Office memo had referred to Moore as prime minister of New Zealand. Edward, having passed on the gaffe, was corrected by a courtier and 'had an explosion of wrath, followed by a very violent fit of coughing'. Within two days the King was dead.[14]

There were two effects. Asquith now had to work with a tyro, and the pressure for respite, if not amnesty, was irresistible. The sharp edges of 14 April were bevelled by necessary humbug and even more necessary concern for the ability of a stamp-collecting former midshipman to cope with a constitutional crisis. The idea of a conference would always be attractive to King George – he would arrange one of his own to take on the Ulster problem in 1914. It had been flown as a kite by both the *Morning Post* and the *Observer*. Indeed Garvin, in a burst of lachrymose grandiloquence, wrote that 'if King Edward upon his deathbed could have sent a last message to his people, he would have asked us to lay party passion aside, to sign a truce of God over his grave, to seek . . . some fair means of making a common effort for our common country'.[15]

This was in line with the sweet, viscous norm of press response to deceased royalty, and the cry for reasonable people to get together had all the force of banality behind it. The 'Truce of God' tinkled about in general comment at the time rather in the way the 'Queen of Hearts' has done in the late 1990s. Anyway, the Tories were losing in Parliament and over negotiations might get something back.

Lloyd George, who had perfect shoals of his own fish to fry, urgently argued for a conference, and the Liberal right wing, Haldane and Grey, ardent drafters of plans for things, were just as keen. Perhaps the strongest motive for acceding to a search for the 'Truce of God' was that people wanted it. As T.P. O'Connor put it in a letter to Redmond after listing the conflicting opinions of the Liberals he had gathered in, 'They all think that the conference should be offered, mainly because public opinion in England demands it and secondly because it is an excuse for the postponement of the General Election.'[16]

The main effect of the conference was to take up six months' time and to give Lloyd George's experimental and managerial impulses an outing and the events of 1916 an intriguing rehearsal. As far as resolving the Lords dispute went, the negotiations – involving Asquith, Lloyd George, Crewe and Birrell on one side and Balfour, Lansdowne, Austen Chamberlain and Lord Cawdor on the other – seemed at times to be doing serious business.

Conservatives had the least trouble making some show of concession on numbers in the Lords. Lansdowne approved of their being reduced 'with the new House containing the *fine fleur* of the old'. He agreed that 'heredity alone should not determine membership;' that it should be 'substantially reinforced' by 'the introduction of a popular element from outside', and that a balance should be struck 'to exercise the functions appropriate to such a body fairly as between the two great parties in the state'.[17] That last observation was slightly opaque, but broadly, both Tories and the Lords, both of whom Lansdowne handily embodied, could move on membership further than they ever would on function.

And Lansdowne objected successfully to the suggestion that the conference should meet sooner in the pleasant surroundings of Lord Crewe's country house. Much gentle amusement has been had by historians at Lansdowne's fear that the negotiators might be thought to have been seduced by Crewe's champagne. But there is a serious side to it. Moneypenny, the joint biographer of Disraeli, speaking to Sir Almeric Fitzroy at the end of 1910 and reflecting on the rejection of the budget, summed up a fact of Tory life at that time. 'Supineness in high quarters,' he said, 'had allowed the Tory Press to prejudge the liberty of choice open to their leader, so that when the moment came for a descision, he had no alternative but to give effect to the foregone conclusion of his followers.'[18]

Not being seen to enjoy Crewe's civilised hospitality while talking conciliation was not a quirk of Lansdowne's, prudent though he was. Newton, his biographer, writing after the First World War, recalls his own mission to agree best treatment of prisoners of war when he had found more concern on his return with whether or not he had shaken any German hands than with what would happen to the prisoners. Enough of the Tory press already talked a half-crazed Manichean language as alien to Lansdowne and Balfour as to Asquith. Confronted with the likes of Fabian Ware of the *Morning Post* or Leo Maxse, the leadership reaction reminds one of Belloc's Lord Hippo facing his bookie –

> Lord Hippo simply turned and ran
> From this infuriated man.*

When it came to powers, the Tories, having made so much play about 'tacking', wanted a formal division of legislation into three categories: financial, ordinary, and constitutional.

---

* Belloc at this time had been Liberal MP for Salford South since 1906 and would not contest in the second 1910 election. His comic verse *Book of Peers* was largely inspired by the events of this period.

The Tory memorandum to the conference would have the Lords give up all claim to veto pure financial measures. But who would adjudicate on purity, certify legislation as untacked?

The option most quoted in this private and under-recorded series of discussions was a joint committee of the Commons and Lords, seven men from each party with the Speaker holding the casting vote. But they reached no resolution about the balance between the two Houses. Then again, Austen Chamberlain was concerned to bar from financial status and immunity any legislation affecting property or, as he put it, 'important social or political changes through expropriation of differentiation against any class of owners of property'. If accepted, this would have marked not so much the reform of the Lords as a constitutional castellation of wealth against any measure of redistribution. It would also have strengthened the Tariff Reform case to which Chamberlain was devoted by blocking off an alternative source of revenue. The Tory remedies in conference were at any rate consistent with their rhetoric as an opposition.

The proposal for handling what was called ordinary legislation which might fall foul of the Lords was to be a joint session of both Houses, 'the nucleus of an imperial senate',[19] as Lord Esher grandly put it. This got nowhere for the good reason that no agreement could be reached on membership, the government insisting on a heavy thirteen-to-two preponderance of full Commons and a body of representative peers. Put in brute arithmetical terms, the Tories would not go below eighty peers and the government would not budge above forty-five. There was little point in joint sittings with no agreement about who should sit.

As for constitutional legislation, the Tories were engaged in a flirtation with the referendum. After two rejections by the Lords, a bill proposing constitutional reform should be referred to 'the people', as so many Conservatives had lately taken to calling voters. But how were such bills to be identified? Asquith favoured a pre-emptive (and narrow) list of topics, notably those affecting the Crown. The Conservatives were apprehensive of Home Rule, as well they might be, having done so much to advance it. They did not want Ireland allowed a measure of self-government merely because the House of Commons had willed it twice. Lloyd George suggested, as a one-off fix, that for the Home Rule Bill in prospect a Lords rejection might be followed by another election which, if won by the government, would allow the bill to proceed as ordinary legislation, joint committee and all. But the Conservatives would not countenance Home Rule for Ireland with whatever safeguards or fall-backs or, it seemed, in any circumstances at all. This was taking place privately before the savage Ulster commitments of 1912–14.

Yet not all Conservatives were quite the indelible Ulster patriots, gun-runners and Protestant martyrs they would become in public during those demented years. F.E. Smith dismissed Home Rule as 'a dead quarrel for which neither country nor the party cares a damn outside of Ulster and Liverpool'.[20] Within two years, Smith KC, improbably on horseback, would accompany General Richardson in his inspection of Ulster Volunteers and earn the soubriquet, 'Galloper Smith'. It was the same highly secular Smith, appealing to 'the souls of Christian people' in a Welsh disestablishment debate, who brought upon his head the advice of G.K. Chesterton: 'Chuck it, Smith.'

But Smith was being sensible in 1910, and was joined by other Tories, like Alfred Lyttleton and Garvin, for whom Tariff Reform was simply more important. A number of Tories had discovered 'federalism', an idea which comes and goes among the generations. Present in our own time, it had been the pet scheme of James Bryce in the nineties. Home Rule as part of a wider scheme which still asserted the union provided one group of Conservatives with an escape route from the Irish preoccupation.

But the fluidity of mind which this represented was as

nothing next to the molten brass of Lloyd George's August memorandum. (The conference was a leisurely affair and had adjourned at the end of of July.) Lloyd George set down his proposals during August at his home at Criccieth on the Lleyn Peninsula) The word 'revolution', endlessly invoked like salad garnish by Conservative peers and journalists to describe the incremental changes, social and constitutional, of both budget and Lords reform, could have been used without extravagance to describe Lloyd George's plan. He wanted a coalition government bringing together the first-rate men of both sides and dropping 'the duffers'. He was prepared to surrender to the Tories a measure of Tariff Reform, naval expenditure and the national military service which certain of them sought as both military preparation and a strengthening of the moral fibre of the working class. He had in mind compromises over both education and licensing, going over the heads of the 'faddists' of both parties. In return he wanted Conservative support for a social programme – national insurance provision for the unemployed, a major liberalising of the Poor Law and the giving of attention, in the way of a hundred politicians since, to 'technology'.

All of this was fascinating, if only tangential to a study of Conservative attitudes, though the Tory response as the Lloyd George memoir trickled through to them (which was pretty much what it seems to have done to Asquith) was instructive. The memo divided imagination from routine politics, quickmindedness from steady pursuit, opportunism from principle, flash from steady. It contained very little Liberalism – Lloyd George was cooling fast towards free trade – considerable elements of socialism, empirically selected and set to use, and, with its compulsory military service clause, a touch of that 'national' politics which would become so unpleasant an aspect of the twentieth century.

Ironically, however, such a coalition would take peacetime form, a rather ghostly one, in the benign and genuinely conciliatory hands of Stanley Baldwin twenty-one years later, as the National Government, something neither harsh nor notably effective. The supreme irony of the Lloyd George memo, if it had been accepted, was that the dealings behind closed doors of politicians of supposedly opposed parties would have shattered constitutional practice and all the forms of democracy in ways to make demotion of the House of Lords look incidental.

The appeal of Lloyd George's thinking was first of all to Smith, his personal friend and a man who similarly combined glittering and abrasive partisanship with shallow party roots. He thought that 'a great sigh of relief would go up from business England if a strong and stable government was formed', adding that 'at the worst, it would enable us to fight against opponents whose most formidable leaders were discredited and under circumstances which might lead to another period of Tory ascendancy'.[21]

Smith gloried in cynicism, and Lloyd George – variously 'the cad in politics' and 'that scoundrel from Wales' – would be similarly damned. But that would hideously undervalue a man who bubbled ideas, thought across a wide social horizon and was vested with genuine creative statesmanship. He would also convince Austen Chamberlain, Joe's unaccountably decent and upright son and Smith's opposite – 'Austen always played the game and always lost.'

Without overdoing amateur psychology, Austen had emerged from paternal domination into a position among leaders and he was vulnerable to anyone able to cast awe. 'Filial piety,' said A.G. Gardiner, contemplating him, 'is a good thing, filial servitude a bad thing.'[22] In that other coalition of the First World War, he would become Lloyd George's loyal and devoted supporter and would decline to join the Tory secession of 1922. Also on-line with the chancellor was Bonar Law, who would shortly become the most ferociously partisan (and constitutionally oblivious) of Tory leaders as the settler cause in Ireland increasingly obsessed him.

Balfour indicated some sympathy with what was being

offered, but sensibly and professionally, wanted to know who was offering it. It surely wasn't Asquith, who had seen a copy unofficially but was not given one by Lloyd George until the autumn. Asquith and Lloyd George were as unlike as two political colleagues can ever have been. Asquith was a patient man, a bridge-player, a player also of long scenarios, very conscious of when time was on his side, as it was now. He was an incrementalist rather than a visionary and his friendships, though they extended to Conservatives, were with the likes of Balfour, another cool, cultivated man.

Asquith, as Roy Jenkins argues, was a better radical in circumstances like these. He might go through a fit of depression, but having picked himself up and made his dispositions and alliances, he would go steadily on to his objective. He was conventional where Lloyd George was inspirational, but with no less intelligence. Asquith drank quietly; Lloyd George, genuinely abstemious, seduced to wide private knowledge. But politically, Asquith was monogamous. It was the right virtue for 1910 for the Liberal Party and for government. The Lords veto had to go; so had British government of Ireland. Federalism represented intelligent politics, rescuing rational Tories from an irrational commitment. Why else would Edward Carson hiss his apprehension to Lady Londonderry: 'I hate the whole situation?'[23] But exactly like Home Rule, *au nature* it would never pass the clenched will of Ulster self-absorption. The pity of the times was that both reforms could not have been telescoped and accelerated.

A compromise between reform and reaction would work in the sterile circumstances of a war, against which, ironically, Lansdowne of all people would cry out in an heroic letter to *The Times* in 1917. In peace it would have meant a burst of activity on certain issues and immobilism on a string of others, with members looking over each other's shoulders at the worst option Smith saw of a new ascendancy, Tory or Liberal. There would have been conflict and impasse still, but conflict and impasse in one office.

Asquith did not expect Lloyd George's activities to come to anything. As for Balfour, he was much preoccupied at this time with not playing the role of Sir Robert Peel, something which echoed Salisbury's resolution not to think generously about Ireland when Gladstone had first proposed Home Rule. It hadn't done the Tory Party any favours, Salisbury had said, and Balfour, faced with the Lloyd George plan, now feared similar consequences.

Balfour in coalition with Asquith made a certain sense: two moderate men happy to 'wait and see', Asquith's stock phrase, and going forward – slowly. A coalition of supposed extremists like Lloyd George, a real one in Law and a flashy figure like Smith was a mute expression of hostility to both Asquith and Balfour, but could not exist without the permission of both. The outcome was effectively one of Asquith looking at Balfour, Balfour looking at Asquith and both shaking their heads.

Back with the ostensible business of reconciling only the House of Lords, Ireland would demonstrate the impossibility of even the smaller aspirations. How would Home Rule be handled when the Lords rejected it? The Liberals were willing to face an election after Lords rejection *this time* but would not establish this as a general rule as the thing dragged on, as it foreseeably would.

The Tories would accept only a rule for all bills. Asquith reasonably observed that his side had given away as much as it should. Almost certainly, from a straight Liberal point of view, having fought the battles of the previous five years, they had conceded too much. As he put it in a friendly letter to Balfour, 'The proposal now under consideration would include in the same category all Reform Bills, big or small (including the abolition of plural voting), all forms of Home Rule from pure Parnellism to the most modest voting, and indeed practically all measures of *political*, as distinguished from social or economic change.'

And he added a simple truth: 'It is here where the shoe

pinches so acutely that the party foot would in our view reject it as a misfit.'[24] Balfour's party shoe hardly allowed him to walk. The number of peers was still irreconcilable, Lansdowne's specific area of chronic immobilism, Home Rule, played an important part in denying acceptance and after a last joint meeting on 8 November, it was agreed that the talks had failed.

Asquith was able with an almost acknowledged relief to do what he had always wanted to do: proceed to a Parliament Act to end for good the hereditary chamber's block on government.

20

'A Senate of Kangaroos'

Asquith was no sooner out of the delays imposed by Lloyd George's schemes and the confirmation of irreconcilability than he was afflicted with the nervous anxiety of George V. Self-preoccupation in George was a factor of fear rather than comfort. He was too readily led; also afflicted, as we shall see, with a troublesome choice of personal guides.

The government's position was neatly caught in a conversation between Morley, now president of the Council, and Sir Almeric Fitzroy. 'I put it to Lord Morley that the tactics of the opposition were to defer a General Election till the new year, and the tactics of the government to get it over by Christmas; on which he remarked drily, "You have described the situation exactly."'[1] Asquith was looking to a dissolution which he could hardly be refused. He was also looking to those guarantees of the creation of sufficient peers to end the Lords veto and thus pass the Parliament Act itself.

The King hated the idea. It would be the undermining of the old hierarchy by the figure standing at its head. He was made anxious by any criticism of himself by peers and leading Conservatives. This example of literal peer-group pressure would be rebuked by John Morley at the very end of the crisis when, to a King worried about aristocratic alienation, he contrasted hard words at the Carlton Club with the opinion of the people.

We are talking estates of the realm: King, Lords and Commons. The small 'c' conservative mindset of 1910 took as its point of abhorrence and avoidance the French Revolution. And the Liberal, Irish and Labour majority in the Commons seemed to be asking, 'Qu'est-ce que le Tiers Etat?'* That question had been resolved in France in ways leading to extreme unpleasantness.

George understandably wanted to know what he should do. There was never any question of refusing a dissolution, but it was constitutionally possible on paper to refuse the guarantees. Except that Asquith was in no position, thus denied, to jog along legislatively with an innocuous something else. He had taken very good care in April to foreclose any option of not pressing Lords reform by way of a Parliament Bill. Refused a dissolution, he would resign and Arthur Balfour would have to be invited to form a minority government. This option, as we have seen, had been delightedly run over by Austen Chamberlain to Balfour – what to do to replace supply which Asquith would surely block? The Rothschilds? The Bank of England? If the King started this chain of action by refusing Asquith his guarantees, events would become as febrile as Austen's imaginings. Conservative rhetoric about revolution might take physical form. It wouldn't have, of course, given the stoic nature of the ruled, but the King was still looking at a full-dress constitutional crisis, and he knew it.

Francis Knollys knew it even better. The former secretary to Edward VII, now jointly serving George V, was about to give an object lesson on the role of a constitutional monarch when the head of state must actually make a decision and is not obeying a clear convention. He takes advice about

* The full quotation from the Abbé Sièyes is. 'What is the Third Estate? Nothing? What should it be? Everything.'

which convention he will be guided by. George had available to him the guidance of his own private secretary, Bigge, later Lord Stamfordham. But Knollys, having served Edward throughout, had the authority and, as it turned out, the guile. There had been a preliminary meeting with Asquith after which his characteristically cautious avoidance of an instant request for guarantees had been happily misunderstood as no request at all. But the requirement had to come, whatever the prime minister's sense of delicacy.

The royal response was clumpingly unhelpful. 'His Majesty regrets that it would be impossible for him to give contingent guarantees and he reminds Mr Asquith of his promise not to seek for any during the present Parliament.'[2] The King confused Asquith's earlier readiness not to demand guarantees operative in the current Parliament with a very different need to have them *made* while that Parliament sat.

Asquith's delicacy did not extend to the unqualified surrender which George was uncomprehendingly demanding. He had made his commitment on 14 April and the paint keeping him in that corner was still wet. He called a Cabinet at once, asked for and got a full Cabinet position stating that 'in the event of the policy of the government being approved by an adequate majority in the new House of Commons, His Majesty will be ready to exercise his constitutional powers (which may involve the prerogative of creating peers) if needed, to secure that effect should be given to the decision of the country'.[3] But it was intimated that it was not necessary for the undertaking to be made public in advance.

George was advised by an outraged Bigge to refuse and told by a cool Knollys to accept. A day was spent resolving which advice would prevail. Knollys won, but only by cutting a major corner and suppressing evidence. The issue hinged upon the existence of an alternative once Asquith, as he was certain to do on such a refusal, had handed in the seals of office. Would Balfour form a minority government? If so, as the constitutional jargon puts it, the King's government would be continued. However, Knollys assured the king that Balfour would not. He knew otherwise; he had been present at an extraordinary meeting on 29 April convened by the Archbishop of Canterbury at which Balfour had made it clear that he would form a minority government in the event of the creation of peers proving an obstacle.[4] Knollys did not tell the King this; neither did he inform Balfour of the possibility of such a request. The secrecy involved in the request probably arose in deference to George's feelings, but it also left Balfour unable to assert his readiness.

Knollys was backed at this time by Lord Esher, the professional court eminence, in a memorandum of 14 November playing down the consequences of the Parliament Act. 'It does not strike a deadly blow at the influence of the House itself . . . and the hereditary principle is not . . . in any way infringed.'[5] When Balfour heard of Knollys' action long afterwards, he was suitably outraged. He would write to Bigge on 1 August 1911, a few days before the balloon finally went up with the Lords' debate on the Parliament Bill, 'Had I been asked to form a government in order to protect His Majesty from giving a promise not merely that a Parliament Bill should be passed over the heads on the Lords, but that it should be passed in a form which by implication carried Home Rule with it, I should not only have formed a government, but I should have had great hopes of carrying the country with me.'[6] One can doubt the last point, since Conservative rhetoric throughout the second election of 1910 was full of the horrors of Home Rule, and much good it did them.

What Balfour had been denied was the forming of a government at the invitation of the King after the King had refused a recently re-elected prime minister the means to accomplish a reform which had lain at the centre of the election. That new government would have been without supply – no reason existed for Asquith, his party and its allies to authorise funds for a government imposed by the King. After whatever Rothschild or the Bank of England had given Balfour to buy time for interim administration and call for a dissolution, the country would be facing an election in which the peers-versus-people argument had been escalated to King and peers versus people.

Knollys did not suppress Balfour's intentions out of partisan sympathy with Asquith's government or its proposals. He acted as an intelligent, small 'c' conservative on behalf of the capital 'C' Constitution which unintelligent capital 'C' Conservatives talked so much about. He was also anticipating Lord Hewart's famous dictum about justice 'not only being done, but being manifestly seen to be done'. King George might not have intended to show favouritism towards either the Conservative Party or, more uncertainly, the House of Lords. But in sending for Balfour at this point he would have been universally perceived to have done so.

The prime minister could, of course, have a dissolution from him as Balfour would be doing in these circumstances. But a dissolution without guarantees was useless to Asquith. He would be fighting a second election with every prospect that it would precipitate a third. Given such a nonsense, coupled with the royal rebuff, the point of equal treatment over dissolution would be meaningless. And the public, which would register a million-vote drop in participation at a mere second election, would see its rulers, King, Lords and Commons, displaying a collective incompetence which intelligent tenders of the status quo like Knollys recognised as destructive of political stability.

The reality was that George and his advisers should have assented when first asked. Indeed, it is very hard to see why Asquith and King Edward between them had not managed to crunch on the issue before the first 1910 election. The issues were clear enough, and a single election a sufficient test of public will. On the other hand, a second election called by Balfour would, in the hands of Lloyd George, be representable with very little *hwyl* as the entire Establishment, King and Lords conspiring against radical politics, an alliance of Crown and coronet against reform and the unprivileged citizen.

The Edwardian-early Georgian era was the least blissfully serene and socially idyllic period imaginable, for all the Pimm's and striped blazers at Maidenhead. It was the time of the Osborne judgement, (the legal obstruction of trade-union representation), and of a bitter strike in the Welsh coalfield which had led to the stoning of passenger trains and riots in Cardiff. A favourite figure at court was the the Marquis de Soveral, ambassador of Portugal. Asquith had called on the King of Portugal during his May cruise. By November that monarchy had been overthrown. Intelligent Conservatives try very hard to avoid provoking a sequence of events which ends in the streets with the whole political order having bottles thrown at it.

Put brutally, the House of Lords had pushed its luck – and pushed Balfour at the same time. It had broken a 200-year convention. An election had not deprived the Liberal government of a Commons majority. Lords and opposition had not been able to accommodate a compromise over the summer. A hereditary chamber was now blocking the road to Commons legislation a quarter of a century after a broad popular suffrage had put the Commons on to a comprehensive basis of representing the people. The Lords had had their chance and had muffed it. Francis Knollys concerned himself about the standing of the King at the apex of a society whose order was not assured. Sitting on Balfour's undertaking and pushing the King firmly towards compliance with the wishes of his ministers and a majority of the House of Commons, he put a term to the crisis, a limit to its rage, and he entrenched kingship at the moment when politics and society were both being amended.

When Asquith's act finally passed the now apprehensive Lords in August 1911, some peers would be cut by other peers and yet others struck off invitation lists. Charles Whibley would accuse Asquith of treason. But this rage existed in a medium-sized section of the upper class. It was far and away the best place for it. Knollys had recognised that constitutions survive by changing and had made discreet arrangements to facilitate such a change. The art of *suppressio veri* has rarely been put to better use.

Given the tools, Asquith could finish the job. (This his home secretary would say in 1940, but we come before him.) But Lansdowne and the Lords were insistent that the Parliament Bill should at least be submitted to them, something agreed reluctantly by Crewe, leader of the Lords, with the proviso that there should be no amendments. Rosebery at once proceeded with his own proposals, which would become in effect the election manifesto of the unelected House and would be heavily cited by Tory speakers on all hands. A future House of Lords would 'consist of Lords of Parliament (a) chosen by the whole body of hereditary peers from amongst themselves and by nomination by the Crown (b) sitting by virtue of offices and qualifications held by them (c) chosen from outside. 'Lansdowne, speaking in the debate, glossed this, suggesting that half the reformed House might be hereditarians 'familiar with country life, familiar with mangement of landed property' rather than 'veterans with a distinguished record who have arrived at a time of life when they would look naturally for repose'.[7]

It was to be, in short, a golf club relaxing its rules, but with a hereditary committee, and the heavily escutcheoned would dominate the greens. Yet it was a lot more than anyone had felt like allowing Rosebery in February, when his ideas had been put out to rust. It was taking place on the sardonic nod of Balfour. Echoing that cynical pessimism of his uncle Salisbury, Balfour said that he didn't think the present Lords could be bettered, but they might thus get a Lords which might last another fifty years. It was also, for all its self-serving, a more elaborate and fussily complicated readjustment of that perfect constitution than Asquith's straightforward proposals on the veto. But this last throw was directed at the election to help Balfour argue that reform was underway anyway.

The election which followed has been widely characterised as outstandingly dull, but any reading of the contest yields indications of a shift in the argument, clarity from Asquith, a strategic retreat by Balfour which would make him new enemies very soon, much devilment from Lloyd George and no end of harmless fun. Among the fun was a two-column advertisement in *The Times* proclaiming:

> To The Electors Of The United Kingdom
> The Brewery Debenture Holders Committee
> ask you to use your Vote and Influence to Defeat
> Government Candidates at the General Election

It gives a number of reasons for so doing, most reasonably, if extravagantly, 'the oppressive taxes and duties on licensed properties embodied in the last Finance Act', and the belief that the Liberals would now 'redouble their effort to tax the trade out of existence'. But it added: 'The avowed intention of the present Government is for the extinction of the Second Chamber or to so limit its powers that socialistic or confiscatory legislation which has never been submitted to the electors may be passed without check by a scratch and log-rolling majority of the House of Commons.' To this is appended, in bold type: 'The last Finance Bill could not have been passed except by the Irish Vote which was opposed to the Budget, but given as one of the terms of the bargain for Home Rule.' The appeal continues:

> If the powers of the Second Chamber are so crippled or extinguished, the property and liberty of the nation will be at the mercy of any temporary but omnipotent majority of the House of Commons. Such uncontrolled power is equally dangerous whether it be in the hands of a Monarch or a Cabinet. On the Other Hand by means

of the Referendum proposed by the Unionist Party, the will of the People will prevail and justice be done to all subjects of the realm.

In conclusion The Brewery Debenture Holders Committee earnestly request all holders of those securities who own Motor-cars to place them at the disposal of their local Unionist Offices in this great crisis.[8]

The referendum as applied to constitutional reform would now be a leading Conservative weapon. The Lords had offered their own reform of themselves, so what was the fuss about? But dangerous ideas like Home Rule must not pass without resort to referendum. Lloyd George, speaking at Llandrindod Wells, made a sortie against the whole idea. 'It is a dodge to put the poor man more than ever at the mercy of the monopolists (cheers) handing over government to the great plutocracy, like America, where great trusts subscribe clandestinely and secretly [unlike the upright Brewers' debenture-holders] large sums of money to run elections and the people are entirely at their mercy.' While he was about it in mid-Wales, Lloyd George could not resist a dig at Balfour. 'Will he now put his actual Tariff Reform Bill to a referendum? How much would it put on the price of food? How much would it burden manufacturers?'[9] It isn't clear whether a referendum had been any part of Lloyd George's own memorandum-writing plans for a partial acceptance of Tariff Reform.

In fact, Balfour was all set for a bold retreat. Asquith, addressing 8,000 in the railway sheds at Reading, a venue and attendance unlikely to be repeated, directly challenged the Conservative leader to put Tariff Reform to the popular single vote. The message, quickly relayed by the technology of the day to Balfour, who was addressing another monster meeting, held more conventionally in the Albert Hall, drew the answer that he had 'not the slightest objection to submitting the principles of Tariff Reform to a referendum'.

Indeed he didn't. The best-known joke about Balfour concerns him many years later asking his niece and biographer, Blanche Dugdale, 'Was I for or against Tariff Reform before the war?' and getting the answer: 'That's what we all wanted to know.' Balfour was incapable of taking an ideology seriously, but to many of his party, protection as enunciated by Joseph Chamberlain was very much the Marxian dialectic of history to Marxists. He had gone along with the zealots and seen them work the destruction of free-trade Tories and sharpen that spirit of jagged-edged inveteracy which would characterise the party until Baldwin's time.

Given the chance, he was very ready to push the sacramental truth into the long grass. He was taking his cue from Lansdowne, who had never really liked protection and whose earlier submission had been far less lighthearted. Lansdowne, in a speech of 22 November, had said provocatively, as he proclaimed his new constitutional reformism, that a referendum could settle the one issue on which the two Houses now disagreed. Conservative candidates who took seriously the effect of the Food Bill arguments in losing them votes in January responded. Even Garvin of the *Observer*, Chamberlain's apostle to the Sunday press, came out with a catchphrase to match his earlier 'Truce of God'. It was 'Trust the People' – and Winston Churchill would use that in the distant future as well. With Garvin editorialising and writing privately urging a referendum, and with only Lansdowne, that free-trader *in pectore*, to consult, the temptation to Balfour to be shot of the charge of shrinking the worker's loaf was irresistible. F.E. Smith, a man of easy opinion, offered a personal view to a Liverpool audience. He was happy to have a referendum.

The message brought by electric telegraph from Reading did not fall on unprepared ears. Accordingly Balfour was able to make his commitment and bring his audience to their feet to show suitable rapture at a massive retreat on the central point of policy. Austen Chamberlain, that faithful son and player of the game, could only look on, protesting.

Meanwhile Lloyd George, having outraged the sensibilities of King, dukes and *Times* at Limehouse, went on another frolic in Mile End. That newspaper's reporter at the Paragon Music Hall, where Lloyd George spoke to 5,000 on 22 November, noted 'an audience restless and unenthusiastic when hearing detailed defence of his budget, [and one which] showed no trace of excitement when he explained the sources of Mr Redmond's dollars, but they became keenly attentive and fiercely demonstrative when he began a violent attack on the aristocracy greatly to the liking of the "East enders", as the chairman, Mr B.S. Straus, called the audience.'

Lloyd George might have been naughty, but some of his irresponsible arguments had the advantage of plain truth, as when he discussed 'certain tribes in the world – savage tribes – who are addicted to devil worship'. The Conservatives were like that, 'unable to get along without bogeys. In the last election the Germans were the bogeys; in 1900 it was the Dutchmen [Afrikaners]; in 1895 it was Irishmen; in 1885, it was Mr Joseph Chamberlain. Now, having exhausted the list, they are going back to the Irish again.'

They were indeed. Lloyd George's great friend F.E. Smith had only the day before invoked John Redmond and the funds he had recently raised in the US and Canada. 'It was Mr Redmond's programme that Mr Asquith unfolded on Saturday; it was the uglier portion of Mr Redmond's scheme that he kept out of sight; and if he remains in power after the election he will be Mr Redmond's lieutenant as he is now his advocate.' It was no longer, said Smith, 'a question of the constitution or the House of Lords or the Unionist Party or anything. It is a question of whether this country is to control its own destinies or whether it is to be dominated by foreign influences controlling Mr Asquith and his Cabinet.'

Lloyd George in Mile End contemplated that Irish bogey; he had changed rather. In the past 'he was – remember – a midnight assassin, ragged, tattered, fierce. But the Irishman of today is a gilt-edged bogey. He is framed in a ring of dollars.' Then, flying high on whimsy, he turned to Australia, a country unblessed by aristocracy and thus civilisation. What should Australia do to be saved? What did they need to make an aristocracy? Well, he said, in England's case, a few shiploads of French filibusters came over from Normandy. They killed all the owners of property they could lay their hands on, they levied tax on surviving owners at 100 per cent. Unfortunately, their descendants had been so engaged in cutting each other's throats that there were very few of them left. Did the Australians have anything like that?

'"Well, we had the bushrangers a few years ago, but they only stole cattle."

'"Oh," we say, "cattle won't do. It must be land."

"Well anyway," say the Australians, "we hanged the last of them a few years back before they had the opportunity of founding a family."'

But, asks Lloyd George, wouldn't they like to be governed by proper aristocrats, who he defined as those who 'pick the most ancient stock in the land, land which they own but take care not to cultivate themselves. They may hunt, ride, shoot, recreations of that sort.'

'"No thanks," say the Australians. "We'd sooner be ruled by a senate of kangaroos."' [10]

In fact, although he raised his largest cheer in Mile End by observing that aristocracy was like cheese – most valued when it was oldest and highest – the Lloyd George demagogic style is mostly charming, quick-witted and, to a grown-up opponent, all part of the political art. That did him no good, however, with the *Times* leader-writer, who discerned 'rabid Billingsgate' in his 'vituperation of aristocrats and owners of land'. And watching a clever politician amuse a working-class audience by sending up the ladies and gentlemen, the editorialist rumbled on, part bishop, part tummy, to pronounce that the country was now 'left prey to any scheme of spoliation with which a demagogue may arouse the worst passions of the multitude who know not their right hand from their left'. [11]

Times reporters were commonly an improvement on the red-faced norm of the leader-writers' room. And one report in particular drily demonstrates an old-fashioned gentlemanly style encountering that multitude and its worst passions – and not having the blindest idea of how to talk to it. 'Lord Rosebery,' wrote a reporter, 'who has long been acknowledged as public orator of the Empire, has lately taken on the the duties of political adviser to the businessmen of Great Britain . . . he had declared against the serious encroachments which the newer Liberalism was making upon personal liberty and was in the middle of a sentence about Irish dictatorship when, from the back of the Hall, arose shouts of "No Politics."' Rosebery explained that he could not manage without politics, but 'he interpreted the word according to the original Greek . . . More howls greeted him as he continued to discuss the subject.' Rosebery 'rebuked Mr Lloyd George for his Mile End speech and unconsciously gave the cue for the raising of three hearty cheers for the chancellor of the exchequer by dissentients.'

At times the reports, with their accounts of high periodic bombast imploding under derision, sound like Dickens – the hustings at Eatanswill, perhaps. But nobody could say that, choking on his own syntax, Rosebery didn't try.

> There is a danger to our liberties greater in one sense, more degrading than any that I have mentioned, one to which if we submit, we must submit to be called a nation of slaves. I mean that Irish dictation (cheers) subsidised by foreign gold by which it is attempted, not for British purposes (cries of 'Rats' and 'No politics') to subvert the constitution of this country by a hurried and unparalleled election . . . Great Britain invaded by an emissary subsidised by foreign money.'[12]

The oddments of newspaper coverage included a running item on 'politicians indisposed'. On 1 December this covered

the Earl of Onslow, who was still recovering from an operation for a defect of the vocal cords, and the statement that
Lord Cawdor had tonsilitis. Birrell appeared everywhere,
limping and carrying a stick, having been kicked to the ground
near York Steps by suffragettes who, in a gentler age, might
only have written to the *Guardian*. *The Times* also reported
defections, announcing on 26 November that 'Sir J.D. Rees,
formerly MP for Montgomery Boroughs, has just crossed the
floor.' He had 'given up a safe seat because . . . he did not care
a brass farthing about Liberal or Conservative . . . the country
was being hurried into single-chamber government and Home
Rule to the detriment of the country and injury to trade.' This
was happening 'because there are a few politicians who love
the people to the tune of £5,000 a year for themselves and
see their offices slipping away from them.'

Then again, 'Mr E. Singleton, one of the leading Nonconformists in south Somerset, has announced his intention of
supporting the unionist candidate because as an Irishman
he feels that Home Rule will be Rome rule.' And 'Mr H.B.
Money-Coutts feels he is a man in the desert. There is no
longer a place in politics for an ardent Liberal and free-trader.
Lloyd George has gone out of his way, not once but often, to
stir up envy, hatred and all uncharitableness between class
and class. His vituperative course can only be intended,
insofar as a plain man can judge, to end in the black abyss
of the social revolution.'[13]

Sir Henry Page Croft was concerned for George V. 'The
sovereign, in the one year when Britons throughout the world
would desire to give peace, is to suffer vexation and be
harassed by the Little Englander–American alliance which
for years has misgoverned this country.'

For the Primrose League, met in an earlier chapter, Lord
Ronaldshay MP said that

in the fight which has been forced upon them they will
stand by their religion, by their constitution and by

their Empire against what will be done at the bidding of an Irish political tramp [Redmond] who has returned with his pockets laden with American gold, of a swash-buckling politician from Wales, and from an amateur working man from Scotland [Keir Hardie], enjoying trips round the world at the expense of the genuine working man and who might be described as 'the Mad Mullah of the political situation'.

The Church Defence Committee and Protestant Alliance called for 'Immediate action in support of candidates' in their 'several districts whose Protestantism is above reproach.'[14]

The scattered *obiter dicta* of the election help one understand Arthur Balfour, whose tone of permanent *ennui* at the stupidity of other people becomes more sympathetic. Balfour's valet was everywhere. Speaking in Nottingham, the Unionist leader ran through the proposed reform of the Lords which he had privately hoped might let the Upper House survive another fifty years. 'The numbers in the Upper House should be diminished and heredity alone should not give a title to a seat in the House. It should be composed of ex-officio members, some elected within, and peers elected from outside by outside machinery.'[15]

It was far from clear, but it was as certainly moderate as it was unimaginably remote from the hand played by Balfour when he had waved on rejection of the budget a year before. And it only made any kind of sense if Balfour could actually win this second election. Meanwhile, he had to be satisfied with a resolution passed at his meeting against Home Rule as 'a policy tending toward the weakening of the union with Ireland', and with the assurance of the chairman of the Conservative National Union that Balfour and Lansdowne both enjoyed the ardent and enthusiastic support of their followers.

They might have done, though from the fury soon to come from the right directed at 'Iscariot' it would show itself in peculiar ways. What Balfour would not have was enough ardent and enthusiastic support from the country to make any difference at all to the House of Commons. The Liberals lost 3 seats net, going from 275 to 272, Labour put on 2, bringing them to 42, and the Irish nationalists moved from 82 seats to 84.

There were thus 398 members of Parliament committed to the agreed course available before the January election, and they were committed now to granting Home Rule to Ireland. Against that the unionists who, including the Speaker, had had 273 seats, now had 272. In terms of futility the Lords and Unionist exercise of 1910 was complete. The unreformed House of Lords was now set to lose what it would have kept if the budget had been passed grumblingly through: its veto on non-money legislation. The battle fought was a war lost, but the ability to recognise this unpleasant fact would now be the line dividing the Unionist party. What had been a constitutional crisis would soon turn into a very nasty domestic scene.

21

'These Degrading 500 Peers'

An immediate reaction to the election was a speech from Lansdowne of such grudging resistance that it might with advantage have been muttered. On the constitutional question the decision would not be final; the relations between the two Houses, and between those two Houses and the people, could and would be remodelled on Unionist lines; but Home Rule, once given, could not be withdrawn, and its passage over the heads of the people and against their wills would be one of the greatest crimes in history.[1]

The second half of that sentence is the incorrigible County Kerry landowner to whom the Easter Rising, a war, several hundred dead, Irish independence and another war would come as a painful revelation. The first part was a futile piece of foot-dragging which would give colour and legitimacy to that defiance of reason which would swell into defiance of Lansdowne himself and genteel riot in the late summer of 1911.

Lansdowne, returning to his own basic good sense this side of the Irish Sea, would eventually have to help put out the fire he was now perfunctorily blowing upon. The Marquess had excellent abilities, but he lacked the cynical touch, almost amounting to indifference, which distinguished Balfour. He had been rightly reluctant to rat on a good cause, free trade, so he was now unhappy at ratting on their lordships' immemorial rights, a thoroughly bad one and, more to the point, a cause lost.

Putting Lansdowne together with the timid, unhappy George V was a recipe for heavy-duty incoherence in high places. The creation of peers loomed. That, wrote Lansdowne, noting his conversation with George, 'was a step which I felt sure HM would be reluctant to take, and his ministers not less reluctant to advise; and I thought it not unfair to say that up to a certain point we should be justified in bearing this fact in mind when considering whether it was desirable to offer resistance to the government proposals.'[2] Lansdowne was taking a position between self-deception and, in cricketing terms, a refusal to walk. The grounds for such prevarication would be that when Asquith proposed a creation of new lords, he didn't mean it. The prime minister's civil and understated style of communication was wasted on some people.

Lansdowne dreamed on about the possibility of another election 'for the purpose of safeguarding the constitution against a violent change during the time which, if the bill became law, would pass before a reformed House of Lords could be called into existence, a new issue of the kind I contemplated might arise'.[3] Would the King really think of creating 500 peers to resist that?

While Lansdowne cogitated on delay, and ceremonial England busied itself with preparations for the crowning of King George, the *National Review*, house journal of the coming revolt against the Unionist leadership, fulminated and threatened. The Parliament Bill now being put to the Commons again was a simple matter of 'the three "D"s – i.e. the Demagogues, the Decoys and the Dummies . . . to exploit the coronation in order to establish themselves permanently in office and open the floodgates of snobbery, jobbery and robbery'. In a style which would shortly intensify, the *National* warned against soft Tories, the 'hands-uppers' and 'white-flaggers' and 'the counsel of the craven who are as active on the back stairs as they are shy of the footlights'. If they should prevail and 'the Parliament Bill be allowed to slip through Parliament, the three Ds would forthwith take the necessary steps to secure permanent power, whence nothing but bayonets could dislodge them'. What was in prospect, wrote Leo Maxse, was the establishment of

an Absolutism in this country as complete as the Absolutism of Russia, with the difference that our Autocrat would consist of a caucus-ridden House of Commons instead of a Sovereign. The new autocrat would instantly be impelled by the laws of self-preservation to take all the necessary steps to fortify and perpetuate itself, and in a very short time it would be as difficult to dislodge as the Tsardom. Government of the people would have passed away until the moment it was resumed by force or we became a conquered country.[4]

In all that paranoia expressing the broad view of the dominant right wing of Unionism there are two references to military force being used against the government. Willoughby de Broke, Maxse's great friend, would in due course harbour such thoughts and establish his British League with armed action half in mind. Over Ulster, the Unionist party would connive at militarised revolt and intimidation. Benito Mussolini was at this time editing a socialist newspaper, but in the teeth of anachronism, the as yet not conceived word 'fascism' comes to mind.

Meanwhile, Maxse looked forward to a 'Co-optation [sic] Bill' probably already drafted by Winston Churchill giving the Commons the right to forgo by-elections and co-opt new MPs, increase salaries tenfold and appoint a Speaker whose eye would never be caught by a Unionist. All that was wanted to prevent 'a dictatorship of needy, greedy adventurers' would be 'the House of Lords hesitating to reject the Parliament

Bill'. Lansdowne was playing for time, Maxse making his own flesh creep. The ever-durable Conservative Party was going to need all the craven white-flaggers it could find on its own back stairs to avoid an anticipatory convergence of ship and iceberg.

Meanwhile Asquith, in his placid, inveterate way, got on with business. The Parliament Bill – in essentials the placing on statute of the convention against Lords power over money bills, the downgrading of their veto on general legislation to a delaying power and, to assuage the single-chamber talk, reduction of seven years of an elected House to five – was carried by the Commons at first reading on 22 February by a majority of 124.

The second reading concluded on 2 March after four days' debate. Austen Chamberlain, for the opposition, spoke on 27 February of 'one of the gravest and most momentous questions with which it [the House] has ever been concerned. They were being asked to replace 'an unwritten and elastic constitution which has grown with our growth, developed with our development and adapted itself on the whole smoothly to the changing times' with 'a rigid formula'. And with the rigidity, said Austen sententiously, 'comes brittleness'. Given the House of Lords' overriding of a 200-year convention, this was a marked case of *chutzpah*.

Chamberlain wasn't impressed by the mandate or the majority. 'Well, the advocates of womens' suffrage claim that they also have a majority in this House – a majority much bigger than that of the government for this bill.' Did they also have a mandate? Of course not. In polite and sane form, Austen voiced the same fat-boy anxieties as Maxse – single-chamber government, a despotic majority in the House of Commons, a despotic government controlling such a majority. And invoking Gladstone and his whips pushing Home Rule eighteen years before, he applauded the Lords' power of bringing about dissolution. Fear of dissolution had caused the Liberals to overrule Gladstone's wish for it. 'They have tarred themselves with the Home Rule brush. They knew they were in danger of losing their seats because they were so tarred.'

The Lords (in conjunction with Joseph Chamberlain) had used their prerogative to kill off Home Rule for the interim. But what was Home Rule but the growing with our growth, developing with our development, the elastic constitutionalism which Austen had just extolled? And the delay about to be practised over the next three years before the freezing of the question at the outbreak of war would, with the events of 1916, leave the 'Constitution' entirely rigid and remarkably brittle. Spared this foresight, Austen came back ponderously into his home key with the orator's reiteration, telling the government: 'You battle in vain against the walls of a Constitution which has grown with our growth which has . . . brought to the service of the state every element of national greatness, and which has known how to preserve order in the midst of national progress, and defend and reform against revolution.'5

The debate ranged about. Balfour of Burleigh was about to introduce in the Lords a bill providing for referendums. William Brace, a Labour MP, commented that he did not object to a referendum as such. As a trades unionist, he didn't object to arbitration, but he didn't support it until he knew the terms of reference. 'The word "referendum" is a good word and it rolls well off the tongue,' but the all-important question was 'What is going to be referred? If we have a referendum in the future, will the House of Lords be the final authority to arrange the terms of reference?'6 Brace had no horror of single-chamber government but he didn't think that we would get it. But if the referendum were a replacement for the House of Lords, that member of the Labour Party would be for it.

Stephen Gwynn, the nationalist representing Galway, said something which in the light of the events of 1912-14 was rather prophetic. 'Hon. members talk as if the power of delay for two years meant nothing. Do you think it means nothing in our apprehension of the chances of Home Rule?'[7] Chambers, an Ulster member, informed the government that they were 'marching through rapine to the dismemberment of the Empire . . . tearing down the Constitution with the assistance of the Irish party and, having done that, they are going to dismember the Empire and cast off those who have been loyal and true . . . they are going to throw us over to the wolves.'[8]

Occasionally *Hansard* shows the perspective of an empty chamber. The Earl of Ronaldshay was interrupted by George Lansbury during a disquisition on the general revolutionary iniquity of things contrasted with aspects of the Greek and Norwegian constitutions. 'These are "revolutionary proceedings", we are told, and no one here to stop them. There is but one member on the other side.'[9]

Alfred Lyttleton, for the Tories, quoted Milton. 'Lords and Commons of England consider what nation it is whereof ye are the Governors, a nation not slow and dull, but of a quick, ingenious and piercing spirit,' and wondered how, during the summer conference, they had 'wholly failed to come to some arrangement upon this matter'. It was the way with milder Tories like Lyttleton and Balfour to strike a moderate tone, applaud all sorts of reform and wonder in a pained way at the government's stiff-necked insistence. Lyttleton also foresaw the future diminution of the Lords. 'I can imagine the Hon. member for Leicester (Mr Ramsay MacDonald) getting up when such a proposal was made. He would address a popular assembly, in say three or four years' time, which had tasted absolute power. Whoever heard of a popular chamber which had tasted the sweets of absolutism which had ever resigned them?'[10]

Sir Gilbert Parker, Tory MP and novelist, touched on the effect upon social tone of creating a wave of new peers. 'I think the country would suffer a humiliation unequalled in our parliamentary history if, for this partisan purpose, these degrading 500 peers were appointed. Napoleon's nobles of the First Empire would look like Planatagenets beside them.' As well as the usual charges of suspending the constitution and bringing in 'an era of wanton power', Sir Gilbert thought the government 'would have produced a degradation of parliamentary intelligence'.[11] (Asquith's private list of individuals contemplated for elevation if the need came included, in addition to Thomas Hardy, Bertrand Russell, Gilbert Murray, Sir Thomas Lipton and General Sir Ian Hamilton.)

A Liberal, Hugh Edwards, following him had a quotation: 'Here lies the corpse of the House of Lords. During the time of its existence, it has protected every abuse and sheltered every privilege; it has denied justice and delayed reform; irresponsible without independence; obstinate without courage; arbitrary without judgement and arrogant without knowledge.'[12] These were the words of Austen Chamberlain's father, Joseph, long ago in the days when Joe Chamberlain rather than single-chamber government or Home Rule had been the bogey of the unionists.

Captain Charles Craig from Ulster smelled radical conspiracy. Nothing since 1906 had been accidental: 'The agitation against the House of Lords which has resulted in this bill has been engineered in a very skilful way from the beginning.' The five bills rejected by the Lords since 1906 had been 'drawn up in such a way, their provisions were so drastic and far-reaching, it was known beforehand by every member on the front bench opposite that the House of Lords would be bound to reject them . . . The government determined for some reason I have not fathomed to get rid of the House of Lords altogether and they deliberately started sending such measures up to them.'[14] Ulster paranoia has always been in a baroque class of its own and Captain Craig continued for six and a half more columns of *Hansard* about the contingent iniquity of Home Rule. Dr Charles Leach, a Liberal, provided a useful list of the House of Lords' historic refusals: the Reform Act, Jewish and Catholic emancipation,

Nonconformists' rights to conduct marriage and burial ceremonies or to occupy public office and latterly, the South African settlement and old-age pensions.[14]

W.E. Guinness, a Tory, fell back into the seventeenth century and the excesses of the Long Parliament and quoted Cromwell, 'who cannot be suspected of very Conservative views', on MPs: 'Their pride and ambition and self-seeking ingrossing all places of honour and profit to themselves and their friends.' He called for 'some authority and power so full and so high as to restrain and keep things in better order and that may be a check to these exorbitances.'

Early twentieth-century debate was creditably flecked with allusions to events and people of whom late twentieth-century legislators may well never have heard. But teaching Asquith good constitutional practice by way of Oliver Cromwell was taking things a bit far.

Inflamed by the historical company he was keeping, Guinness denounced the prospective peers of creation in Maxse's terms as 'dummies', and proceeded to similar bloodshot conclusions. 'If the government are relying in their hope of resisting true reform on the action of the marionettes, let them remember that "they who take the sword shall perish by the sword"; that the weapon of constitutional violence can be used a second time and used against those who forged it.'[15] And he went on to hint at the comic-opera possibility of a Tory counter-creation.

Late on the third day there was a tiny exchange involving Asquith and a Tory MP, J.A. Clyde, which allowed Asquith to say almost everything about the House of Lords in one word:

Mr CLYDE: The complaint has really never been against the power of the Second Chamber, the complaint has been not that there is too great power in the Constitution, but that the brakesman has not yet had your confidence.

The PRIME MINISTER: Both.[16]

There was another terse exchange when Walter Runciman, now president of the Board of Education, put it to the Conservatives that they had lost.

> Mr RUNCIMAN: They appear seriously to have forgotten that on three occasions in a General Election, they have been totally defeated. It is not a chance majority that is now in power; it is a majority which has three times received authority from the constituencies.
> Lord HUGH CECIL made an observation which could not be heard by the Official Reporters.[17]

Some backbench comments had a scholarly ring. Henry Ingleby, another Conservative, quoted, then proclaimed, 'There we have Mr Pitt on the one hand and Mr Burke on the other as witnesses of the value of our splendid constitution. And again let me quote Polybius . . .' And what did Polybius say? 'With the government of the multitude and the destruction of the aristocracy comes every species of violence.' For himself, Mr Ingleby observed,' We want to preserve the aristocracy because it is the main prop of the throne.'[18]

From a very different point of view Philip Snowden, the future orthodox chancellor, but away from the treasury a vigorous and sharp-tongued socialist, put the argument back where it had come from – Lloyd George's budget. 'The House of Lords . . . did not reject it because they believed like Lord Rosebery that that budget was the end of all things . . . they knew that that was only the beginning of greater things. The reform of the House of Lords is a simple desire on the part of the aristocratic and plutocratic interests of this country to strengthen the second chamber, so that it will be a far stronger protector of their interests.'[19]

The Labour members tended rather to be prayed in aid by Tories as 'the multitude' in personal form. Claude Lowther made inquiries. Had not Keir Hardie said at Chester-le-Street,

'I regard the existence of a king as a proof of lunacy among the people'? Did not the milder Will Thorne say in Nottingham, 'I believe the Lords, monarchy and Church will all go at the same time'? Mr Lowther thought that if 'the one and only barrier between the country and socialistic anarchy' were abolished as the Parliament Bill sought to do then, 'we have the Commons thus left at the mercy of the first effective mob-monger'. The government were going to create 500 peers whose only qualification for a seat in the Lords was their blind, servile allegiance to party.

Alternatively, perhaps, you wish for an aristocracy of brains ... But if you establish your aristocracy of brains think in what a ridiculous position you will place this House! ... I say that the House of Lords, through the dignity of its debates and through its expert knowledge, has won for itself the admiration and respect of every parliament in the world.

An hon. member mumbled, 'Then why do you want to reform it?'[20]

The effective climax of the debate came with the opening speeches of its last day from Balfour and Asquith. Balfour was mild and speculative, casting a sad eye back on the hereditary principle and its enormous appeal to 'the ordinary man'. 'If you tell him that what reason really requires of him is to regard himself as being represented in an assembly for which he has perhaps given a vote for a candidate who has been rejected and in which the majority hold views in which he does not share, he would say, "They do not represent me; they are no better than I am; I differ from them; why should I obey them? Give me the old plan – my nation, or my tribe, or my clan, or my sept."'

In the light of the 20 million men about to start dying three years later for their tribe, clan or sept, he had a point of a desolating sort. It was also the comment of a high-octane obscurantist, primal slime being something we try to rise out of.

For Balfour, the hereditary principle was the universal mortar. It was to the Crown and not 'your transient majority' that 'the domnions beyond the seas or our fellow-subjects in India look'. All popular democracy was flawed. Someone had said, 'We want the will of the people,' by which he meant 'the will of the majority in this House for the time being'. Essentially Balfour argued for a sort of philosophical inertia, but he talked a measure of sense as he did so. Politics was not as important as politicians made out; majorities exaggerated the strength of public feeling. A few votes shifted so power moved from side to side. That was as it should be, sustaining stable government. But people didn't vote for specifies, education bills or licensing bills. There was no voice of the people there, and the House of Lords exercised a natural corrective, unfair, perhaps, he acknowledged, against radical governments, but really it was only enthusiasms that were being seen off. The real function of the House of Lords was to ensure very great caution over matters to do with the constitution.

Part of Balfour's charm was to take over the enpurpled bluster of Lord Halsbury or Claude Lowther and make it seem essentially reasonable. So the Lords' action in breaking precedent and stopping a finance bill was handled in these terms. 'I think it utterly absurd to say that the transfer of these few votes at a General Election under the violent influence of some hope, fear or passion of the moment is to give a universal power of attorney to any government to do exactly what it likes with the British constitution.' He was opposed, and 'always have been opposed to this talk or overtalk about mandates. Let me add that I think the system of pledges at elections is carried much too far – I think it is a great and growing evil.' Far more than he was a Unionist or indeed a Tory, Balfour was a Conservative, given to seeing the connection between progress and a secularised notion of original sin. He might well have said, 'In order not to fall into a hole don't dig at all.'

Upon that pessimism about a parliamentary system caught up in mandates and promises, he rested a Balfourian cool support for the referendum, a mechanism of negative virtue. 'It takes away from us the unlimited power we ought never to possess and it leaves us the power we ought always to possess – the power of determining absolutely what shall be the administration.'

When Balfour applied his refined thinking to Ireland, refinement quickly broke down, quite ruining his peroration. By reason of their dependency upon the Irish nationalists, the government were attempting 'to make fundamental changes in the constitution of which they are guardians, and openly say they are going to force them through one branch of the legislature by coercion, as they have imposed them on the country by fraud. (Hon. members: 'Order' and 'Withdraw'.)

The Speaker was then asked by a Liberal, Dalziel, if it was in order to use the word 'fraud' about individuals and political parties. The Speaker in a hapless moment said that when applied to individuals, the word was certainly unparliamentary 'but when applied to a party, I do not think the expression is out of order'. Irish members at once stood up and said, unanswerably as to parliamentary order, 'The Tory Party are frauds.'[21]

It was symbolic: Balfour as contemplative negativist thinker had great appeal and charm, however isolated from events. When he undertook the rant which his own football crowd expected, he finished in an undignified heap.

Asquith, speaking next, tackled the Tory calls for delay while the Lords was reformed in their way. They had become ardent Lords reformers; so had the Lords. Yet Balfour was saying that the Lords had been right all along to reject the Education Bill, Licensing Bill and budget. We had exactly the sort of second chamber which every rational democracy ought to desire. It has a clean bill. Every count in the indictment against it fails ... They have done right, says the Hon. gentleman. They have done what they ought to have done. The country has endorsed their view ... After three general elections in each of which the House of Lords has been conspicuously rebuffed, the country has endorsed their view! But he says they do not look well on paper. They are difficult to defend when you come face to face with hard-headed voters in Lancashire and Yorkshire. So let us put something in their place which will do the same as they do, but look a little more plausible and presentable ... Now we know the real inwardness and the true meaning of the desire of the Tory Party to reconstitute the second chamber.

And gently chiding the 'master of nebulous dialectic', Asquith quoted from Balfour's Manchester speech of October 1906: 'The chamber of review which we are now fortunate enough to possess is not quite one which would be easily improved even by the most ingenious constitution-mongers amongst us. It stands impregnable, not merely upon its historic past, but upon its present utility.' Yet as for the Tories now, 'Whatever else they are doing, they are constitution-mongering.'

Lucidity has its own splendours, and Asquith was putting together with perfect clarity the entire argument. He had nothing to retract; he had always taken this view. The Commons must be first in legislation; the functions of a second chamber were 'consultation and revision and, subject to proper safeguards, of delay. The body doing that should be small and it should not rest on a hereditary basis. Above all, unlike the current House of Lords, it should not be governed "by partisanship tempered by panic".'

All that being so, he and his government were not inclined as requested 'to wait, to hold our hands, to put this bill aside until some vast and formless change in the whole structure and mechanism of the constitution has been thought out and then worked out.'[22]

It was an elegant way of saying 'Nothing doing', which in the circumstances was the only thing to say. The Conservatives had constructed for themselves a doctrine of the Upper House which made it a guardian of the people's will, an instrument of inquiry into the true purpose of the nation, something it could do to yet greater perfection by referring difficult things to referendum. It was like a man bankrupt to the sum of £100,000 raising a loan of half a million for the purpose of expanding trade. The government would not only get their bill at that and later readings, they had won the argument.

The attempt in the Lords to reform the Lords defensively, to evade the consequences of acts done by the unreformed Lords, would still be made, but it would follow with extraordinary muddle. Lansdowne had been quite seriously ill and, in his absence, various well-intended mice tried to play. Balfour of Burleigh, who could claim to have warned Lansdowne privately and the Lords publicly not to jump into the pit they were now in, offered on the next day, 3 March, his 'Reference to the People' Bill. It took the referendum an enormous distance. Either House of Parliament could command a reference to the people in the event of dispute. For that matter, 200 MPs acting together could conjure one up even without a dispute between the parties. Lord Balfour's common sense operated best in the negative sphere. Favoured by many peers who had given no attention to his earlier advice, this genuinely revolutionary measure was given a first reading, but it went no further. Lansdowne had recovered and, recognising the limits of a constitutional picnic, requested Lord Balfour not to push this measure.

When it fell to Lansdowne on 8 May to put up the agreed reform rescue package, his moderation buttered few parsnips on either side of the debate. The House envisaged would be cut to 350 members, with only the new category of 'lords of Parliament' being summoned to attend. A hundred of these were to be elected by the generality of hereditary peers. The criterion would be distinction, either in public service – those generals, colonial governors and ambassadors about whom Curzon had rhapsodised – or expressing an old-style territoriality or by way of lords lieutenant and chairmen of county councils (a very lordish thing at this date). Another 120 peers would be elected by a college of MPs grouped by locality; and a third group, also of 120, would be appointed by the government on a strict basis of party proportions. Rather fewer spiritual lords, the bishops having been unsound in the conflict, but a good quota of law lords completed the mix.

Lansdowne stood sweetly between stools. He had ended the hereditary principle, banishing more than half the peers altogether and letting others back by a byzantine mixture of nomination and closed election. But he had kept a Tory majority for the purpose of stopping 'radical' legislation. As he candidly explained, given the present government majority of 126, there would be a unionist majority of eighteen, 'not, I venture to say, a very large majority for a body whose duty is admittedly the duty of revision and delay'. Lansdowne was not a humorous man, but there was something of a tease in his next words. 'And my lords, are we quite sure that we could always depend on that majority? I doubt myself whether there is anything which could be fairly described as a standing party majority in such a House. In such a House, carefully selected, evenly balanced with heavier responsibility, you would find that what I may fairly describe as the cross-bench mind would very often prevail.'[23]

If Lansdowne was being flirtatious, the chances of the government spokesman Morley flirting back were nil. The Unionist leader had contrived in what he called his Reconstitution Bill to abandon the hereditary principle while leaving the Tory Party a short-handled weapon against reform legislation. The Lords Reconstitution Bill was a baroque construction for a narrow (and obvious) party purpose. The *Morning Post* denounced, it, Maxse quoted *Through the Looking Glass* – lines about 'dying my whiskers green' – and once Morley had spoken, it was going nowhere. It existed to stop the Parliament Bill. It furiously changed the Lords membership in order to keep its powers stolidy the same. Morley's words were terminal. 'The noble Marquess's bill may or may not be a good bill; an adequate and sufficient bill in itself and on its own merits. It may or may not prove to be a possible supplement or complement to the Parliament Bill, but there is one thing which it cannot be. It cannot be a substitute or an alternative for the Parliament Bill. That is the definite position.'[24]

Various things would be said by peers, notably Willoughby de Broke's polite accusation that Lansdowne was introducing 'a measure which, in my opinion, will destroy the constitution and abolish this historic House for no adequate reason except as a tactical measure for securing the support of some electors while, at the same time, appeasing those who desire not reform, but single-chamber government'.[25] But the words of the debate had been made irrelevant. All that remained was the brute option of accepting the Parliament Bill or resisting it to the point where the Lords was swamped and degraded by the people whom Mr Lowther thought made First Empire nobility look like Plantagenets.

The coolest and best judgement of it all came from Fitzroy. Clerk to the Privy Council, younger son of a duke, descendant of Charles II, Sir Almeric was hardly a Jacobinical figure. 'Lord Lansdowne made the best case he could. As a parliamentary swordsman distinguished for consummate dexterity, he never acquitted himself better, but to the question, to what profit, no adequate answer is returnable. His scheme from the first could not have been expected to supersede that of the government.'

Fitzroy added a couple of days later, 'I had a long talk with Charlie Helmsley, who is quite of my opinion that the present position of the Tory Party is very hopeless and, in language I might have used myself, attributed it to the ghastly error committed two years ago: the damned consequences, in short, had overtaken its authors.'[26]

Fitzroy was sufficiently a lover of tradition to know that the House of Lords had its roots in 'the *curia* of the Norman kings, with its feudal tradition as a court of vassals expanding into the *Magnum Concilium* of the Plantegenets'. He also knew that the House of Lords 'at times slowly and reluctantly – at others freely and generously – has moulded itself to the desire of the nation; but time has dimmed what it could not destroy and secular prestige withers before the constant censorship of popular opinion.'

Fitzroy had no doubt that he had watched while 'the opposition leader with balanced phrase, graceful diction and judicial restraint pronounced what was in effect a sentence of death upon the oldest legislative chamber in the world'.[27]

22

'Traitor, Traitor, 'vide, 'vide'

The term 'long hot summer' could have been designed for 1911. It was a season combining political tension with meteorological excess. The coronation of 22 June took place ahead of the last stage of the Parliament Bill, with the Lords stage as final hurdle, or triumphal arch, as the case might be. It was also a time for enacting other controversial measures: Lloyd George's National Insurance Act and a Trades Union Bill to offset the Osborne judgment made against political contributions to political parties.[1]

The government, feeling that it had jumped, or rather crawled, through quite enough hoops in the seventeen months since the budget had been rejected, made grateful use of all the procedural devices of acceleration it could lay its hands on. There were 900 amendments, mostly Tory, but by use of the Kangaroo, which grouped and skipped where the guillotine sliced, these were disposed of in ten days.

Calls for the government's guidance to the Crown on assent to be replaced by the Privy Council, or alternatively that a tribunal made up of judges and those colonial governors again, were remaindered. So were the notion of the liberal Tory, Sir Alfred Cripps, that some subordinate title should be given to acts of Parliament passing into law unblessed by their lordships

334

and Lord Hugh Cecil's call for a secret vote at third reading to frustrate that caucus against which Conservatives now railed and which, in his municipal days, Joseph Chamberlain had invented. Balfour, feeling that enough from Lord Hugh was too much, withheld official support for the latter. Defeated on a division was a sizeable Liberal revolt (137 strong), led by Sir Henry Dalziel, which would have cut the delay allowed to the Lords from three sessions to two. In the light of the nervous distress soon to be imposed by resistance to Home Rule, Asquith must have lived to regret not nodding Sir Henry through.

It remained to the unreformed Lords to make its amendments. *Punch*, moderate to liberal in outlook at this time, showed two peers in coronets and shirtsleeves making ready behind a wall of sandbags:

> *First Peer*: What about the White Flag?
> *Second Peer* (reaching into an ammunition box marked 'Amendments'): Well, I dare say it'll come to that in the end; but we may as well loose off this stuff first.[2]

Punch's peers are affable sorts with a nod at the Emsworth style. Willoughby de Broke of the British League and the study of genetics was in earnest. To the embarrassment of Lansdowne, he moved an amendment that no bill twice rejected by the Lords should receive royal assent until it had been approved by the voters at both a General Election and a referendum. This, he said proudly, was a root amendment which, as Lansdowne had to point out, could not be made with second reading passed. Ignoring such niceties, Willoughby pressed to a division. Time was when he had come down on the early train from Warwickshire to join another 400 foxhunting peers at Lansdowne House to receive the Marquess's instructions, a time when no one wanted long debate to delay the lunch provided at the Carlton. On the present occasion he called out only seventeen rebels, but he was acting independently and made clear that night his readiness to move rejection of third reading.

Lansdowne's moderation was largely technical sophistication. For across the six days from 28 June, their lordships constitutionally uprooted most of the bill, inserting a committee of both Houses to determine what might be a money bill, creating whole categories of bills which would fall outside its scope. Nothing affecting monarchy or Protestant succession, or creating any Parliament or council in any of the three kingdoms, or deemed by that committee of the two Houses to be a matter of great gravity would automatically be granted exemption from veto. But these were the moves of the moderate Tory peers, Cromer and Lansdowne himself. The extremists had hardly started.

Reacting with unnecessary awe to the coronation, John Morley had remarked, 'What a moment to die.' A growing number of peers concurred. The high-class gossip Fitzroy was taking in at this time was instructive. Lord Bath told him at Mrs Pitt-Rivers' reception that 'the wiser course would have been for Lord Lansdowne to wash his hands of all responsibility and, by declining to move amendments, to reserve his freedom of action against the time when his party should again be in power.' Lord Lansdowne had, he regretted to say, 'yielded to pressure from advocates of more violent courses'. Bath ran through the players: Selborne, who 'in season and out of season, was urging resistance', was 'blind to the handling of the present difficulty but . . . his persistence makes him formidable'. Balfour, said Bath was 'in favour of prudence'; Curzon and St John Broderick took the same line. Bath, and those who thought like him, 'realised that no substantial advantage was to be gained by prolonging the struggle'. They were 'making themselves accomplices in a step which would destroy the historic peerage of the United Kingdom and substitute for its prescriptive splendour a titled mob without faith, distinction or responsibility.'[3]

The weather got hotter and legislation progressed. If

Asquith stayed firm, the Lords would have to choose between the white flag and the ammunition box. And, despite self-comforting talk among peers about bluff, Asquith, the player of long slow games, had not the faintest intention of being anything else. The Cabinet minute to the King, sent a week after the Lords depredations, is crisp. 'The Bill might just as well have been rejected on Second Reading.' The amendments would be 'rejected *en bloc* by the Commons and a complete conflict between the two Houses will have been created . . . a third dissolution is wholly out of the question. Hence in the contingency contemplated, it will be the duty of Ministers to advise the Crown to exercise its Prerogative so as to get rid of the deadlock and secure the passing of the Bill. In such circumstances, Ministers cannot entertain any doubt that the Sovereign would feel it to be his Constitutional duty to accept their advice.'[4]

'Contingency' is a fine word. Like a sexual euphemism, it tactfully indicated the act which dare not speak its name. Creation of peers, like procreation itself, had to be spoken of in code. Asquith gracefully moved the decanter round the table to the tremulous King. 'In such circumstances, Ministers cannot entertain any doubt that the Sovereign would feel it to be his Constitutional duty to accept their advice.' The hemlock stood at George's right hand.

Before drinking, George, as he told Asquith through Knollys, wanted to wait until the Commons had thrown out the Lords amendments. That was allowed. Creation, embarrassing to Asquith, could wait, but certainty of creation was something else. Just as it would have made sense for Lansdowne to keep out of amendment-making, it would have made sense to let the Unionist leadership know the hard realities as soon as George's painful consent had been extracted. What Knollys had known the King must do must be made known now. Belief in the possibility of bluff was a mist which had to be lifted.

That message delivered, Fitzroy was witness to its effect.

He observed 'the point and piquancy' of the meeting of peers at Lansdowne House. But 'the problem the peers have to solve lies in a nutshell'. They should ask themselves if any election would produce a different result from December – two by-elections had done nothing for the unionists. If it would not, 'the only conclusion they can draw is that their duty lies in giving effect to the popular voice, however distasteful to themselves.'[5]

The constitutionally dogged Lansdowne had to be convinced more urgently than the constitutionally sceptical Balfour. Who better to carry the news than Lloyd George, the rejection of whose budget had set off the whole pageant? In the words of Newton, Lansdowne's biographer, 'On July 18, Mr Lloyd George met Mr Balfour and Lord Lansdowne and stated that a pledge to create peers had been obtained from the King as far back as November: that nothing would induce the Government to run the risk of losing the Parliament Bill in the House of Lords; and that the Government were reluctant to create Peers.'[6] The Conservative leaders were also told that, on 24 July, Asquith meant to combine announcing the government response to Lords amendments with a public statement of the intention to create peers. Time would be granted before disposal of the amendments for negotiations which might allow for some concession on Crown and Protestant succession legislation and the joint committee replacing the Speaker as definer of legislative categories.

This was all unofficial, but if Lansdowne wanted a formal letter to himself ahead of that day he could have it. Asquith was treating the Lords courteously, but Lansdowne complained that the amendments should come back to the Lords with a reasoned statement of objections. What was offered was 'entirely inconsistent with the consideration which one House had a right to expect at the hands of the other.'[7]

It was left to Knollys to pick up the negotiations. Lansdowne complained that the proposed announcement 'could not fail to have a most exasperating effect upon those peers who were already inclined to oppose the passing of the Parliament Bill at whatever cost'. He asked to be allowed to tell them himself at a peers' meeting. Lansdowne was already telling Newton that he feared a revolt in his own ranks. The idea of *en bloc* rejection by the Commons made him apprehensive and Knollys, in the courtly, disingenuous way of this sort of discourse, said that 'he had no idea that any procedure was likely to be followed', that the King was reluctant and that he, Knollys, hoped an intimation of last-resort creation would do the trick. He even suggested that a creation as small as twenty would be enough, which it wouldn't.[8]

The third reading now passed the Lords quickly with a brief exchange of severities between Lansdowne and Morley. Yet the amendments remained in the air with the prospect of a body of peers insisting on their return upon a division. It was time for Asquith to write a letter which probably should have been written back in November when the King had agreed in principle. This stated that 'the government will advise the King to exercise his prerogative to secure the passing into law of the bill in substantially the same form in which it left the House of Commons and His Majesty has been pleased to signify that he will consider it his duty to act upon that advice'.[9]

We had come at last to 'contingencies'. F. Anstey's novel of thirty years earlier, *Vice Versa*, contains the line: 'Drastic measures is Latin for a whopping.' So was 'contingencies'. Lansdowne, knowing that, proceeded immediately to a meeting of peers. Their lordships were seeing their illusory battlements of Asquithian bluff and the backstop resistance of the King dissolve into the air. At Lansdowne's meeting, people said predictable things. St Aldwyn, declared: 'Although we might be applauded for our courage if we "died in the last ditch", the deliberate judgement of the country, when it has had time to reflect, will be against us.'[10] Selborne, about whom Fitzroy and his friends had shaken their heads, said: 'No courses could be more disastrous than that of surrendering until the opponents of the bill were actually outvoted in the House of Lords.'[11]

Lansdowne himself, beginning to dispel his self-deceptions, thought 'the more prudent course might be to allow the bill to pass, the peers, of course, making it clear that they accept no responsibility for it'. He was now talking about future things that might be done by way of redress under a Unionist government, not necessarily fantasy, though no succeeding Tory government would ever show much enthusiasm for the requisite resurrectionary legislation.

In fact, as Lansdowne had hinted privately to Newton, the real division would now be within Conservative ranks. Bedford, Salisbury, Halsbury and Willoughby de Broke had spoken along the same 'no surrender' lines as Selborne, now immured in his bitter certainties. And earlier, during the third reading debate, old Halsbury had fired off the sort of broadside for which this particular loose cannon was becoming famous.

'I should like to know what man with the spirit of a man in his heart would consent to sit in an assembly mocking the actuality of debate when at the end of it, he is obliged to submit to what the minister for the time being thinks proper to dictate.' He was concerned that the people of the country did not understand what was going on in Parliament. 'They do not know . . . the Constitution of the Country is in peril. The passing of this bill unamended would mean the destruction of the Constitution and threaten the destruction also of the liberties, aye, and the lives, of His Majesty's subjects, wherever they are. It is the most momentous piece of attempted legislation I have known in the course of my long life.' He could not believe that 'men familiar with Constitutional principles should have contrived such a mass of unconstitutional, bitter and selfish proposals'.[12]

For Halsbury, the proposed creation of peers was 'a gross violation of parliamentary decency'. He went on about 'injustice and tyranny' and his 'solemn duty to God and my country'. The immediate duty was to vote against the bill at the next opportunity. This would come with the return of the Lords amendments. Halsbury had been born in 1823, nine years before the Great Reform Act, though his language – that 'aye' and a profusion of 'forsooths' – had the ring of 200 years earlier, and he would quote, not for the first time, from a statute of Edward I, trumpeting that 'the disppearance of an act of Parliament by desuetude is unknown to English law'. But quite what even Halsbury meant by the 'destruction of the lives of the King's subjects' who could guess, unless Halsbury had been listening to the armed-rising talk in which Willoughby had wistfully indulged and which would feature more often when the scene shifted to Ireland. To listen to Halsbury was to understand the fix Lansdowne was in.

But that was where Lansdowne's own foot-dragging resistance and belief in government bluff had put him. From now on, there existed a diehard party bent upon pulling down the pillars of the temple and getting on television. On the other hand, Lansdowne, attending that meeting after noting in a private minute St Aldwyn's plea for realism and recognition of the impossible, added: 'Lord Curzon spoke with much ability in the same sense.'[13] This was to be of enormous importance, for Curzon's line of thought, though in a more sharply defined way, had paralleled Lansdowne's own and would continue to do so. That line had been a wiggly one whose course, very roughly, was: 'Fight the corner defiantly; Asquith's bluffing so just keep going; oh no he isn't; very well, we should be awful fools to push our luck any further; lets cut our losses.' Or, as he put it a letter to Violet Cecil, 'Many of the Lords are d—d fools', adding that the resisters would 'dwindle daily as they are brought face to face with facts.'[14]

Curzon would be the exact opposite number of Willoughby de Broke, who would whip and organise for the irreconcilables. Both had energy and clear purpose, but Curzon had *The Times*, whose proprietor, Northcliffe, he had won round to editorial support. Using *The Times* himself, through the letters column, Curzon set out his stall on 23 July. It was cowardly to retreat, was it? He was 'not aware that the Duke of Wellington, when he bent his head in similar circumstances, was ever tainted with cowardice ... the greater courage is that which is willing to be miscalled cowardice, to face estrangement and to endure reproach sooner than advise a course which, stripped of its superficial appearance of valour, is found to be indifferent to the permanent interests of the state'.[15]

Curzon, although his own roots were those of the very backwoods peerage in which Willoughby rejoiced and which now lay like a 4-ton log on a railway line, had created his own aura of grandeur and not-to-be-argued-with self-confidence. As A.G. Gardiner would note, 'Curzon's superiority was aggressive and self-conscious. It was not merely implicit, it hit you in the face. He moved through life as if it were a Roman triumph arranged to celebrate his magnificent transit through time.'[16]

These were qualities which made enemies on the assembly line and would deny Curzon the premiership. But at this time, such loftiness and self-assurance were exactly the requirements of the quotidian business of persuading the House of Lords to be sensible. Lansdowne, though he now understood the situation, had been weakly strong and was still distinctly limp, while Balfour, at this very moment, was engaged in the worst kind of silly cleverness. A decisive lead to the shadow Cabinet being perfectly essential, Balfour began his comments to colleagues by first suggesting that talk of the diehards defending the pass at Thermopylae was 'for music hall consumption'. But having started at the provocative end of strong, he collapsed into saying that it was all right to play up to 'the music hall attitude of mind' providing that 'the performance was not too expensive' – i.e., that it did not 'swamp the House of Lords'. He added that the creation of fifty or a hundred peers was 'a matter of indifference'.[17]

It wasn't just that the inertia principle had a disciple

in Balfour; he advertised his inactivity. There was a full-blown crisis running in his party and his immediate response invoked the words used to him five years earlier by Campbell-Bannerman – 'Enough of this foolery.' It left the shadow Cabinet split wide open, with Austen Chamberlain, F.E. Smith, Salisbury and others joining Halsbury and Selborne in their ditch, while Derby, Bonar Law, Long and Middleton urged acceptance of the Parliament Bill.

Among the peers themselves a great body of defections had left Lansdowne leading a residue; fortunately Curzon offered to take charge of it. He also strengthened Lansdowne's own resolution in the face of the right. As Balfour put it, with languid admiration, Lord Lansdowne would not budge. 'George Curzon won't let him; won't leave him.'[18] Curzon was assigning his own clear imperious purposes to the cause of moderation – just what it needed.

Meanwhile, in the Commons, an outing by the junior branch of the diehards did everything that could be asked to discredit the hard line. On 24 July, Asquith was due to make the statement to the Commons about the government's approach to the Lords amendments. It was never made. As 'Toby MP' put it in *Punch*: 'Since the free fight on the floor of the House that disgraced the session of 1893, nothing has equalled the tumult that filled the chamber this afternoon.' Toby (Henry Lucy) continues in the semi-cablese style, flecked with pet names, which marked that famous column.

Premier rose amid storm of cheering from his own supporters. Taking up sheet of manuscript, placed on brass-bound box as he entered, he smoothed it out and the cheers subsiding, began his speech. Instantly uprose from group behind Front Opposition Bench, on which Prince Arthur [Balfour] lolled with languorous air, cries of 'Traitor! Traitor!' Shout taken up from front benches below Gangway.

COUSIN HUGH [Cecil] in corner seat, pale to the lips,

with blazing eyes and frail form shaken by tempestuous passion, led the rally. [There were also cries of 'Let Redmond speak,' the next hatred getting itself warmed up. Despite the Speaker making his 'earnest appeal for preservation of order' it was impossible for Asquith to get a hearing.] EDWARD CARSON moved adjournment of debate. Speaker ready at every turn pointed out that the debate had not yet been opened. F.E. SMITH waved both arms in eloquent, though inaudible argument. All the while in corner seat sat COUSIN HUGH, like the bird of evil omen perched on the bust of Pallas above the chamber door, forlornly croaking "Vide, 'vide, 'vide' . . . Premier took no more notice of him than if he were a fly settled on somebody else's nose . . . For full forty minutes the struggle lasted – a hundred men against one. At last with angry gesture, the PREMIER rolled up his manuscript and facing round to his supporters, protested 'I am not going to degrade myself by futher endeavouring to press arguments on people who are evidently not willing to listen.*[19]

Shrewdly, Asquith's chief whip, Elibank, moved around the back benches enjoining a perfect silence for Balfour when he should speak. As Toby put it, 'Elibank was seen fluttering round dove-like, with olive branch in his beak. Effect marvellous. Prince Arthur was listened to in silence, an unexpected reception he gratefully acknowledged.' In that silence Balfour would be unable to disguise either his embarrassment at what he could not control or his unwillingness to disown it.

The hysteria of the Unionist right could have had no

---

* Lord Hugh Cecil, for all his antics – so identified with him that the phrase 'the Hughligans' had earlier been coined for his group – had charms denied to most of the diehards. One cannot be altogether against a man who, on descending from his first bus, reflects on his own high Anglicanism and naïveity at large: 'I descended by way of what, with my ecclesiastical predilections, I should call the West Door.'[20]

more vivid public display. Asquith's daughter, Violet, less ironic than Toby, said that they 'behaved – and looked – like mad baboons'. They were doing Asquith's work for him – and Curzon's. Birrell, speaking a few days later to Northamptonshire Liberals at Althorp, observed that the rioters 'had not even had the excuse of losing their tempers; it was a carefully planned, cold-blooded orgy of stupidity and ruffianism'.[21]

The *National Review*, by contrast, had no notion of forty minutes' continuous screaming being bad tactics, never mind bad manners. It spoke of 'the historic scene of 24 July, when at last the House of Commons found tongue and for once really represented public opinion'. But by this time, the *National* was beside itself with rage, venting much of it on the Tory leadership. Exempting only the *Morning Post*, *Pall Mall Gazette*, *Standard* and *Globe*, it also turned on the mainstream newspapers, including *The Times*, which Curzon had won round. It spoke with the flash of an incisor of 'the scuttle press', which 'generally has one common interest, namely to hold the system familiarly known as Foozle and Boozle and to represent the Foozlers and Boozlers as the only people who count in public life'. This was 'the present rotten system, under which political parties and governments are either run by the Rt Hon. A.J. Foozle and the particular coterie of which he is the centre, or by the Rt Hon. H.H. Boozle and Co., who have succeeded in getting their noses into the public bin'.

The *National* now openly hated the Tory leader. A.J. Balfour was A.J. Foozle, his supporters white-flaggers, while its own faction were 'the stalwarts'. Certain of conspiracy everywhere, they viewed Curzon, 'who has played perhaps the worst part of anybody in the crisis', in the livid perspective of paranoia. Curzon, Lansdowne and Middleton couldn't just have changed their minds or realised that the game was up. It could only be that while 'delivering brave speeches declaring their readiness to die in the last ditch, they were privately preparing to surrender on the first plausible pretext'.

As for Asquith, he had

> openly sold his country, for which he cares nothing, his party, for which he cares little, and himself, for which he cares much, to the Dollar Dictator [John Redmond] and the apostle of dynamite. He has bartered the British Constitution against the votes required to secure for him and his needy, greedy colleagues the enjoyment of the princely fortunes which for some accountable reason are lavished upon Cabinet ministers ... Mr Asquith has, deliberately and in cold blood, devoted his talents to lowering the position of this country in the eyes of the civilised world and risking our credit and security by the establishment of single-chamber government under which the narrowest majority in one House, elected by the most corrupt means, can establish an autocracy such as we have not seen for 250 years which then ended, as this will end, in bloodshed ... In a word he has sold his soul for five thousand a year. His government has hounded one king into the grave and has betrayed another by traitorous advice. He has smashed the British Constitution to oblige the enemies of Britain; he is preparing to install another Transvaal at our doors.

That expectation of violence again, but then, Leo Maxse was the master of the psychotic style.

It was also natural that what struck the prejudiced Violet Asquith as the behaviour of baboons was recounted by him as something of a triumph. There were, he said, 'limits to what human nature can endure, and to us the marvel is not that the Unionist Party should have at last found tongue to protest against the sale of the country by the Foozles and the Boozles, but that they should have been able to remain silent so long while one Front Bench attacked the Constitution with vigour and malignancy and its self-appointed defenders could never be got to take off the kid-gloves'.

Praising the 'courage' of Lord Hugh and the help he had had from Carson and Smith, the *National* went on to sum up: 'The outbreak of July 24 was a revolt against the Caucus. It was not, as the pundits of the press will have it, a mere exhibition of Tory hooliganism; rather was it the indignation of honest men who resented being sold to their enemies.'[22]

But Maxse did have an apt quotation – from a Liberal newspaper, one of which it approved and which almost certainly reflected the truth. 'Probably, however,' the *Daily Chronicle* had said, 'the exhibition in the House of Commons, though ostensibly directed against Mr Asquith, was in part at least, addressed to another quarter. It was intended, we may reasonably suppose, as a demonstration against what is called 'Lord Lansdowne's policy of surrender' in the House of Lords.'[23]

So it had been, and for the last three weeks of a crisis which had run for twenty-one months, resistance to the 'radical party' government would take the form of a hand-to-hand knife fight among titled Conservatives; a Hobbesian conflict amid the red upholstery, the war of lord against lord.

23

The Captain of the Rats

To the *National Review* Balfour had become 'the titular leader of the Unionist Party now openly hand in glove with toe-the-line Asquith'. He 'had been kept straight for one day [Monday 24 July] by the demonstration against Mr Asquith, but no one expected him to remain straight'.[1]

Indeed not, for Lansdowne, with Curzon at his elbow, had made clear in a minute to peers that acceptance of the Parliament Bill was the only course.

> It is a choice whether by desisting from further opposition, we shall render it possible for His Majesty's government to carry the bill in the House of Lords as at present constituted, or whether by insisting on our amendments, we shall bring about a creation of peers in numbers which may overwhelm the present House and paralyse its action in the future without in any way retarding the passage of the Parliamentary Bill. I have come to the conclusion that the former alternative is preferable in the interests of the House, the Unionist Party and the Country.

He acknowledged and wanted his party to recognise 'that we are no longer free agents'.[2]

Balfour, after his flippant memo about music halls – which Curzon had managed to stop him from circulating – produced a long letter to his friend Newton and for publication. The key phrase was 'I agree with the advice Lord Lansdowne has given to his friends'. And he ended with the observation: 'It would, in my opinion, be a misfortune if the present crisis left the House of Lords weaker than the Parliament Bill by itself will make it, but it would be an irretrievable tragedy if it left us a divided party.'[3]

Even wearing his straightest face and in this most reasonable and necessary of damage-limiting causes, Balfour could not stop the too-blatant cynicism from forming a slick on the surface of his good sense. He was saying privately that he thought that parts of the Conservative Party had gone mad and nothing in their conduct over the next fortnight would contradict him. When the diehards – or 'ditchers', as they were called in honour of the last ditch and in contempt of Curzon's 'hedgers' – met to proclaim their solidarity at a public function, the so called Halsbury Banquet, they did so in effective secession from the party that Lansdowne and Balfour led. The organiser of the banquet, something arranged at short notice at the Hotel Cecil, was Willoughby, in association with F.E. Smith, Selborne's son Wolmer, and Smith's recently elected brother, Harold. Willoughby was now indispensable and centre stage – a dog, this foxhunting man would have acknowledged, having his day.

As he would later confirm, the entire ditcher/diehard movement was a thing of the last three weeks before the final vote. And with Lord Leith's house and that of the Duke of Westminster used as committee rooms and assembly points, he busied himself organising runners to canvass for revolt among the peerage of their neighbourhoods. Notable among these were Saltoun, Ebury, Bathurst, Raglan, Ampthill and Rothes.[4]

On the 25th a statement of intent by the diehards went out signed by Halsbury, Selborne, Salisbury, Willoughby,

Mayo and Lovat. It declared 'the barren power of two years' delay reserved to the House of Lords' to be 'unworthy of consideration', and proclaimed with touching confidence, 'We believe that we are supported in our resistance to it by half the nation, and that a majority of English men and women deeply resent the violence that is being offered to the constitution.'[5] What they believed the Scots, Welsh or Irish to think, their lordships did not say.

Willoughby's short-notice invitations were bearing fruit. 'It simply rained letters,' he said. The Halsbury Banquet attracted a good attendance. Roy Jenkins puts it at 600, though with an ironic shortage of lords – only forty in all. It was chaired by Selborne with Halsbury himself at his right as guest of honour and main speaker, and a top table completed by Austen Chamberlain, Milner, Edward Carson, Smith, Salisbury, Pretyman (a Tory MP who had made a stir with his opposition to the budget), the Dukes of Bedford and Portsmouth, Cave, a future lord chancellor, the Dukes of Westminster* and Somerset, the Earls of Scarborough, Plymouth and Winchester and J.H. Campbell KC.

The emotional mood surrounding the speeches – which take up a full page of *The Times*, with regular interpolations of '(cheers)' and '(loud cheers)' – is caught in the response to a passage of Lord Selborne in one of these bracketed spasms. 'The scales are dropping from the eyes of the electors. Our duty as trustees is plain – to stand by the amendments the House of Lords has made unless and until outvoted in the lobbies. (Loud cheers, most of the company rising and waving dinner napkins enthusiastically.)'[6]

Selborne had opened the proceedings ecstatically. 'We are now in the middle of a revolution (cheers). We know it. The

---

* This Westminster was the ignominious 'Bendor', so called after his racing colours, an activist diehard close to Selborne. But he is perhaps best remembered for informing against his brother-in-law, Lord Beauchamp, for homosexuality, driving him into exile and drawing from George V the remark – about Beauchamp, naturally – 'I thought men like that shot themselves.'

electors of the country are only just beginning to realise it. It is our duty to make this ominous and fatal fact known to them (cheers).' This revolution was not, Selborne continued, 'being compassed by shot and shell. Effectually it is being compassed by falsehood and fraud (loud cheers).' Making a point which had already appeared in the diehard letter, he welcomed the creation of peers. It would 'hallmark the revolution as a revolution' and would 'tear aside the veil of the government's hypocrisy'. Selborne then offered a toast to Halsbury for 'his conduct in the crisis of his country's fate'. He concluded: 'I give you the toast of the Constitutional Cause coupled with the name of Lord Halsbury. (Toast drunk amid scenes of enthusiasm, the company rising from their seats and cheering vociferously.)'[7]

One ironic feature of the banquet was the deference shown at the start of all speeches to Lansdowne and Balfour – great and good men both, splendid leaders both, not a word against them – before each speaker urged a course at 90 degrees' variance from what Balfour and Lansdowne had asked of them.

Halsbury, speaking second with the gnarled elaboration he mistook for courtesy, shrewdly reverted to Lansdowne's own earlier pronouncement on government legislation. 'Nothing is safe,' the leader had said. 'The crown is not safe, the constitution is not safe, the union is not safe, the Church is not safe.' It was an effective thrust. Lansdowne, and to a lesser extent Balfour, had paddled among the grotesque end-of-the-world orotundities which Halsbury and his fellow diners were still talking. As a professional politician of some sophistication, Lansdowne understood the difference between a flourish of bogey talk and devout belief that, in the person of H.H. Asquith, the Reds were coming. Eloquence is a cross of lath, but Lansdowne was nailed to it.

Halsbury's antique and extremist mind applied itself to the possibility of the impeachment of Asquith. 'Such things as impeachment have been known,' he said, alluding to the

1711 crisis. 'But the act deserving impeachment ought to have been resisted. Did you vote against it? . . . You knew it was wrong, you denounced it as wrong, you said it was an outrage on the constitution.' He would say to Lansdowne and Balfour, whom he so respected, 'You had the power to vote and had not the manliness to do so.'

Pausing only to comment that the last creation of peers, under Queen Anne (implemented by Tories!), had been 'utterly disgraceful and an outrage upon the Constitution', Halsbury concluded by calling the Parliament Bill 'the most corrupt measure that I believe can be found in English history'.[8] He then sat down to prolonged and fervid rapture and a subsequent proposal, clean out of W.S. Gilbert and just averted, that he should be taken home to Kensington in triumph in an open cab drawn by a team of peers.

Wyndham, man of culture, poet, anti-semite, nurser of grudges, perhaps as alienated from moderate Tory politics as anyone and 'the most handsome man in Britain', was the most biting about his (unnamed) leaders. His friends, 'having made up their minds, were not prepared to close them for extensive alteration and repairs and put their consciences into commission. And their belief was that the future of the country was at stake'. Some names, of course, had only to be mentioned to get a music-hall response. 'Mr Winston Churchill (hisses) has publicly proclaimed that so much power was to be left to the House of Lords and if they were to use what was left, they would be held up to contempt for petulant and irritating employment of functions they should have abandoned.'

Wyndham also had an ingenious defence against the charge of disloyalty. Although he thought the division in the Unionist party was 'touched by tragedy', was it not a rebuttal of 'that foolish jibe that the House of Lords is only a wing of the Carlton Club, an annexe of Lansdowne House? They are now refuting that insult in the steps they are taking.'[9]

The Duke of Northumberland said what everyone, starting

with Selborne, seemed to have been saying all evening – that the House of Lords were 'Trustees for the Nation' – and added his own twist: 'As trustees for the good of the country they have no right to relinquish that duty whatever the consequences. Indeed,' continued his Grace, providing an inadvertent epitaph on the whole saga, there was 'these days altogether too much thinking of consequences'.

The Lords was 'on the whole, the best deliberative and legislative assembly the world has ever seen (cheers)'. He also invoked Oliver Cromwell, whose assaults upon the constitution had been 'rather more humble than those of the present prime minister with his proposals for the creation of Brummagem peers'. The Trustee for the Nation had a phrase for this sort of thing. 'We are suffering the effects of unparalleled democracy.' And it was endured 'under the rule of a despotic prime minister'. The function of the rebels was to have 'provided the unionist party with a backbone'.[10]

Milner, now a viscount, also stressed the trustee theme. They were trustees for the nation, and were they to give up, 'more pliable trustees' would be appointed. 'Very well, let the government appoint agents of its own to do its evil work.' Milner found it harder than most men to go through the fatuities of undying admiration for Lansdowne and Balfour. They had 'badly miscalculated, a miscalculation rendered only worse by large pronouncments of the heroic stand they were going to make on some future occasion'. Milner's savage contempt for weakness, of however sensible a sort, then broke surface. 'The spectacle of men in full retreat turning to hurl defiance at those upon whom they have turned their backs is not an inspiring spectacle.'[11]

A message of support had been read out from Joseph Chamberlain, still dedicated, in his seventy-fifth year and paralysed by a stroke, to a life's work of destroying party leaderships. His son, Austen, contributed a decent attempt at an inflammatory speech. But Austen was not a man to be

altogether taken seriously. Gardiner's scathing judgement fifteen years later lingers in the mind. 'He is the last reminiscence
of Victorian correctitude left in the House of Commons.'
Gardiner was reminded of the 'Dignity' half of Landseer's big-
dog-and-little-dog picture, *Dignity and Impudence* – decent,
kind, honourable, without his father's malice, but a victim
until the day awful old Joe died of not so much filial loyalty as
'filial servitude'.[12] But at the Halsbury Banquet, the big, kind
dog tried to bark fiercely. This was 'a revolution nurtured
in lies and promoted by fraud and only to be achieved by
violence. Such a revolution cannot endure' he said, moving
into the declamator's subjunctive, 'unless we be false to the
faith that is in us (cheers).' The government had been 'playing
and are playing a game of gigantic bluff. They do not wish to
create peers.' They talked of 100 to 200 incomers. 'I say that
is bluff and fraudulent bluff.' That was the Austen Chamberlain
who 'does not say foolish things, but does say platitudes with
aggravating solemnity.'[13]

Carson was the real, deadly puff-adder thing, advising the
Lords to tell Asquith, 'We shall walk out and leave you to
create your harlot peers.' Asquith was bent on 'destroying
a constitution which has stood for 700 years, couldn't do
it without creating peers and only then by adding men
who are willing to sell their honour for a coronet (loud
cheers).'[14]

The dinner was attended by Jack Sandars, Balfour's friend
and secretary, who noted the concern about the exertions
of Curzon and Middleton not just to abstain, but to vote
with the government. Lansdowne, Austen told him, should
express his displeasure at anyone voting for this 'noxious
measure',[15] something passed on by the wind-borne Balfour.
But Lansdowne, with Curzon beside him, did not see why,
with the diehards going off on a line, Unionists disagreeing
with them should not follow one of their own.

Wyndham was snarling to friends about 'an abdication of
leadership'.[16] He took a generally violent view of Curzon: it

was all snobbishness on Curzon's part. 'He could not bear to see his order contaminated by the new creations.'[17]

In the latter part of July and the first few days of August the two camps were making calculations on the backs of envelopes about the likely response to the late line of Lansdowne and Balfour, acceptance of the bill. In the days when Tory peers had gone to Lansdowne House for directions, managers would have required only a general abstention. But this was no longer the body which Lloyd George had called Mr Balfour's poodle. Whether we see it as disturbed Alsatian or yapping Yorkie, it had been growling all night at the Halsbury Banquet. In fact it had become apparent that the built-in Conservative majority, about which Liberals had been complaining since at least 1860 (Gladstone's paper duties), could give a mere faction of the opposition a majority over the party of government. The rebellion against the Tory leadership actually demonstrated the full strength of the case against the unreformed Lords. Given quadruple superiority over a reform government, and with the 300 and more who would abstain, it could potentially beat it with several arms tied behind its back.

The possibility of a creation of peers *before* the debate existed. It would have had the sovereign virtue of creating a government majority without delays for the controversial legislation to come, Welsh disestablishment – 'the Church is not safe' – and Home Rule – 'destruction of the Empire'. Brisk legislation without delay might have brought the Ulster micro-patriots to some sort of accommodation; delay would allow the drilling and the gun-running to assume their menacing shape. But the short arguments against an instant mobilisation/nobilisation of Thomas Hardy and Gilbert Murray were obvious enough. Better the threat of packing the Upper House than the fact of packing it.

Then again, Asquith had to live with dim, touchy George V, preoccupied with his own feelings and frightened of criticism from the nobility. Constitutionally, George was the wife worried about what the neighbours think. He had to be assuaged by rolling adjustments in Asquith's statements to the Commons about his role in the affair. And Crewe, who had collapsed and nearly died earlier in the year, had to be dragged out of convalescence to speak in the pre-vote censure debate the Unionists were staging so as to put a gloss of 'natural and legitimate reluctance' on George's actions. This raised an unwelcome element of speculative doubt among Unionist peers, anxious as ever to believe it was all bluff. George's dull concern that *he* should be absolved by yet greater emphasis on that reluctance, would, if further complied with, have put a serious weapon into the ditchers' hands. George, in Halsbury's language, lacked manliness.

More importantly, he lacked the wit to see that from his own point of view, he had everything to gain by a clean, decisive cut which settled the affair. And Asquith, as irritated as that eirenic character let himself become, drew a line. 'To be led into public discussion about the feelings and motives of the King or his view about the policy of the government would . . . be even less in the interests of the King than of the government.'[18] An intelligent monarch less obsessed with how he looked was an asset not to be hoped for.

Accordingly, prior creation was ruled out and, the Lords' amendments having been rejected by the Commons* with just enough minor exceptions to please the King, Morley, as Lords leader, did his arithmetic about the likely vote. He canvassed the nominal Liberal peers and received assurances from eighty. This was better than he had hoped for, but his view at the end of July was that without forty votes from the other side of the floor, the bill would fail, leaving the whole intolerable cycle to be run again and the new Lords – helots, puppets or Brummagem – to be brought forth. However, by 4 August he was beginning to think,

---

* Hugh Cecil used the amendment debate to prophesy accurately enough the coming criminal conspiracy in Ulster, and to exult in it.

fallaciously, that he might just get through on government steam and abstentions alone. Meanwhile, someone on the government side told Lord Newton, a moderate, who told Lord Lovat, a ditcher, who told Selborne, the arch-ditcher, that the government was relying on the bishops.[19]

As such numbers were crunched and Willoughby and his runners moved and wrote excitedly around, and gossip of an Epsom nature,* which their lordships must have appreciated, pushed the odds for success and failure of the motion around, it became clear that abstention, like patriotism, would not be enough. The sacrifice of voting *with* the government, *for* revolution and the destruction of the constitution would have to be made by someone – a statistically sufficient number of someones.

Curzon had been working hard at abstention. This was, after all, the party's correct line, in spite of Balfour's vaporousness, and he was able early in August to publish a list of 320 pledged to just that. Getting votes across the floor was a difficult undertaking, especially since, as a member of the shadow Cabinet, Curzon was not free to cast his own vote this way. But since a steady succession of rustic noblemen had been coming up to take the parliamentary oath in response to Willoughby's circular, he was clearminded enough to have no qualms whatsoever in organising people to do it.

To the diehards, rich in vicious epithet, these vote-shifting Tories were 'the Rats'. Curzon, taking the view that he was not leaving the ship so much as refitting it for easier waters, was happy to be non-playing captain of the Rats. And like Willoughby, concerned in the words of Wyndham 'to find peers who will fight to the end even if the leadership counsel surrender', he was entirely in earnest. Curzon would make

---

* Carson, finding a couple of the younger peers comparing the odds, snarlingly reproved their levity. 'Betting! Is that all you can think of when the constitution is in the melting pot?'[20] Carson's Dublin accent, so strange in its militant Orange milieu, did not make him *that* sort of Irishman.

enemies in this campaign who would at least contribute to his later failure to become Tory leader. It is part of his appeal that he seems never to have given personal advantage much thought. He was convinced of the commonsense necessity of saving party and House from themselves and he got on with the job, disinterestedly raising promises from forty peers. Curzon might be deathly proud, but he lacked the limp vanity of Balfour and the furtive anxiety of the King.

A great deal turned upon figures who were being watched by other doubters. The Duke of Norfolk would have preferred to have abstained and had, typically, been given no help at all by Balfour when he asked for advice. But he was expected to bolt into the diehard camp if any Unionist voted with the government. As Norfolk had a following as premier duke and leader of the Catholics, it was hoped in diehard circles that he might carry as many as a dozen ditherers with him into rebellion. This was the risk attached to organising a transfer vote, but one which Curzon was ready to take, especially as the Duke had enemies as well as friends, and there were diehard doubts about having him on the team. As things turned out, the Duke, though he went into the ditch, was reckoned to have taken only three followers with him.

Such sophistications had to be brushed aside, and Curzon and Middleton worked the circuit for transfers. They were dealing with a middle more than usually undistributed. Middleton, dining at Lord Cadogan's, found that none of his companions, who included a former chancellor, viceroy, lord lieutenant and prime minister (Rosebery), had yet decided which way to vote. All of them – St Aldwyn, Minto, Cadogan himself and Rosebery – finally undertook to vote with the government, though not all of them turned up in the lobbies.[21] Loyalty to the leadership, for all the rage and hatred which Leo Maxse was now pouring on A.J. Foozle, was still a factor. General Lord Roberts, a more amiable man than his admirers, wrote apologetically to Balfour hoping that, despite his vote, goodwill might soon be restored.

This was not the reaction of Gwynne, editor of the *Morning Post*, writing to his less moderate proprietor, Lady Bathurst. 'Always remember that defeat of the bill means the political death of A.J.B., therefore the struggle has to be kept up with full strength.'[22] In fact the bill would pass, but Balfour would move from inertia to 'political death' quite voluntarily. Loyalty was strong enough for it to have been a notable achievement for Willoughby and Selborne to have won over Lord Northcote, who earlier had been ready to act only with 'the approval of our responsible leaders'. Then, despite the fact that his wife was a 'hedger', the term covering acceptance of the bill, he was drawn into the ditcher camp.[23] Another factor, one particularly helpful to the hedgers, was the bishops. Curzon was able to indicate quite early ten firmly committed ecclesiastical rodents.

Meanwhile, by way of therapy, on the day the Commons dealt with amendments, Curzon called a motion of censure in the Lords. This was directed at Asquith's conduct and afforded Curzon the chance to give a cool performance. He amended the letter of Junius to the Duke of Grafton – 'You began by coercing the King; you ended by betraying the people.' This was not, he argued, a case like the Reform Act of 1832, 'a measure which the great mass of the people earnestly desired',* and he quoted, naturally enough, Dicey. The professor of law who thought Irish Home Rule without all-union consent worth armed resistance unsurprisingly took a low view of the legitimacy of a parliamentary coalition containing the Irish.

Home Rule had in fact hung over the argument at least since the first election of 1910. Curzon wound up in good, slightly simulated, Tory style. 'To utilise the prerogative of the Crown and the creation of peers to pass a measure like Home Rule before it has been again referred to the people would, I

---

* Halsbury would later point out that he remembered the Reform Bill riots. He would have been eight years old.

submit to your lordships, be a public crime.' The government were going 'to usurp the prerogative of the Crown in order to deny and to extinguish the prerogative of the people. That is the nature of the offence for which we on this side indict you in this debate. It is an offence which I believe the people of this country will never forgive; and when they realise it – and it may be sooner than you expect – they will rise in wrath and tear your ill-omened work to pieces.'[24]

Crewe replied for the government and through the silk of his habitual pleasant charm dropped a nasty hint intended to discourage talk of bluff. 'If we are to be forced, to my keen personal regret, into giving advice which would have the effect of the creation of peers, we cannot pretend that the number so created could necessarily be limited by any newspaper list . . . all such lists will have become, if the lamentable necessity arises, altogether irrelevant.'[25]

Halsbury made a speech full of legal geology. He denounced the creations of 1711 and compared the Liberal government with the French revolutionaries. His overall stand on Lords reform was best summed up by Loreburn, the lord chancellor, who spoke after him. Halsbury's gist, he said, was that 'it is unconstitutional for the only pressure which can be put on this House to be put upon this House under any circumstances'.[26] There was another brisk moment from Loreburn when he was interrupted by Cadogan challenging the legitimacy of the Commons majority.

> Earl CADOGAN: But you lost 110 seats, I think, in obtaining that majority.
> The LORD CHANCELLOR: Is a Liberal government not entitled to govern with a majority of 125?[27]

Lansdowne, speaking last, made the inevitable point that what the government had obtained from the King was not 'any "cast-iron scheme of legislation to be rammed through Parliament". That is quite true. It is a *carte blanche* scheme and the blank cheque . . . has to be filled up by His Majesty in accordance with the directions of his advisers.'[28] The size of that cheque had been varying from speaker to speaker for some weeks now, with early talk of ten to twenty growing to 400 to 500.

The vote on this ghostly occasion, 8 August, registered the censure of the government by their lordships' House by 281 to 68. It was a gesture, and the source perhaps of some emotional satisfaction. But with temperature flickering during that unEnglish August between 97 and 100 degrees Fahrenheit, the real contest would take place over the next two days, when the government would seek so to alter the House of Lords as to deprive it – apart from that delay which Halsbury had called worthless – of any other possible satisfaction.

24

'Mild Uproar and Cheering in the Streets'

By October *Punch* would be carrying a cartoon of Edward Carson as a Red Indian – a role to which his lean features were suited – head and ear to the ground, declaring, 'Time to begin the war dance two years away.' That apprehension had run through the latter part of the Lords crisis and would appear again in the final debate. But for the moment, *Punch* was concerned with the weather.

> *Perspiring Customer*: P-H-H! Bring me something cool.
> *Waitress*: Yes, sir. Would you like an ice?
> *Perspiring Customer*: No, no. Something cooler than that.

Or as *Punch*'s Toby MP put it, 'Thermometer marks 97 in the shade, 131 in the sun, 181 in the House of Lords.'

Punch also saw Halsbury as 'a sort of Wellington', on a black horse talking to a sceptical peer. 'Up Lords and at 'em.'

'At whom?'

'Well, I want to damage the government for choice; anyhow damage somebody.'[1]

In the chamber, the Duchess of Somerset had sent sprigs of

heather to friends among the diehards, while in awful antici-
pation of Mr Mandelson several government peers wore red
roses.[2] Lansdowne, upon whom the light burden of directing
inbuilt resistance during little sessions at Lansdowne House
now rested like a Promethean punishment, rose to speak.
He stressed the effect of new creations: 'The whole of the
exiguous safeguards which are left us by the Parliament
Bill might disappear altogether ... I am haunted by my
apprehension of the spectacle which will be presented to the
whole civilised world and to the rest of the British Empire if
the threat of HMG is carried into effect ... We should have
exclaimed and poured forth volumes of ridicule and contempt
if such a thing had happened in the Republic of Venezuela.'

They faced what he could only call 'stupendous political
corruption. If it is not accomplished, 500 English [there we go
again] gentlemen will not have taken their seats in this House
upon conditions in which I can only describe as humiliating
and disgraceful.' Lansdowne seemed at times to have a whiff
of *Iolanthe* in his nostrils, the House of Lords as chorus
singing a comic song. The fear of being made collectively
ridiculous undoubtedly weighed more heavily with him and
his supporters than the usual charges of destroying the constitution. He also picked up Willoughby's talk of 'using main
force', stating, 'However I may be thought pusillanimous, I
prefer parliamentary methods.'

He quoted Winston Churchill's ebullient reference in the
Commons to 400 to 500 creations with a shudder which
comes off the printed page, and tried to draw Morley as to the
full peer-planning of the government, something with which
Morley declined to oblige him. Lansdowne's final point, with
Ireland very much in mind, was that this was not the end of
the constitutional struggle and that the Lords must make the
best of things and keep what powers they could. 'We may
be worsted in this encounter, but we are not going to be
annihilated.'[3]

Halsbury was his usual self – 'turgid rhetoric and senile

violence', Sir Almeric called it.[4] The man who fifty years before had defended the rebel-lynching Governor Eyre of Jamaica, was permanently astounded at radical impudence and, unlike Lansdowne, not troubled at the prospect of appearing ridiculous. 'Let the government take the responsibility of introducing 400 or 500 peers – I care not how many . . . It is as if a highwayman came and said, "Give me your watch or I will cut your throat," and if you did not give him your watch that you are the author of your own throat being cut.'

As for the idea that this little divergence from Lansdowne 'as, I confess I read in a vile journal whose principal idea is to get advertisements in some way or another, that it was part of a conspiracy against my noble friend and against the distinguished leader in the other House to obtain from them the leadership, forsooth!', such thoughts could only originate with 'the degraded journalist'.[5] (*Punch*, a week or two later, would show Balfour and Austen Chamberlain in seventeenth-century costume with Balfour echoing Charles II to his brother. 'Do you think they would kill me to make you King?').

The Archbishop of York, Lang, a *politique* if ever there was one, expressed himself with marvellous and uncharacteristic succinctness. 'It is unreal at the present time to discuss either the bill, however deplorable, or the amendments, however admirable, because we know perfectly well that the bill must, and the amendments cannot, become law.' Thus was Occam's razor drawn across the throat of rational resistance. Thereafter Lang did a good deal of chuntering at the government, but he had made his point and underlined it by reminding the peers that they wanted to cripple Welsh disestablishment and Home Rule ('searching criticism and delay where delay would be most useful'); no point, then, in giving up what nobbling powers they still had. And with all the bathos at the service of a prelatical politician in the second decade of the twentieth century, Lang invoked those 'times when it may require a higher courage . . . when it may win a truer victory, times when in the service of the King and the country, "He that ruleth his spirit is better than he that taketh a city." [6]

Sharp-edged prudence was thus astutely dipped in molasses, and the Archbishop undoubtedly made himself useful. Salisbury, by contrast, said that he had never 'stood at this table with feelings of more poignant regret than I do at this moment', and was then lachrymose for three quarters of a column of *Hansard* about his division from Lansdowne. On the constructive side, he could see no objection, now that Asquith had destroyed the constitution, to a Unionist government creating another 500 peers to put things right. St Aldwyn, the perennial Tory moderate, would later observe of this bizarre proposal that 'exercise of the prerogative would almost certainly kill the prerogative for the future'.[7]

Lord Ribblesdale came after the Archbishop, and Salisbury like iced oxygen. Aristocrat of aristocrats, master of the buck-hounds, famously painted at the artist's request by Sargent, spoken of in France as '*ce grand diable de milord Anglais*',[8] and, very incidentally, Asquith's brother-in-law, Ribblesdale embodied the insouciance and confidence which gave the British upper class what can only be called class. He sat as a Liberal, finding bristling reaction rather vulgar, and mocked the apocalyptic anxieties of stress cases like Selborne.

Ribblesdale had always been good value for money. He had said during the budget debate that Lloyd George struck him as a combination of pantaloon and highwayman, but that he saw nothing in this budget to justify the fuss that was being made. He was even better this time. 'It is driven in upon me that the constituencies have ceased to care very much about the House of Lords. We get on very well at hunting and bazaars and those kind of things, but I rather feel that our time is up as far as regards the constituencies.' The Tories should understand that if there had been a dissolution they couldn't have 'won an election on the cry of the House of Lords . . . I am afraid that with dear food round your necks and the House of Lords on your backs you are not likely to win an election for some little time to come.' It was time, said Ribblesdale 'to beat a dignified but determined retreat'.

As for the shock-horror aspect of peer-creation, Ribblesdale came as close as a hereditary baron can to saying 'Come off it.' It was 'the only way in which you can bring about a parliamentary arrangement at all and I venture to ask the House, "Why not?" . . . The new peers would probably be what is called a very nice body of men. I should regret as much as anybody a comic-opera creation of peers and I feel that the classical and aesthetic sense of the prime minister would make such a thing repugnant to him.'

Ribblesdale reckoned that the constitution would get on all right 'because to my mind, our unwritten constitution is an area congenial to these time-to-time adjustments and working agreements'. Things would happen 'which will jar on the nerves of people like myself . . . but I really cannot believe in the very large words which are employed as to our degradation and so on, or accept the phrases used by Lord Selborne and Lord Curzon.' He advised those two 'super-peers', as he cheekily called them, that 'your lordships' House will become more like family solicitors who warn and delay and advise and confuse their clients, but who do not decide and never accept any responsibility. But after all, solicitors are reassuring and indispensable people and held in general esteem.'[9] If the House of Lords had been capable two years earlier of thinking like Ribblesdale, the hole they were in would never have been dug.

Instead they were fulminating at the bottom of it and it was time for Willoughby to intervene. Willoughby had no cant, least of all about representative institutions. 'You may claim majorities if you like in favour of the Parliament Bill at a dozen General Elections, but that will not alter my view and I do not think it will alter the view of Lord Halsbury . . . We will continue to resist the abrogation of the constitution as long as we have any power left in us to do so.' As for the main force Lansdowne had quoted against him, he had been talking about 'the main force of the creation of peers and the overbearing of this House by introducing into it an unlimited number of new peers'. The government might as well have 'called a regiment of dragoons in to make the House of Lords do what the radical party wants it to do'.

Willoughby was perplexed at the bishops and used some wonderfully plain language. 'If they desire to remain an established Church in this country they can only do so through the agency of the Tory Party, which is the only agency, as Lord Beaconsfield used to say, by which you can maintain an established Church.' So, 'if you believed that the established Church is bound up with the existence of the Tory Party, then right reverend prelates may be placing themselves with regard to the protection they may expect to receive from political parties in the future in a very equivocal position indeed'. ('Nice little diocese you've got here, reverend.') Willoughby then dwelt upon salvation – in secular form. They should just remember, he said to the people he suspected of constituting the majority against him, that their 'only hope of salvation . . . is to stand up for the party which is the trustee of the ancient constitution of this country and the bulwark of the Church'.

Willoughby might have been simplistic in his fixed-wing constitutionalism, but his narrow coherence could score points against Lansdowne. 'I believe I am as intelligent as some of my neighbours in my own part of the country, and I do not see how any ordinary man can possibly understand a man talking one way and voting another.' But at bottom, where it mattered, Willoughby envisaged a Lords primacy over all this elections and democracy stuff: 'All these conventions with regard to the Cabinet representing the electors and the electors representing the nation are only applicable to ordinary legislation and become tyrannical if used to push through extraordinary legisla-tion.'

And when, as now, that legislation was 'not only extraordinary, but in our view absolutely unthinkable and impossible, then we cannot entertain that affection for representative government which we normally extend to it'. As he had said, majorities in favour of the Parliament Bill in a dozen elections would not alter his view. And Willoughby's view was that fighting was the option. He had said more than once that the whole crisis was like the challenge at public school, 'Will you fight, or will you take a licking?' And viewing his leaders, he was reminded of 'the native who was so humble in his demands on the Almighty that when he met a bear walking in a wood, he knelt down and prayed that divine providence would at least not be on the side of the bear'.

Ready to stonewall, to appeal to the Committee of Privileges – pretty much anything, as he cheerfully conceded – Willoughby sent the Lords into its dinner break rather anticlimactically, asking for rejection which would 'force a dissolution of Parliament or postpone this bill and afford a chance of something turning up which may prevent its turning into law'.[10]

When the House resumed it must have been cooler, but the tone of His Grace of Bedford hardly demonstrated this. 'It is useless to try to delay the constitutional crisis when it is upon us. Much better meet it now. Let the peers be actually created. Let that creation advertise to the whole Empire the violence done to the constitution and that at a moment when half the people are already opposed to this revolution.' The bill itself was 'an act of violence to the constitution without any parallel in our history. But if the country is to learn the lesson, it can only be taught by an act of violence.'[11] Since unwelcome legislation was excitedly called 'violence' by diehards, one assumes charitably that the Duke was characterising rejection and a counter-creation of Tory peers as violence rather than thinking wistfully about something else.

Lord Newton, Lansdowne's friend and biographer and a

general voice for sense, quoted from the Liberal press on the idea of peer-creation.

> 'A large militant influx of young Liberals and radicals of a quite different type from those Liberal absentees who have served their cause so poorly during the struggle' – rather unkind to noble Lords opposite – 'would make a startling change.' I believe that these passages reflect absolutely accurately the view which is entertained by the extreme supporters of the government, and I would urge with all respect upon my noble friends that they should pause and consider deeply before they take the fatal step.[12]

The permanent split within the great family of Russell climaxed towards the end of the day when Ampthill, diehard, was followed directly by Earl Russell, advanced radical. Ampthill regarded this Parliament Bill as 'a crime . . . the gravest political outrage that has ever been perpetrated short of bloodshed, and we regard the objects of the bill as utterly corrupt'. For him the outcry of the Lords was analagous to the cries of 'the woman who attempts to hold the armed burglar who has broken into her house. Her cries may possibly bring the police and if the ruffian is then brought to justice other people will be saved from outrage at his hands.' (There is at least a B.Litt. dissertation to be written on the criminal metaphor as applied to the government of H.H. Asquith.) Ampthill rumbled on about the outrage done to the King and the humiliation inflicted on the Lords 'by the mere threat to create "puppet" peers'.

As for the government, Ampthill compared them with 'the directors of a commercial company who have adopted questionable methods of finance or of trade, perhaps to gratify the cupidity of the shareholders'. Such men had 'no alternative but to go on with their trickery unless they wish to make a clean breast of it'. The Lords should make their stand, said Ampthill, 'not for any privileges of its own or for the personal rights and privileges of its members, but actually for the liberties of the people'.[13]

It was odd to find Ampthill in this company. He had inherited the title from Odo Russell who, in a brilliant account of his time as ambassador in Rome, had depicted the papacy in its post-*risorgimento* sulk huddled under Pius IX in baroque atria while that Pope, as devoted to the fixed order of things as Willoughby, hurled disregarded encyclicals at the Asquiths of secular Italy.

Francis Russell, the 2nd Earl who had pushed his grand-father's Reform Bill Whiggism far beyond the famous finality, spoke next. The Russells had once all been found on the same side of debate. If he were to use 'what is nowadays the standard language of political controversy, I suppose I should hurl the word "traitor" across the House. Apparently, the word "traitor" is now used to describe a person with whose political views you disagree at the moment.' And Russell, politer and milder than in his intervention during the budget debate, pointed out that the censure motion was something of an own goal. Censure had been defeated in the Commons. In the Lords it had passed 'by an enormous majority, but nobody cares a snap of the fingers'.

As for the supposed lack of public clamour as shown for the Reform Bill, a recurring diehard point, Russell was clear. 'The country is convinced, and has been convinced since the time of the last election, that the Parliament Bill will become and must become the law of this country; and I am perfectly certain that if the country thought that the Parliament Bill would be impeded on its way to the statute book, noble lords opposite would have had as much effervescence as they would desire on the part of the people.'[14] This, like Ribblesdale's cool words, amounted to the bitterest of all judgements: that the House of Lords, whatever its theoretical powers, did not actually matter very much; that the constitutional devaluation had already taken place.

The second day's debate was opened by Middleton, a Lansdowneite and not the most tactful of men. He was anxious about caterer's logistics. 'The House holds 275 members and consists of 600. Increase the number to 900 and you will have three men for each place.' He alluded directly to the rounding up from their harvest activities of rural nobility not much seen in the sophisticated settings of St James or Westminster, 'who perhaps have not been heard in this House at all and who are among the less experienced members of your lordships' House . . . these half dozen or ten men are going to dictate to 400 men who disagree with them.' Middleton feared the country would be dismayed to learn that 'the insistence of five or ten men who are, to say the least of it, of first experience in public affairs, has been allowed to counterbalance the opinion of 400 men who undertook to stay away and not insist upon the vote.'[15]

Quite why inexperienced, and indeed stupid, peers should not have their votes counted, Middleton did not make clear. But apart from affronting men in whose hair he detected straws, he was making an inadvertent point against the entire Upper House. It was not only hereditary, but voluntary, and among those voluteering, often amateur. Unionist control worked through an oligarchy of activist gentlemen whom practice had enabled to cope with the bowling of players less diabolic than that complained of in Asquith. Gentlemen and players could be understood, but Middleton in his anxiety had invented a third category: 'other gentlemen'.

At some urgent insistence from Rosebery and Lansdowne, Morley, who had not planned to speak so soon, now made his contribution. Wearily he observed that 'the Greeks of classical times had trilogies – three dramas forming a whole – and you may have three or four'. This stage of the current drama would conclude that day, 'and speaking is not needed by us at all events'. But then, 'dramas were made not by words but by situations'. Lansdowne had asked for more information on the creation of peers. Very well. 'If the bill should be defeated tonight His Majesty would assent to a creation of Peers sufficient in number to guard against any possible combination of the different parties in opposition by which the Parliament Bill might again be exposed a second time to defeat.'[16] The House now had certain knowledge, if indeed it had not had certain knowledge from Morley's earlier statement. Anyone on the Unionist side who spoke after Morley had no last scruple of excuse for arguing from 'Asquith's bluff'.

Milner had first go. What was proposed added 'enormously to the outrageousness of the proceedings', but it shouldn't change the way they voted. Resisting to the end would 'be better for the country, for the wholesomeness of our political life and for the honour and character of all those concerned in this transaction'. Milner was not irrational, merely an intelligent man temperamentally harsh, but he was drawn readily to the paranoid style. Suppose when Home Rule legislation came up and the Ulstermen were raised to feverish resistance (something he was to play his part in doing), he could see how the government might behave. Would they not be preparing to urge on the sovereign that delay in settling the matter was dangerous and might lead to bloodshed, and that if the House of Lords was not prepared to pass the measure at once, they would advise the sovereign to exercise his royal prerogative to override the opposition of this House? 'If we give way today, we shall be exposed to the same threats again and again in the future.'

What Milner wanted was for the government to be pushed towards taking dire steps and to lose authority by doing so. 'Once you swamp this House by a large creation of peers in order to ride down their opponents, the storm of odium that will be aroused will prevent any ministry in the future from abusing the royal prerogative in a similar manner.'[17] As a theory it was a mixture of the Leninist worse-means-better theory, and 'When I'm dead you'll all be sorry.'

Camperdown, who had been rather violent back in the days

of the unspeakable budget but who had been cooling for some time, made the first Unionist commitment to voting with the government. He did so by taking on the Duke of Norfolk. The Duke had written to the press to say that he preferred to abstain, but if any Unionist voted for the amendments 'he himself would vote in the other lobby and would do all that he could to bring into the other lobby as many as he could. Camperdown took civil umbrage at that. The Duke of Norfolk was in effect disfranchising people like himself. 'You are not to vote; if you do vote, then I shall take a lot of peers into the other lobby.' He 'hated and detested the bill', but like the rest of the Lansdowne mainstream, he detested creation more and would push that logic to the point which Curzon had been urging.[18]

An irritated Norfolk sarcastically thanked Camperdown for sharing his (Norfolk's) thoughts with the House. Given the perfidy of the Liberal government and the sending of 'four or five hundred coroneted individuals up the classic hall of Westminster to find seats in your lordships' House'[19] purely to deny amendments to a bill, he was going to vote with the diehards.

It was left to the Duke of Northumberland to provide the poster painting for the diehards, saying things that nobody, not Willoughby nor Selborne, had dared to utter or indeed quite think. There had been all this talk about the precedent of 1832 and the Reform Act. 'There was some interest aroused in the country and very unpleasant interest, too. The country was very nearly on the edge of revolution then; but as far the present bill and the Lords were concerned nobody cared a brass farthing.'

For himself he didn't see why the Lords had bothered with a committee stage; the bill should have been thrown out at second reading. He would have divided the House, but 'the loyalty to our much respected chief was such that nobody would bell the cat and so we went into committee'. The House of Commons did not represent the feeling of the country; the first thing Campbell-Bannerman had done when he came to office was to declare war on the House of Lords. As for the election, 'the whole country had been well bribed by the chancellor of the exchequer'. It was a great pity the Lords had given up its powers over money bills. As for the new creations, 'it might be difficult afterwards to express in adequate language the contempt I feel for them'. That wasn't all. 'Those who procure their presence here are in my opinion still further degraded. Procurers generally are more degraded than those they procure. But my lords, are we to be degraded by their presence? Can you be degraded by the presence of the degraded?'[20]

The contribution of the Earl of Meath is described by Roy Jenkins in *Mr Balfour's Poodle* as 'a speech of remarkable stupidity'. Meath, Reginald Brabazon, a former ADC to Queen Victoria who owned 15,000 acres in Ireland and Herefordshire, thought that 'we have had a revolver of the very latest construction presented at our heads and we know now that the revolver is loaded and is about to be discharged . . . but my lords, principle is above tactics.' The government, he added, were 'putting enormous power into the hands of the Cabinet. And what, may I ask, is the Cabinet? Is the Cabinet recognised by the constitution of this country? It is a junto, a subcommittee of the Privy Council – that is all, although no doubt it has the confidence of the sovereign.' Lord Rosebery had said that 'by yielding in 1832 we obtained a further existence of eighty years'. Meath thought that had been a bad mistake. 'I wish to goodness we had never had those eighty years. If only in 1832 a real fight had been made we should have been a real live assembly at this moment.'

As it was, 'is it worthwhile for the sake of a few years' existence to go on without any power or real authority whatever, as a sort of painted fortress? . . . Shouldn't we say to the government [the ones with that revolver], "Force us. We are not going to yield until you fire. Do your worst"?'[21]

The Archbishop of Canterbury, Davidson, set an example

of promised and delivered brevity by taking up only half a column in *Hansard* to say that he couldn't 'hold the position of one of those who might have averted the calamity and did not'.[22] He would give his vote against retaining the amendments. There was a nasty moment for those who gushed about the ancient courtliness of the House when Lords St Leven (diehard) and Heneage (hedger) both stood up and, in the way of any degraded puppet procured by a Liberal government, refused to give way. St Leven, when he did speak, remarked charmingly that he was loyal to Lansdowne, really, only going a bit further as he found it difficult to stop.

The final contest, after a verbal vote and before the division, concerned, suitably enough, the 'super-peers', Curzon and Selborne. Curzon spoke with what reads like quiet insistence. His remarks in denunciation of the government were perfunctory and his appeal was to peers' sense of rational self-interest and dignity. The term 'damage-limitation' was unknown to Edwardians, but that was the essence of his function. And perhaps his key point was aimed at turning peers away from their cloistered view of their own standing: 'At the bottom of my heart I cannot help thinking that the country . . . so far from believing that HMG had resorted to an action which is ridiculous, would say that the peers, who had twice stood out against HMG and been defeated, were finally being hoisted with their own petard.' As for ridicule, 'I think it might conceivably recoil on the heads of noble Lords on this side of the House.'

Curzon also tackled head-on the term 'revolution' which had become the buzzword of fretting noblemen in the previous few weeks. They had certainly made their point. 'But if they think the country is likely to be brought more face to face with revolution because 400 or 500 gentlemen are going to troop into this House and sit on the benches opposite, I respectfully differ from them.' If they voted to retain their amendments they 'would be making an enormous and gratuitous addition to the power for mischief of the party opposite'.

On the matter of loyalty to their leadership, Curzon quoted Salisbury from the day before. '"The country only understands deeds; it utterly despises words."' Well now, what about these protestations from diehards of their loyalty to Lansdowne?

Curzon however, for all his broad sense, had not lost his aristocratic sublimity. He looked upon creation as something 'which must effect the pollution – perhaps that is too strong a word – the degradation of this House'. He directed his plea to a minority, 'the eighty or ninety or a hundred members of your lordships' house . . . [who could] dictate an action for the whole of the House . . . I do not suppose that a more momentous division will ever have taken place in the House of Lords.'[23] They were starting afresh to build a new constitution. God knew how they would do it. At this point, Curzon's sweetness and light were interrupted by a snarl from the higher peerage. The Marquess of Bristol called out: 'It is because 400 peers are going to run away tonight.' There was then a brief playground exchange invoking the Duke of Wellington (Curzon), who retreated and Lord Nelson (Bristol), who did not.[24]

Curzon's peroration had been spoiled, but he had made his point. Selborne, who concluded, was short but memorable, and his words have often been quoted. 'We ourselves as legislators are doomed to destruction. The question is, shall we perish in the dark by our own hand or in the light killed by our enemies?' He also said – and viewed through the prism of the best part of a century of parliamentary government since 10 August 1911 it is the measure of his overwrought obtuseness – 'I believe that a single chamber – naked, as Lord Rosebery would say – would be safer for the country than a constitution with a House of Lords emasculated according to the bill. Therefore the government's creation of peers has no terror for me.'[25]

The division was called. Davidson, the Archbishop of Canterbury, moved around shepherd-like, and a slight check in the flow of the government's supporters gave the impression that the bill had been defeated.[26] As John Morley recorded in his diary: 'For three or four hours from my announcement in the afternoon, the result was still to all of us profoundly dark; and dark it remained in the dead silence broken only by the counting of the tellers, down to the very moment of fate.'[27]

Violet Asquith, a more volatile personality than Morley, recorded 'one of the most thrilling evenings of my life'. She quoted 'little Benn', the future 1st Viscount Stansgate, who 'told me in the lobby two minutes before [that] we should be defeated'. She 'went through all the emotions of defeat until three minutes later a man rushed through with the news the government had won – by 17 as we afterwards found – 114 diehards, 131 Gov . . . Mild uproar and cheering in the streets'.[28]

'We were beaten by the bishops and the rats,'[29] said George Wyndham with his usual affability, adding that the bishops 'were selling the Crown and the Church to men who despised them'. At the Carlton after the vote, cries of 'Traitor' and 'Judas' were vented on those who had followed the leaders of the Conservative Party. For the diehard press, Garvin's *Observer* would speak of 'the ignoble band, clerical and lay, of Unionist traitors who had made themselves Redmond's helots'.[30] And Whibley would write in his *Blackwood's* column, 'Musings Without Method', 'Mr Asquith has committed his crime, without reason and without excuse. In callous contempt for England and her traditions, he has set himself above the Constitution, above the Parliament which he has destroyed, above the People. At every step he has been guilty of deception and chicane. If the wholesome methods of old were still in force, he would stand at the bar of the nation an impeached and guilty Minister.'[31]

Meanwhile, an analysis of group voting shows thirteen bishops voting positively for the government (three from conviction, ten for Curzon's reasons), and eight Dukes in the ranks of the diehards. But along with the hedgers were the rats, thirty-seven unionists specifically walking into the government lobbies. Without them, and without Curzon's exertions and his steadying of Lansdowne, a minority faction of the Unionist party would have defeated the government. In which case the bill would have been re-presented, procedurally accelerated and a new House, degraded by the presence of Thomas Hardy, would have passed it.

The House of Lords, which, with a little sense of political perspective and knowledge of its own limitations, could earlier have kept all its formal powers to be used sparingly but with effect, did at last save its face. It did not die and would soon give a demonstration of envenomed obscurantism in the cause of delaying Irish Home Rule and advancing Irish independence. It lived, in fact, to do its bit for Sinn Féin. But as unreason subsided beween the wars, the House of Lords would pass into an odd compromise position of its own. 'Out on its feet in the thirties,' according to the private judgement of the same Lord Salisbury who had died so hard in 1911, it became largely decorative. But it was not not swamped. Instead, lapped after 1963 by slow tides of incremental degradation in the form of life peers, it actually became rather useful and, delaying as it did Margaret Thatcher's abolition of London local government and resisting a harsh Criminal Justice Act, has been by no means an illiberal institution. At the time of writing a government supposedly bent on reforming the House of Lords seems less certain than Asquith (or Macmillan, who instituted the life peers) of quite how to do it. Degradation has worked rather well.

PART III

Irish Home Rule
1912–14

25

Andrew Bonar Law

E ighteen years had passed since the defeat of Home Rule
in 1893, when Conservatives, lords and Queen, all in
their proper places asserting an immutable *status quo*, had
succeeded in bringing about the final departure of Gladstone,
rightly perceived as a danger to civilisation as they knew it.

Defeat and departure had been followed – after the perfunctory blip of continued Liberal government under the
unmemorable (and unLiberal) Lord Rosebery – by the return
to power of Salisbury with Arthur Balfour at his right hand
and his brother, Gerald Balfour, as chief secretary for Ireland.

There is a tendency to talk about Ireland at this time as
being in a state of hiatus. Parnell was dead, the second Home
Rule Bill had failed, the violent tradition was drawing a long
breath between Fenianism and Sinn Féin; meanwhile all the
exciting things in Ireland were literary and artistic. Irish
labour and socialism made a measure of inspirational and
well-deserved trouble through the agency of James Larkin and
James Connolly. Meanwhile, folklorist Ireland was coming
into focus with the Gaelic League, a tantalising mixture of
'Back to Cuchulain' and Black Studies. This cult, which told
its disciples to go west, not to California but to Connaught,

would find expression in the early asinine pronunciation of Patrick Pearse: 'I often fancy that if some of the Old Masters had known rural Ireland we should not have seen so many gross and merely earthly conceptions of the Madonna as we have.'[1]

The fashionable Celtic twilight was promoted by the likes of Lady Gregory, relict by a late marriage of that much older Sir William Gregory who, during the famine, had denied relief to peasants earthly enough to own a quarter of an acre. It would in due course join hands with Sinn Fein and that other asinine remark of Pearse, that 'violence is a cleansing thing', in the vision of Eamon de Valera – less twilight than fog – one of pious violence and maidens dancing at the crossroads. The violence trembled beneath the kitsch, witness the clerical novelist Canon Sheehan in *Graves at Kilmorna* (1913): 'I have never thought of anything higher or greater than to strike one smashing blow for Ireland and then lie down to die on some Irish hillside . . . The country has become plethoric and thus indifferent to everything but bread and cheese. It needs bloodletting a little. The country is sinking into the sleep of death; and nothing can awake it but the crack of the rifle.'[2] This was a sort of recreational death, chatter not very different from the sentiments of Lord Kitchener a year later.

In the course of all the rhetoric, the actual earthly population of the real and miserably impoverished west would migrate to Kilburn and St Helens. Yeats, terse for once about politics, would say it all:

> Yes Ireland shall have her freedom
> And you still break stone.

The reality of Ireland – a pre-industrially poor country with a capital city enjoying the highest mortality figures of any in Europe and more of the huddled masses inscribed below the Statue of Liberty than any government knew what to do with – remained: a problem, a question and continuing, unresolved, fretful politics.

There were at this time also half-sensible, partly constructive things being done. William O'Brien, the editorial
lieutenant of Parnell, a bad team player on terms of running
ill will with colleagues, but an intelligent, creative man, set
up the United Irish League with 100,000 members, and
concentrated on utilising the Land Purchase Acts – which,
at reasonable prices, were (literally) cutting the ground
beneath the ascendancy – and on exercising power through
the recently created County Councils. O'Brien was also the
one nationalist leader to recognise that Ulster unionism was
there and not to be flapped away with a heroic phrase.

What had gone out of Irish politics for the interim was
the immediacy and stress of the Parnell era. It wasn't just
the absence of a tall, gaunt, black-bearded man speaking
with mesmeric urgency. There wasn't the fear and conviction
generated by the Land League that something very big must
be done and urgently, or poverty and anger would generate
their own explosion. The grimmer parts of rural Ireland
had looked then creditably like the very pattern of Marx's
doctrine of immiseration – things getting worse and worse
until revolutionary consciousness was raised to the point of
revolution. Ironically, people like Jim Larkin, who thought
revolutionary conditions existed, were in unamiable agreement with George Saintsbury pouting over a vintage about
the threat from Jacobins.

Tralee and Ennis are, of course, classically *not* what Marx
had in mind – centres of regions at once backward, rural,
unalienated and pious. They were just unspeakably poor and,
in ways Marx hadn't thought of, getting poorer, through
falling product prices on a glutted market improved by a
dab of renewed potato blight in the south-west. The Land
League had been a fair shot in the Marxian revolutionary
scenario, though actually the circumstances producing it were
the price paid by the rural poor for something sustaining
urban capitalism – cheap food.

It had all been handled by Gladstone and Balfour with a

mixture of amelioration and force. The Mitchelstown shootings defended by Balfour were the nearest we came to the 'really good massacre' yearned for by Leslie Stephen, but a succession of land purchase acts had put land, however unprofitable, under the feet of tenants and Balfour had sensibly spent money on small-scale rural and coastal developments. It wasn't the coherent grand thinking which advocates would make it out to be, rather a hand-to-mouth response to different emergencies, but it served. The bitterest edge was taken off the knife. Ireland retreated in the Westminster mind from crisis to question, and with that comfortable malaise, the Irish Question, government could jog imperceptively along well enough.

The whole Home Rule agitation, despite being frustrated of Home Rule itself, had shifted British government attitudes massively. Balfour, who would live until 1930, would observe with some complacency as the Irish Free State functioned and got along, that he had made all of that possible. Up to a limited point he had – in conjunction with Gladstone and Morley's land reforms – but he had spent money and bought out ascendancy landowners in the bloodshot conditions then prevailing *after* Parnell and because of him.

As for Irish leadership, the split between Parnellites and anti-Parnellites took ten years to fully resolve itself, but although the parliamentary representation contained talent enough – Dillon, Healy, O'Brien and more – cohesive was the last thing it was. Agreed leadership finally came at the end of the century to the forty-three year-old John Redmond. Redmond, though personally loyal to Parnell, had more in common with Isaac Butt. Gentlemanly, profoundly decent, parliamentary in the slightly debilitated way of which that institution approves, straight, uneasily capable of rant for the rural (and American) market, otherwise orotund and statesmanlike, this Wexford Catholic was a barely concealed Anglophile while the cricketing Anglican from Wicklow unaffectedly loathed the English. Above all, Redmond was willing to treat and reason.

In choosing him the Irish Party knew what they did. Redmond more than anyone represented the continued alliance with the Liberals. Parnellism proper after the great divide of 1890 had been rejectionist, embittered towards all English connections, inclined almost prophetically for 'ourselves alone'. But common practicality meant the Liberal alliance. And Redmond, who would be in his natural element with civilised Liberal Englishmen like Asquith and Birrell, was the man for that unromantic course.

After 1895 the Conservatives were under less pressure than before, and Salisbury, ageing, immobilist and detesting the Irish, was an obstacle. Even so, Gerald Balfour with the agreeably decorative Cadogan as viceroy, had a creditable record. Not obliged to do the Cromwellian bits with which his brother Arthur had delighted Ulster and Tory journalists, he spoke in October 1895 of being 'very glad if we were able by kindness to kill Home Rule'.[3] Although it got him into all sorts of trouble, it was in some ways a good thing to say, or at any rate to be thinking, but it implied more coherent purpose than there was, and more than Salisbury had sympathy or imagination for. It left the Tories looking Machiavellian when they were putting sensible bits and pieces together.

The Land Act of 1896 and the act of 1899 establishing agricultural and technical training were worthwhile and constructive affairs, while the Local Government Act of 1898 was, ironically, a Tory follow-through of Chamberlain's thinking while still a Liberal. And it was a marginal measure, however much sacred sovereignty was retained, of Irishmen governing Irishmen, which was a start, perhaps a precedent.

Accordingly, the nationalists set about winning council elections – 551 to the 125 of unionists (86 of those in Ulster). And this had been brought about by a Conservative government, a *unionist* government with a large majority owing no votes at Westminster to the Irish. In fairness, local government derived from the need to equalise rating for landlords between Ireland and the mainland. The protagonists of a hard line, Lord Londonderry and Sir Edward Carson, Balfour's prosecuting counsel in the late eighties, now solicitor-general, created rows in Cabinet and walked out of things, denouncing the councils as 'mere handmaidens of the National League' and the sort of thing 'we might expect from a Parliament in College Green'.[4]

One thing expected from College Green which Gerald Balfour was stopped from giving was more money for Catholic education, including an effectively Catholic university in Dublin balanced by a broadly Protestant one in Belfast. The objection did not come from Carson or Ulster so much as from English Tories badly upset by 'ritualism' being insufficiently persecuted in the Church of England. It was a step, several steps, too far for the Tory Party at large. In their resistance should be included a resentful Salisbury, whose 'bare toleration' of his progressive Irish ministers Cadogan recorded.[5] In its self-absorption the episode is reminiscent of the reason given by Herbert Morrison in 1951 for not joining the initial Europe of the Schuman Plan: 'The Durham miners would never stand for it.'

But Salisbury's elderly sourness was of less importance than the indifference of Carson. Edward Carson minded the County Councils very much and the education spending hardly at all. With such a measure of real self-government achieved, serious power was passing in the south to Catholics. The Protestants of the south, moving out, disburdening themselves of estates, were an accredited minority in that territory. Carson, himself a southerner, a Protestant Dubliner, concentrated his mind on arithmetic and directed his energies upon Ulster, where the arithmetic was good.

For all the rhetoric quoted in previous chapters about standing on a precipice, England in danger, Jacobin conquests, repeal of the union and the unfitness of the Irish for anything, the Gerald Balfour–Cadogan regime of liberal practicalities did *not* kill Home Rule by kindness, though it created a fair measure of goodwill. It offered some of the things Home Rule would have brought about and enough Home Rule in small, sovereignty-respecting parcels to make an incremental adoption of the full-dress thing a logical development. As was remarked by an Irishman, if the Conservatives had proposed Home Rule, Ulster would have had to have grinned and borne it. Instead, the logic of Randolph Churchill in 1886 would in due course come home. Not least in the bottomless if unconscious cynicism which Churchill had embodied when he took to calling Ulster Presbyterians 'a dominant and imperial caste' in 1886, having called them in 1885 'foul Ulster Tories who have always ruined our party'.

The Protestants were, of course, quite capable of admiring themselves without encouragement from Tory politicians. Birrell, who in 1907 would go with a loyal sigh to the chief secretary's lodge, would sum them up in the autumn of 1913 in a memo to Asquith.

It is a splendidly prosperous province in the Protestant parts with mills and factories by the side of the rivers and plenty of employment for the young . . . And then if you wind up as we did in Belfast, which is really a great Protestant effort, with a town hall as fine as Glasgow or Manchester and shrewd, level-headed businessmen managing its affairs, you realise what a thing it is you are asking these conceited, unimaginative Protestant citizens to do, when you expect them to throw in their lot with such a place as Dublin, with its fatuous and scandalous corporation and senseless disputes about the Irish language![6]

Birrell had earlier in the same draft recorded something of the ascendant mentality.

It is an odd country. I have just had a visit from the

Tory Lieutenant of County Sligo who wants troops sent at once to Sligo to protect the Protestant minority. I asked what risk they ran. He replied quite simply: if the Catholics are handled roughly in Belfast and its neighbourhood, there would be reprisals in Sligo. I said he might rely upon it that if the Catholics of Belfast were ill-treated, HM's government would dispose of their military forces throughout the north of Ireland in such a manner as would ensure protection to all law-abiding citizens. Thereupon he became very angry and wanted to know how people who flew the Union Jack could be treated as rebels![7]

The Protestants of nine-county Ulster were geographically grouped together. They formed a majority in four counties of Ulster, about half the population in two more and a diffuse minority in three outer counties. Unlike the scatter of their co-religionists in the south, they could get themselves elected, give or take a little gerrymandering, in six. This was the territory to defend, and if Canon Sheehan could talk wistfully about the crack of a rifle, the profits of linen and shipbuilding would shortly make a Hamburg cargo of good-quality German rifles dock at a northern port.

While Conservative England was prejudiced against Roman Catholics and ritualism in the Church of England, Liberal England, pretty much including Nonconformist England (and Wales), was disposed to be tolerant and for that reason unable quite to understand Ireland. Hartley Coleridge had remarked that he was never sure which of Catholicism and Protestantism had done more harm to Ireland. This, as Patrick O'Farrell comments, is to miss the point that Catholicism and Protestantism *are* Ireland. And as Birrell had also said in that memo assessing the Ulster mentality, 'At the bottom, the moving passion is hatred and contempt for the papist as a papist: at the top it is contempt and fear of the papist as a man of business.'[8]

And the irony was that religion was growing more important. The Irish parliamentary party, though made up largely of Catholics, had not been clericalist, and cast in tricky Westminster waters among English apprehensions, its members had gone out of their way to stress an Erastian view of Church power. The reality back in Ireland, a peasant country with real domestic command in the hands of parish priests, was a large measure of clerical authority and authoritarianism, quickly reasserted after the fall of Parnell. The division which continues to this day in the Republic of Ireland, between liberal and secularising, though often observant, opinion and the Church's correct line, was there. And increasing clerical domination would come to fruition in the thirteenth-century role of Archbishop John Charles McQuaid at the prime ministerial shoulder of de Valera.

The flavour of what was being fashioned was perfectly caught by Colm Toibín in his brilliant novel *The Heather Blazing*, in which a young man on a political platform stresses Fianna Fáil's clericalist tradition. 'We know, our history tells us, about the persecution of religion in his country. We know of the time when the priests had to flee from house to house. We respect our priests for that, and we don't fly in their faces now, like some others do. We don't start telling the bishops what to do, because we know our history.'

Enough Catholic bigotry and triumphalism existed to set against the bigotry and triumphalism preached from Presbyterian pulpits in County Antrim. And clerical attitudes at this time were vividly coloured by Rome's experiences at the hands of the *risorgimento* and the Church's identification in France with the narrowest reaction, the alliance of château and presbytery, with a dab of anti-Semitism thrown in. (A nasty little burst of persecution aimed at the inoffensive handful of Jews in Limerick, something got up by a poisonous priest, was denounced by local Church of Ireland clergy and by Michael Davitt, the old Land Leaguer and socialist. But the hierarchy flinched from using its authority to rebuke it.)[9]

The Church feared freemasons and liberals and looked at an expanding electoral/democratic process with no more enthusiasm than the Marquess of Salisbury. The ironic fact of the Irish Church's rigid, apprehensive reaction co-existing with what was seen in English Tory eyes as dangerous radicalism only added to a general confusion. The leaders of English Conservative politics had nothing to fear from the Roman Catholic Church in Ireland except an immoderate conservatism. But they were settled into a course of biological empathy with Ulster. Randolph Churchill's speeches had lain on deposit and had been added to by the party's leading figures, very much including Salisbury himself.

The Asquith government did not, to put it mildly, rush headlong into Home Rule. Liberals had been bitten and ground down twice before. And as long as the House of Lords subsisted to do what Dicey considered its constitutional duty, there was every reason to put off another rejection by dukes and barons of legislation advanced by an elected Parliament. But the Parliament Act had changed all that.

The necessity for Asquith to assert the powers of Commons over financial legislation was never going to be made narrowly so as to leave the peers their veto in non-fiscal matters. The Irish members had, after the January 1910 election, been necessary for that legislation, and a party committed to Home Rule, however nervous about it, could not have flinched from going forward dangerously.

Ironically, from the moment that he set the Lords on to the Education Bill, Balfour had begun the process which would lead to the Home Rule legislation and indeed to Irish independence. Balfour had called up the dukes and had seen his party swell with frustration into a mood of unreasoning rage. Now the dukes had been put in the shunting yard and the right wing was ready to turn on Balfour.

Defeat over the Parliament Act involved the Tories in losing two elections in a year as well as seeing the Lords stripped of their veto. The mixture of bitterness and abandon flourished in the *Morning Post* and the *National Review*, organs of the right. And then, as now, the right of the party knew what it wanted. The party was happiest preoccupied with itself and part of the preoccupation became the damning of Balfour.

The Tory leader had always had problems with the Tory Party. He was cleverer than they were, had wider sympathies and a decent hinterland – poetry, philosophy, Jane Austen and the new man, Bernard Shaw. In addition to his earlier enjoyment of Handel and Bach he had latterly become, appropriately, amid the tumult, something of a Wagnerian, making the pilgrimage to Haus Wahnfried. He would also have the imaginative capacity to be stopped dead in his tracks at a first meeting with an inorganic chemist from Manchester, Chaim Weizmann, from which initial conversation worldwide developments would flow with that Balfour Declaration upon which the state of Israel was founded. 'We all agree,' wrote Asquith to his wife, 'that A.J.B. is head and shoulders above the rest of his party.' Such a view in the eyes of an opponent is never a good sign.

But Balfour had lost those elections and that constitutional contest. And he had been a man to kindle respect rather than affection. Lloyd George, always a dispassionate judge away from a public platform, said, 'I could work with Balfour. Personally he is kind, but his underlying sense of class superiority is the trouble with him. He is kind and courteous but makes you believe he is a member of a superior class.' The Conservative Party liked a lord, but seeing themselves, in Fitzjames Stephen's phrase, as 'a belligerent civilisation', they were looking for a thug.

'BMG,' wrote Leo Maxse of the *National Review*. 'Balfour Must Go.' The *Morning Post* curled lip and rolled drum. Walter Long, a key colleague, resigned by way of a brutal letter. Something called the Halsbury Club, made up of militant right-wingers, was formed in celebration of the aged reactionary who had lead the resistance during the constitutional crisis. None of this was imperative. Balfour did not have to go, but scornful as ever, he went. The Conservative Party, torn on the matter of his successor between Austen Chamberlain – as much for continuity with Balfour as with his father – and the squirearchical stereotype Walter Long from the party's right, produced, as so often, a compromise, Andrew Bonar Law.

Law was not precisely a thug. His private style was soft-spoken and civil, if uninteresting. But he was not distracted by refinements or by Jane Austen. A teetotal widower grieving for the wife who had died two years before, Law disliked conversation, detested art and theatre and so loathed music that when he was awarded an honorary doctorate at Cambridge some years later, Trinity College curtailed the accompanying service to save him the pain of organ and choir. Of the listed distractions of Edwardian politics, 'women and champagne and bridge,' Law liked bridge.

Leopold Amery, a young and rising Tory of a furiously partisan sort, examined the two men. Balfour he compared to a virtuoso on the violin discursively developing an unexpected but intriguing theme. But Bonar Law's style 'was like the hammering of a skilled riveter, every blow hitting the nail on the head'.[10] There were a lot of riveters in Belfast, mostly Protestants of an unrelenting sort, and the steel discs they hammered out in the shipyards were frequently kept for later use by the handful against 'papishes' and other undesirables. They were known as Belfast confetti.

Bonar Law's father had not been born in Belfast, but in Coleraine, County Londonderry, a Protestant town not notably more relaxed in outlook. And he had been the minister – in Canada, where Law was raised – of a Free Church of Scotland congregation, the ultra-dogmatic 'Wee Frees'.*

---

* Not that Law, despite his manifest empathy with Ulster Protestant intolerance, actually believed in God. Devastation at his wife's death ran as deep as it did because he did not allow himself any delusion about an afterlife.

Law stood at an interplanetary distance culturally and temperamentally from the worldly sensibilities of A.J. Balfour. But something else had changed as well as the leader of the opposition. The Parliament Act had done more than shift the unimpeded passage of money bills from convention to statute, it had made all legislation free to pass after two rejections. The House of Lords was now weaker than it would have been if the budget had never been challenged. What Dicey had described as 'its constitutional duty to reject a Home Rule Bill' was now barred by law. There could only be a delay. However heckled and fretted, Home Rule would go through. And the Tory Party, behaving like a JCB in a tea tent, had, by bringing about elections, done just enough to deprive Asquith of the absolute majority with which that low-temperature politician had confined the urge to bring in Home Rule. With the Liberals now dependent for continued office upon the Irish members, even the gentlemanly and accommodating John Redmond would demand Home Rule.

Conservative rage would now bring on everyone's head a course of events actually more controversial than the budget-plus-Parliament Act struggle. That party, thrashing furiously about in a wilderness it did not recognise as defeat in elections, had chosen for leader an honest man of near-depressive grimness and a vein of fanaticism. About him danced mischief-makers like the alcoholising dazzler Fredrick Edwin Smith, affecting the mad mood of the hour; bitter and immobile Ulster landowners such as the Duke of Abercorn, the inveterately organising Captain James Craig and especially the Marquess of Londonderry, for whom the word 'reactionary' hardly suffices.*

Most important of all, he would be thrust into close alliance

---

* Birrell would be respectively optimistic and crisp about these two last. 'My friend Captain Craig, who is I believe a Christian – odd as it may sound – is ready to listen to reason. Londonderry is a cur and his wife a clever woman.'[11]

with Edward Carson. Carson – a hypochondriac who lived to the age of eighty-three, a law officer, law-breaker, exonerater of Archer-Shee (the Winslow Boy) and the man who chopped Oscar Wilde fine in the witness box – followed a steady doctrine of ferocity. Like Danton (and Goebbels), he believed exclusively in attack. There is a tendency to see the Edwardian age through its talents and glamour with metaphors involving the word 'golden'. There was talent enough, much of it at any rate gilded; but the period from 1909 to that outbreak of war so pitifully saluted was one of pressures – social, economic and Irish – met by fear and distilling, on the political right, a contempt for law and civility: the nearest thing to a genuinely fascist mood in the shrewd history of British Toryism. The combination of this party, these two men, Law and Carson, and the Ulster mentality – paranoia modified by blazing rage – would produce the worst political chemistry in British politics this century.

The representative figure – with the prime minister – on the other side was the chief secretary, Augustine Birrell. Birrell has had neither a friendly nor an attentive press. Because the ultimate crisis of 1916 blew up under his stewardship, it became convenient under what would then be the wartime coalition to make him the scapegoat. Tory historians were naturally unfriendly. And the opinion which instinctively derides the Ulstermen as bullfrogging brutes – George Dangerfield in his *Strange Death of Liberal England* – is lightly dismissive, while *The Times* on Birrell's death in 1933 and later the *Dictionary of National Biography* would variously describe 'a lightweight', and, charmingly, 'an intellectual coon'. Being a wit and a literary critic, he could surely never understand rough politics.

Birrell understood a great deal. He was clearminded and being a better Liberal than many of his colleagues, was enthusiastic for the reform. Unlike most of his predecessors, he actively liked the Irish. Himself, as he said, in origin a 'Nonconformist of Nonconformists', he had a soft spot for

Catholics (as, in a time of much casual anti-Semitism, he had for Jews). He would make a point, as Balfour had been the first to do, of travelling throughout Ireland, especially in the hard-driven west, recognising with some pain the wonderful effect of Asquith's 10 shillings of old-age pension on dismally poor old couples living in cabins in the less hopeful parts of Mayo and Clare.

An intensely bookish man, Birrell had read deeply on Ireland before taking on the job, from Edmund Spenser's pamphlet of 1595 through the writings of rebels and nationalists – the *Jail Journal* of John Mitchell, Michael Davitt's speech before the Parnell Commission and his *Leaves from a Prison Diary*. Always a fair man, he had also read Froude's *English in Ireland*![12] Over his years in the post, the first nine starting in 1907, Birrell had rescued the 1903 Land Act of his Tory predecessor, Wyndham – financially ramshackle and dependent on a falling stock – by extracting treasury backing, and he reinforced the act with powers of compulsory purchase. While an attempted Councils Act had fallen between two stools, he finally created the university which had been hanging fire so long, formally non-denominational but essentially the Catholic University, with newly established colleges in Dublin, Cork and Galway.

Humour is not lightly forgiven in politicians. Adlai Stevenson, the wittiest of presidential contenders, would be told by his handlers that America didn't like jokes. The man who said that a jackdaw should should be kept in the Cabinet room to say 'Ireland' at stated intervals to keep ministerial minds on the subject, spoke with an irony and deftness nowhere evident among his opponents. But the larger aspect of Birrell's rule was its mildness and sympathy, something acknowledged after independence by hard-line men of the rising. Pierce Beazley, biographer of Michael Collins, wrote in 1926,

There exists a a curious idea in England to this day that Mr Asquith and Mr Birrell were in some mysterious way responsible by their 'tolerance' of the Irish Volunteers for the insurrection of Easter Week. I can testify that the biggest obstacle that we had to contend against was the cleverness of Mr Birrell's policy. The one thing that would have rallied support to our side was drastic coercion on the part of the English government, but Mr Birrell cleverly contrived to appear as not interfering with us while taking care we were effectively silenced.[13]

Another republican, P.S. O'Hegarty, in his *Victory of Sinn Fein*, reckoned that 'Birrellism' might have held Ireland for England if it had not been succeeded by repression and the mailed fist. And looking back in 1952, O'Hegarty would write: 'Birrell's mild, apologetic, non-aggressive administration entirely bamboozled Irish public opinion and the Irish parliamentary Party and brought nationality into the greatest danger in which it ever stood.'[14]

But the notion of frustrating violence by cleverness and making a looser union work through sympathy would be doomed by insensible repression after 1916. And the prelude to that disaster would be a campaign largely directed against cleverness and sympathy.

26

A Besieged City

Gladstone had written in a pamphlet published two months after the rejection of his first bill that after a few years of 'constitutional and peaceful action, of steady and free discussion, then the walls of Jericho would fall "not in blood and conflagration, but at the trumpet's peal."' That sanguine hope had been followed by a further rejection, an ocean of hostile and fearful rhetoric and the foregathering of the Tory press and a pride of Oxbridge intellectuals rumbling against Home Rule. And it had seen the Conservative Party erect immutable union as both tactic and principle.

On and off for twenty-five years, with brief respites for an assault on free trade and the invasion of the Transvaal, Home Rule had dominated British politics. As for blood and conflagration, although so far they had not got beyond Colonel Saunderson's blustering talk, Lord Randolph had not quoted 'The Battle of Hohenlinden' at the Ulster Hall for nothing. Years of *talking* violence had left the Ulster Protestants, like the nationalists, equally and dangerously vulnerable both to taunts of making empty threats and the urge to fulfil them. This time round, as Asquith prepared a third Home Rule Bill, the bluster would be upped to preparation for war, and the Conservative Party and its leaders drawn into the physical threats.

The first shots were fired in in September 1911 when 50,000 men marched under the eye of a large gathering of spectators to assemble on the stepped lawns of Craigavon, home of Captain James Craig. These, as an admirer remarked, formed 'a sort of natural amphitheatre offering ideal conditions for out-of-door oratory to an unlimited audience'.[1] Craig would subsequently organise resistance while Carson articulated it. Edward Carson, who resembled the cinema Sherlock Homes, played by Basil Rathbone, lank and tall with a face for ever thrust forward, would not be a presence lightly forgotten as he made his pledge.

I know the responsibility you are putting on me today. In your presence I cheerfully accept it, grave as it is, and I now enter into a compact with you and every one of you, and with the help of God, you and I joined together ... will yet defeat the most nefarious conspiracy that has ever been hatched against a free people ... Make no mistake; we are going to fight with men who are prepared to play with loaded dice. They are prepared to destroy their own constitution, so that they may pass Home Rule, and they are prepared to destroy the very elements of constitutional government by withdrawing the question from the electorate ... Mr Asquith says that we are not to be allowed to put our case before the British electorate.

Very well, by that determination he drives you, in the ultimate result, to rely upon your own strength, and we must follow all that out to its logical conclusion ... That involves something more than that we do not accept Home Rule. We must be prepared, the morning Home Rule passes, ourselves to become responsible for the government of the Protestant province of Ulster.*[2]

* Ulster as Carson defined it – with nine counties – was 43 per cent Catholic, but a subsequent prime minister of Northern Ireland, Lord Brookeborough, would speak of 'a Protestant Parliament for a Protestant people'.

Two days later, 400 delegates from the Orange lodges, Unionist clubs and the Unionist Council passed a resolution to take immediate steps to frame and submit the constitution of a provisional government to come into being when a Home Rule bill passed and to be in force 'until Ulster shall again resume unimpaired her citizenship in the United Kingdom'.[3] This was to practise with a vengeance the Welsh rugby quip about getting your retaliation in first. The Parliament Bill had been signed five weeks earlier, and the introduction of the Home Rule Bill was still seven months away. The Craigavon rally was followed, at Easter 1912, a few days before first reading and four years before another Easter, by the meeting on the Belfast agricultural Show grounds in the suburb of Balmoral. In the words of A.T.Q. Stewart, historian of the struggle, it was 'a solemn occasion, no less than the wedding of Protestant Ulster with the Conservative and Unionist Party.'

It was literally a demonstration in that it demonstrated power: 100,000 men took part in a march-past, seventy trains had brought in the participants, and under a 90-foot flagstaff there was unfurled, at the moment a resolution against Home Rule passed, a Union Jack 48 feet by 25. Nothing about that day would be notable for quiet good taste or understatement.

As befitted a wedding, bride and groom both brought a party: seventy mainland MPs for the Conservatives headed by Law. Law instinctively spoke the language of Ulster – resentful, bad-tempered, historico-reminiscent and slammed shut on the world.

> Once again you hold the pass, the pass for the Empire. You are a besieged city. The timid have left you; but you have closed your gates. The government have erected by their Parliament Act a boom against you to shut you off from the help of the British people. You will burst that boom. That help will come and when the crisis is over,

men will say to you, in words not unlike those used by Pitt, you have saved yourself by your own exertions – and you will save the Empire by your example.[4]

Calling up the historical paraphernalia of the Siege of Derry in 1690, Law sounds very much like an Afrikaner politician invoking Blood River and the Voortrekkers. The air of Ulster and Britain would fill with like maunderings for the next two years until they were muted by trench fire.

In July 1912 the monster meeting transferred to Britain with a great gathering of Tories at Blenheim Palace. A law might be passed in the Commons but it would not be binding, and if Ulstermen used force against it, the Conservative Party would support them. The loss of the Lords' veto and the role in this of Irish votes, the inability of the Tories to get the dissolution which a Lords rebuff would have guaranteed, brought Law close to a position of regarding constitutional law as suspended. The monster meeting intimating the threat of force through street armies was a formula with great potential. The Conservatives of 1912 were playing with a fire which in other places at later dates would get hotter.

Such readiness for menacing assembly derived from the intensity invested in fighting that Parliament Act. But also in the air was an idea suggested long since by Dicey. The Vinerian professor, in his concern for an England which nothing but the efforts of every unionist in the land could save from destruction, had of course wanted, back in 1893, to have the House of Lords, if the Commons persisted with such evil legislation, 'append to any Home Rule Bill which they were prepared to accept, a clause which might make its coming force depend upon its, within a limited time, receiving the approval of a majority of the electors of the United Kingdom'.[5]

Following this advice, the Lords, in their own committee stage of the Parliament Bill in 1911, had carried just such an amendment saying that any bill 'affecting the Protestant succession or which makes provision for Home Rule in

Ireland, Scotland or Wales or which raises grave matters where the country has not been consulted, will not become law until it has been submitted to and approved by the electors in a manner to be provided by statute', meaning a referendum.

Asquith, as we have seen, having come through two dissolutions and two elections, had responded by requiring of the King the creation of a majority of peers under the royal prerogative. It was this which set off the famous emotional breakdown by Conservatives in the Commons, Lord Hugh Cecil and those cries of 'Who killed the King?' This outburst was a rending of garments as the Lords veto finally came to be buried. The constitution, at the urgent self-destructive urgings of both Conservative Party and peers, had been changed historically.

The Conservatives, having seen the Parliament Bill then pass the Lords unamended, suffered a kind of phantom pregnancy. With the Lords veto gone and the referendum amendment rejected, they persuaded themselves that constitutionally, they had in some way a moral right to either referendum or dissolution. The Parliament Act had sprung from resistance to a budget. It had been created because of an archaic attempt to stop a money bill, but it had gone beyond getting a finance act on to the statute book.

Their lordships had lost more than the convention-barred powers which they had attempted two centuries late to reassert. Antiquarian resistance having thus misfired, Asquith did not intend to suffer further assault. The prime minister had few things in common with Oliver Cromwell (better spoken of in Ulster), but he had treated the House of Lords like one of those captured royalist castles that Cromwell would disable for future defence by shattering the walls. Technically it was called 'slighting' or 'degradation'.

We have seen Tory spokesmen in 1886 talking uneasily in the wake of the third Reform Act about democracy as a threat. Unsure of how to play the new age, they now oscillated between Lords supremacy and populism by way of the referendum. It was an opportunism born of raging frustration. No one caught it better or more extravagantly than Kipling, in a poem for the occasion published in the *Morning Post*:

> Rebellion, rapine, hate
> Oppression, wrong and greed
> Are loosed to rule our fate,
> By England's act and deed . . .
> . . . Before an Empire's eyes
> The traitor claims his price
> What need of further lies
> We are the sacrifice . . .
> . . . We know the hells declared
> For such as serve not Rome—
> The terror threats and dread . . .
> . . . What answer from the North
> One Law, one Land, one Throne.
> If England drive us forth
> We shall not fall alone.

Was Redmond 'the traitor'? The mood, and Kipling with it, were mad enough to think so. Hysteria begets hysteria. Kipling's friends were already engaged in rebellion. Very little rapine is involved in extended local government and enhanced fiscal powers. 'The traitor' Redmond was almost embarrassingly fond of England and loyal to the British imperium. Cardinal Michael Logue lacked credibility for intending hells. Kipling could write like a serious poet and like a talented but unstable fourteen-year-old.

But he caught (and helped whip up) a mood – among Tories and their press quite as much as anyone in northern Ireland – one of impotent rage. The union Parliament, Pitt's creation, put together after the rising of 1798 (and thirty years later amended unwillingly to begin the enfranchisement of Catholic

Irishmen), was creating a new dispensation, however mild and moderate, and using precisely those Catholic Irish votes. Parliament Act and Home Rule had become entwined with each other and the fears and doctrines of a professor of law provided a justification for straightforwardly illegal actions. The mood was as fraught as Kipling's verse. There wasn't a House of Lords able to stop Home Rule; an attempt at stipulating a referendum had been rejected, not least because two requests for a dissolution had already been granted. It was thus in order for a former law officer to tell an Ulster rally that power should be seized. The twist in the Conservative mind in autumn 1911 was grievous.

The mind of Ulster was no prettier, but far less complicated. Sir Henry Robinson, adviser to the chief secretary in Dublin, passed on to Birrell an inspector's report ahead of a meeting which Winston Churchill, a rather strenuous Home Ruler, proposed for Belfast in October.* Since that meeting had been announced, reported Sir Henry, nearly 5 tons of nuts and bolts had gone missing from the shipyards, extracted, he feared, for non-industrial use. Belfast confetti was being laid up.

Birrell quietly persuaded Churchill to hold his meeting in a safe place. 'In Belfast all depends on locality and the character of the surrounding streets.' (Then as now.) He added, 'My own belief is that if you hold a midday meeting in a tent, no blood will be shed.' But he did not expect an attack on the military. 'The idea that the Protestants of Belfast, however excited, would begin by fighting the soldiers is absurd. In Belfast two mobs are necessary, a Catholic mob and a Protestant mob – it is they who fight and the military who seek to prevent them from murdering each other.'[6]

---

* Carson, Churchill had said cheerfully, was commander-in-chief of only half Ulster. What about the other, Catholic half? At this time and for some time to come, Carson, Craig and Law would claim the historic Ulster, nine counties including Catholic Cavan, Monaghan and Donegal, but they had no more than a two-thirds majority even in the six remaining.

When Carson, at another meeting in Portrush, had talked about the unionist organisation as the only influence controlling public violence, while denying any intention to fight army and navy, a voice in the crowd had called out: 'They are on our side!' That was shortly to prove true of a group of officers, but the Ulstermen would leave nothing to chance and prepared to be their own military.

A Protestant account, Lord Cushenden's *Ulster's Stand for the Union*, mentions the origins of what would soon be the Ulster Volunteer Force. 'It had been noticed that a contingent of Orangemen from Tyrone attending the Craigavon rally displayed a greater degree of smartness and precision, both in their marching and and their turn-out generally, than was usual. Upon inquiry it transpired that these men had for some time been learning the elements of military drill.' He continues, without irony, 'They had done so quite voluntarily and without any designs of an ulterior nature whatever. To the enthusiastic Ulsterman the idea possessed the most attractive features.'[7]

The legality of the act had been tested with a lawyer, James Campbell (later lord chancellor of Ireland under the wartime coalition!). In Campbell's legal opinion, again given with irony suspended, two JPs had 'the power to authorise military exercises within their jurisdictions upon the condition that such proceedings are consonant with constitutional intent'.[8] And to Ulstermen, words such as 'constitutional' and 'loyalist' had whatever meaning they, like Humpty Dumpty, chose to give them.

Churchill's meeting duly took place – in a marquee on the Celtic football ground in what might be called the wrong part of Belfast: western and Catholic. But it was a rare instance of provocative behaviour by a Liberal minister. Asquith's instincts at all times were Brer-Rabbitish – to lie low and saying nothing. Such an approach normally gets credit for depth and longsightedness, and Roy Jenkins, in his *Asquith*, argues that the prime minister could hardly have done anything else. Early concession on Ulster, as proposed by a Liberal backbencher, Agar-Robartes, would have shown weakness in the face of the drilling and Asquith's instinct was to play everything long, quiet and official. He would win any contest in Parliament, so keeping to the admittedly dreary Westminster path was to get to the destination. He had, after all, won the Parliament Act conflict by exhaustive and admirable patience.

But this approach was coupled with a strong impulse on the part of ministers, much encouraged by Redmond, to think of the whole Ulster military undertaking as bluff. This was intensified by lack of intelligence. The Liberals knew more about Ulster than Gladstone, who had come to the province as a historical theory, but they didn't know enough. Birrell felt this keenly and minuted in July that he had been reading for five years reports about secret societies in the Catholic south, but 'I think the time has come when the same microscope should be employed in another part of Ireland if that be possible; and information collected as to the "goings-on" in parts of Ulster of clubs and organisations which have lately been supplied with arms and are being detailed for eventualities. These "secret societies" are for the moment at all events, of greater importance than those whose movements are recorded in these reports.'[9]

But the Ulster Protestant network had not jumped up from nowhere. The Ulster Unionist Council, which brought together various groups, including the Orange lodges, had been a product of the earlier crisis of 1904–5, when the under-secretary in Balfour's administration, Sir Anthony MacDonnell, had written a document floating a form of modified Home Rule. And the Ulstermen were as agitated as much as they were because the Parliament Act had removed Ulster's longstop.

Their lordships had dispatched Gladstone's second Home Rule Bill amid laughter by a majority of over 419. But it had been Redmond's votes which had ensured that the House of Lords would never cast another veto. The delaying time substituted was thus an allocated period in which a Home Rule Bill could be stopped by a variety of means other than the House of Lords – the threat of force, force itself, men drilling with the blessing of two JPs, a provisional government or guns firing bullets.

There is a temptation to blame Asquith for not invoking the Ulster opt-out from Home Rule sooner than he did. He had made clear his readiness to do so to the King. Why not trade sooner rather later? But the bill itself was so modest. The Ulstermen couldn't really mean to fight a shooting war over such limited devolution, could they? Back in the nineties, Colonel Saunderson had talked windily of military resistance and, rightly, nobody had taken it seriously. A sheer inability to believe in the violent threat played its part in Asquith's want of response.

Birrell was less confident than most of his colleagues. His under-secretary, Sir James Dougherty, was convinced that the whole campaign, the lawns of Craigavon and all, was pure bluff, and Sir James, though a Liberal Home Ruler, was an Ulsterman, and a former Presbyterian minister! Birrell was uneasy. It was not easy to judge the extent of feelings in the north-east, he said in a Cabinet memorandum which he also sent to the King. There had been killings in Belfast before and public rage was being stirred. He wanted the noise made in Ulster taken seriously, but not in ways to frighten the horses, or the King.

Anyway, you had first to identify Ulster. Carson was talking nine counties, which was ridiculous and coolly known to be ridiculous by Carson, who was simply bargaining. At this time there were seventeen nationalist parliamentary seats in historic nine-county Ulster to only sixteen unionists. Four counties would be mooted, raising the question of partitioning Tyrone and Fermanagh, both genuinely mixed in religion.

Two things were certain: the Protestants violently rejected Home Rule from Dublin and the Protestants were no more

than a majority of the population of Ulster, however narrowly defined. From which advantage they regularly ill used
Ulstermen of the other confession. The proper object, knowing
what we know about subsequent Protestant lordings-over and
exclusions, might well have been three and a half counties
(omitting South Armagh) plus a wiggly line in the west.

Not acting sooner was for Asquith also a function of the
possible withdrawal of Redmond's votes in the Commons.
But however exasperated he was, Redmond would never
kill Asquith in order to establish the drab, virulent kingship
of Bonar Law. The question lingers why Asquith never
contemplated a 'powers-for-territory' deal. So modest a bill
could have been topped up in compensatory ways with each
or all of immediate RIC control, an improved financial
package or more fiscal independence. A twenty-seven- to
twenty-eight-county Ireland so enabled would have been a
tempting offer. And since Ulster opt-outs would later be rung
from Redmond across the long struggle anyway, a clean-cut
deal across the rhetoric (and the county lines) – deeper Home
Rule across narrower boundaries – looks like the best, most
imaginative response.

As it was, Asquith was committing himself to an agonising
process of legislation, including a guillotine in slow motion,
with most of the process run again each year to use up the
Lords' delaying power – all this in face of a quite literally
irresponsible opposition which played at sedition while the
northern Irish component of it marched, drilled, armed and
complained.

Speaking of which, he had also to deal with the King.
George V was laborious in his response to his clear duties
and preoccupied with his personal position and security.* The
temptings of lobbying Tories to effect the dissolution
of Parliament to which they believed they had a right and

---

* Exactly as he would prove when the question of asylum for his cousin,
Czar Nicholas, would be put to him and funked.

for which they yearned, attracted him. And, as with Lords Reform, Asquith would be given a hard time keeping the constitutional head of state functioning as constitutional head of state.

As for the parliamentary process by which Home Rule should be granted, the Conservatives were one degree readier for irrational action precisely because Irish votes, those of members of Parliament elected under the union, had helped carry the Parliament Act in the Commons. Balfour's patronising remarks during the report stage of the 1893 bill – that somehow Irish votes were alien and not part of our system – had been impertinently disregarded. The Irish members sitting in the Westminster Parliament under the Act of Union (1801) had voted in divisions. It was outrageous. And among Conservatives, the idea that Irish support for a Liberal government and its reciprocation somehow constituted a conspiracy, so Irish votes shouldn't count, was a long-running fallacy. An expression of their mood would come later in debate when a Unionist demanded that the Union Jack should fly from the Irish Parliament House during each session. The flag, replied the chief secretary, was a noble and great one, but 'compulsory loyalty is as impossible as compulsory religion or compulsory Greek'.[10]

From the start, Asquith, loaded dice, nefarious transactions and all, was privately ready to make concessions to Ulster. The prime minister's message to the King in February 1912, after extensive debate in Cabinet, was that although the initial bill should apply to the whole of Ireland, the Irish leaders must understand that the government reserved the right to make any changes which either fresh evidence or the pressure of British public opinion made expedient. Quite specifically, Asquith was ready to give special treatment to some Ulster counties, either by amendment or by not pressing the full terms of the Parliament Act, giving the Lords a kind of courtesy veto.

The bill itself was hardly radical. The two proposed Irish Houses in Dublin would stand under the King, the powers

devolved were those of 1893 while war, peace, army, navy,
treaties and honours were reserved from Dublin. And the
College Green Parliament would not handle land purchase,
public loans, tax-collection – other than postage, and, by historic irony ahead of the Easter Rising, the Post Office Savings .
Bank. For an immediate period of six years, the Royal Irish
Constabulary would continue under British control before
transferring to Dublin. Beside such modest concessions to
self-government, the British government would now make
a stab at settling Westminster representation. There having
been no Irish MPs there for the 1886 bill and the full quota
of eighty in 1893, Asquith settled on a compromise number
of forty-two. Moderation does not come any better.

That was sadly remarked upon during first reading in
a speech from William O'Brien, who could not follow
Redmond's words to the party convention that Ireland looked
forward to 'the greatest charter ever offered to her, one
resulting in the greater unity and strength of the Empire'.
If, said O'Brien,

> the Irish people are to be asked to accept this bill as a
> complete and final satisfaction of Irish national rights
> and demands, it will involve a degree of renunciation
> by Irish nationalists of the old school of those dreams
> . . . for which many generations of the best men of our
> race were proud to risk their liberties and their lives. I do
> not think we are changed, can ever possibly be changed
> in our readiness to incur risk for Ireland but we . . .
> have been changed in our eagarness for a genuine and
> enduring peace with the people of England and what
> was once called their garrison in Ireland.[11]

The bill, he pointed out, though offering 'a large and
courageous and perhaps generous proposal of administrative
Home Rule and of local, purely local, legislative power, does
not offer anything in the remotest degree approaching to that

national independence which was declaimed against at Belfast the other day . . . This Home Rule Bill, if I understand it rightly, is not repealing the Union; it is not colonial rule any more than it is an Irish Republic; it is a federal devolution pure and simple.'

Drily, O'Brien recalled that a few MPs like him remained who had heard Joseph Chamberlain in 1886 during the debates on Gladstone's first bill offering to withdraw his opposition if the Irishmen would accept Canadian provincial Home Rule. They could have settled for that then and it would have passed.

'The present bill' he said, 'unquestionably introduces the essential features of Canadian provincial devolution.' Irishmen not migrating to that province, as had once been urged on them, could now be their own Manitoba. O'Brien would have liked 'fiscal independence, full and at once' with 'the Irish Parliament raising their own revenue and without surrendering customs to the Imperial Parliament'. Nor, with such limited devolved power, was he happy at cutting the Irish Westminster contingent. Nevertheless, he was resigned to making the best of things: 'In my judgement, the success of an Irish Parliament will depend to a large degree upon its being won by consent . . . I mean carried by a larger degree of acquiescence and goodwill on the part of the better thinking men of the Protestant minority in Ireland.' Securing that goodwill and co-operation would be 'of infinitely more permanent value to Ireland than any mere politician's point about whether this or that particular power was given to or withheld from the Irish Parliament. I for one would be prepared to go to any reasonable lengths, and even some unreasonable lengths, to secure that co-operation and goodwill.'

There is something poignant in that speech. O'Brien had a more critical mind than Redmond. He was conscious that Asquith's Home Rule distinctly under-egged the pudding. However, like the rest of the Irish members, he wanted what the constitutional process would agonisingly permit.

But if the Irish MPs would accept a third of a loaf, they did want a whole island; and the appeal to the goodwill of the better-thinking men of the Protestant minority was the forlorn plea of men trying to keep some sort of Ireland together. Four years after these April speeches would come the Easter of men with guns.

The preoccupation at this time of both the Irish Nationalist Party and the Liberal government was to stress the reasonable minimalism of what was being done. Winston Churchill, later in the debate stressing that Ireland's demands had become steadily more moderate, would give a little advance notice of a speech of his twenty-eight years later, saying, 'Never before has so little been asked, and never before have so many people asked for it.'[12]

But there are some people on whom moderation is wasted. Sir Edward Carson had already launched himself into what O'Brien called his 'extraordinary and misguided' position. That was courtly understatement. Carson was talking war. James Craig spoke in the same first reading debate in ways which illustrate the Ulster perception. Southern moderation to Craig was incitement to northern inactivity. The demand for Home Rule had gone down. There was little for the Irish to complain about, why bother with Home Rule?

> If land purchase had been permitted to take its ordinary course, and if the few small and trifling grievances in Ireland – small matters connected with the pay of teachers, with local administration and with the examination of private bills without the expense of coming here – had been settled and we had been allowed to go on as we were, I have no hesitation in saying that any discord in the relationship as between the various sects and creeds in Ireland would have been removed and peace would have settled down in the country.

It was Craig who, long after partition had settled him in

as prime minister of Northern Ireland, would claim grimly never to have knowingly given employment on his estates to a Roman Catholic!

He had his own definition of Ireland. It was absurdly overrepresented. 'Whether you look at Ireland for administrative purposes or from the point of view of railways or county council work or industries, it is only a little bit larger than the county of Yorkshire.'*

The language, as it was with almost everything Ulster Protestants had to say at this time, was violent and livid. Asquith quoted Bonar Law's speech earlier in the week. The bill was 'nothing better than the latest move in a conspiracy as treacherous as has ever been formed against the life of a great nation'. Meanwhile, 'the present government turned the House of Commons into a marketplace where everything is bought and sold ... In order to have a few months longer in office, His Majesty's government have sold the constitution.'

'We have sold ourselves?' mocked Asquith. 'This, Mr Speaker, is the new style.'

JAMES CRAIG: It is the truth and you do not like it ...
ASQUITH. This is all very well for Ulster, but what about the House of Commons?
BONAR LAW: I have said it here.
ASQUITH: Am I to understand that the Rt Hon. gentleman repeats here or is prepared to repeat on the floor of the House of Commons—
BONAR LAW: Yes.
ASQUITH: Let us see exactly what it is: it is that I and my colleagues are selling our convictions.

---

* Such geographical triumphalism, such sizeism, is not dead. I was once confronted on a television programme with Norman Tebbit, who said in response to something done by the Irish government, 'Well, they're only a County Council.'

BONAR LAW: You have not got any.

ASQUITH: We are getting on with the new style.[13]

Interestingly, at this stage, Carson, speaking in the Commons in the same debate, was distinguishable from Carson on a public platform. (Law, on the other hand, not a man for nuance, produced the same sullen truculence everywhere.) He, Carson, made the sound point that Gladstonian finance would never have permitted in a Home Rule Ireland the medley of reforms with land purchase at their head which had taken place in the twenty-seven years since 1886. With £115 million (some £6 billion of today's money) spent on land purchase, he had a point. Carson also put perfectly civil arguments against the federal solution for all Britain which was heavily canvassed at this time.

He looked to future costs and the likely lack of control over them and noted the lack of safeguards over the new university, which the Irish Cardinal, Logue, with the usual archiepiscopal crassness, had sworn to make Catholic. But Carson, in the Commons, spoke rationally; the fires of the monster meeting were banked. Indeed he touched on Ulster only at conclusion. The Ulstermen had come into the union in 1801:

> They came in and got satisfied under your rule and became loyal and because they did, now you tell them to go out . . . We at all events in this matter have a plain and a ready duty before us. It is to oppose this bill with all the energy we can at every stage and at every moment it is before the House . . . We believe it to be a fatal bill for our country and an equally fatal bill for yours, and above all things, we believe it to be involved in the greatest series of dishonourable transactions that have ever disgraced any country.

Eleven and a half *Hansard* columns of rational discourse

were concluded with a softly spoken commitment to total resistance and a sudden, spat-out twist of venom. As an admirer had described him, 'The rich southern voice, the simple moving phrases . . . the lack of gesture or histrionics and then perhaps the concluding sentence, suspended while in a still intense pause he surveys his audience – and then like a pistol, shot the final word.'[14] His conclusion also contained that phrase 'our country'. To the Dublin-born Carson 'our country' ostensibly meant Ireland. But Ulster was taking on the dimensions of a country, and Carson was leading it.

Backbench argument on all sides tended in these debates to dive into archives and fish out old speeches, speeches which thrillingly unmasked the true, sinister purpose of the other side. Ronald McNeill, the future Lord Cushenden, who would shortly leave Winston Churchill bleeding from the bound copy of Commons orders which he flung at him, had scoured the far corners of the Irish provincial press to prove the real feelings of the Irish behind John Redmond's affable words about British institutions. Redmond had earlier been quoted as saying, 'We are entirely loyal to the Empire as such and we desire to strengthen the imperial bonds through a federal system of government.' He had subsequently denied using the words.

MCNEILL: Then there is the *Enniscorthy Echo*, which said, 'We publish today a statement that will astonish and pain every nationalist in County Wexford.'
JOSEPH DEVLIN: What did the *Skibbereen Eagle* say?*
MCNEILL: I am sorry I cannot gratify the Hon. member with what the *Skibbereen Eagle* said, but I will gratify him to the extent that I can tell him what the *Connaught Champion* said: 'Bewilderment is the only

---

* A standing Irish joke is an editorial in that newspaper in which the editor had written during an international crisis, 'The Czar of all the Russias should know that the eye of the *Skibbereen Eagle* is upon him.'

word which can describe the feelings of the supporters of Mr Redmond at his profligate barter of what
he proclaimed to be his unalterable principles a few
months ago.'[15]

The repudiation, said McNeill, was made 'because you
have got that opinion in Ireland which is utterly disloyal to the
Empire and is not going to strengthen its bonds . . .' McNeill,
an Ulsterman representing a Kent constituency, turned to his
own country. 'If I have not said much about Ulster it is because
I cannot trust myself to do so. I do not believe . . . as regards
Ulster I should be capable of the necessary restraint to keep my
language within the limits of order . . . Hon. members below
the gangway [where the Irish sat] . . . look upon Home Rule
as an extension of liberty. We look upon it as a degredation
of status.' It was because Ulstermen were 'proud of being part
of the United Kingdom and do not wish to lose that status,
that we object to proposals of that sort'.

The date for commencement of the bill fell 'on a very
significant anniversary. It was on the 11 April just fifty-one
years ago, that the first step was taken in the great American
Civil War . . . I pray God that on this 11 April, fifty-one
years later, the prime minister may not by his action have
been setting his hand to a similar tragedy.' That threatened
comparison had already been made outside Parliament and
would be used over the next three years by more important
Ulster figures than McNeill. It would be invoked by the leading
men in Conservative politics on the mainland, not least by the
leader of the Conservative Party.

This was the first day of legislation which, by reason of
the Lords delay substituted in the Parliament Act for the
veto, would go through the full set of parliamentary hoops
three times, and the note of hysteria struck at Craigavon had
already been echoed and would be sustained.

27

Bowler Hats and Wooden Rifles

The parliamentary process would continue – first and second readings, committee stage, Lords and report – most of it again and again. But beside the passing into law of legislation with a clear parliamentary majority, there ran a parallel, a campaign which was extra-parliamentary and increasingly anti-parliamentary.

Something of the mood of Ulster, making allowances for aristocratic disgust, can be found in the memoirs of Lord Ernest Hamilton, brother of the Duke of Abercorn: 'When I saw Members of Parliament [*sic*] who called themselves Englishmen systematically taking the side of their country's enemies and yet being saluted by policemen and going about the streets with whole skins, I felt I was in a world for which I was not fitted.'[1]

And something of the mood of British Conservative opinion, making allowances for nothing, lies in the sulphurous pages of *Blackwood's* in an unsigned piece, almost certainly by the viperous Whibley. Was Asquith a touch bland and disappointing to nationalists as a Home Ruler? On the contrary, he was selling England out for votes:

The democracy whose name is ever on the slavish lips

of the Radicals, is bidden to stand aside. There are now two parties to the contract – Mr Asquith who represents the Cabinet and Mr Redmond who represents the dollars of America ... 'What have I to gain?' Asquith asks virtuously, 'and what have my colleagues to gain?' They have gained the support of eighty henchmen and some years of office. And we cannot imagine any advantage nearer to their hearts.

Was William O'Brien complaining of Canadian provincial devolution? Nonsense, the Irish were robbing us. 'And at the same time we proclaim Ireland a 'nation', we are to confess without sorrow or shame that she is an insolvent nation. She is to be free, not merely to manage her own affairs and to oppress Ulster, but to put her hands in the British till.'[2]

This was an Ireland 'who henceforth will be protected for nothing by the army and navy of Great Britain and who will retain no further responsibility for the National Debt. Ireland in future shall tread the primrose path ... others shall earn her spending money, others shall defend her against foes. And she will have nothing left to do, save oppress Protestants, bait landlords and prove to an admiring world that she enjoys all the benefits of "freedom".'

Then there was religion: 'If Mr Redmond has his own way, the Protestants of Ireland will be handed over hand and foot, not to the priesthood of Ireland, but to the Vatican.' And anyway, the evil wouldn't stop at Asquith's Bill. 'In October last, Mr Redmond unveiled a statue purchased with American gold in memory of Mr Parnell ... The truth is that "federalism" will never satisfy those who prate of "nationhood".'

As for defence, the nation was in danger. 'Not one word has been said to allay our just fears for the future defence of the Empire, not a single word to justify the new and perilous policy of disintegration.' And it would lead to war. 'Yet so monstrous is the levity of Mr Asquith that for the sake of a compact which will keep him and his colleagues in office a year or two longer, he will imperil the sovereignty of the Empire and make civil war an imminent possibility.' Or, to put it with less restraint: 'An Ireland hostile and independent will weaken us immeasurably in the face of Europe . . . the granting of Mr Asquith's Home Rule to Ireland can make nothing certain save civil war.'

But anyway, it would never happen. 'The Home Rule Bill will follow its brothers of 1886 and 1892 into the night and will survive only as a curiosity neatly bottled and labelled in a glass case of political antiquities.'

Blackwood's was still fighting the battle against any form of Home Rule. Conservative even in its Conservatism, it had not in 1912 cottoned on to the fact that the argument was shifting, retreating into the redoubt of Ulster, an Ulster waiting to be defined. Resistance would, slowly but perceptibly, become narrower, less rhetorical and altogether more serious. Southern Protestants influential in the Conservative Party, like Lord Lansdowne, a Fitzmaurice and a Kerry landowner, came to realise that nothing would be done for the southern Protestants. Too few, too scattered, asking too much in the way of reasonable demands, the largely Anglican southern minority lacked the geographical concentration which would make that special ego-zealotry of the Ulster Protestants such an effective weapon.

Lansdowne might effectively be joint leader of the Unionist party with Law since he led them in the Lords. And Law, an honourable man by his narrowly focused lights, would admit privately in 1913 that any outcry for southern loyalists would have 'a very violent echo in England', because all these years 'we have fought Home Rule as bad on national and imperial grounds as well as from the point of view of Ulster.' But, he added, 'if the question were left to the electors . . . they would decide that Ulster must not be coerced; but I think also that they are so sick of the whole Irish question that they would vote in favour of trying an experiment so long as the Ulster difficulty was solved.'[3]

'Experiment' is an unusually euphemistic, not to say weasel word for Law. He was slipping without acknowledgement into acceptance of Home Rule for the south; and Lansdowne, for all his commitments, could not stop the argument shifting to the exclusive interests of the north-east. Ulster would fight, or at any rate might well fight, but it would be for Ulster. Twenty years before, Lord Randolph Churchill, near the end of his sentient life, was told by a Liberal guest, the future Marquess of Crewe and a minister in the Campbell-Bannerman and Asquith governments, that 'the Unionists are making a great mistake in getting so tied up with Ulster and they will pay for it when they wish to settle the question'. Lord Crewe recalled: 'Randolph replied, "We shall tell Ulster to go to the devil," and I said, "That is exactly what you will never be able to do." And so it has turned out.'[4]

Lord Crewe was right. Ulster at this time was rife with paramilitary preparation of those neatly turned-out contingents from the country districts. Returned NCOs with South African War experience worked at Orange halls or on the estates of the Ulster gentry, turning James Campbell's legal opinion to account by providing the essential training which the army of a country normally gives its recruits for the purpose of fighting a war. (And indeed, on the Somme on 1 and 2 July 1916, the trim, well turned-out delegates who had practised with wooden rifles would march into the German machine-gun fire which determined the battle for Thiepval Wood, in which 5,500 men were lost in two days.)

One reason why Ulster could not be told to go to the devil was that she had too many friends and nephews in the British military. Cromwell had been the effective creator of the British army and men from the north-east of Ireland had found it a congenial service, rising to high and extensive rank. It was thinkable to make an approach to one of them who happened also to be commander-in-chief. Ulster leaders were encouraged in this by their Conservative friends in England. There had been formed in March a British League for the

Support of Ulster and the Union with an address in St James's Street. It was the brainchild of a certain Lord Willoughby de Broke. The chief ditcher could claim 120 MPs and 100 peers supporting his League. And one of them, Thomas Hickman, member, interestingly for South Wolverhampton, future Enoch Powell territory, undertook to write direct to a former commander-in-chief.

Lord Roberts of Kandahar was a competent military talent, but in the near-hysterical mood of pre-First World War imperial England, 'Bobs', as he was cloyingly called, enjoyed the sort of hero-worship now given more wholesomely to pop stars. He was probably more adulated than a genuinely great soldier like Wellington. Roberts ducked out of the invitation to command seditious forces drilling with wooden rifles in County Fermanagh. But, keen to help, he recommended for the post General Sir George Richardson, who complied, though he was less of a fire-eater than the people he would soon find himself inspecting. As Colvin, the egregious biographer of Carson, would put it, this veteran of Waziri campaigns and the Boxer War before he finally settled in Poona was 'as completely at home with the Ulster volunteers as with the tribesman of the Tirah or Zhob Valley'.[5]

In September 1913, the Belfast division of the UVF, as it styled itself, would hold a review on the Balmoral grounds used for the earlier rally. General Richardson inspected the troops, accompanied by a mounted figure, the inspecting general's galloper, an opposition frontbencher newly returned from defending his friend Lloyd George and other Liberal ministers in the legal actions flowing from the Marconi scandal – Mr F.E. Smith.

But for the moment, Ulster Protestantism occupied itself with religious rather than military pageantry. The usual word employed by outsiders of Ulstermen – as it is the usual word for the personality of Andrew Bonar Law – is 'dour'. More apt than most stereotypes, the adjective misses a certain gift for self-dramatisation and sense of theatre in the Province.

This would show itself in response to the mood of violence mounting across the summer.

An attack by a group of marching Hibernians – the Ancient Order of Hibernians, otherwise the Molly Maguires, Catholic equivalents of the Orange lodges – on a Sunday School excursion parading Union Jacks had been followed by a shipyard riot in which Protestants terrorised and drove out Catholic workmates (more confetti being thrown), and finally by a football riot when a Celtic–Linfield match turned into a battle at half-time, banners and flags being reinforced with weapons to cause sixty casualties.

In looking for a pageant, Carson, in Tim Healy's words, was also seeking 'a safety valve for the Orangemen'.[6] Searching for ways to highlight resistance through an oath ceremony and lacking a form of words, he took the advice of a Belfast businessman called Montgomery. 'You couldn't do better than to take the old Scotch Covenant. It is a fine old document, full of grand phrases and thoroughly characteristic of the Ulster tone of mind at this day.'[7] As blissful admissions go, that does very well. The National Covenant sworn to in 1638 belonged in the world of the Thirty Years' War, witch trials, dragonades in Languedoc, massacres at Drogheda and Wexford, James II resisting good advice from the Pope and the sort of Scottish Calvinism that gets Scottish Calvinism a bad name. As a snapshot of the 'Ulster tone of mind today', calling in aid the Scottish Covenant pictured militant anachronism, not to say ancestor-worship.

The words of the original proved too heavy and ornate, so what would be called 'the Covenant' was in fact a new document. But the word itself served great psychological purpose, adding grim lustre to the ceremony, a mass public signing with drums and banners scheduled for 28 September, which was now designated 'Ulster Day'. The text, describing Home Rule as 'subversive of our civil and religious freedom, destructive of our citizenship, and perilous to the unity of of the Empire' spoke for 'men of Ulster, loyal subjects of

His Gracious Majesty King George V, humbly relying on the God in whom our fathers in days of stress and trial confidently trusted'. Ulstermen do few things humbly, and trust no one at all. But for the purposes of demanding with menaces, religious phraseology did a good deal for the tone.

And the menaces were clear enough as the signers undertook

> through this our time of threatened calamity to stand by one another in defending for ourselves and our children our cherished position of equal citizenship in the United Kingdom and in using *all means which may be found necessary* [author's italics] to defeat the present conspiracy to set up a Home Rule Parliament in Ireland. And in the event of such a Parliament being forced upon us, we further solemnly and mutually pledge ourselves to refuse to recognise its authority.

The 'threatened calamity' was the granting of Canadian provincial devolution to Ireland. The position most cherished by Ulster Protestants was the steady keeping in their place of those unequal citizens, the Roman Catholics of the north. The whole screed caught the tone of Ulster very well – unctuous, religiose and, while munching the word 'loyalty', contemptuous towards all British law inconvenient to Ulster interests.

The covenant itself was a piece of theatre slowly built up by performances in outlying districts before a grand climax in the capital. The principles paraded around the outposts of the plantations, starting from Portora Hill near Enniskillen, then advancing on Lisburn – a town with a significant Catholic population, which was marched through under torchlight by men with wooden rifles in earnest of the real things to come, accompanied by a fife-and-drum band playing 'Protestant Boys'.

At Portora, Carson spoke of being at 'one of the outposts,

nearer to the zone of danger and among the enemies'.[8] In Portadown, he had an escort which presented wooden arms, and when he inspected them royal-style, a Union Jack was dipped. If all this was threatening, there was also a comic element. Not only were the rifles wooden; also wheeled on at Portadown were 'two pieces of ordnance, the guns being made of wood painted a steel-grey colour' accompanied by an ambulance van and nurses. *The Times*, a friendly recorder of the events, remarked that the Ulstermen were well placed for their show: 'The southerner has a dread of making himself ridiculous which the northerner does not share. The northerner's lack of this feeling gives him the advantage in a crisis like the present.'

Ridiculous or not, as the Covenanters processed at similar grand public meetings involving British Tory politicians through a string of towns, the menace was clear enough: menace attended by ceremonial Presbyterian theatre. At the conclusion of the provincial run, the show was brought to the Ulster Hall. A great ceremony had been devised, something which would fluctuate uneasily between municipal pageant and 'the Triumph of the Will'. A yellow banner supposedly borne before William III at the Battle of the Boyne was put, together with a silver key, into the hands of Edward Carson by a Colonel Wallace, one of the commission of five leading the movement. Captain Craig then took and loosed the flag and held it out, saying, 'May this flag ever float over a people that can boast of civil and religious liberty.'[9] A northern Catholic newspaper observed: 'If that flag ever saw the Battle of the Boyne, all we can say is that the man who manufactured it deserves undying fame for the strength and durability of the material.'[10]

The next day, 18 September – Ulster Day, as it had been proclaimed – was begun inevitably with a religious service in the Ulster Hall; then, after one of those bowler-hatted Ulster marches which have defied ridicule for eighty years, the solemn signing took place at Belfast City Hall. Attended by Mayor and corporation, poor-law guardians and members of the water board, all by way of an early photo opportunity under the 39,000-candlepower glare of electric lamps, the document itself lay, symbolically perhaps, upon a Union Jack.

Lord Cushenden (otherwise the excitable MacNeill), sympathetic chronicler of the revolt, gave a keen account.

> No man but a dullard without a spark of imagination could have witnessed the scene presented at that moment without experiencing a thrill which he would have found it difficult to describe. The sunshine sending a beam through the stained-glass window on the stairway threw warm tints of colour on the marbles of the columns and the tessellated floor of the Hall, sparkled on the Lord Mayor's chain, lent a rich glow to the scarlet gowns of the City fathers and lit up the red and blue and white of the imperial flag, which was the symbol of so much that they revered to those who stood looking on. They were grouped in a semi-circle behind the Leader [sic] as he stepped forward to sign his name ... there they all stood, silent witnesses of what they all felt to be one of the deeds that make history, assembled to set their hands each in his turn to an instrument which, for good or evil, would influence the destiny of their race; while behind them through the open door could be seen a vast forest of human heads, endless as far as eye could reach, every one of whom was in eager accord with the work in hand and whose blended voices, while they waited to perform their own part in the great transaction, were carried to the ears of those in the Hall like the inarticulate noise of moving waters.[11]

The paranoid style was on full-dress parade in its natural home.

Carson, followed by another yellow banner decorated with a red star and the cross of St George, walked to the table and signed. Marshalled in batches of 400 or 500 at a time, simultaneous signatures were then inscribed. Not at all mindful of ridicule, a Major Frederick Crawford signed the covenant in his own blood. But then, Major Crawford, of whom more later, had said a few months earlier that if Ulster were put out of the union he would 'infinitely prefer to change his allegiance from King George to Kaiser Wilhelm'.*

He was not alone in this sentiment, already, as we have seen, expressed by Thomas MacKnight. James Craig, the impresario of the covenant, had told a London newspaper that the German Emperor would be preferred in Ulster to a government headed by John Redmond. The loyalty of Ulster was strictly Pickwickian. When the war against Germany did come, Lord Aberdeen, the Liberal viceroy, was told by one loyalist group: 'We are making garments and bandages, but they will all be sent to London for I would not like to think that any of our things would be used by nationalists.'[12]

Outside in the street, the Conservative journalist J.L. Garvin observed the marchers and the crowds with rapture. 'No one for a moment could have mistaken the concentrated will and courage of these people. They do not know what fear and flinching mean in this business and they are not going to know.'[13]

When Carson left for the docks to make his departure on a ship called the *Patriotic*, he did so to the beating of drums, and found his cabin decorated with roses. And to the sound of the mass singing of 'O God, our Help in Ages Past' and, of all things, 'Come Back to Erin', he was gone, only to arrive in Liverpool an hour or two later to encounter a reception

---

* The same Frederick Crawford, as a young man during the fever of Gladstone's second Home Rule Bill, had unsuccessfully approached a wealthy peer, Lord Ranfurly, for £10,000 to pay for the hire of a yacht from which the prime minister, holidaying in Brighton, might be kidnapped and 'removed to a South Sea island'.

party carrying Union Jacks, banners commemorating William III, brass and concertina bands, an address by the champion of Protestant Toryism on the Mersey, Alderman Archibald Salvidge, and a second rendition of 'O God, Our Help in Ages Past'.

Conservative involvement wider than that of Alderman Salvidge – in Parliament and the press – was something else. F.E. Smith, who would become General Richardson's galloper, had discovered that his birthday coincided with the Battle of the Boyne and had joined the pre-signing rambles. He had also been told in a letter from Edward Dicey, as fervent as his brother, that 'Home Rule is intended by the coalition to ruin the power of England'.[14] Smith gave the Ulstermen what they wanted to hear.' For how long have you nourished the dreams of the patriotism of your youth out of that deep well which inspired [sic] the Battle of the Boyne? . . . But you cannot live for ever, however glorious they may be, on the memories of your ancestors. It is time for you – listen to me – to make history for yourselves.' Carson's biographer, Colvin, detected failure by the London barrister to make contact: 'Mr F.E Smith, brilliant, impetuous, a Rupert of the platform, yet somehow not altogether favoured in Ulster, which may have been puzzled by oratorical fireworks or may have felt instinctively that he had no bottom of seriousness.'[15]

The Tories also responded by sedulous imitation, staging their own mass meeting in England, another monster rally on ducal turf, this time in the Duke of Marlborough's grounds at Blenheim, where Law, sullen, vengeful, unnerving, showed a bottom of seriousness by advocating simple insurrection. The speech is famous. Before he was leader,

> I said that in my belief if an attempt were made as part of a corrupt parliamentary bargain – to deprive their men of their birthright, they would be justified in resisting such an attempt by all the means in their power, including force. I said it then and I repeat now,

with a full sense of the responsibility which attaches to my position, that in my opinion, if such an attempt is made, I can imagine no length of resistance to which Ulster can go in which I should not be prepared to support them and in which, in my belief, they would not be supported by the overwhelming majority of the British people.[16]

Cheered in ways familiar from the reception of most platform infamies, he had put himself on the record at Blenheim as endorsing armed rebellion against lawful government, which meant endorsing the killing of its soldiers – British soldiers.

Law meant what he said. Smith, who followed him, probably did not mean it when he shouted 'Should it happen that Ulster is threatened with a violent attempt to incorporate her in an Irish Parliament with no appeal to the English electors, I say to Sir Edward Carson, 'Appeal to the young men of England.''[17] In a court of law, Smith's spongiform ambiguities could have been defended with optional readings; Law, on the other hand, had made an uncomplicated proposal for sedition. The young men appealed to might have only been invited to another monster meeting. 'Force', specifically included by the unsubtle Law, lacked nuance. The view expressed by Birrell later in the campaign got the balance of bluster and real purpose right. 'This isn't bluff,' he later told Asquith in a note of the Ulstermen themselves. 'Many of them would fight and die like heroes, but it's politics and they are almost all deeply persuaded a dissolution will intervene, and until that is over, they needn't make their wills or say more prayers than usual.'[18]

Carson, less than a fanatic, though he did a very good impression of one, was gambling; gambling upon the political damage done to Asquith's government bringing about the dissolution sought by both Ulstermen and Conservative politicians – not least from the actions of a jittery George V, upon whom Law was naggingly at work. Carson struck a lot of attitudes – very hard, but he never quite stopped being a Conservative politician. It is difficult to believe that under a Tory leader remote from Ulster prejudices, he would have played the same hand quite so remorselessly. In fact, the immediate numbers signing the covenant were well below the sensational level: 471, 44 in Ulster, was something less than full-hearted assent, especially as, in a burst of progressive practice, the covenant had been thrown open to women. In Britain and the south of Ireland, where books had been opened and a sympathetic assocation formed, the total signatures collected, according to the devoted unionist Henry Maxwell, amounted to 19,162 – a modest number given Conservative connivance and the belief of the opposition that the country yearned in equal passion to free Ulster and elect the Tories. It was not so much figures as the ferocious conviction of the believers which counted, a conviction which brooked no law and knew no limits.

Carson used menaces and displayed verbal contempt for law, but one is never quite sure whether rider or tiger is determining the route. Back in December 1912, he had threatened Britain with the raw will of Ulster Protestantism.

My own people in the north of Ireland come up to me and say – they don't argue very much – 'I should like to tell you, Sir Edward, what they were saying about you here after your speech last night.' I asked them what it was, and they say, 'Well, a good many of us think you are going too slow.' Then sometimes, as I walk through the streets of Belfast, a man will come up to me – mind you, they are a serious lot of people – and without any idea but extreme gravity, he will say, 'When are you going to give the word, Sir Edward?' I tell him to go home and behave himself, but I don't know how long I shall have the power.[19]

There was a good deal of Spenlow and Jorkins about this: 'I

would be more reasonable, but my business partner, he's the hard man.' Except that, as Carson was finding out, Jorkins *was* a hard man, and more than a little mad.

By spring 1914, against the 1,000 regular troops and the local policemen, the province would have 23,000 trained volunteers under command – 'Ourselves alone' was a slogan with wide application in Ireland. Moreover, parallel with theatre ran serious actions, albeit actions running through hands both highly influential and a little unhinged. In this crisis the preposterous had a way of overlapping with the sinister and criminal. Dummy rifles, bowler-hatted guards of honour and light streaming through town hall stained glass to illuminate the signing ceremony below are one thing, a trained armed force is another. If the Conservative Party in the sour style of Bonar Law was finding the parliamentary authority assembled through three reform acts an uncomfortable fit, there were people in the aristocracy and imperial administration to whom it was essentially contemptible.

Alfred Milner, so prominent in the South African war and its miseries, was an English sketch for those 'strong men' who would adorn the first half of the century. He was, aptly enough, a protégé of Joseph Chamberlain. Rotten radical politicians had made an unnecessary public sensation about Chinese coolie labour in South Africa, the pro-consul's pragmatic revival of slavery. A disgusted Milner lived in semi-retirement, but the freedom of an imperial and dominant caste from integration with Ireland's own Bantu was near his heart. In December, he wrote to Carson, 'It would be a disaster of the first magnitude if that "rebellion" which would really be the uprising of unshakeable principle and devoted patriotism – of Loyalty to Empire and the Flag – were to fail! But it must fail unless we can *paralyse the arm* which might be raised to strike at you. How are we to do it? That requires forethought and organisation *over here*.'[20]

One option was for that fellow-travelling British organisation the British League to turn its young, fit supporters into additional troops to go to Ulster in support. But the main mechanism would be the Union Defence League, for which right-wing press publicity was solicited by Milner. Before the world war intervened a statement was issued avowing that passing the Home Rule Bill 'without submitting it to the judgement of the Nation is contrary to the spirit of the constitution', and that 'accordingly I shall hold myself justified in taking or supporting any action that may be effective to prevent it being put into operation and more particularly to prevent the armed forces of the Crown being used to deprive the people of Ulster of their rights as citizens of the United Kingdom.'[21]

But Milner and his friends did not stop at threats to do unconstitutional things in defence of their private definition of the constitution. He raised money from dukes and other reliable sources, including an incredible £30,000 from Kipling, who 'knew the hells designed for they that serve not Rome'. More cash and serious talk about drumming up volunteers came when Milner circulated his colonial contacts in the armies and governments of the Empire. Much of the money would go into the patriotic purchase of German guns. He was also ready to organise insurance for officers who resigned their commissions rather than 'violate their consciences'.

To similar ends, Carson and Law had again enlisted the former head of the army. A letter written in the name of old Field-Marshal Roberts sought to tell officers in the Territorial Army (which the hated Liberal government had created for national defence), that in circumstances of civil war the old business of obeying orders would not be quite the binding thing they might think. 'It is a soldier's duty to obey,' said Roberts or his draughtsman,

> but if and when the Civil War breaks out, no ordinary rules will apply. In that case the soldier will reflect that by joining the Army, he has not ceased to be a citizen and if he fights in such a quarrel, he will fight on the side he believes to be right. If the attempt be made to

coerce Ulster, Civil War and nothing else will inevitably
follow. Ulster will not be fighting against the Crown or
the Flag, and it will be idle to describe such men as 'the
King's enemies'.[22]

Asquith would shortly speak of the general's 'senile frenzy'.
  The idea mooted was that this letter should appear in the
press at the same moment as Law published an amendment
to the Army Act to be put to the Lords. As the diary of Sir
Henry Wilson noted, 'The proposal is for the Lords to bring
in an amendment to the effect that the Army shall not be used
against Ulster without the will of the people expressed at a
general election.' Wilson, an intriguer's intriguer, was happy
with this, though as chief of the imperial general staff, he was
conscious that such an amendment might give rise to minor
difficulties. 'We discussed it all backwards and forwards,
the handle it will give against the Lords, the possibility of
no Army remaining after April 30, the effect abroad; but I
am convinced Bonar Law is right. Desperate measures are
required to save a desperate situation.'[23]
  Desperate it surely was, since given a sequence of the Lords
accepting the amendment and the government rejecting the
bill in that form, their lordships could for two sessions refuse
to pass the bill, something they were quite mad enough to do
at this time. Then the rules of military discipline by which
soldiers are commanded, not being renewed, would be put in
suspension and the soldiers given the legal status of civilians
serving by consent. No left-wing troublemaker could have
asked for more. And this was being planned in the early
months of 1914.
  The idea slightly scared the people engaged on it, as well
it might. On 16 March 1914 Law, writing to Sir Henry
Craik, said: 'Here is a method strictly constitutional, for
nothing is clearer than that the method by which the Army is
maintained has been adhered to for the express purpose of
putting a check on the Executive Government preventing it

from using the Army against the will of the People.' And on the 18th, Wilson records a dinner with Carson, Milner and Jameson (of the Raid). 'They all agree the Lords must amend the Army Annual Act.' But while using the army as a weapon against an elected government was acceptable, what couldn't be risked was a split in the Conservative Party. On 20 March, Law wrote privately to Croal, the editor of *The Scotsman*, 'It would be fatal to do it if there were any serious opposition to it in our ranks and I think there is a sufficient amount of that feeling to make it impossible to do it.'[24] Law, coming part way to his senses, would be saved from the humiliation among his conspirator friends which would have been caused by climbing down from an act of criminal irresponsibility. He would also be saved by another grotesque act committed by a clique of senior military men which would enter history as the Curragh Mutiny.

It was the misfortune of Asquith to have promoted an exceptionally able man, R.B. Haldane, from war secretary to lord chancellor and appointed in his place Colonel Seely, a rather lovable, brave soldier with no political sense and that feebleness in civilian dust-ups which often seems to afflict brave officers. The *dramatis personae* at this time also included an exceptionally silly senior officer, Sir Arthur Paget, who had a predilection for rather girlish fits of apprehensive honour; another general, Sir Hubert Gough, who, talking sense during the First World War would be disregarded and badly treated, and when talking Ulster particularist rubbish at this time would be taken all too seriously. And hovering around like a malignant office politician was the deeply unpleasant and ill-intentioned figure of General Sir Henry Wilson.

The idea obsessing a significant tranche of the military command was that in some way they were likely to be sent north to crush Ulster. Now, there was, under the laid-back Asquith and the sensible Birrell, never any prospect that British troops would be ordered from their base near Dublin to do anything of the kind. But there *was* a Cabinet committee concerned with defending arms depots in the north. Since it was entirely thinkable that illegal imports might be followed by illegal raids, guard reinforcements on those stations were intended. They were to be sent from the military base at the Curragh, north of Dublin. As the volunteer force outnumbered the army locally, it was the least that could be done. Also Churchill, first lord, had responded to prospective gun-running Churchillianly by moving ships into coastal waters and, later in the crisis, would utter the sort of stern words which across history have been uttered by men in no way placed to enforce them. Grave matters were being raised, said Winston, which would be put to the proof – a silly thing to say given the absence of any credible means to hand for proof-putting.

The (optimistic) reality was described by Birrell at the height of the crisis. 'The forces of the Crown,' said the chief secretary, would 'never be used in Ulster except for the legitimate purpose of maintaining unbroken the integrity of His Majesty's dominions, of assisting the civil power in the maintenance of law and order, and of securing to every minority, be it large or small, be it Catholic or Protestant, the protection to which it is entitled against the fury of the religious bigot or the savagery of the political partisan.'[25] Actually Birrell was overstating the extent of military commitment. Catholic shipyard workers driven out of their jobs during a riot against 'papishes' had little hope of protection from His Majesty's forces.

But General Paget, collecting his orders to do precisely that job of reinforcement, extracted from the feeble Seely the undertaking that 'where officers have direct family connexion with the disturbed area in Ulster . . . they should be permitted to remain behind'. Paget told seven of his senior officers, one of whom, Hubert Gough, an Ulsterman, canvassed *his* officers, many of them in fashionable regiments and rich enough to afford cashiering. Having asked them what they wanted to do, Gough reported to HQ, asked for more information and notified Paget in a gentlemanly way, expressing regret that 'if the duty involves the *initiation* of active military operations against Ulster, they would respectfully, and under protest, prefer to be dismissed'.

The entire crisis invites General de Gaulle's comment not long before the coup of 1958, 'If there is a government it will govern and the army will obey. The army only rebels when it is frustrated in its natural instinct to obey. If there is no government, the army will assume power in Algiers and, as for me, seeing that there is no longer a state, I will assume power in Paris in order to save the Republic.'[26]

Assuming power to save the Republic, like setting up a military force to hold Ireland for the Empire, is elegant cant, but the Ulstermen and the Conservatives had done their bad-tempered best to hollow out government authority. Asquith, called from Lord Sherfield's bridge table to receive Paget's telegram, looked as much *fainéant* as insouciant, though his immediate reaction was cool enough. 'The military seem to have thought,' he wrote to his correspondent, Venetia Stanley, 'that they were about to be ordered off at once to shed the blood of the Covenanters and they say they never meant to object to duty like the other troops in protecting depots and keeping order.'[27]

Unfortunately, the crisis had also touched the slow, plaintive mind of George V, 'grieved beyond words at this disastrous and irreparable catastrophe which has befallen my army'. Nagged by the King and threatened by Bonar Law with a parliamentary explosion, Asquith told his friend on 22 March: 'The military situation has developed as might have been expected and there is no doubt, if we were to order a march upon Ulster, that about half the officers in the army – the navy is more uncertain – would strike. The immediate difficulty in the Curragh can, I think be arranged, but that is the permanent situation and it is not a pleasant one.' You could say that again. Under far more duress than any plaintive soldier, Asquith was obliged to substitute inoffensive

434

orders. Shortly afterwards the Cabinet authorised Gough to say that the whole matter was a misunderstanding, but that nevertheless, it was

> the duty of all soldiers to obey lawful commands given to them through the proper channel by the Army Council, either for the protection of public property and the support of the civil power in the event of disturbance, or for the protection of the lives and property of the inhabitants . . . That is the only point . . . and the Army Council has been glad to learn from you that there never has been and never will be any question of disobeying such lawful orders.[28]

This was the sort of thing Asquith was good at: damage limitation, forms of words deftly saving the face of the government and making the army as a whole look undisturbed, except by a blip, in its seamless adherence to orders. But Seely and Morley, quite unauthorised, in response to calls from Gough, added two paragraphs asserting the right 'to use all the forces of the Crown in Ireland . . . to maintain law and order and support the civil power in the ordinary execution of its duty', but they had no intention whatsoever of taking advantage of the right 'to crush political opposition to the policy or principles of the Home Rule Bill'.[29] Gough, with the graceless inveteracy of Ulster, said the words were not good enough, and demanded written assurance that the last paragraph meant that the army would not be used to enforce Home Rule in Ulster. Sir John French, the commander-in-chief, loyal but not clever, endorsed the statement to this effect, and Gough carried his piece of paper back to Ireland.

Effectively the ability of an elected government to give orders to the military had been surrendered. De Gaulle's notion that 'when there is no government the army will assume power in Algeria' was being anticipated. Gough, badgering

435

two weak ministers and a military colleague, French, softer than himself, had given the army – on paper and for a very few days – the sort of powers which might be accomplished by a coup d'état.

Asquith, who could be decisive when he had to be, realised that Gough's rewriting of the law must be disowned. To that end, he gently edged French and Ewart, another general present at the Gough exchanges, together with his calamitous war secretary, into resignation. And after a short look around, he took the War Office into his own hands. Obliged under the law of the day to seek re-election, he was, though unopposed, to encounter a display of spontaneous popular enthusiasm in Edinburgh and in his Fife constituency agreeable to see on the other side after the number-bullying of Carson's street and stately home populism.

But although damage had been limited, it was damage still. The idea that officers might treat orders as a buffet lunch had appeared in full public view and the arrogance of Carson, Henry Wilson and the men talking openly of creating a provisional government for Ulster had been reinforced. The only satisfaction was that the Tories would muff their political chance in the Commons and that Carson at this time would make his own empty threats of returning to Ulster to form a government and do nothing to consummate them.

But running through the Curragh Mutiny was another thread, one of compromise over Ulster, reasonable in itself but made deeply damaging by Gough's revolt and by the self-pitying inability to cope with crisis of a King limited in outlook, anxious, viciously lobbied and struggling imperfectly to understand. For the further history of the third Home Rule Bill is one of a scramble for compromise.

28

Hon. Members: 'Traitor!'

Well before the Curragh Mutiny took place, steps were already being taken to seek a compromise over Ulster – with minimal help from Carson and Law. The attempt was made against a background of vituperation in Parliament and press, intrigue at court and refusal by the opposition to respond to major concessions.

The bill itself, after inordinate witter in the committee stage, finally passed the Commons on 16 January 1912 with a majority of 109. It was then rejected by the Lords by 326 votes to 69. But although it had to come round twice more under the terms of the Parliament Act, it was not, blessedly, then subject to committee. Accordingly, the bill would now come back a second and a third time before leapfrogging the Lords veto, leaving opponents at home as well as in Ulster in much the same vixenish mood they had shown at the start.

Charles Whibley* of *Blackwood's* expressed the general Tory rage at the new dispensation.

---

* A familiar figure in this narrative, Whibley would become friend of T.S. Eliot in the 1920s during his 'Mussolini good thing, hang Mrs Thompson' phase.

Our tyrants care not whether the country is for them or
against them. They have suspended the constitution . . .
[The Parliament Act] has taken away from us the chief
safeguard of our liberty, an appeal to the country and
it has enormously strengthened the hands of our tyrants
. . . the House of Commons has been brought indeed by
Mr Asquith's revolution to a state of nullity. An era of
unreality enwraps all its proceedings. It has ceased to be
a deliberative assembly.[1]

This was nonsense, and of course the Tories, by trying on a
resurrection of convention-barred powers for their own ends,
had brought major constitutional changes on their own heads
– 'Tu l'as voulu, Georges Dandin.' Parliament at this time,
displaying so much virulence over three sessions, would have
seemed a strange place – and a mad one. As for 'Parliament
ceasing to be a deliberative assembly', the Tories appeared at
times to have given up deliberation.

On 13 November 1912 Asquith had moved the rescission
of a snap vote of two days earlier by which the opposition
had amended the financial element of the bill. Events and
words spoke the Tory/Ulster mood. The yearning for an
election which they had persuaded themselves they would
win was very high. The snap vote had elated them to delusive
expectations. They anticipated an election over the defeat and
in acknowledgement of the strength of the current trend, yet
here was Asquith, in all his maddening calmness, gracefully
rescinding the vote and quoting back at them Balfour's speech
when in a similar fix back in 1905. Balfour's old words
mocked the new high constitutional tone of his colleagues.
The then Tory prime minister had thought the idea 'that a
Ministry kept in office by a majority in Parliament ought to
consider in addition to the views of that majority, precisely
how the tide of public opinion is flowing so far as the
direction and strength of that tide can be judged by the
course of by-elections' to be 'an absolutely novel principle

– a principle which so far as I know has never been suggested by any responsible Minister of the Crown, either in public or private.'[2]

He had been right. Asquith had a Commons majority and a mandate. The situation is familiar today, and such exchanges, beginning with calls for resignation, usually amount to desultory and ritual games of House of Commons table tennis. But that was hardly Law's way. In his speech he compared Asquith with Cromwell (a hero to this opposition in the Irish context). 'Tyrannical governments,' he said 'and above all, revolutionary governments, have always chafed against restriction.' But Law was silken compared to James Craig.

A man for physical action, contemptuous of these constitutional refinements and bubbling with menace, Craig spoke his mind. Ulster members were 'in a very awkward position in connection with the whole of this dirty business from start to finish'.[3] Graciously, if with doubts, they had resolved to keep to parliamentary rules. 'Rightly or wrongly, we came to the conclusion that as far as possible we would conform to the dignity and rules of this House and preserve our attendance in order to drive the present government from power.' But having struck a blow 'at the very heart of the bill', they had been frustrated. 'The prime minister says that even that victory is now to be snatched away from us. But he is not going to do this constitutionally; he is going a step further in shattering a constitution which I thought he had brought to the very gutter. What does it mean? It means that the attendance of hon. members on this side is useless while the government have behind them a party subservient to the last degree and are supported or led by Irish members below the gangway.'

Craig, the earnest non-employer of Roman Catholics on his estate, disliked contradiction, of which there is a good deal in Parliament. His friends 'lay open to the grossest taunts and insults from members on the other side'. They were 'met in the most flippant and jeering way with members of the

Cabinet sitting there and grinning like apes at us'. He was tired and wouldn't stand for it.

> The north of Ireland will be forced from under the shelter of Great Britain and from under the British flag, and will have to go. In future we will have to take our orders from the hon. and learned member for Waterford [Redmond] and the nationalist rebels.*
>
> That is the position I say so far as I am concerned – and this is a serious statement – I am tired: I repeat it, I am tired. I believe that my proper place and the proper place of all the other Ulster members is among their own trusty friends in the north of Ireland, for I believe that this government is not to be treated as a government, but is to be treated as a caucus led by rebels. The only way to treat them is for us to go back quietly and assist our loyal friends there to make what preparations are necessary.

Craig's sullen rage was infectious. A few minutes later, while a Tory member, Pollock, was renewing the attack on Asquith – 'quite ready to throw aside every possible precedent in order to maintain his own contemptible position' – the skies broke in ways best set out by *Hansard*:[4]

> SIR WILLIAM BULL, COLONEL CHALLONER AND OTHER HON. MEMBERS: Traitor, traitor!
> Mr SPEAKER: If I knew the hon. member who made use of that expression—
> SIR WILLIAM BULL: I did.
> COLONEL CHALLONER: I did.

---

* Ireland had not rebelled in any meaningful sense since 1798, but Ulster Unionists always cultivate a taste for anachronism. To this day they speak of the Republic of Ireland – established under that name in 1949 – by its treaty title, the 'Free State'.

Mr SPEAKER: I tell both members that it is not a parliamentary expression.

Mr CHARLES CRAIG: How can hon. members be expected to use parliamentary expressions under circumstances such as these?

Mr SPEAKER: However strongly hon. members feel they have been treated, they are not entitled to use that particular word.

Mr CHARLES CRAIG: I echo everything that has been said by the hon. member.

(HON.MEMBERS: Traitor!)

Mr SPEAKER: What hon. members used that expression?

SIR WILLIAM BULL: I used it.

Bull was suspended for the rest of the day, but the mood of the evening did not lighten. Pollock continued, and told colleagues that if they passed Asquith's resolution, 'They will have declared that we are no longer a deliberative assembly, but that we are all sitting here merely to register the decrees of the executive of the day'. He was followed by Henry Page Croft,* for whom 'the action of the government today sounds the death-knell of parliamentary government and of representative government . . . the name of the government stinks in the City of London . . . the government have reduced this House to a sham and a fraud. There is not a single member opposite who does not sit there by trickery. There is not a single member opposite was not elected on a pledge to destroy the hereditary principles of the House of Lords' – a pledge Page Croft complained had not been redeemed. This was

no longer a representative assembly because it is absolutism gone absolutely mad.

---

* Twenty years on, Stanley Baldwin would advise the young R.A. Butler to avoid extremes 'between Henry Page Croft at one end and Harold Macmillan at the other'.

There is no Bourbon who does not turn in his grave when he sees how absolutely he has been beaten at his own game by the Prime Minister. Even Metternich was at least honest. He did not pretend to be a people's man . . . The government now think that they are in the position of the Czar and that there is no one to consult except themselves . . .[5]

By 8.30 another Tory, Hewins, had described the House of Commons as 'the greatest of English [*sic*] possessions; it represents the quintessence of national feeling,' and had informed Asquith that he had 'no business to trample on the honour of the country'. Although he knew that 'there are hon. members on that side and hon. members sitting on the front bench opposite who perhaps have not got that feeling about English traditions that we have on this side'.

Hewins knew the government would infallibly be destroyed – 'directly they try and explain these things to the British working classes, do you think they will show any mercy to men who threaten the constitution of the country?' But he begged them not to pass the resolution 'to prevent this disgrace and dishonour being put upon the House of Commons'[6]

When, after that burst of tremendousness, Rufus Isaacs, the attorney-general – who might have been in Hewins' mind as 'not having that feeling for English traditions' – tried to speak, he was met with continual noise and shouts of 'Adjourn!', 'Civil war!' and what *Hansard* describes as follows:[7]

Mr RONALD MCNEILL: Why do you not sit down? (Interruption) . . .
Mr SPEAKER: In my opinion grave disorder has arisen, and under Standing Order No.21, I adjourn the House and suspend the sitting for an hour.
Sitting accordingly suspended at half past seven o'clock p.m.

At eight thirty, Isaacs again tried to speak, creating a dia-
logue of:

> SIR RUFUS ISAACS: Mr Speaker
> (Interruption)
> HON. MEMBERS: Sit down.
> AN HON. MEMBER: There is your parliamentary machine
> broken.

There was half a column in the same constructive vein,
including the cry from Carson 'No more business in this
House!', which seems to have been taken up as a chant
before the Speaker, at 8.36, ruled that 'it is quite obvious
that the opposition having determined not to allow further
business, I am compelled to say that a state of grave disorder
has arisen and, under Standing Orders, I must adjourn the
House until tomorrow.'[8]

The matter of McNeill's question 'Why do you not sit
down?' and the following interruption is clarified at columns
2088–9 of *Hansard*.

> I desire in a few words, Mr Speaker, to give something
> in the nature of a personal explanation of an incident
> which occurred after the adjournment of the House
> last night . . . Political feeling was very high and taunts
> were exchanged between members upon both sides of
> the House. Under the influence of a momentary loss of
> self-control, I regret to say that I discharged a missile
> which struck the first lord of the Admiralty.'[9]

McNeill then apologised to his victim, Winston Churchill,
who gracefully accepted it.

Unionists had cheered the second adjournment, and when
Churchill and John Seely were spotted, there were cries of
'Rats', at which Churchill had waved his handkerchief. Then,
in the words of Lord Blake, Law's biographer, McNeill

'seized the Speaker's copy of the Standing Orders and hurled it with great accuracy at Churchill's head'.[10] But loss of self-control was neither momentary nor confined to this Ulster member. Law, speaking the next day at the Albert Hall, could manage no more than, 'I did not suggest a disturbance, but I have this responsibility; I did not attempt in any way to interfere with what my colleagues desired to do ... I did not try it, and under similar circumstances I never shall try it.'[11] Opposition loss of control was official.

But the oppressive ranting mood which Whibley voiced and which an eruptive opposition acted out reads even more strangely in conjunction with the comfortable readiness of 'our tyrants', especially the 'traitor', Asquith, to consult and accommodate over Ulster. The prime minister had made his reserve position clear in the initial 1911 outline of the bill to Cabinet. In the latter part of 1913 he would take definite consultative steps with the leadership of the opposition.

The government *might* make changes over Ulster if it had to. But no government wished to be held to ransom by the sort of posturings currently taking place, especially when they strayed outside the roughest sort of democratic protest and turned first to drilling, then to talk of provisional government. The people tired with Parliament would soon flaunt rifles and ammunition purchased in the Kaiser's Germany, whose soldiers leading Ulstermen said they preferred to see in Dublin than an elected government. As, obviously, all the Irish nationalists were bitterly opposed to concession. It was a thin enough bill already and their understandable Irish view of Ireland as one country was fixed.

There was a practical need for the economic contribution of the north and there was that ill-used Catholic population. But against all argument for the integrity of the bill came the King. George V had a tenuous hold on the purposes of constitutional reform and a tendency to see the amenable Redmond as a rock of contention. He would nag his ministers to extract more from Redmond, who from any Irish point of view, was already dangerously overextended in the concessionary direction. George had inflicted an unnecessary second election in 1910 over the Parliament Bill. Though trying honestly to be a constitutional monarch, he was a natural Tory, much lobbied by Tory public figures, colonial and military, and deferentially indulgent to Carson. His letters and minuted conversations with Asquith and Birrell make reference to Sir Edward Carson being 'put in an impossible situation', as if Carson occupied any position in which he had not coolly placed himself. Throughout 1913, as the covenant was launched and the arms conspiracy took shape, ministers considered the options.

Immediate assessment of the state of affairs came from the chief secretary. Birrell, in March 1913, took the threats seriously. His briefing indicated that the Ulster revolt had created a dangerous situation, but in a very fluid way. The talk of civil war was irrational and fluctuating. At one moment it was imminent, the next it would be thought that if a single citizen were to be shot by a British soldier the whole enterprise would collapse. We shouldn't, he thought, rule out a declaration of a provisional government, at any rate for Greater Belfast, where the protest was concentrated.

But all commercial argument went against it. Belfast was a commercial city with money to lose, and a vitally important part of her business was with the rest of Ireland. As for when an explosion was most to be feared, actual elections looked like the probable trigger. It would be very hard to hold elections in Ulster for a Dublin Parliament without disproportionate military and police supervision and obviously, the covenanters would try to sabotage the machinery of any newly established Irish government. And as he would say in his memoirs, Birrell was 'not a believer in the gospel of bluff'. As for the extent of the risk, it would be hard to assess, but that risk had been increased by the stirrers-up, Ulster and Tory, and their propaganda, too much of which, he murmured, was already influencing the King.

The King, of course, was part of the problem. So Birrell, called to the Palace in July, found George frightened and wobbling. 'Somebody of importance,' he minuted Asquith, had

> told the King that in addition to the 100,000 poor Irish nationalists who have long made my native city of Liverpool joyful, there were another 100,000 Orangemen, all well-to-do citizens who on passage of the Home Rule Bill, would desert their homes and flock to Belfast to fight all and sundry. I found it very difficult, believing as I do that there are grave possibilities of riots, bloodshed and even worse incidents of religious strife and hatred in North East Ulster, to stem his tide of hearsay. But I think I partially succeeded in putting forward the following point of view: that it was the plain duty of these potential rebels and advocates of civil war, mutiny and the setting up of an independent government which must involve the commercial ruin of Belfast, to place before Parliament . . . a proposal of their own for their future government . . . This seemed a novel point of view.

The trouble with George V was self-concern. Without himself thinking himself selfish, he thought chiefly about himself. 'His Majesty said a great deal about the awkwardness of his own position and his determination to look at it from his own point of view as King and left in my mind the clear impression he was being pressed to entertain the idea, though not able quite to see how it could safely be done, of forcing a dissolution next year.'[12]

The King dropped this hint, but his badgering was of a tentative nature and as he didn't spell it out, Birrell didn't feel free to answer what hadn't quite been asked (Asquith would do this magisterially later). But his analysis to Asquith of a suitable reply was prophetic. 'I would have said that if the Home Rule cause was in the ordinary course of political events in England postponed for a few months or years, there would be no great disturbance in Ireland, yet if it were defeated by an unconstitutional or unusual action, risking its speedy ultimate success, the rage would be universal.'[13] Artillery bombardment, imposition of matial law, the shooting of citizens on the street and sixteen executions in the early summer of 1916 followed by the imposition of a form of military government under the Defence of the Realm Act, could be called unconstitutional and unusual.

The government had trouble with the King because Law was making trouble. In the perfectly proper conversations held by the leader of the opposition with the King, Law was trying perfectly improperly to persuade the head of state to dismiss the government. At a Buckingham Palace dinner as early as May 1912, he had said to the King,

> Your only chance is that they [the government] should resign within two years. If they don't, you must either accept the Home Rule Bill or dismiss your ministers and choose others who will support you in vetoing it: and in either case, half your subjects will think you have acted against them ... They may say that your assent is a purely formal act and that the prerogative of veto is dead. That was true as long as there was a buffer between you and the House of Commons, but they have destroyed this buffer and it is true no longer.[14]

The obsessive belief that removal of the Lords' veto had destroyed the constitution, which appears in speeches, articles and pamphlets throughout the whole three-year period, is the true north of Conservative compass-reading for the duration. As we have seen, the idea of a hereditary chamber able to brake legislation might, at a time when the hereditary element was better regarded, have been defended credibly, but for the inconvenient fact that across the previous half-century, and at an accelerating rate, the House of Lords had become a one-party assembly. What had been done in the Parliament Act had lodged in the mind of the unaffectedly outraged Law. His private approach to the King was followed when George asked for more with a memorandum on 31 July signed by Law and Lansdowne.

The King now addressed Asquith on 11 August echoing Law: anything he did would offend half the population. One alternative would alienate the Ulster Protestants 'from me . . . No sovereign had ever been in such a position'.[15] Kindly and politely – this was another thing he did supremely well – Asquith explained to the King the position of the King. The royal veto had been unthinkable to monarchs back to and including George III, apart from William IV, who had sacked Melbourne and put in Peel. Peel wasn't able to govern, Melbourne had come back – for five years – and the Crown had been damaged. The Parliament Act concerned itself entirely with relations between the two houses. If the Crown did not stick to the constitutional precedents, it would turn into 'the football of contending factions'.[16]

But George went on worrying and sending memoranda, anticipating what would happen at the Curragh with his concern for the army and its tender religious conviction and disinclination to police its own people. Would it be 'fair to the sovereign as Head of the Army, to subject the discipline and indeed the loyalty of his troops to such a strain'?[17] Such perception as that reveals reflects the fact that the swarm of elders advising the King included any number with military connections.

Asked to think about the wishes of Irish people at large, George wondered, like any Tory backbencher 'if the demand for Home Rule [was] as earnest and as national today as it was in the days of Parnell'. For himself, he was 'assured by landowners in the south and west of Ireland, that their tenants while ostensibly favourable to Home Rule, are no longer enthusiastic about it and are, comparatively speaking, content and well-to-do.'[18] In a few years' time George V would be called upon to give his assent to the treaty creating an Independent Irish state constitutionally attached to the British Empire by a strand of coloured cotton.

Parallel with hints about dissolution, he had canvassed the idea of an inter-party conference. Asquith thought this only possible given a shared base for discussion – acceptance by the Unionists of the principle of Home Rule. The implication of a conference was of course the exclusion of Ulster, and its flip side: the abandonment by the Unionist Party of the Protestants of the south. Asquith was finally edged into parlay by the enthusiasm of Churchill for a deal and the intervention in a disobliging letter to *The Times* in the autumn of 1913 from Loreburn, lately lord chancellor, the bitterest opponent when the bill was first drafted, of any excluding of Ulster – a letter proposing a conference on excluding Ulster!

It was not a helpful experience. A private conversation between Asquith and Law took place on 4 November at the Home of Law's friend, Aitken, now Lord Beaverbrook, another Canadian Ulsterman. Law rejected in advance any thought of Ulster having its private Home Rule, wanting all legislation to stay with Westminster, and asked for Post Office autonomy to be dropped from the bill, something about which Asquith had no qualms. On the geography of exclusion, Asquith pre-emptively quashed, and Law acquiesed to, all ideas of a nine-county Ulster. Unresolved discussion was of a four-county Ulster, with Tyrone and Fermanagh problematic. Back in 1911 there had been talk of what was called 'County Option', local plebiscites. Birrell, who was in favour, had reckoned, allowing for the moderate Protestant vote which did exist, that local plebiscites might leave only Antrim (including Belfast) and Down outside.

But the reasonable discussion between leaders would tear its trousers on the belief, conceived by Law, that in the area of consensus he had been given a hard promise to be advocated by Asquith to his Cabinet, while Asquith thought in terms of neutral reporting to them. Law, quick on the draw over his honour, would later choose to treat this as a breaking of a word. As the Cabinet held diffuse opinions and had to consult Redmond, satisfaction would always be difficult. Yet Asquith would now listen to the proposals of Lloyd George for the 'temporary exclusion' of the Protestant counties of Ulster for five or six years, something he had raised back in February 1912. It was a postponement of the crunch, and as such, attractive to the men facing it. Asquith, having communicated to the Irish leader his fear of Home Rule opening in bloodshed, undertook to Law 'to discuss plans for its temporary exclusion or separate administrative treatment'.[19] This was to drag Redmond at the wheels of the Cabinet and against Irish feeling, but was not enough for King or opposition leader. A further meeting with the leader of the opposition let Law indicate his side's rejection of mere temporary exclusion. It had to be permanent.

Asquith tried again, this time with Carson. Ulster was offered by the prime minister a different option: an Ulster – her boundaries to be defined later – would be covered by the Home Rule Bill and have its representatives sit in Dublin, but could exclude its geographical area from any Irish bills on anything worth legislating about: tax, religion, education, industry and land tenure. The proposals were made on 23 December and on the 27th Sir Edward dismissed them. Carson was asked on 2 January 1914 to make his own counter proposals, and on the 7th declined to do so. On 15 January, Law, authorised by Asquith, announced that the negotiations had taken place. Unauthorised, he stated conclusively that they had failed.

There are times when Law's conduct stops being dull and obsessive and begins to look fly. In November he had written: 'From a party point of view, I hope the Nationalists will not agree, for, if they do, I am afraid our best card for the Election will have been lost.'[20] Now, aware of the King's susceptibility to the idea of dissolution, he invited George, via his secretary, Stamfordham, to inform his ministers privately, with a public option later, that it was their duty to hold an election before final passage of the bill. The King's limits were reached by this particular piece of brass neck and he declined to oblige.

Whatever criticism might be made of Asquith for his leisurely approach to the whole business, he had by the end of 1913 met the requirements of the King and indeed Loreburn to the extent of indicating to Ulster, by alternative routes, liberation from all and any of her reasonable fears. The final offer – so reminiscent of a European Union opt-out demanded by clamorous British Conservatives – pushed nationalist loyalty further than self-respect would permit. An Ulster leadership which had been anxious only to pre-empt its several bogies of 'Rome Rule' and southern intrusion could have congratulated itself on a splendid deal and closed with Asquith. But the Ulster view was pathological in its contempt and fear of the south. And as indicated by Law's advance rejection of Ulster's own self-government – the option favoured by Redmond of 'Home Rule within Home Rule' – the full imperial connection was a non-negotiable requirement.

But perhaps the Ulster leaders might be excused their arrogance, for they had long been flattered and made heroes by a Tory press to which Asquith, however bending and accommodating, was an object of round and monotonously repeated abuse. The *Saturday Review* is an excellent guide to Tory attitudes. This was the same *Saturday Review*, taken weekly by a solid Conservative public, in which, twenty-five years earlier, George Saintsbury had snarled against that unlikely Marat, John Morley.

The *Saturday* was as keen as Law to play the royal card. 'But how should the Crown assert itself – of its own motion or at the behest of ministers? . . . It is unseemly that the Crown should ever appear to be reposing confidence in Ministers of whom the country does not approve.' Admittedly Queen Victoria had never dissolved Parliament off her own bat, 'but it would be wrong to infer from this negative action of the Crown that its right to take positive action has fallen into complete abeyance or even that such actions are only taken on advice ... We must never forget that that it [the prerogative] is an appenage [*sic*] of the Crown and not of ministerial office.'[21]

As for Ulster generally, the paper gloried in it as an expression and paradigm of pure brute power. In June that year it had been rapturous:

> How Belfast shows up the House of Commons. While the House gibbers having tied its own hands, the people of Belfast are acting without noise and without show. They are preparing for the worst ... Here at any rate are people in earnest! People who not only have strong opinions, but are willing to back them with their lives. No one now talks about the Belfast men bluffing. Right or wrong, these men mean to have their way.'

And it was all 'having a great effect on public opinion here. There is something so very different in their conduct from mere political agitation. The public is so sick of political agitation that it spontaneously sympathises with any people who will fight for what they believe to be their right instead of just talking about it.'[22]

By September the paper was referring comfortably to a 'reign of terror'. When the bill finally passed, 'fighting will have begun or will certainly begin immediately throughout Ireland perhaps even in England or Scotland. The passions of the people have burned to fever heat. Religious animosities such as we have not seen since the reign of James II and the trial of the seven Bishops, will have come into play. The Battle of the Boyne and the Siege of Londonderry may have to be fought all over again.' And why should all this be happening? Because Asquith 'will not even risk the two years loss of the sweets of office in order to save his country from such ills.' *Chutzpah* hardly says it.

But the *Saturday* foresaw national resistance. 'As England and Scotland are mainly Protestant and Scotland is largely Presbyterian, it must always be exceedingly unlikely that the people of England and Scotland will ever consent without such frauds and jockeying to hand over the loyalists of Ulster to the tender mercies of the Molly Maguires.'

At the start of October, four days before Asquith wrote to Law proposing a meeting, it marvelled: 'The wonderful scene of the [military] review in Ulster last Saturday shows what a voluntary army can do in the way of accurate machine-like drill and discipline once the passion of the thing is in it.' After regretting that the Territorial Army, recently created by the Liberal war minister, Haldane, could not be formed on the same passionate basis, the paper went into celestial mode: 'We have in Ulstermen today what Kinglake found in the cavalry of the Crimea – that innate warlike passion, the gift of Heaven, it would seem, to chosen races of men.'[23]

Although Ulster armed and marching against the government of the United Kingdom was a wonderful sight, blame for what might follow naturally belonged with Asquith and his colleagues: up to their eyes in foreign causes, bullying the poor Protestants of Country Antrim and refusing the referendum or election which Tories demanded and giving such provocation. 'These men who have protested so loudly against coercion when the victim is a Bulgarian, intend to coerce their fellow subjects . . . Perhaps when Ulster has been goaded into active resistance then government will at last be driven to test public opinion. They may be doubtful as to the result of a referendum now, but there will be no need of a referendum then.'

'Things,' continued the *Saturday*'s hissing menace, 'will have got beyond mending by constitutional means.'[24] Suitably, it quoted Carlyle, never one for constitutional philacteries, who 'speaks somewhere in his great book on Cromwell's letters and speeches, of a "steadily regimented thing" and of the profound impact which must attach to that. "A steadily regimented thing" exactly expresses what goes forward with the force of a high tide in Ireland today.'

The *Saturday* ran paramilitary exaltation in harness with a wish to make our flesh creep:

> This Ulster business simply is a thing about which it is not in us today to doubt at all. We are absolutely and completely convinced that it is a danger of deadly earnest and that it threatens, unless it is settled, to end shortly in that – in the modern English understanding – almost unthinkable thing, stark mad civil war. Civil war would not mean horrible ruin and chaos in Ireland alone: it would grow such a rank, wretched crop of hates and spites through England, Scotland and Wales and the whole nation that the Empire might easily be shaken and enfeebled for a long time to come.

Oddly, as it talked civil war and demanded surrender to the splendid army which threatened it, for 'who but those with lips of brass' would give orders to fire on it, the *Saturday* found room on another front to denounce the government for caving in. Certain suffragettes who had gone on hunger strike were being released by the home secretary, Reginald McKenna. This was done under the so-called 'Cat and Mouse Act', which allowed the women to be released on licence, resume normal eating at home and to be liable for re-arrest. It was a crass piece of legislation much belaboured by good suffragists then and since, but for the now coercive *Saturday*, 'What is the Cat and Mouse Bill in reality but a caving-in measure? That cat will be found to have caved in to the mouse. It is not a despotic Mr McKenna who has coerced Mrs Pankhurst and the hunger strikers but they who are coercing and controlling a dead-beat Mr McKenna who has caved in to them.'[25] Presumably, if the home secretary had let the women die, that would have shown two of its favourite qualities, 'pluck' and, aptly, 'manliness'.

Something else, a diversion but instructive of the mood – the pre-First World War mood, a civilian enthusiasm for all things warlike, high on force, soldiering and clean-limbed strength – comes in another item, a ripping yarn straight out of *Boys' Own*. In the same issue which saw in Ulstermen 'that innate warlike passion, the gift of Heaven it seems, to chosen races of men', the *Saturday* was busying itself with another hero, a colonial officer, Lieutenant Corfield.

It wrote sublimely that 'some people at least who care for England have not read without emotion the blue-book this weekend on the Camel Corps reverse in Somaliland. It is too clear that Mr Corfield made a mistake in hurling his little force at the massed dervishes. He was warned not to do so by Captain Summers. Corfield, bravest of the brave, died in the thick of the fight. He was of that class of Englishmen who does not fear many men or things.' And the *Saturday* took the shortest possible time – that between issues – to blame the Liberal government. 'It was this government's scuttle from Somaliland which put Corfield into a position where he must either rashly dare or submit his flag to a loss of prestige . . . Had he succeeded at Burao, his exploit would have ranked with Nelson's blind eye at the telescope or Drake's singeing of King Philip.'[26]

This is newspaper patriotism, the sort of thing which Kipling, on one of his better days, had attributed to 'jelly-bellied flag-waggers'. But there were some people who actually behaved the way the *Saturday Review* talked.

29

Changed Utterly

A last attempt would be made to meet George's wishes. In April the King wrote to Asquith begging him to concede most of Carson's terms: six counties of Ulster to come out of the bill with no time limit. The letter was expressed in familiar regicentral terms. 'Surely you could persuade Mr Redmond and his friends to go to this length for the sake of the peace the whole country is longing for . . . You appreciate I know, the terrible position in which I shall be placed if that solution is not found.'[1]

Before this could be responded to, a telegram from Belfast informed the chief secretary that

> about 8pm last night a large body of the Ulster Volunteers Force armed with truncheons, numbering 800 mobilised at Larne under Sir William Adair and Major McCalmont MP. They drew a cordon round the harbour and vicinity and allowed no one to pass except a few on business; police and customs officers particularly excluded; signals from the sea had been observed and large numbers of motor cars arrived. Two steamers, believed 'Mountjoy' and 'Millswater', discharged cargoes of what appear to be arms and ammunition

which were conveyed away by motor cars. Reporting fully today. Telegraph and telephone communication interrupted.'[2]

Major Frederick Crawford, the signer in blood and earlier aspirant kidnapper of Gladstone, had already, back in 1906, responded to the mere election of a Liberal government by advertising 'in French, Belgian, German and Austrian newspapers for 10,000 rifles and two million rounds of ammunition'.[3] The change in Ulster unionism's outlook is illustrated here. In 1906 Crawford was considered a crank and made to resign from the club from which his advertisements had been placed. By 1911 he was leading Carson's escort to the City Hall – chief bowler hat, as it were. He was also on the committee of the Ulster Council, but although rehabilitated, he was still an initiator. The actual impetus to buy arms to menace the British government began with Crawford himself.

The Ulster Volunteer Force, which had been trimly presenting arms with wooden dummies (pitch-pine 1s 8d, spruce 1s 6d),[4] was now to have the real thing. When Crawford had taken fellow members of the Ulster Council aside and shown them samples of the German guns he had already purchased, some of them had resigned, but his initiative was accepted and followed. Had not Charles Craig MP said that while Ulster should try to educate the British electorate, £10,000 spent on rifles would be a thousand times stronger than the same sum spent on meetings and pamphlets.[5]

Crawford showed a good many signs of being on nodding terms with insanity, but then, as he had played with fantastical schemes on and off for more than twenty years, he knew quite enough about the arms market and could do the business. He had handled small consignments already, but his move now was for a coup. As the ardent partisan Henry Maxwell puts it, 'Major Crawford submitted a daring proposal and upon its acceptance by the committee, set out at once for

Hamburg where he saw a certain Hebrew, a dealer in firearms who embodied the exact opposite of those characteristics wherewith the critics of his race are wont to impugn it.'[6] This was Bruno Spiro of Benny Spiro and Co., Adolphsbruck 911, with whom Crawford had already had dealings.

He also called on Carson and left his own account of the meeting.

> I so well remember that scene. We were alone; Sir Edward was sitting opposite to me, his face was stern and grim and there was a glint in his eye; he advanced to where I was sitting and stared down at me and shook his clenched fist in my face and said in a steady determined voice which thrilled me and which I shall never forget, 'Crawford I'll see you through this business if I should have to go to prison for it.'[7]

Crawford had hired a Newcastle collier, the *Fanny*, and put a servant of the Antrim Iron Ore Company in charge of her. The *Fanny* was scheduled to rendezvous with a tug-drawn train of barges loaded with arms at the German military port of Kiel, at an agreed point between Fünen and Langeland in Danish territorial waters. Danish officials smelled a rat and were not encouraged by a cover story about a cargo bound for Iceland, which was currently making Irish-class trouble for Denmark with its own separatist movement.

They confiscated his papers and forwarded them to Copenhagen. Crawford spoke briskly to God. 'I went into my cabin and threw myself on my knees and in simple language told God about it: what this meant to Ulster, that there was nothing sordid in what we desired, that we wanted nothing selfishly. I pointed out all this to God, and thought of the old psalm, "O God our help in ages past".'[8] Cometh the hour, cometh the loon.

To rejoin Maxwell: 'After a night of mental agony picturing the fiasco in which he must now involve Ulster and her leaders, Major Crawford threw a gage to fortune and sailed next morning without papers as a pirate of the seas.' After many hazards involving weeks of patient and persevering work both afloat and ashore while the *Fanny* under different aliases steamed thousands of miles round the coast line of Britain, her cargo was safely transferred one night into the holds of the *Clyde Valley*.

How this was to be effected would almost make a brilliant 'thriller' in itself, were it to be told in full, but be that as it may, the *Clyde Valley*, renamed for the occasion the *Mountjoy II*, came slowly alongside the quay at Larne on the night of April 24th and Major Crawford could congratulate himself upon the successful execution of a feat, the like of which can have fallen to few men to perform and for the success of which his own indomitable purpose was alone responsible.[9]

One aspect of Crawford's indomitable purpose in the course of a tortuous journey was to put a loaded revolver to the head of his captain, Falck, who wanted to dock at Dunkirk to get medical help for Crawford, who was suffering from enteric fever.' Captain Falck,' said the indomitable Ulsterman, 'I know I am alone amongst you and your foreign crew, but I am a match for all of you if you attempt to interfere with my orders. I will shoot you or any of your crew who interferes as dead as a herring.'[10]

The guns would eventually be landed at Larne, where an elaborate operation, cutting telegraph wires and virtually cutting off the port to evade the British authorities, would see the guns brought ashore. It was indeed very much like a thriller and, as commentators have said to the point of monotony, worthy of John Buchan – an uncertain compliment. It may have been a splendid boys' story but it was one with dismaying implications for grown-ups. It also anticipated another indomitable running of arms for a patriotic purpose, that to be undertaken by Sir Roger Casement.

Ulster, for all her self-preoccupation, could not drill and not be seen by other Irishmen who might also drill; it could not bring in arms without those other Irishmen also bringing in arms. The entire Ulster show – rally, marching and gun-running – had been splendid theatre, but for some time now it had won notices outside the province.

John Redmond, representing mainstream, moderate national-ist opinion, the cautious ally of cautious British reformers, had sought an Ireland with limited autonomy under the Crown, a rational objective buttressed by a sensible parliamentary deal. To Tories both objective and coalition were corrupt constitutional outrages; to Ulstermen they were the crimes of Hell sent by the Pope of Rome. And to an important minority of Irish nationalists they had begun to seem like small beer.

Eoin MacNeill was an Ulsterman himself, from the ancient enclave of Catholicism surviving in the glens of Antrim. He was also an academic, an Irish language enthusiast and a Celtic archaeologist, exactly the sort of man to be kept at arm's length from politics, soldiering or the example of Major Crawford (though MacNeill had the sense of humour and lacked the mad glint which Crawford and some of MacNeill's own supporters had been respectively denied and given). But the trim and smartly drilling volunteers had impressed the professor. He had written an article in the newspaper of the Gaelic League, a piece which noted that the British army was not being used to prevent the enrolment and training of troops. The legal cover for the UVF was that it existed 'to hold Ireland for the Empire'. Very well, was the professor's response; in effect, nothing stopped the rest of Ireland – Wicklow, Cork, Kerry and such riffraff – from creating *their* volunteer force, also to hold Ireland for the Empire. It did not matter, MacNeill genially explained, for *what* Ireland was held, what counted was who did the holding! 'Three cheers for Carson,' he said at a meeting in Cork, where those slow to catch his affably Machiavellian drift nearly rioted. The original article was entitled, by way of a historical prophecy 'The North began'.[11]

In October 1913 a manifesto was issued calling for the establishment of a volunteer force; a vast meeting in Dublin in November realised 4,000 recruits and the National Volunteers had been created. Birrell, who knew his Irish history, explained to the Cabinet that this echoed a name going back to the eighteenth century, a term resonating out of the misty time of Rober Emmet, Lord Edward and the Rising. The volunteers might be a random mix. But military instructors with British army experience now began to drill men in the south. They recruited from the green youth movement established in 1909 by Countess Markievicz (Constance Gore-Booth, a green daughter of the Ascendancy) in opposition to the Baden-Powell imperial lot. There were also now Irish Republican Brotherhood elements who had been drilling, secretly and illegally, without the approval of two magistrates. They would now drill openly and as legally as mattered 'to hold Ireland for the Empire'.

A shift was taking place. All the energies of southern Catholic Ireland had been directed through constitutional channels. Much of its talent, supplemented by idealistic products of the southern Ascendancy, had gone into a cultural nationalism, language, art and theatre, which in good old Marxist terms was raising the consciousness of Ireland – middle class first. Meanwhile, Protestant Ulster and the Tory Party had responded to constitutional legislation with shouts of 'Traitor!', 'Revolution!' and – rather more in Belfast than in London – 'Kill the Pope.' The Ulstermen who had made those several statements preferring Kaiser Wilhelm to John Redmond with devolved powers had been marching and arming men with prominent members of the British shadow Cabinet applauding. As the grant of Canadian provincial devolution now in committee dragged its slow length through an eternity of allotted days, the notion of doing something *un*constitutional for Ireland looked increasingly attractive to culturally aroused bourgeois and old Fenian alike.

Patrick Pearse wrote plays and poems and had been conducting a couple of progressive schools, running up losses and teaching Irish culture. He was on the Dublin Castle intelligence list, but the idea of this physical force William Morris sparking a revolution was – quite reasonably – thought ridiculous.*

The same intelligence had long and correctly dismissed the IRB as a bunch of no-account reminiscent drinkers. But since 1911 the IRB had been in the sober hands of young zealots determined to create a fighting force. And if Carson's people could get foreign arms, so could his admirers in the south. With the example of the Ulster soldiery before it, the 'brotherhood' was on the way to turning into an 'army'. Along with a future civil servant of the Republic, Bulmer Hobson, a Quaker who would quaintly look after the procurement of guns, were Tom Clarke, an old-school Fenian, and the scarily fanatical Sean MacDermott, both of whom would die in 1916 before the British firing squads which would create the sovereign Irish state.

Carson's rhetoric on armed force inclined to a certain furtive mystique. 'You are our great army. It is on you we rely. Under what circumstances you will have come into action you must leave with us ... You must trust that we will select the most opportune methods, if necessary taking over the whole government of this community in which we live.'[12] But armed, trained, psychologically prepared for both war and secession, Protestant Ulster had broken the rules of parliamentary politics. To adopt the words of a Tory idol,

---

* More reasonable than the derision of the Austrian foreign minister, Count Berchtold, at the thought of Herr Bronstein, habitué of the Café Central in Vienna, being any sort of threat. Trotsky was hotter subversive stuff than Pearse any time.

Pitt, the bringer of Union, they were saving Ireland by their example. Though it would soon be a terrible salvation. If arms could come ashore at Larne, they could come ashore at Howth. If General Sir George Richardson could inspect Ulster forces, Colonel Maurice Moore, commander of the Connaught Rangers (rtd.) could inspect nationalist troops. Here were 4,000 troops recruited in an evening for him to look over.

Meanwhile, Carson's bark about 'taking over the whole government of this community where we live' had far more appeal to a man like Patrick Pearse than anything John Redmond could ever say or do. Carson was, in MacNeill's words, 'a realist who had shown the Irish people the way to assert their manhood and their right to arm themselves in defence of their liberties'.[13] Or as Birrell put it, 'The Irish have a great facility for hating and admiring each other at the same time. The recent gun-running exploit of the Ulster Volunteers excited as much admiration amongst the lodges of the AOH [Ancient Order of Hiberinians] as in those of the Orange faction. "Well done Ireland" was the general verdict.'[14]

In the interim, official nationalism – Redmond and the parliamentary party – managed to get control of the volunteers, subsuming them officially for their own purpose of never having to use them. And ironically, although the volunteers had the appearance of a force to fight Ulster for a united Ireland, the mentality of people like Pearse could not see Ulster as an enemy. The compliment of imitation was paid, the blinding hatred never returned. Pearse and his friends were given over to Anglophobia. Boringly, 'England' was proposing greater self-government for Irishmen and Ulster leaders were denouncing the act as treason, betrayal, death and damnation. He sailed on in his own cloud of unknowing. The British could not constitutionally have good intentions. They were to be damned for seeking alternative methods of control while he blessed

Ulster for her heroic stand against the English who were the enemy.

Men made obtuse by preoccupation, as Pearse was, tend to think in perfect circles. In an article he wrote without irony: 'You are creating a Provisional Government of Ulster – make it a Provisional Government of Ireland and we will recognize it and obey it.'

'England,' said Pearse, had 'governed Ireland through the Orange Lodges, she now proposes to govern Ireland through the AOH. You object, so do we. Why not unite and get rid of the English? They are the real difficulty: their presence here the real incongruity.'[15] Any liberal Englishman reading Pearse must have felt like the equally well-meaning but beaten-down academic in the mid-1960s raved at with charges of 'repressive tolerance'.

Imperception takes many forms. Gladstone knew about Ulster in the era of her disputes with Westminster government in the late eighteenth century. Exposure to Ulster's kaffir notion of the rest of Ireland by the editor of the *Northern Whig* had not really cured him of optimism. For Redmond, the assumption was that Ulster wasn't serious and would fit in with a share of Canadian provincial devolution precisely because it was so modest a thing. Pearse, and the much saner MacNeill with him, thought that the Ulstermen were rebels first and that all rebels shared an enemy.

The undistributed middle of this thinking was Ulster's feeling for Catholic Ireland: 'At the bottom the moving passion is hatred and contempt for the papist as a papist: at the top it is contempt and fear of the papist as a man of business.' Birrell, who had said that, had gone on to assess the possibility of a war. 'I don't think it is possible to exaggerate the strength of these top and bottom emotions, and if the Protestants don't fight, it will simply be because they can't; and I don't see how they can, in any tented-field sense of the word, but short of "the pomp and circumstance of glorious war" they will do whatever hatred can.'[16]

Among the possible actions which the Ulster volunteers might take once Home Rule became law, so Birrell was told, was the appropriation of police control of the streets and seizure of the Customs House and the Post Office in Belfast! The other fear which the chief secretary reported was what he called 'the wildfire scenario'. 'The common talk of the heads of the Ulster police is that at any moment some trifling incident of everyday Irish life where whisky is an ingredient may begin troubles which would spread "like wildfire" from county to county.'[17]

It would take more than a trifling incident, but the incendiary potential is all caught there, and in Pearse and his group, epigones calling up armed men, a mechanism existed. It was still remote from being a credible force; it would take a mountain of British military stupidity in the fraught circumstances of world war – bombardment, reprisals, executions, more crowds fired on – to provide the explosive for Pearse's detonator. But already he signified something. The terrible charm of war was descending on Ireland's particular disputes as it came down generally upon Europe. Rupert Brooke would soon write: 'Now God be praised who has matched us with this hour.' Crawford and Pearse thought much the same thing.

A race was being run in parallel and its stage points should perhaps be marked. On the constitutional/parliamentary front, the Home Rule Bill passed the Commons on its first post-Parliament Act circuit on 16 January 1913; it was rejected in the Lords on 30 January, passed the Commons again on 7 July and was rejected by the Lords on 15 July. It passed the Commons a third time on 25 May 1914. A government amending bill temporarily excluding part of Ulster was passed by the Commons on 23 June. On 8 July the Lords altered this to define and indefinitely exclude a nine-county Ulster, something shelved by the government. A conference between interested parties was held at Buckingham Palace, where it failed to reach agreement, between 21 and 24 July.

Meanwhile, in respect of accumulating force, the Ulster Volunteers had been officially formed in January 1913 and, the Irish Volunteers in November of the same year. Crawford ran his guns to Larne in April 1914, guns came ashore at Howth near Dublin on 26 July. There is a last sentence to add to that dual catalogue. On 4 August the United Kingdom and Germany went to war.

The government had been in a dreadful bind through the early months of 1914. They had pulled back from the coercion of Ulster partly because Asquith was a parliamentarian playing a parliamentary hand which he knew he could win in Parliament, partly because martyrdom was something the Ulster leaders yearned for and would milk by the dairyful. And at an unacknowledged level, they flinched from those who shared the assumptions of the Sligo lord lieutenant that you don't repress people who are flying the Union Jack.

Ulster had assumed the Carlylean-Prussian qualities of 'a steadily regimented thing' as admired by the *Saturday Review*. Some other Irishmen were minded to be their own steadily regimented thing. And with timing as deadly as Crawford's they would move while grave civilian deliberations were taking place. The bill itself was introduced into the Lords on 23 June. Asquith had previously seen Carson and Law and had offered an amending bill granting undefined temporary exclusions. The Lords instantly made that nine-county Ulster exclusion without local option voting or time limit. The government was willing in principle, dragging John Redmond after it, to exclude certain counties for a period of time, perhaps with local plebiscites. The notion of four counties and that wiggly line through Fermanagh and Tyrone began to look like a serious proposition. Asquith's leisurely parliamentary approach appeared to be working. The time now seemed right for the conference the King longed for. Asquith, Lloyd George, Redmond and John Dillon would meet Bonar Law, Lansdowne, Carson and James Craig at Buckingham Palace under the chairmanship of the Speaker, Lowther. The conference literally ended in tears – Carson's, according to Redmond – after they had come to grief over the topograpical detail which Churchill would immortalise as 'the dismal steeples of Fermanagh', or in Asquith's words, at 'an impasse with unspeakable consequences which to English eyes seems inconceivably small and to Irish eyes immeasurably big'.[18] The partition of those two nicely balanced but spottily distributed counties stymied all best efforts and the conference broke up.

That was the jaw-jaw of negotiation, and it concluded on 26 July. On the same day something happened which made a bleak mockery of negotiations chaired by the Speaker of the Commons and gave melancholy plausibility to Pearse's Anglophobia. Arms came ashore at Howth, north of Dublin. They had been bought in Hamburg – which gratefully armed both sides – by Darrell Figgis and Erskine Childers. No secret was made of the importation. Volunteers marched back to Dublin 'through a low quarter of the City'[19] and the assistant commissioner of police, Harrell, did what decisive people had urged upon the government in the north. He used police and soldiers to stop the march and take the guns.

The volunteers dispersed but kept their new guns, and one military detachment on its way back – Scottish Borderers under a Major Haigh – was pelted and blocked on Bachelor's Walk, Dublin, north of the Liffey. There then happened what keeps happening in Ireland, India and other places where authority is not always appreciated. In the tradition of Mitchelstown, which is also the tradition of Bloody Sunday, troops opened fire. Three people were killed and thirty-nine wounded, probably, on the evidence, as a result of half-orders half-understood rather than deliberate fire. Henry Maxwell reports in his masterful way, treading metaphor underfoot, 'But in the ensuing days, short as they were before the Ship of State – around whose helm the mutineers and the officers stood so tense and preoccupied – was drawn within the maelstrom, there occurred yet another incident which the disaffections of Irish blood were to mortify into a fresh gangrene of the body politic.'[20] The incident, he adds, in contrast to his account of the indomitable Crawford, 'was the outcome of Casement's and MacNeill's treachery'.[21]

Birrell, whose whole policy had been directed at avoiding all tails of all dragons, instituted a commission and in due course sacked Harrell. H. Alison Philips, a dedicated unionist commentator, observed: 'The effect on the moral [sic] of the police was disastrous, for henceforward it was felt that no action could be taken by them even in grave emergencies, without risk of being "broken" by the government.'[22] If the thought occurred that the Larne and Howth importations were much of a dangerous muchness, Phillips had answers. 'The Larne volunteers . . . had been able to justify their action in some sort by the judicial decision which had declared the Arms proclamation illegal. But this decision had been reversed by the Dublin Court of King's Bench on 15 June and the act of the Irish Volunteers was therefore one of ostentatious defiance of the law; for the Proclamation remained until its withdrawal on 5 August.'[23]

All that mattered about Bachelor's Walk was that it fulfilled the Pearse–Sinn Féin emotional requirements that England should be to blame. The south had imitated the north, which had got away scot-free – and the south had forty-two casualties from British soldiers firing on a crowd.

Another commentator, one inclined to understatement, was H.H. Asquith. 'The malignity of fortune could hardly have devised a more inopportune coup and how the devil the soldiers came to be mixed up in it at all, still more to fire their volleys, at this moment passes my comprehension . . . But of course it has left enormous exasperation behind in the mind of the Dublin populace.'[24] As much might have been said about the Londonderry shootings more than fifty years later.

In the recent wonderful production by the Royal Shakespeare Company of *Love's Labour's Lost*, skilfully and credibly set in Edwardian Oxford, the lines

> Come Sir, it wants a twelve month stir
> And then 'twill end

uttered in the context of summer 1914, are followed by a frozen tableau, the darkening of the sky-drop and the distant thumping of artillery. So it was with Ireland. The bill formally became law and the amending bill promised to follow. Ireland was to have Home Rule with a six-year, six-county opt-out, but none of this would operate for the moment. The assassination of Archduke Franz Ferdinand brought the hour with which that generation was to be matched (and buried in neat rows), and God was to be praised.

The sequence of what happened in Ireland can be recounted fairly quickly. John Redmond, by instinct, for all the moronising of the Tory press, an Irishman for the Kingdom, gave unequivocal support for the war and rapidly found himself a hero to Conservatives. In fact he had done his moderate cause no immediate harm. He supported recruitment, and Irishmen in the early term of the war went in great numbers to join. His idea was that volunteers north and south, from standing poised against each other, would unite and find comradeship in the struggle against the Kaiser – a touching aspiration; not absurd, but harder than it looked.

In much the same spirit, Conservatives were invited into the Cabinet, Carson, as senior law officer, hilariously among them.* Redmond was three times pressed to join too, but whatever his other mistakes, he declined to participate in what would become a Conservative government headed by Lloyd George. But 'he hears from John Dillon three times a day . . . urging him to make an anti-Conscription harangue in the

---

* 'Asquith,' said Birrell, who loathed the coalition, 'was as untrusting as a young woman making up her mind whether she will have rubies or diamonds in her engagement ring.'

House'.[25] The Irish pressures were stronger and mounting, and they would break him.

The situation would have been comic if it hadn't been so many other worse things. There was an army of Irishmen. It had been formed in hostile parallel with the Ulster troop as gesture, menace and potential in a civil dispute. Government in Westminster – which now included the men who had fought savagely against Home Rule and had invented (and trained and armed) volunteers – demanded that southern Catholic recruits fight at Mons and the Marne for that government and for a United Kingdom which in peacetime Tory rhetoric was usually 'England'.

There were takers, but never enough for that cannibal war, and the authorities, nagged by the egregious Kitchener, contemplated introducing conscription. Redmond would not touch that. But he made a speech at Woodenbridge, County Wicklow pledging Irish troops for service beyond the immediate defence of Ireland, in France and Belgium. If the union had meant more than it did, an undertaking to fight in the general defence of Britain in France would have been a commonplace. Irishmen were in the trenches anyway. But the speech proved more potent than the practice. The argument that this was a British war undertaken far off for British ends was powerful. Ireland was, as her Tory critics observed, notoriously disloyal. The scroll decorating Galway Town Hall inscribed 'God save Ireland from the Huns'[26] was not calculated to create loyalty, and Redmond, appearing under it for an earlier rally, lacked force.

His decline as a focus of authority and that of his party with him is often dated from the Woodenbridge speech. The temper of Ireland was more nationalist than that of the leader of the Nationalist Party. Even so, 200,000 Irishmen would join up during the war, compared with the estimated 14,000 Irish Volunteers, the group which after Woodenbridge had split from the National Volunteers. The British, especially the military, were angry at the rate of recruitment which declined as the war went on. In this they echoed other national leaderships in that war. Dr Bautze, chairman of the military medical board in Hasek's *The Good Soldier Schweik*, put well enough a real-life Austrian military view of the Czechs. '*Das ganze Tschechische Volk ist eine simulantenbande!*' – 'The whole Czech nation is a pack of malingerers.'[27] (A Czech legion actively fighting *against* Austria would give that people enough credit with the winning side for them to become Czechoslovakia at Versailles – simple treason in Austrian terms, and prospering.)

Increasingly, as the awful war continued, the Irish, bidden by scrolls about saving Ireland from the Hun to go to the recruiting station, abstained. By 1917, Irish recruitment represented just under 5 per cent of the male population, against 17 per cent in England, Scotland and Wales.[28]

War is the opportunity of revolutionaries, and in the case of Pearse, dreamers of nightmares. At the funeral in 1915 of O'Donovan Rossa, himself no small bagpipe, Pearse put down a marker. The ceremonies of this drunken dynamiter, author of *Prison Life*, who over fifty years had quarrelled with anyone who was anyone in Irish revolutionary politics and had been old hat before Parnell's time, were deployed by the poetical schoolmaster to make that call for blood. 'Life springs from death, and from the graves of patriotic men and women spring living nations.' It was absurd, but like many absurdities, potent.

Pearse had said a lot of things in the couple of years since he joined the IRB in 1913, among them that 'it would be better that Dublin should be laid in ruins than that the existing conditions of contentment and confident security within the British Empire should continue'.[29] There was also a lot of bad Christianity knocking about – Christ-sacrifices to be made and so on. There was a distinct tendency, wonderfully facilitated by executions and imprisonments after the Rising, to cry too often, not wolf, but Christ. Pearse's view on death chimed entirely with the signature-in-blood mentality.

In fairness to Pearse, not something easily achieved, this sort of nonsense was cleaner in the mouth than the style of some of those directing operations in the First World War, such as Field-Marshal Robertson, who said that we were a country standing at the gaming tables and that with our deeper pockets we could wager more lives. And Pearse's flammable fantasy only echoed other men's rhetoric. After all, Carson and Law had *talked* civil war for three solid years. And what had the *Saturday Review* written in this same year, 1913, of the Protestants of Belfast?

> Here at any rate are people in earnest, people who not only have strong opinions, but are willing to back them with their lives. No one now talks about the Belfast men as bluffing. Right or wrong, they mean to have their way. One feels it instinctively . . . The public is so sick of political agitation that it spontaneously sympathises with any people who will fight for what they believe to be their right instead of only talking about it.

But that wasn't all the *Saturday* had said. The article continues: 'What if we asked the Nationalists to do the same? What if they burn their boats and refuse to acknowledge the Imperial writ if Home Rule is not carried? They will do nothing of the sort.'[30]

That challenge and a score like it express a steady contemptuous belief that the 'manly', 'plucky' soldiering and bullying part of life belonged with the superior and occupying race. They were now being answered in their own heroic, bone-headed language. Such talk was a sort of poking through railings asking to be bitten. And as the war passed, enough of the mood changed among enough Irishmen for biting to be an option. The actual numbers available were modest. The Irish Volunteers, the harder faction, which split away, was a small splinter of the National Volunteers. The IRB was perhaps 2,000 strong by 1916. But a sense of trouble was there too.

In late 1915 Birrell wrote:

During the last few *weeks* I have been reading nothing
but uncomfortable figures about the Irish volunteers
who are steadily, month by month *increasing* ... The
newspapers are poor enough both in circulation and
ability but reading them as I have to do, I think I
notice an increasing *exaltation of spirit* and growth of
confidence in some of the better written articles which
indicates more *belief* in the possibilities of the future
than was the case 6 months ago ... and having regard
to the uncertainty of our military operations, gloomy
possibilities in the East and elsewhere, parliamentary
upsets and so on, I feel the *Irish* Situation one of actual
menace.[31]

Birrell would be caught out (and handily damned) on the
specific rising, reserving a move against Sinn Féin by a
fatal twenty-four hours. But on the general direction he
sensed what was coming.

Exaltation of spirit was the whole function of Patrick Pearse.
Armed rising, with or without active German involvement,
was talked in IRB circles. It was rejected by MacNeill but
embraced by a military subcommittee which, rather like the
generals shovelling men into trenches and graves, became a
law unto itself. Yeats's endlessly quoted poem was only half
right. The people he had met at close of day were, James
Connolly excepted, a crankish lot endowed with suicidal
courage and a talent for nursing hatreds; intolerant, fussy,
imperious puritans – perfect blood sacrifice material. But
Yeats says 'All is changed, changed utterly,'* and that, when
the suppression of the rising was concluded, was pretty much
the literal truth.

* Yeats's often fatuous muse, Maud Gonne, wrote to him to say, 'I do
not like your poem. It is unworthy of you and unworthy of the event.'

The rising itself – seizure of not only the General Post Office in what was then Sackville Street, but Stephen's Green, Boland's Mill in Sandymount, the *Evening Mail* offices and, with pleasant incongruity, the Jacobs Biscuit Factory – was serious but not desperate. It took Sir John Grenfell Maxwell and an artillery bombardment to achieve that.

The events of 22 to 29 April are a succinct narrative: the capture near Tralee of Sir Roger Casement carrying arms by way of a German submarine; the precipitation into a coup by Pearse and (probably) the yet madder MacDermott of MacNeill's plan for a march; the taking of those strong points at a time when garrisoning was at an exceptionally low point (many of the officers had gone off to the races); the bringing in of General Maxwell; the siege of the rebels; the catching of Sherwood Foresters in a killing fusillade from the canal bridge at Lower Mount Street; and finally, a British use of artillery which razed much of central Dublin. Of the rebels, 450 were killed and 2,614 wounded, while among official forces, 116 soldiers and 16 policemen were dead.

The rising had not been popular. Rebels led away were hooted at and spat on. But blood sacrifice it was all to be. Martial law included a measure of martial lawlessness, like the random killings of householders in North King Street. Among the dead was Francis Sheehy-Skeffington, a non-violent and very popular figure who, while trying to prevent looting, was murdered by a deranged officer, Bowen-Colthurst. Exaltation of spirit would come with executions conducted according to proper procedures under emergency regulations and thus spaced out across a fortnight. It was reasonable justice to shoot after trial people who had started an armed rebellion during a war, but it was unimaginably stupid politics. Professor Philips was shocked at the shock. 'That the sentences, according to the codes of all civilised countries, were just made no difference. Public opinion swung suddenly round.'[32]

But the formal killing of men by firing squad over a

fortnight, with every other new day a gobbet of authorised death to be announced and read in newspapers, was a brisk formula for making heroes of the men shot and new enemies for the men shooting. The wounded Connolly being taken out on a stretcher to execution was an image to linger in a country notoriously susceptible to images. Pearse's talk of bloodshed being a sanctifying thing did not mock him when his own came to be shed. It validated everything he had said and turned rant into prophecy. The young man out of Turgenev had been transformed into an icon. The degradation of Roger Casement in being hanged as a traitor after prosecution by Galloper Smith, now a law officer, and in the passing round of the 'black diaries' demonstrating his homosexuality, a piece of business more than ordinarily sordid, placed another martyr in a separate niche a little way off.*

John Dillon, Redmond's lieutenant, always less tractable and accommodating than Redmond, made a speech in the Commons during the May days of executions. 'The horrible irony' was that by giving soldiers a free hand 'you are making yourselves the instrument of your own worst enemies to defeat your own policy.' Effectively, in that speech, Dillon also endorsed the rebellion.

But the government was now full of Tories, supporters of the Ulster *défie*, Law, Long, Smith and – touted for strong man and premier by a yellow press daily yellower – Carson himself. They too were in a state of exaltation. The soft, sane, tolerant line towards Ireland embodied by Birrell would be replaced by, as it were, the smack of firm government. H.C. Duke, a Conservative nonentity, became chief secretary, but for a while, General Maxwell, exercising powers under DORA and the Crimes Act of 1887, handled things alone.

---

* The question of Casement's sanity was mooted, as was that of Bowen-Colthurst, the officer who had murdered Sheehy-Skeffington. Casement was hanged; Bowen-Colthurst was found guilty but insane and soon released, living to become a bank manager.

Maxwell was not an exceptionally stupid or brutal general, but enough stupid and brutal things were done and exceptional qualities were not now needed to alienate Ireland. There were ninety death sentences originally, but after Asquith's intervention on 12 May – symbolically, characteristically, on the right side too late – they stopped at fifteen. But it is not in the way of seventy-five reprieves to be remembered or to decide history. Probably Ireland was conclusively lost by then. But the conduct of Duke helped things along. 'Honest and intelligent men can always agree on some solution,' he announced blithely, excluding Sinn Féin from consideration. One Irish historian has characterised Duke's policy as 'pin-pricking coercion'; another speaks of his 'almost inconceivable obtuseness'.[33] Duke's skills at conciliation were aided by the intervention of the Tories at Westminster seeking to extend conscription to Ireland.

Ironically, the first victims of that sudden swing of opinion which surprised Professor Philips would be the National Party. Redmond was dead prematurely in 1918 and already seen as tainted with Britishry. Moderate men no longer looked big. Fringe Anglophobia, promoted by Pearse and Sinn Féin before the war, was, after the artillery bombardment and executions, mainstream opinion. The Church, never on good terms with the parliamentarians, began to exert power. Part of the Church attitude was narrow and atavistic. Most of the rebels, Connolly and Tom Clarke apart, were earnest Catholics deferential to priests. The rebel spirit of exaltation, now strewn with martyrs and shrines, was highly sympathetic – enough bishops came out very early for the rebels. And anyway, and conclusively, Ireland for a long time to come would be quite naturally a clerically minded country of small landholders.

Another Duke first, the death through force-feeding of the hunger-striking rebel commander Thomas Ashe, was followed by a full-dress Fenian-style funeral with a Catholic bishop taking part. A different bishop, Fogarty of Killaloe,

wrote to the press: 'It is horrible that the country has to stand
silently by listening to the moans of the decent young Irish
boys who are being slowly done to death behind the walls
of Mountjoy Prison by the brutal tyrants.'[34] That overused
expression 'national unity', dear to Conservatives, exactly
described the situation.

Henry Maxwell describes things in his own way: 'Ashe
however had a weak heart and as a result no doubt of these
measures, the poor wretch died some hours after the food had
been administered . . . Tremendous capital was made out of
the affair, and the wickedness of the Government was upon
every tongue . . . The Bishop's words were well attuned to
the note of rising hysteria which was in a short while to
plunge the whole of Ireland into that frenzied madness of
destruction.'[35]

If this were not enough, an attempt was made in 1918 to
arrest the leadership of Sinn Féin for alleged involvement with
Germany. What happened was what was bound to happen.
One set of leaders, de Valera and Arthur Griffith, gained great
prestige by being locked up by the British, while new men
like Michael Collins got on with the job of quartermastering
a revolutionary war. The National Party, with the Church
against them, John Redmond no more and the mood of
the country turned away by the unfortunate deaths of poor
wretches and the hysteria of bishops from all accommodation with the British, would be forewarned by a series of
by-election defeats, and in the election of 1918 be reduced to
six seats, with Sinn Féin winning seventy-three. Which seats
they declined to take up, establishing Dáil Eireann, their
own parliament, while they set about creating a network
of local courts.

Ironically, with the demise of the party of Home Rule
and Sinn Féin proclaiming a state and in the field waging
guerrilla war, Conservatives became convinced of the need for
Home Rule. Any number of options, dominion status and
federalism among them, rattled around like dice in a box,

but Walter Long, of all people – a right-wing Conservative with Ascendancy credentials and former Unionist member for Dublin County – declared that Home Rule, object of so many million words of Conservative obloquy, must be maintained and that the extremists who had replaced a party willing to work it must be destroyed.[36] Moderation was to be enforced.

Per contra, Lloyd George, Home Ruler, early advocate of an Ulster opt-out, most flexible of politicians, would fall necessarily into the rhetoric of the Conservatives who in December 1916 had made him prime minister. 'We have murder by the throat,' he said at one juncture, while Smith, now Lord Birkenhead, would acknowledge that 'a small war' was going on in Ireland. In his days as Smith, Birkenhead had been free, like other oppositionists, with talk of 'civil war'. This war, in which a high proportion of Irishmen supported irregular forces against the United Kingdom government, was not what they had had in mind.

It was a brutal little war on both sides. The policy of picking off men in uniforms undertaken by the IRA, as it had become, and 'Red Sunday', the Dublin massacre with axes of seventeen military cadets, were less than Christ-like. Between January 1920 and July 1921 (the date of the truce), 160 soldiers and 400 policemen were killed. The intimidation and enforcement of the Land League, which had been evidence in Unionist speeches and newspapers against Home Rule for forty years, had finally come back after a long era of law and reform. And it had come back in spades, though it was not much advocated as 'a cleansing and a sanctifying thing'.

Meanwhile Ulster did a little killing of her own. No one can describe it as well as Henry Maxwell.

That counter-terror followed upon outrages in the North is of course not to be disputed. A strong minority fighting for its very existence is likely to adopt rough and ready measures of self-preservation. Nor is it likely in the heat of provocation to exercise that degree of discrimination which will enable it to differentiate between passive foes and active enemies. There can be no question but that entirely inoffensive Roman Catholics were sacrificed upon the altar of republican cowardice.'[37]

Another report is more specific. '10,000 Catholics were expelled from their employment, Protestant mobs wrecked and looted the property of Catholics, 40 Catholics were killed between July and November 1920.'[38]

This was to be a war of targeted killings and often random reprisals. Field Marshal Wilson favoured 'shooting by roster'[39] – something akin to to Mr Alan Clark's more recent proposal for going in there, shooting perhaps 600 people and having no more trouble. In practice, with police resignations reaching understandably high figures, their supplements – the Auxiliaries and, more famously, the Black and Tans (the idea of General French, now Viceroy), recently demobilised men looking for adventure – were more promiscuous in killing. The Black and Tans have been compared with the German *Freikorps* flourishing at the same time. And in the Irish conflict, they won an evil reputation, not least in the inadvertent mouths of would-be defenders.

Winston Churchill, writing, as he supposed, sympathetically, said, 'They acted with much the same freedom as the Chicago or New York police permit themselves in dealing with armed gangs. When any of their own men, or police or military comrades were murdered, they "beat up" the haunts of well known malignants or' – he added thoughtfully – 'those who they considered to be malignants, and sharply questioned suspected persons at the pistol's point.'[40]

The war had its affinities with Vietnam. Despite the 1918 election, Sinn Féin, like the Viet Cong, were less than universally supported across the country, collecting in January 1920 only 572 local government seats to other parties' combined 872, but they controlled much of the country much of the

479

time. Above all, their enemy, enraged and uncomprehending, gathered membership for them by random acts of stupid reprisal. The two-sided murderousness of it all, later given definition by Sean O'Casey in *Juno and the Paycock* – 'Take away our hearts of stone . . . an' give us hearts of flesh!' – climaxed on 21 November 1920. The IRA shot eleven unarmed British officers in the morning; in the afternoon British troops fired into a football crowd, killing twelve.

The IRA, like the Viet Cong, won the propaganda war. They had the American interest and the growing sickness at it all of parts of the British press. Defence of action proved counterproductive. Speaking of the Black and Tans and Auxiliaries, Lord Curzon, like any State Department spokesman in the late 1960s, would say, 'These men . . . are fighting the battle not merely for their own lives, not merely for Ireland, not merely for the British Government or the British Empire, they are fighting the battle of civilisation.'[41]

It became, like Vietnam, a war it was imperative to get out of. It could, of course, be fought physically, but not with the current resources. During the world war Kitchener had sought to poach policemen for the front. In 1921 it was suggested that 250,000 soldiers should be sent to Ireland! Long's version of Home Rule had become law in 1920, but as its machinery was boycotted, the country could now be governed only by martial law.

The objective of an Ireland closely associated with Britain, enjoying a set of granted freedoms – Canadian provincial devolution, or a little better – was dead. It could have been had peacefully if the opposition had shown understanding on any of three occasions in the thirty-five years since Gladstone's mad, senile impulse. It couldn't be had now.

Envoi

With the Irish treaty died a tradition of masculine politics in which words like 'pluck' and 'manliness' were common currency. The Conservative opposition had become a component in a coalition government fighting one of the great wars of all history. 'All is changed utterly' may have become a glib and rhetorical phrase, but changed it was. Yet the Great War, as it was properly called, was, surprisingly, not the chief reason. The last worst follies of the British in Ireland – the rule of Secretary Duke, the conduct of the Black and Tans – came *after* that war.

The men and the instincts adoring the peerage, killing the budget, inciting Ulstermen to armed resistance and talking civil war, would slip from the public stage. Selborne, Willoughby de Broke and Salisbury were marginalised, though Leopold Amery would carry the banner of that sort of politics in the 1920s and people like Henry Page Croft made backbench patriotic noises. But Stanley Baldwin, with his instinct for conciliation, his patriotism muted to an affectionate contemplation of the Worcestershire horizon and his perfect lack of rage, was prime minister and embodied the era. It was not so much that the game was up as that it had left everyone exhausted.

Across the nearly two decades of Conservative government that followed, there would be no question of reviving the powers of the Lords. As for the twenty-six counties of Ireland, Salisbury would write to Selborne: 'Have things really been allowed to get to such a point that we must accept whatever terms de Valera chooses to impose? (He may be induced by Smuts to limit his demands).[1] Salisbury had also talked to Carson about reconquest of Ireland, 'and it appears that it would require 15 divisions'.[2] Selborne, diehard of diehards, contented himself in his reply with his own interpretation of the historical significance of 1914–18. 'England is so immensely great at this moment that I doubt whether the dominions or foreign countries think that England is humiliated by it.'[3] 'England' might not be humiliated, as this headless victor put it, but any thinking Conservative must have known that the Tories were. Tory policy had been directed from Gladstone's first words in 1886 to saving the union. They might have developed that policy to saving a looser but still functioning union working with Irish partners. (Plaintively, after the Easter Rising and enlightened by force, some of them would try.) But instead England had narrowed her focus to Ulster, the frantic, flippant preoccupation of Randolph Churchill, and that province had done very well. James Craig and Brooke, his successor, would establish a Protestant parliament for a Protestant people for the best part of fifty years before the events and deaths which have dominated the last thirty. Ulster now had her own corner of mastery. She had played the Tory card and it had proved to be an ace.

If the Conservative Party had shown wisdom and discretion, Ulster might have been a grumbling part of a loosely linked Irish autonomy, or enough of her might have been attached to Westminster by local option, or any of the deals rolled by Asquith might have been concluded. Instead there was to be violence, and Ulster had created the conditions for violence. At the outset she had talked it. In conjunction with Law's Tory Party, she had orchestrated and recruited resistance to modest, contemptible, civilised measures. Now, as before, nothing could be done until Ulster was settled, so with the usual complaining ill grace, Ulster accepted a parliament of her own. It was of the size required: six counties, 66 per cent Protestant, compact enough, secure (given gerrymandering – 77 per cent of the seats), but with enough Catholics to misgovern. The treaty which Lloyd George, with the latest chief secretary, Hamar Grenwood, in tow, would negotiate agreed to a twenty-six-county Ireland, dominion status in name, independence in practice. A split and further conflict would be engineered by de Valera, obsessed, like Enoch Powell, with the forms and titles of sovereignty – the sacred name of 'Republic'. Kevin O'Higgins, minister of justice and defence, would put down that vicious little war with seventy-seven executions. But de Valera, who had said that he cared nothing for politics, would live to misgovern Ireland on and off for decades by way of protectionism, clericalism and stale exaltation.

Irish independence was an inevitable, right, desirable thing; modern Ireland a highly sympathetic and now very successful country. Given early and effective achievement of Home Rule without Ulster (or without a carefully drawn sub-Ulster, a 'Prodestan'), a sovereign independent Ireland, might still have occurred, but later, through amicable separation.

Furious and irrational resistance to an Ireland given even a form of autonomy would create two small savage wars, one of which may have concluded in 1998. From Salisbury to Law and Carson, reaction brought enmity and death, and they had heirs.

A revisionist (and Conservative) theory puts inordinate stress on every element of party calculation which may have influenced Gladstone, and which certainly weighed with Asquith. It also approves Balfour's modest claim to have done it all by his land reforms – to have achieved the

Irish government of Ireland which he bitterly opposed by way of equipping a landholding economy.

Balfour's reforms, begun by Gladstone and concluded by Birrell, were in his case undertaken in consequence of the agitation to which Home Rule had also been the response. They were adapted as an alternative to Home Rule and through the folly of his own party and successor they became instead the provisioning of a sovereign Irish state. As for coalitions and deals by which a party sympathetic to an idea accelerates legislation to win the general support of another party, that atrocious thing has been encountered in politics.

Home Rule was, in fact, the only policy of wisdom. Back in 1886 this was perhaps wisdom of a visionary nature; by Asquith's time it was common sense. But the Conservatives, proclaiming themselves the Conservative and Unionist Party, proved a match for wisdom of either sort, and recurringly from 1886 to the First World War, invested febrile energy in resisting sense.

What would have been open to Britain and Ireland if the Conservative Party had been ordinarily realistic and sympathetic to the peoples of the union was an Ireland devolved but not independent. It would have cost us a measure of money under our own increasing social budget, but somewhat less than we have since spent on institutionalised emergency. Given no encouragement to illegal acts by the Conservatives, Ulster would have been obliged to negotiate a loose attachment garlanded with guarantees. But in practice she would have been able to call many shots at College Green, including the wise veto of protection, if, in the absence of de Valera, that folly had arisen.

Any full-dress upper-case Independence would have been for a southern component only, with every economic argument discouraging it. (The submerging in Ireland of the persuasive *economic* case for union was the particular idiocy of the Unionists.) But had independence come, it would have been at a later date, in a cooler time and by consent, and the narrow, fearful northern government of a minority by a minority would not have engendered the low-intensity war of the last thirty years. The Protestants of the south, in a state so linked and affiliated, would not have suffered the discreet pressure and discriminations of a small country free to be narrowly clericalist. And crucially, the present late decent relations between Britain and Ireland would have started fifty years earlier.

Instead, the Tories of 1912, talking 'treason', 'precipice' and 'madness', used their lordships' remaining powers of delay to enhance the threat to civil government of the armed resistance they had conjured up. The Conservatives proved at last godparents to an independent state preponderantly governed over thirty years by the surviving IRA commander in the Easter Rising. No course of conduct could, in the humorous-patronising sense, have been more Irish. But then, 'Tory' is a word of 'Irish' derivation.

Source Notes

PART I IRISH HOME RULE 1886 AND 1893

1 'A Separate Nation? Surely Gladstone Could Not Mean It'

1. Tom Corfe, *The Phoenix Park Murders*, Hodder and Stoughton (1968), p. 39.
2. R.F. Forster, *Modern Ireland 1600–1972*, Allen Lane (1988), p. 324.
3. Ibid., p. 351.
4. Quoted in Corfe, op. cit., p. 44.
5. R.F. Foster, 'Varieties of Irishness': essay in *Paddy and Mr Punch: Connections in Irish History*, Allen Lane (1993), p. 27.
6. Quoted in Corfe, op. cit., p. 51.
7. Ibid., p. 53.
8. Ibid., p. 54.
9. Roy Jenkins, *Gladstone*, Macmillan (1995), p. 537.
10. Corfe, op. cit., p. 154.
11. Quoted in Corfe, op. cit., p. 54.
12. Quoted in Foster, *Modern Ireland*, op. cit., p. 401.
13. Letter to Katharine O'Shea, quoted in Foster, *Paddy and Mr Punch*, op. cit., p. 43.
14. Quoted in Corfe, op. cit., p. 56.

2   Long Surgical Knives
1. Jenkins, *Gladstone*, op. cit., p. 475.
2. Ibid., p. 471.
3. Conor Cruise O'Brien, *Parnell and his Party*, Oxford University Press (1957), p. 85.
4. Lady Gwendolen Cecil, *Life of Lord Salisbury*, Vol. III, Hodder and Stoughton (1931), p. 281.
5. James Anthony Froude, *The English in Ireland*, Longman Green (1881) pp. 4–5.
6. Waldo H. Dunn, *James Anthony Froude: A Biography*, Clarendon Press (1963), p. 377.
7. Froude, op. cit., p. 10.
8. Ibid., p. 9.
9. Ibid., p. 11.
10. Ibid., p. 11.
11. Ibid., p. 12.
12. Ibid., p. 13.

3   The Kite and Joe
1. Jenkins, *Gladstone*, op. cit., p. 523.
2. Lady Gwendolen Cecil, op. cit., p. 159.
3. Ibid., p. 158.
4. Ibid., p. 161.
5. Jenkins, *Gladstone*, op. cit., p. 541.
6. Michael Balfour, *Britain and Joseph Chamberlain*, Allen and Unwin (1985) p. 167.
7. Jenkins, *Gladstone*, op. cit., p. 472.
8. *Pall Mall Gazette*, quoted in James Loughlin, *Gladstone, Home Rule and the Ulster Question 1882–93*, Gill and Macmillan, Dublin (1986), p. 65.
9. Loughlin, op. cit., p. 70.
10. Ibid., p. 80.
11. Ibid., p. 80.
12. Quoted in Loughlin, op. cit., p. 85.
13. Ibid., p. 86.
14. Quoted in Balfour, op. cit., p. 156.

15. Ibid., p. 180.
16. Ibid., p. 181.
17. Loughlin, op. cit., p. 93.
18. Ibid., p. 93.

4 Red Ruin
1. *Saturday Review*, 27 February 1886.
2. *Northern Whig*, 2 January 1886.
3. Quoted in Jenkins, *Gladstone* op. cit., p. 552. PD cols 1036–85.
4. Ibid., p. 553.
5. Gladstone, PD 10 May 1886, col. 599. (Speech cols 574–603 passim.)
6. PD 13 May 1886, cols 912–32 passim.
7. PD 10 May 1886, cols 603–22 passim.
8. PD 10 May 1886, cols 622–32 passim.
9. PD 9 April 1886 cols 1181–1207 (Chamberlain).
10. *Saturday Review*, 27 February 1886.
11. *Saturday Review*, 6 March 1886.
12. PD 10 May 1886, cols 638–51 passim.
13. Report in *The Times*, 16 May 1886.
14. Ibid.
15. Letter to Carnarvon, March 1890, quoted in John Wilson, *C-B: A Life of Sir Henry Cambell-Bannerman*, Constable (1973), p. 103.
16. PD 21 May 1886, cols 1667–82 passim.
17. Lady Gwendolen Cecil, op. cit., p. 305.
18. Jenkins, *Gladstone*, op. cit., p. 556.
19. Ibid., p. 558.
20. Wilson, op. cit., pp. 99–100.

5 Roaring at Ballymena – and Belfast
1. R. Lucas, *Colonel Saunderson*, John Murray (1908), p. 85.
2. Speech at Ballykilbeg, 1882, ibid., p. 67.
3. Letter in *Northern Whig*, 7 January 1886.

4. *Northern Whig*, 8 January 1886.
5. Loughlin, op. cit., p. 163.
6. Ibid., p. 165.
7. Ibid., p. 166.
8. Ibid., p. 164.
9. *Pall Mall Gazette*, 14 February 1886.
10. *The Times* 16 February 1886.
11. Quoted in R.F. Foster, *Lord Randolph Churchill: A Political Life*, Clarendon Press (1981), p. 240.
12. *The Times*, 23 February 1886.
13. Loughlin, op. cit., p. 225.
14. Ibid., p. 226.
15. *The Times*, 23 February 1886.
16. *Freeman's Journal*, February 1886.
17. Foster, *Churchill*, op. cit., p. 256.
18. Ibid., p. 256.
19. Ibid., p. 256.
20. Quoted in Foster, *Churchill*, op. cit., p. 232.
21. Foster, *Churchill*, op. cit., p. 257.
22. Quoted in Foster, *Churchill*, op. cit., p. 259.
23. Foster, *Churchill*, op. cit., p. 258.
24. Quoted in Loughlin, op. cit., p. 168.
25. Ibid., p. 169.
26. Loughlin, op. cit., p. 170.
27. Quoted in Loughlin, op. cit., p. 161.
28. Ibid., p. 160.
29. PD, 7 June cols, 1168–84 passim.
30. Foster, *Churchill*, op. cit., p. 262.
31. Ibid.

6 **Tragedy Before Legislation**

1. T.P. O'Connor, quoted in Max Egremont, *Balfour: A Life of James Arthur Balfour*, Collins (1980), p. 83.
2. Ibid., p. 87.
3. Ibid., p. 123.
4. Foster, *Modern Ireland*, op. cit., p. 421.

5. Loughlin, op. cit., p. 215.
6. *The Times*, 18 April 1887.
7. *The Times* 19 April 1887. Both quoted in O'Brien, op. cit., p. 207.
8. F.S.L. Lyons, *Charles Stewart Parnell*, Collins (1977), p. 425.
9. Ibid., p. 426.
10. Jenkins, *Gladstone*, op. cit., p. 569.
11. Ibid., p. 572.
12. Ibid.
13. Ibid.
14. Francis Birrell, *Gladstone*, p. 125. Quoted in Jenkins, op. cit., p. 573.

7 Preparing and Bringing in the Bill

1. Jenkins, *Gladstone*, op. cit., pp. 598–99.
2. Quoted in Loughlin, p. 243.
3. MacKnight, *Ulster As It Is*, Macmillan (1896), p. 296.
4. Ibid., p. 299.
5. Quoted in Loughlin, op. cit., 280.
6. Letter written by Mary Arnold-Foster, quoted in Loughlin, op. cit., p. 249.
7. Quoted in Loughlin, op. cit., p. 245.
8. Loughlin, op. cit., pp. 257–60.
9. *Blackwood's* magazine, October 1893.
10. Quoted in Foster, *Churchill*, p. 378.
11. *Blackwood's* magazine, October 1893.
12. Ibid.
13. Ibid.
14. Ibid.
15. Ibid.
16. PD, Lords, 6 September 1893, Vol. 17, cols 201–23 passim.
17. Ibid., cols 268–81 passim.
18. Ibid., 7 September, cols 362–80.
19. Ibid., 8 September, cols 609–13 passim.

20. Ibid., cols 617–22 passim.
21 Ibid., cols 622–40 passim.

8   A Belligerent Civilisation: A.V. Dicey and Other Thinkers

1. A.V. Dicey, *A Leap in the Dark*, London (1893), pp. 193–5 and passim.
2. Quoted in Foster, *Modern Ireland*, op. cit., p. 477.
3. Ibid., pp. 581–2.
4. A.V. Dicey, *Fool's Paradise* (1913). Quoted in Ferdinand Mount, *The British Constitution Now*, Heinemann (1992)
5. Sir J.F. Stephen, *Liberty, Equality Fraternity*, London (1873). Quoted in Tom Dunne, 'La Trahison des Clercs', an article in *Irish Historical Studies* 1982–3 to which brilliant essay (pp. 134–73) I am indebted for much of what follows.
6. Quoted in Dunne, op. cit., p. 146.
7. Quoted in Christopher Harvie, *The Lights of Liberalism*, Allen Lane (1976), pp. 26–7.
8. Ibid., p. 27.
9. Sidgwick diary, quoted in Harvie, op. cit., p. 219.
10. Harvie, op. cit., p. 220.
11. Ibid., p. 221.
12. Ibid., p. 219.
13. Quoted in Harvie, op. cit., p. 225.
14. *The Times* 21 January 1886, quoted in Dunne, op. cit., in Harvie, op. cit., p. 147.
15. Quoted in Dunne, op. cit., p. 144.
16. Harvie, op. cit., p. 225.
17. Campbell in *Fortnightly Review* quoted in Dunne, op. cit., p. 159.
18. Dunne, op. cit., p. 162.
19. Quoted in Dunne, op. cit., p. 161.
20. Quoted from *Edinburgh Review* 1887 in Dunne, op. cit., p. 165.
21. Quoted in Dunne, op. cit., p. 165.

22. Ibid., p. 161.
23. Ibid., p. 169.
24. Ibid., p. 170.

9   Mr Gladstone and the Ulstermen

1. MacKnight, op. cit., pp. 392–3.
2. Ibid., p. 393.
3. Ibid., p. 394.
4. 'Ireland as She Is and as She Would Be Under Home Rule', special commissioner of the *Birmingham Gazette* (1893), pp. 289–90.
5. MacKnight, op. cit., p. 387.
6. Ibid., p. 390.
7. Ibid., p. 396.
8. Ibid., p. 190.
9. Ibid., p. 192.
10. PD, Lords, Vol. 17, 1893, col. 646.
11. Loughlin, op. cit., p. 281.
12. Ibid., p. 281.
13. 'Ireland as She Is', op. cit., p. 286.
14. PD, 1 September 1823, Vol. 16, speech cols 1809–25.
15. Ibid., Vol. 11, col. 869; speech cols 855–75 passim (Repeated Vol 16, col. 1780).
16. Leon O'Broin, *The Chief Secretary: Augustine Birrell in Ireland*, Chatto and Windus (1969) p. 31.
17. PD, supra 1 September 1893, col. 1824.

PART II   THE LIBERALS, THE BUDGET AND THE PARLIAMENT ACT

10   'We Are in for a Great Time'

1. Quoted in Gregory Phillips, *The Diehards*, Harvard University Press (1979), p. 151.
2. PD, Lords, 14 July 1913, Quoted in Phillips, op. cit., p. 152.
3. Ibid., p. 153.

4. Egremont, op. cit., p. 176.
5. John Wilson, op. cit., pp. 407–8.
6. Henry Lucy, 'Toby MP' of *Punch*, quoted in Wilson, op. cit.
7. Wilson, op. cit., p. 402.
8. Egremont, op. cit., p. 195.
9. Wilson, op. cit., p. 404.
10. Egremont, op. cit., p. 194.
11. Quoted in Stephen Koss, *The Rise and Fall of the Popular Press*, Hamilton (1981).
12. Wilson, op. cit., p. 475.
13. Letter to Lady Salisbury, quoted in Wilson, op. cit., p. 375.

11 **'Mr C-B Forgets the Danger of Increasing the Power of the H of C'**

1. Roy Jenkins, *Mr Balfour's Poodle*, Heinemann (1954), p. 25.
2. Wilson, op. cit., pp. 549–50.
3. Ibid., pp. 550–1.
4. Quoted in *Edwardian Conservatism* ed. J.A. Thompson and Arthur Mejia, Croom Helm (1988), p. 111.
5. Lord Willoughby de Broke, *The Passing Years* (1924) p. 168.
6. Ibid., p. 169.
7. Phillips, op. cit., p. 113.
8. Ibid., p. 113.
9. Ibid., p. 117.
10. Ibid., pp. 117–18.
11. Quoted in Corfe, op. cit.
12. David Cannadine, *The Decline and Fall of the British Aristocracy*, Yale, New York, (1990), p. 520.
13. Phillips, op. cit., p. 134.
14. Cannadine, op. cit., p. 520.
15. Phillips, op. cit., p. 109.
16. Ibid., p. 109.

17. Cannadine, op. cit., p. 530.
18. Lord Newton, *Lansdowne*, Macmillan (1929), p. 352.
19. Ibid., p. 354.
20. Wilson, op. cit., p. 556.
21. Quoted in Wilson, op. cit., p. 495.

12 'The Real Discussion . . . Must Be Elsewhere'
 1. Wilson, op. cit., p. 503.
 2. Ibid., p. 503.
 3. Cannadine, op. cit., p. 490.
 4. Augustine Birrell, *Things Past Redress*, Faber and Faber (1937), p. 188.
 5. Ibid., pp. 191–2.
 6. Quoted in Wilson, op. cit., p. 555.
 7. Strachey to Maxse, quoted in Egremont, op. cit., p. 209.
 8. Sir Almeric Fitzroy, *Memoirs*, quoted in Wilson, op. cit., pp. 555–6.
 9. Ibid., p. 556.
10. *Punch*, 12 December 1906.
11. Newton, op. cit., p. 358.
12. Ibid., p. 359.
13. Wilson, op. cit., pp. 563–4.
14. Ibid., p. 565.
15. Willoughby de Broke, op. cit.
16. Ibid.

13 Lord Roehampton Strains a Vocal Cord
 1. *National Review*, 1910, Vol. 54, pp. 566–76.
 2. Roy Jenkins, *Asquith*, Collins (1964), p. 167.
 3. Sir Philip Magnus, *King Edward VII*, John Murray (1964), p. 302.
 4. Ibid., p. 302.
 5. Birrell, op. cit., p. 210.
 6. Quoted in Newton, op. cit., p. 369.
 7. Hilaire Belloc *Selected Cautionary Verse*, Puffin (1940), p. 125.

8. Cannadine, op. cit., p. 48.
9. Ibid., p. 48.
10. Ibid., p. 48.
11. Ibid., p. 48.
12. Ibid., p. 48.
13. A.T. Wilson-Fox, *The Earl of Halsbury*, Chapman and Hall (1929), p. 214.
14. *The Times*, 29 April 1909.
15. Ibid., 17 April 1909.
16. Ibid., 3 May 1909.
17. Ibid., 7 May 1909.
18. Ibid., 9 May 1909.
19. *National Review*, Vol. 53, p. 549.
20. Ibid., Vol. 56, p. 36.
21. Advertisement in *National Review*, Vol. 54.
22. *National Review*, Vol. 54, p. 533.
23. Ibid., vol. 53, p. 540.
24. Ibid., June, Vol. 54, p. 175.
25. Ibid., July, p. 731.
26. Ibid., Vol. 53, p. 729.
27. *The Times*, 22 June 1909.
28. *National Review*, July 1909, p. 727.
29. *Punch*, May 1909, quoted in the *National Review*, July 1909, pp. 724–5.

14 'No More Tactics!'

1. *National Review*, Vol. 53, p. 916.
2. Jenkins, *Asquith*, op. cit., p. 198.
3. *National Review*, August 1909, Vol. 53, pp. 913–14.
4. Newton, op. cit., p. 199.
5. *National Review*, Vol. 53, p. 915.
6. Jenkins, *Asquith*, op. cit., pp. 199–200.
7. *National Review*, Vol. 53, pp. 916–17.
8. Jenkins, *Asquith*, op. cit., pp. 199–200.
9. Ibid., p. 200.
10. *National Review*, Vol. 53, pp. 917–18.

11. Quoted in Peter Rowland, *The Last Liberal Government*, Vol. 1, Barrie and Jenkins (1968), pp. 224–5.
12. Magnus, op. cit., p. 528.
13. Quoted in Rowland, op. cit., p. 234.
14. *National Review*, Vol. 54, p. 35.
15. *Times* report, quoted in George Dangerfield, *The Strange Death of Liberal England*, Capricorn, New York (1935), p. 23.
16. Quoted in Koss, op. cit., pp. 552–3.
17. Quoted in Rose, op. cit., p. 138.
18. Newton, op. cit., p. 376.
19. Ibid., p. 377.
20. Willoughby de Broke, op. cit., p. 253.
21. Newton, op. cit., p. 380.
22. Willoughby to Maxse, January 1910, quoted in Thompson and Mejia, op. cit., pp. 86–7.
23. Jenkins, *Asquith*, op. cit., p. 200.
24. Magnus, op. cit., p. 534.
25. Peter Fraser, *Lord Esher*, Hart-Davis (1973), p. 208.
26. Ibid., p. 209.
27. Kenneth Young, *A.J. Balfour*, Bell (1963), p. 290.
28. Ibid., p. 291.

15   'Time Has Touched it With his Finger'

1. Roy Jenkins, *Mr Balfour's Poodle*, op. cit., pp. 84–5.
2. PD, Lords, 22 November 1909, cols 731–50.
3. Ibid., cols 750–60.
4. Ibid., cols 760–70.
5. Ibid., cols 770–74.
6 Ibid., cols 799–806.
7. Ibid., cols 775–85.
8. PD, Lords, 23 November 1909, cols 821–31.
9. Ibid., cols 831–42.
10. Ibid., cols 861–71.
11. Ibid., cols 878–93.
12. Ibid., cols 904–16.

16   A Noble Utterance – a Balaklava Utterance
  1. Rose, op. cit., p. 53.
  2. Ibid., p. 54.
  3. Ibid., p. 76.
  4. PD, 24 November 1909, cols 925–42.
  5. Ibid., cols 942–54.
  6. Ibid., cols 966–78.
  7. Ibid., cols 993–1002.
  8. Ibid., cols 1002–11.
  9. Ibid., cols 1011–16.
 10. PD, 25 November 1909, cols 1023–31.
 11. Ibid., cols 1031–43.
 12. Ibid., cols 1062–72.
 13. Ibid., cols 1080–86.
 14. Ibid., cols 1086–92.
 15. PD, 29 November 1909, cols 1137–53.
 16. Ibid., cols 1156–65.
 17. Ibid., cols 1165–76.
 18. Ibid., Ellenborough, cols 1187–90.
 19. Ibid., Reay, cols 1190–93.
 20. Ibid., Knaresborough, cols 1193–9.
 21. Ibid., Swaythling, cols 1185–90.
 22. Ibid., Ampthill, cols 1199–1206.

17   Lord Curzon and the Old Man of the Sea
  1. PD, 29 November 1909, cols 1206–17.
  2. Ibid., cols 1229–30.
  3. PD, 30 November 1909, cols 1243–64.
  4. Ibid., cols 1264–75.
  5. Wilson, op. cit., p. 256.
  6. PD, 30 November 1909, cols 1279–84.
  7. Ibid., cols 1296–1301.
  8. Ibid., cols 1305–8.
  9. Ibid., cols 1308–10.
 10. Ibid., cols 1310–24.
 11. Ibid., cols 1324–42.

18   Crocodile Shooting and its Difficulties

1. Young, op. cit., p. 291.
2. Koss, op. cit., pp. 564–6.
3. Ibid., pp. 564–6.
4. Quoted in Koss, op. cit., p. 568.
5. Koss, op. cit., p. 568.
6. Ibid., pp. 571–2.
7. Ibid., p. 575.
8. *National Review*, Vol. 54.
9. Ibid., p. 743.
10. Ibid., p. 712.
11. *Blackwood's*, Vol. 87, pp. 160–1.
12. Ibid., pp. 274–87.
13. *The Times*, 10 December 1909.
14. Phillips, op. cit., p. 164.
15. *The Times*, 12 December 1909.
16. Ibid., 16 December 1909.
17. Ibid., 17 December 1909.
18. Ibid., 18 December 1909.
19. Rowland, op. cit., p. 245.

19   Lord Crewe's Champagne

1. Quoted in Rowland, op. cit., p. 243.
2. Ibid., p. 242.
3. Jenkins, *Mr Balfour's Poodle*, op. cit., p. 123.
4. Ibid., p. 126.
5. Quoted in Jenkins, *Mr Balfour's Poodle*, op. cit., p. 124.
6. *Blackwood's*, Vol. 187, p. 307.
7. Ibid., p. 748.
8. Ibid., p. 749.
9. *Punch*, April 1911.
10. PD, Lords, Vol. 5, cols 313–20.
11. Ibid., pp. 320–30.
12. PD, Commons, Vol XVI col. 548, quoted in Jenkins, *Mr Balfour's Poodle*, op. cit., p. 137.
13. Rowland, Vol. 1, op. cit., pp. 298–99.

14. Sir Almeric Fitzroy, *Memoirs*, Vol. 2, Doran, New York (1925).
15. Rowland, op. cit., Vol. 1 p. 302.
16. Ibid., p. 303.
17. Newton, op. cit., p. 400.
18. Fitzroy, Vol. 2, op. cit., p. 424.
19. Fraser, op. cit., p. 214.
20. Quoted in Jenkins, *Mr Balfour's Poodle*, op. cit., p. 159.
21. Rowland, op. cit., p. 316.
22. A.G. Gardiner, *Certain People of Importance*, Dent (1926), p. 96.
23. Rowland, op. cit., p. 318.
24. Ibid., p. 322.

20 'A Senate of Kangaroos'
1. Fitzroy, Vol. 2, op. cit., pp. 422–3.
2. Quoted in Jenkins, *Mr Balfour's Poodle*, op. cit., p. 174.
3. Ibid., p. 175.
4. Quoted in Fraser, op. cit., p. 217.
5. Ibid., p. 218.
6. Ibid., pp. 219–20.
7. Quoted in Jenkins, *Mr Balfour's Poodle*, op. cit., pp. 184–5.
8. *The Times*, 2 December 1910.
9. Ibid., 30 November 1910.
10. Ibid., 23 November 1910.
11. Ibid., 24 November 1910.
12. Ibid., 1 December 1910.
13. Ibid., 21 November 1910.
14. Ibid., 23 November 1910.
15. Ibid., 18 November 1910.

21 'These Degrading 500 Peers'
1. Quoted Rowland, op. cit., p. 340.
2. Quoted Jenkins, *Mr Balfour's Poodle*, op. cit., p. 195.
3. Ibid., p. 196.
4. *National Review*, Vol. 57, March 1911, pp. 6–7.

5. PD, Vol. 22, cols 45–57.
6. Ibid., cols 70–6.
7. Ibid., cols 85–9.
8. Ibid., cols 89–95.
9. Ibid., cols 109–19.
10. Ibid., cols 224–32.
11. Ibid., cols 243–54.
12. Ibid., cols 254–61.
13. Ibid., cols 274–81.
14. Ibid., cols 281–6.
15. Ibid., cols 311–18.
16. Ibid., col. 381.
17. Ibid., col. 429.
18. Ibid., cols 422–6.
19. Ibid., cols 447–56.
20. Ibid., cols 455–62.
21. Ibid., cols 580–81.
22. Ibid., cols 581–9.
23. PD, Lords, Vol. 8, cols 215–36.
24. Ibid., cols 400–8.
25. Ibid., cols 396–403.
26. Fitzroy, Vol. 2, op. cit., pp. 443–5.
27. Ibid., p. 443.

22 'Traitor, Traitor, 'vide, 'vide'
1. Jenkins, *Mr Balfour's Poodle*, op. cit., pp. 205–7.
2. *Punch*, 12 July 1911.
3. Fitzroy, Vol. 2, op. cit., p. 454.
4. Jenkins, *Mr Balfour's Poodle*, op. cit., pp. 213–14.
5. Fitzroy, Vol. 2, op. cit., p. 455.
6. Newton, op. cit., p. 417.
7. Ibid., p. 418.
8. Ibid., pp. 418–9.
9. Quoted in Jenkins, *Mr Balfour's Poodle*, op. cit., p. 219.
10. Newton, op. cit., p. 222.
11. Ibid., p. 422.

12. PD, Lords, Vol. 9, cols 592–603.
13. Newton, op. cit., p. 422.
14. David Gilmour, *Curzon* John Murray (1994), p. 388.
15. Ibid., p. 389.
16. Gardiner, op. cit., p. 66.
17. Gilmour, op. cit., p. 390.
18. Ibid., p. 391.
19. 'Toby MP' (Sir Henry Lucy), *Punch*, 2 August 1911, pp. 83–4.
20. Rose, op. cit.
21. *The Times*, 10 August 1910.
22. *National Review*, Vol. 57, pp. 928–9.
23. Ibid., p. 912.

23   The Captain of the Rats
1. *National Review*, 19 August 1911, p. 937.
2. Wilson-Fox, op. cit., pp. 245–6.
3. Ibid., pp. 246–9.
4. Phillips, op. cit., p. 139.
5. Wilson-Fox, op. cit., p. 139.
6. *The Times*, 27 July 1911.
7. Ibid.
8. Ibid.
9. Ibid.
10. Ibid.
11. Ibid.
12. Gardiner, op. cit., pp. 95–6.
13. *The Times*, 27 July 1911.
14. Ibid.
15. Gilmour, op. cit., pp. 390–91.
16. Ibid., p. 391.
17. Ibid., p. 394.
18. Jenkins, *Mr Balfour's Poodle*, op. cit., p. 247.
19. Ibid., p. 249.
20. Willoughby, op. cit., p. 135.
21. Gilmour, op. cit., p. 392.

22. Phillips, op. cit., p. 134.
23. Ibid., pp. 135–6.
24. PD, Lords, Vol. 9, cols 815–32.
25. Ibid., cols 832–43.
26. Ibid., cols 849–52.
27. Ibid., cols 863.
28. Ibid., cols 865–75.

24 'Mild Uproar and Cheering in the Streets'
1. *Punch*, 9 August 1911.
2. Willoughby, op. cit., p. 301.
3. PD, Lords, Vol. 9, cols 886–96.
4. Quoted in Jenkins, *Mr Balfour's Poodle*, op. cit., p. 255.
5. PD, Lords, Vol. 9, pp. 896–1000.
6. Ibid., pp. 900–7.
7. Ibid., pp. 907–14.
8. Barbara Tuchman, *The Proud Tower*, Macmillan, New York, (1963), p. 15.
9. PD, Vol. 9, cols 915–20.
10. Ibid., cols 930–7.
11. Ibid., cols 937–43.
12. Ibid., cols 949–55.
13. Ibid., cols 959–65.
14. Ibid., cols 965–70.
15. Ibid., cols 994–5.
16. Ibid., cols 997–1000.
17. Ibid., cols 1007–10.
18. Ibid., cols 1012–18.
19. Ibid., cols 1019–23.
20. Ibid., cols 1028–37.
21. Ibid., cols 1049–55.
22. Ibid., col. 1059.
23. Ibid., cols 1064–70.
24. Ibid., col. 1070.
25. Ibid., cols 1072–3.
26. Wilson-Fox, op. cit., p. 278.

27. Ibid., p. 278.
28. Lady Violet Bonham Carter's *Lantern Slides Diaries*, ed. M. Bonham Carter and M. Pottle, Weidenfeld and Nicolson (1996) p. 277.
29. Quoted in Jenkins, *Mr Balfour's Poodle*, op. cit., p. 267.
30. Ibid., p. 267.
31. *Blackwood's* magazine, September 1911, p. 415.

PART III   IRISH HOME RULE 1912–14

25   Andrew Bonar Law

1. Quoted in Foster, *Modern Ireland*, op. cit., p. 449.
2. P.A. Sheehan, *The Graves at Kilmorna 1913*, quoted in Patrick O'Farrell, *Ireland's English Problem*, Batsford (1971), p. 231.
3. Richard Shannon, *The Age of Salisbury 1881–1902*, Longman (1996), p. 452.
4. Ibid., p. 457.
5. Quoted in Shannon, op. cit., p. 457.
6. O'Broin, op. cit., p. 83.
7. Ibid., p. 83.
8. Ibid., p. 84.
9. Article in the *Spectator* 1997.
10. The Earl of Birkenhead, *The Life of F.E. Smith*, Eyre and Spottiswood (1960), p. 172.
11. Quoted in O'Broin, op. cit., p. 85.
12. Birrell, op. cit., p. 196.
13. Quoted in O'Broin, op. cit., p. 217.
14. P.S. O'Hegarty, *Victory of Sinn Fein*, quoted in O'Broin, op. cit., p. 218.

26   A Besieged City

1. Lord Cushenden, *Ulster's Stand for the Union*, quoted in Henry Maxwell, *Ulster Was Right*, Hutchinson (1924), p. 59.

2. Quoted from A.T.Q. Stewart *The Ulster Crisis*, Faber and Faber (1967), p. 48.
3. Ibid., p. 54.
4. Quoted in Robert Blake, *The Life and Times of Andrew Bonar Law 1858–1923*, Eyre and Spottiswood (1955), p. 129.
5. Dicey, op. cit., p. 199.
6. Quoted in O'Broin, op. cit., p. 50.
7. Maxwell, op. cit., p. 62.
8. Ibid., p. 63.
9. O'Broin, op. cit., p. 60.
10. Ibid., p. 57.
11. PD, 1912, Vol. 36, col. 1468; speech cols 1466–74.
12. PD, 1912, Vol. 37, col. 1705; speech cols 1701–22.
13. Quoted in Blake, op. cit., pp. 95–6.
14. Maxwell, op. cit., p. 57.
15. PD, 1912, Vol. 36, col. 1513; speech cols 1505–14.

27 Bowler Hats and Wooden Rifles
1. James Loughlin, article in *Irish Historical Studies* (1995).
2. *Blackwood's* magazine, May 1912, pp. 736–44 passim.
3. D.G. Boyce, 'British Conservative Opinion and the Partition of Ireland 1912–21' *Irish Historical Studies*, Vol. 17, March 1970.
4. Conversation with J.L. Hammond, quoted in Boyce, op. cit.
5. Quoted in Stewart, op. cit., p. 74.
6. Ibid., p. 61.
7. Ibid., p. 61.
8. George Peel, *The Reign of Sir Edward Carson*, P.S. King, (1914), p. 66.
9. Stewart, op. cit., p. 63.
10. Quoted in Birkenhead, op. cit., pp. 217–18.
11. Maxwell, op. cit., pp. 85–6.
12. O'Broin, op. cit., p. 108.
13. Quoted in Stewart, op. cit., p. 65.

14. Birkenhead, op. cit., p. 213.
15. Quoted in Birkenhead, op. cit., p. 212.
16. Quoted in Blake, op. cit., p. 130.
17. Birkenhead, op. cit., p. 215.
18. O'Broin, op. cit., p. 70.
19. *Ulster Guardian*, 7 December 1912, quoted in *Peel*, op. cit., p. 80.
20. Stewart, op. cit., p. 131.
21. Ibid., p. 135.
22. Blake, op. cit., p. 178.
23. Quoted in Blake, op. cit., p. 181.
24. Ibid., p. 181.
25. O'Broin, op. cit., pp. 93–4.
26. Quoted in Frank Giles, *The Locust Years*, Secker and Warburg (1991), p. 311.
27. H.H. Asquith, *Letters to Venetia Stanley*, Oxford University Press (1982), quoted in Jenkins, *Asquith*, op. cit., p. 309.
28. Jenkins, *Asquith*, op. cit., p. 311.
29. Ibid., p. 312.

28 Hon. Members: 'Traitor!'

1. *Blackwood's* magazine, Vol. 194, 1913, p. 416 et. seq.
2. PD, 13 November 1912, Vol. 43, col. 2012.
3. Ibid., cols 2036–9.
4. Ibid., cols 2041–2.
5. Ibid., cols 2045–50.
6. Ibid., cols 2050–3.
7. Ibid., cols 2053–4.
8. PD, 13 November 1912, Vol. 43, cols 2037–54.
9. PD, 14 November 1912, Vol. 43, cols 2088–9.
10. Blake, op. cit., p. 132.
11. Ibid., p. 133.
12. O'Broin, op. cit., pp. 65–6.
13. Ibid., p. 67.
14. Blake, op. cit., p. 133.

15. Jenkins, *Asquith*, op. cit., p. 283.
16. Ibid., p. 284.
17. Ibid., p. 286.
18. Ibid., p. 285.
19. Ibid., p. 291.
20. Ibid., p. 292.
21. *Saturday Review*, 20 September 1913.
22. Ibid., 14 June 1913.
23. Ibid., 4 October 1913.
24. Ibid., 4 October 1913.
25. Ibid.
26. Ibid.

29   Changed Utterly
 1. Jenkins, *Asquith*, op. cit., p. 316.
 2. Stewart, op. cit., p. 91.
 3. Ibid., pp. 90–1.
 4. Ibid., pp. 71–2.
 5. Stewart, op. cit., p. 71.
 6. Maxwell, op. cit., p. 134.
 7. Ibid., pp. 134–5.
 8. Quoted in Foster, *Modern Ireland*, op. cit., p. 470.
 9. Maxwell, op. cit., p. 136.
10. Stewart, op. cit., p. 191.
11. O'Broin, op. cit., p. 89.
12. Stewart, op. cit., p. 72.
13. Maxwell, op. cit., p. 101.
14. O'Broin, op. cit., pp. 100–1.
15. Quoted in Foster, *Modern Ireland*, op. cit., p. 467.
16. Quoted in O'Broin, op. cit., p. 84.
17. Ibid., p. 101.
18. Asquith to Venetia Stanley, quoted in Jenkins, *Asquith*, p. 321.
19. H. Alison Philips, quoted in Maxwell, op. cit., p. 147.
20. Maxwell, op. cit., p. 146.
21. Ibid., p. 146.

22. H. Alison Philips, quoted in Maxwell, op. cit., p. 148.
23. Ibid., p. 149.
24. H.H. Asquith, *Letters to Venetia Stanley*, op. cit., pp. 127–8.
25. O'Broin, op. cit., p. 151.
26. Ibid., p. 163.
27. Jaroslav Hasek, *The Good Soldier Schweick*, trans. Paul Selver, Penguin (1930), p. 66.
28. Foster, op. cit., p. 473.
29. Quoted in Foster, op. cit., p. 477.
30. *Saturday Review*, 4 June 1913.
31. Foster, op. cit., p. 476.
32. H. Alison Philips, quoted in Maxwell, op. cit., p. 178.
33. F.S.L. Lyons and David Fitzpatrick, quoted in Charles Townshend, 'British Policy in Ireland,' essay in *The Revolution in Ireland 1873–1923*, ed. D.G. Boyce, Macmillan (1988).
34. Quoted in Maxwell, op. cit., p. 204.
35. Maxwell, op. cit., pp. 203–4.
36. Townshend, op. cit., p. 187.
37. Maxwell, op. cit., p. 287.
38. Bishop Joseph MacRory (Down and Connor), quoted in O'Farrell, op. cit., p. 292.
39. O'Farrell, op. cit., p. 292.
40. Quoted in O'Farrell, op. cit., p. 245.
41. Ibid. Quoted in O'Farrell, op. cit., p. 249.

ENVOI

1. *The Crisis of British Unionism*, ed. D.G. Boyce, The Historians Press (1988).
2. Ibid., p. 230.
3. Ibid., p. 231.

Bibliography

Asquith, Margot, *The Autobiography of Margot Asquith* (Vol. II), Penguin Books.

Balfour, Michael, *Britain and Joseph Chamberlain*, George Allen and Unwin, 1985.

Bateman, Michael, *This England* (selection of pieces from the *New Statesman*, 1934–68), Penguin, 1969.

Belloc, Hilaire, *Selected Cautionary Verses*, Puffin, 1940.

Biggs-Davison, John, *George Wyndham*, Hodder and Stoughton, 1951.

Birkenhead, Second Earl of, *F.E.*, Eyre and Spottiswood, 1960.

Birmingham Daily Gazette, 'Special Commissioner' of 'Ireland as she is and as she would be under Home Rule', BDG, 1894.

Birrell, Augustine, *Things Past Redress*, Faber and Faber, 1937.

Blake, Robert, *The Unknown Prime Minister: The Life and Times of Andrew Bonar Law*, Eyre and Spottiswood, 1955.

Blackwood's Magazine, Edinburgh, July–December 1893, January–June 1910, July–December 1910, July–December 1911, July–December 1912, January–June 1922.

Bonham Carter, M. and Pottle, M. (eds.), *Lantern Slides: Diaries of Lady Violet Bonham Carter (1904–14)*, Weidenfeld and Nicolson, 1996.

Boyce, D. George (ed.), *The Crisis of British Unionism:*

Lord Selborne's Domestic Political Papers 1885–1922, The Historians' Press, 1988.

Boyce, D. George, 'British Conservative Opinion' and 'The Ulster Question and the Partition of Ireland' 1912–21, articles in *Irish Historical Studies*, 1971.

Boyd, Charles W. (Ed.), *Mr Chamberlain's Speeches*, Vol. I, Constable and Company, 1914.

Butler, David and King, Antony, *The British General Election of 1966*, Macmillan, 1966.

Cannadine, David, *The Decline and Fall of the British Aristocracy*, Yale University Press, 1990.

Cecil, Lady Gwendolen, *The Life of Robert, Marquis of Salisbury*, Vol. III, 1880–86, Hodder and Stoughton, 1931.

Corfe, Tom, *The Phoenix Park Murders: Conflict, Compromise and Tragedy in Ireland 1879–1882*, Hodder and Stoughton, 1968.

Dangerfield, George, *The Strange Death of Liberal England*, Capricorn, New York, 1935.

Dicey, A.V., *A Leap in the Dark*, John Murray, 1893.

Dicey, A.V., *The Law of the Constitution*, Macmillan, 1915, reprinted 1924.

Dunn, Waldo Hilary, *James Anthony Froude*, Vol. II, 1857–94, Clarendon Press, 1963.

Dunne, Tom, 'La Trahison des Clercs', article in *Irish Historical Studies*.

Egremont, Max, *Balfour*, Collins, 1980.

Ensor, R.C.K., *England 1870–1914*, Oxford University Press, 1936.

Ervine, St John, *Craigavon*, Allen and Unwin, 1949.

Fitzroy, Sir Almeric, *Memoirs*, Vols I and II, Doran, New York, 1925.

Foster, R.F. *Lord Randolph Churchill*, Oxford Clarendon, 1981.

Foster, R.F., *Modern Ireland 1600–1972*, Allen Lane, 1988.

Foster, R.F., *Paddy and Mr Punch: Connections in Irish and English History*, Allen Lane, The Penguin Press, 1993.

Fraser, Peter, *Lord Esher*, Hart-Davis, 1973.

Froude, James Anthony, *The English in Ireland*, Vol. I, Longman Green, 1881.

Gardiner, A.G., *Pillars of Society*, Nisbet, 1913.

Gardiner, A.G., *Some Persons of Importance*, Dent, 1926.

Giles, Frank, *The Locust Years*, Secker and Warburg, 1991.

Gilmour, David, *Curzon*, John Murray, 1994.

Harvie, Christopher, *The Lights of Liberalism*, Allen Lane, 1977.

Horne, Alistair, *Macmillan*, Vol. 1, 1894–1956, Macmillan, 1988.

Jenkins, Roy, *Asquith*, Collins, 1964.

Jenkins, Roy, *Mr Balfour's Poodle*, Collins, 1953.

Jenkins, Roy, *Gladstone*, Macmillan, 1995.

Jenkins, Roy (ed.), *Letters to Venetia Stanley of H.H. Asquith*, Oxford University Press, 1982.

Jenkins, T.A., *Gladstone, Whiggery and the Liberal Party*, Oxford University Press, 1988.

Koss, Stephen, *The Rise and Fall of the Political Press in Britain*, Hamilton, 1981.

Loughlin, James, *Gladstone, Home Rule and the Ulster Question 1882–1893*, Gil and Macmillan, 1986.

Lucas, Reginald, *Colonel Saunderson MP*, John Murray, 1908.

Lyons, F.S.L., *Charles Stewart Parnell*, Collins, 1977.

Macknight, Thomas, *Ulster As It Is*, Macmillan, 1896.

Magnus, Sir Philip, *King Edward VII*, Murray, 1965.

Maxwell, Henry, *Ulster was Right*, Hutchinson, 1924.

Morrison, Herbert, *Government and Parliament: A survey from the Inside*, Oxford University Press 1954.

Mount, Ferdinand, *The British Constitution Now*, Heinemann, 1992.

The National Review, March–August 1909, September 1909–February 1910.

Newton, Lord (Thomas Newton), *Lord Lansdowne*, Macmillan, 1929.

O'Farrell, Patrick, *Ireland's English Problem*, Batsford, 1971.

O'Brien, Conor Cruise, *Parnell and his Party*, Oxford University Press, 1957.

O'Brien, Conor Cruise, *States of Ireland*, Hutchinson, 1972.

O'Broin, Leon, *The Chief Secretary: Augustine Birrell in Ireland*, Chatto and Windus, 1969.

Parliamentary Debates (*Hansard*), Commons: 19 April–24 May 1886, 11 August–4 September 1893, 5–22 September 1893, 26 April–29 June 1911, 28 October–14 November 1912, 30 December 1912–17 January 1913; Lords: August 1893, 26 April–29 June 1909, 19 October–3 December 1909, 3 July–2 August 1911.

Peel, Hon. George, *The Reign of Sir Edward Carson*, P.S. King, 1914.

Phillips, Gregory (ed.), *The Diehards*, Harvard, 1979.

Punch, January–June 1886, July–December 1911, January–June 1914.

Ramsden, John, *An Appetite for Power: A History of the Conservative Party since 1830*, HarperCollins, 1998.

Ramsden, John, *A History of the Tory Party*, Vol. II, 'The Age of Balfour and Baldwin', Longman, 1978.

Rose, Kenneth, *The Later Cecils*, Weidenfeld and Nicolson, 1975.

Rowland, Peter, *The Last Liberal Government*, Vol. I, 1905–10, Barrie and Jenkins, 1968; Vol. II, 1911–14, Barrie and Jenkins, 1981.

The Saturday Review, January–June 1886, July–December 1913.

Shannon, Richard, *The History of the Tory Party: The Age of Salisbury 1881–1902*, Longman, 1996.

Stewart, A.T.Q., *The Ulster Crisis*, Faber, 1967.

Thompson, J.A. and Mejia, Arthur, *Edwardian Conservatism*, Croom Helm, 1988.

Willoughby de Broke, Lord, *The Passing Years*, 1924.

Wilson, John, *A Life of Sir Henry Campbell-Bannerman* Constable, 1973.

Wilson-Fox, A.T., *The Earl of Halsbury*, Chapman and Hall, 1929.
Young, Kenneth, *A.J. Balfour*, Bell, 1963.

Quotations from *The British Constitution Now* by Ferdinand Mount (Heinemann, 1992), *The Chief Secretary* by Leon O'Broin (Chatto, 1969), *Mr Balfour's Poodle* by Roy Jenkins (Heinemann, 1953), *The Last Liberal Government* by Peter Rowlands (Barrie and Jenkins), *Ulster Was Right* by Henry Maxwell (Hutchinson, 1934), *The Locust Years* by Frank Giles (Secker and Warburg, 1991) and *A Map of Verona Cape* by Henry Reed (1961) reproduced courtesy of Random House UK Ltd.

Index

Bull, Sir William, 440, 441
Burke, Thomas, 29
Burnley, 279
Burns, John, 190
Butler, R.A., 4, 245, 441
Butt, Isaac, 17, 18, 19, 20, 24,
68, 71, 384

Cadogan, Lord, 358, 360,
385, 386
Caernarvon, 275
Caird, Sir James, 55
Calvinism, 85, 421
Cambridge, 143, 158, 240,
282, 392, 397
Cambridge, Duke of, 100
Campaign for Nuclear
Disarmament, 238
Campbell, George, 146
Campbell, James, 404, 419
Campbell, J.H., 350
Campbell-Bannerman, Henry,
83, 118, 168, 169, 171,
173, 175, 176, 183, 184,
190, 191, 192, 193, 197,
210, 230, 265, 266, 343,
374, 419
Camperdown, Lord, 275, 276,
372, 373
Canada, 56, 64, 65, 66, 71,
146, 311, 392, 410, 417,
422, 449, 461, 464, 480
Canterbury, Archbishop of,
188, 304, 374, 376
Cardiff, 306
Carlton Club, 193, 302, 335,
352, 377
Carlyle, Thomas, 50, 134, 453
Carnarvon, Lord, 30,

31, 32, 39, 40, 41, 47,
65, 93, 98
Carrington, 225, 250, 251
Carson, Edward, 104, 298,
344, 347, 350, 354, 362,
386, 394, 398, 403, 404,
406, 411, 413, 414, 420,
421, 422, 423, 425–30, 432,
436, 437, 443, 445, 450,
456, 457, 458, 461, 462,
463, 466, 467, 469, 472,
475, 482, 483
Carter, Rev. Leslie, 155
Casement, Sir Roger, 460, 468,
474, 475
Cat and Mouse Act, 454
Catholic, 2, 12, 31, 43, 51,
61, 77, 85, 87, 88, 89, 90,
92, 95, 96, 98, 99, 101, 105,
106, 110, 111, 117, 131,
134, 151, 155, 158, 169,
187, 221, 281, 285, 286,
358, 384, 386, 388, 389,
390, 395, 402, 403, 404,
405, 412, 413, 421, 422,
423, 433, 439, 444, 460,
461, 464, 470, 476, 479,
483; emancipation of, 12,
31, 43, 323
Catholic University, 87, 395
Catholicism, 89, 111
Cavan, County of, 86, 403
Cave, 350
Cavendish, Lord Frederick,
28, 29, 42
Cavendish-Bentinck, Lord
George, 165
Cawdor, Lord, 188, 224, 265,
266, 281, 292, 314